Topiltzin Quetzalcoatl

Carvings on lid of the "Box of Hackmack," Late Aztec style. Museum für Völkerkunde, Hamburg, Germany. The feathered serpent, flying downward, is flanked by the two dates most closely associated with both Ehecatl and Topiltzin Quetzalcoatl, One and Seven Acatl (Reed). Photo courtesy of the museum.

Topiltzin Quetzalcoatl

THE ONCE AND FUTURE LORD OF THE TOLTECS

by H. B. Nicholson

UNIVERSITY PRESS OF COLORADO

First printing, 2001; second printing, 2008 (both with color plates)
Third printing, 2015

Published by the University Press of Colorado
5589 Arapahoe Avenue, Suite 206C
Boulder, Colorado 80303

Printed in the United States of America.

The University Press of Colorado is a cooperative publishing enterprise supported, in part, by Adams State College, Colorado State University, Fort Lewis College, Mesa State College, Metropolitan State College of Denver, University of Colorado, University of Northern Colorado, University of Southern Colorado, and Western State College of Colorado.

The paper used in this publication meets the minimum requirements of the American National Standard for Information Sciences—Permanence of Paper for Printed Library Materials. ANSI Z39.48-1992

Library of Congress Cataloging-in-Publication Data

Nicholson, H. B. (Henry B.)
Topiltzin Quetzalcoatl : the once and future lord of the Toltecs / H. B. Nicholson
p. cm. — (Mesoamerican worlds)
Includes bibliographical references and index.
ISBN 0-87081-547-4 (cloth : alk. paper) — ISBN 0-87081-554-7 (pbk. : alk. paper)
1. Quetzalcoatl (Aztec deity) 2. Aztec mythology. 3. Aztecs—History—Sources. 4. Toltec mythology. 5. Toltecs—History—Sources. 6. Manuscripts, Mexican (Pre-Columbian)—History and criticism. I. Title. II. Series.
F1219.76.R45 .N53 2001
972'.01—dc21
2001000483

To the memory of those native, mestizo, and Spanish chroniclers who labored to preserve—often in the face of many obstacles—our knowledge of the most advanced civilization of the indigenous New World and its historical traditions—including the extraordinary tale that is the subject of this book.

ALSO IN THE SERIES

Mesoamerican Worlds

FROM THE OLMECS TO THE DANZANTES

General Editors, Davíd Carrasco and Eduardo Matos Moctezuma

Eating Landscape: Aztec and European Occupation of Tlalocan,
Philip P. Arnold

In the Realm of Nachan Kan: Postclassic Maya Archaeology at Laguna de On, Belize, Marilyn A. Masson

Life and Death in the Templo Mayor,
Eduardo Matos Moctezuma

Mesoamerica's Classic Heritage: Teotihuacan to the Aztecs,
Davíd Carrasco, Lindsay Jones, and Scott Sessions

Tamoanchan, Tlalocan: Places of Mist,
Alfredo López Austin

Topiltzin Quetzalcoatl: The Once and Future Lord of the Toltecs,
H. B. Nicholson

Twin City Tales: A Hermeneutical Reassessment of Tula and Chichén Itzá,
Lindsay Jones

Utopia and History in Mexico: The First Chronicles of Mexican Civilization, 1520–1569, Georges Baudot

Editors' Note

In his enjoyable essay "Why Read the Classics," Italo Calvino lists among his definitions of a classic the following two. First, a classic is a book that exerts "a peculiar influence" because it refuses to be eradicated from the mind and conceals itself in "the folds of memory." Second, a classic is a book that never finishes saying what it has to say. We are honored to present a classic of Mesoamerican scholarship with this publication of H. B. Nicholson's *Topiltzin Quetzalcoatl: The Once and Future Lord of the Toltecs* in our series Mesoamerican Worlds. Many elements of Nicholson's work make it exceptional, influential, and long lasting. Yet it is ironic that his work is already a classic even though it has not been published until now. Let me explain.

Works that rise to the status of "classic" typically do so as the result of years of public critical reading and appreciation. Nicholson completed this project as his dissertation, "Topiltzin Quetzalcoatl of Tollan: A Problem in Mesoamerican Ethnohistory," at Harvard University in 1957. It was quickly recognized by the handful of scholars who read it as the most thorough and insightful analysis of a large part of the Mesoamerican ensemble of primary sources ever done in a single volume. What made his work even more powerful was the sustained focus on a key problem in Mesoamerican studies, i.e., the problem of understanding the role of the Toltec kingdom and especially its legendary priest-king Topiltzin Quetzalcoatl in the history of Postclassic Mesoamerican society and in the encounters between Spaniards and natives in Tenochtitlan. But the dissertation was never published. Nicholson had completed it while on the move from Harvard to several early archaeological projects and on to his first and only job at UCLA, and moved on to many other important projects and essays.

Even though it was often referred to in footnotes and text, it was read by relatively few and never critically evaluated in journals. Those of us who dug into the Harvard archives, or cajoled a copy of the thesis from Nicholson or someone who had it, found ourselves working within a manuscript that was at once a tour de force of focused and creative readings of evidence and a royal guide to the conundrum of Topiltzin Quetzalcoatl. As time passed, this unpublished manuscript influenced, sometimes in a profound way, an array of interpretations of the Toltec and Quetzalcoatl traditions. Scholars such as Alfredo López Austin, Nigel Davies, Eduardo Matos Moctezuma, Eloise Quiñones Keber, Davíd Carrasco, and others depended in significant ways on Nicholson's stunning and eye-exhausting achievement. Either we followed his lead or struggled hard to develop alternative readings of parts of the primary evidence he had mastered. In a way, we stood on Nicholson's shoulders (or at least his research) but without the attendant claim that we could see farther. Rereading the manuscript today I am still tremendously impressed by Nicholson's rigorous contextualization of the evidence and distillation of the Topiltzin Quetzalcoatl material from over seventy sources, including pre-Hispanic pictorials, Sahagún's encyclopedia, colonial histories, Spanish chronicles, and archaeology. Like Eduard Georg Seler, Nicholson has set a standard of description and evaluation that will continue to guide us for decades to come.

For over ten years Luther Wilson, who was at that time the director of the University Press of Colorado, and I tried to persuade Nicholson to review the thesis and publish it in the Mesoamerican Worlds series. Other members of the Mesoamerican Archive's working group supported this effort to bring Nicholson's work to public light. Fortunately Alfredo López Austin lent his encouragement and Nicholson agreed to work with us and prepare the manuscript for publication. With the assistance of Scott Sessions, Nicholson went over the dissertation with a fine-tooth comb, greatly enhanced the bibliography, and prepared a new introduction.

Remembering Calvino, we can say forty-four years after its completion at Harvard, Nicholson's previously unpublished classic is coming out of the "folds of memory" and we can discover just how much more it has to say to us about Mesoamerican history and religion than even H. B. Nicholson and his Ph.D. committee could have imagined.

—Davíd Carrasco and Eduardo Matos Moctezuma

Contents

Illustrations

FIGURES

Foreword

Henry Nicholson's *Topiltzin Quetzalcoatl: The Once and Future Lord of the Toltecs* first came to my attention when he submitted it as a doctoral dissertation at Harvard in 1957 under the title "Topiltzin Quetzalcoatl of Tollan: A Problem in Mesoamerican Ethnohistory." Henry was one of my best graduate students at the time; however, let me state right at the beginning that when it came to Mesoamerican ethnohistory Henry was—and still is—miles ahead of me. After he left Harvard, Nicholson obtained a post at UCLA in which he has served with great distinction ever since.

While Henry and I remained in touch through the years, I don't think Topiltzin Quetzalcoatl would ever have come into our discourse again if it hadn't been for an 1975 issue of *Daedalus*, the journal of the American Academy of Arts and Sciences. This particular number of *Daedalus* was devoted to the theme of "transcendence," especially as to how this historical process pertained to the ancient civilizations of the Old World, particularly those of the last millennium before and into the early Christian Era. Benjamin I. Schwartz, the historian who edited the volume and wrote its introductory essay (Schwartz 1975), defined his use of the term "transcendence" in this context as referring to those movements such as classical Judaism, Zoroastrianism, Buddhism, and Confucianism, and to these we can add early Christianity. Such are manifest at a point in time when there is a critical and reflective questioning of the way things have been done and a vision of how they can be made better. All occur as civilization matures. One might think of them as expressions of the agony of civilization. Did such critiques or processes of transcendence occur in the New World? Although Schwartz does not belabor the point, he stated that "so far as we know" they do not appear in the "Mayan-Aztec civilizations."

I was fascinated by the transcendence concept, and my attention was particularly drawn to Schwartz's comment about the New World Precolumbian civilizations. Was there nothing comparable here to what Schwartz and his colleagues were describing for the Old World? I thought then of Nicholson's Topiltzin Quetzalcoatl thesis and went to the library for my first look at it since Henry's doctoral presentation. This led me to some related writings by Henry and others. While such brief study hardly qualified me as a scholar of Mexican ethnohistory, I was becoming more and more fascinated with the subject. I corresponded with Henry, telling him what I was up to. As I remember, he was slightly amused by this sudden foray of mine in a direction in which I had shown no previous interest; nevertheless, he was sympathetic and encouraging. So I went ahead and wrote my little paper, "Mesoamerican Civilization and the Idea of Transcendence," and the editors of *British Antiquity* were kind enough to publish it (Willey 1976). Looking back on it now, I am glad that while I will never claim any great competence in Mesoamerican ethnohistory, I learned a little something about it. Better yet, and while this may be debated by some, I think I made a case for the Native American scene with Topiltzin Quetzalcoatl, who, in his opposition to the prevailing dominance of war and human sacrifice, "rose transcendent over the contemporary darkness with his millennial vision of the a bright future."

—Gordon Willey
HARVARD UNIVERSITY

Prologue

Prologues are usually written to explain why a work has been published; to present readers with pieces of a reality that, although external to the content of the book, serve to explain or justify it. Prologues speak, from the outside, of the existence of hidden springs in the mechanism of the text or of deep impulses in the mind of the author. With prologues, one attempts to provide readers with resources bringing them closer to history or to the logical or aesthetic intimacy between the author and his work. One attempts in this way to help readers extract from between the lines the underlying elements necessary to reach higher levels of comprehension or emotional participation.

With my prologue, I would like to fulfill the habitual requisites of this type of foreword. However, my prologue is anomalous for two significant peculiarities: the first, because I do not intend to justify the publication of the book; on the contrary, I reflect upon the strange fact that this magnificent study was not published earlier; the second, because I do not find any satisfactory response to explain the lack of publication.

We begin with the second peculiarity to quickly resolve this problem. For many years, we specialists, who knew the work *Topiltzin Quetzalcoatl of Tollan: A Problem in Mesoamerican Ethnohistory*, asked the author why the manuscript remained unpublished. H. B. Nicholson's vague answers indicated to us only that he had no desire to publish his book. He kept his motives to himself, the very same ones that we, unaware of their character, considered a priori inadequate. We friends and colleagues insisted on the need for the original to go to press; but we no longer bothered the author further by asking the reasons for his reticence, a matter that we understood was of such a private nature that it obliged our discretion. Finally, H. B. Nicholson agreed to publish his work. Why didn't he make it widely available earlier to all those interested? This no longer matters; what counts is that insistence in this case bore fruit.

The history of the work is unique. In September 1957, H. B. Nicholson presented *Topiltzin Quetzalcoatl of Tollan* as a thesis, one of the requirements to obtain a Ph.D. in the Department of Anthropology at Harvard University. The topic chosen by Nicholson is one of the most interesting in the history of Mesoamerica. In effect, the Tollan-Quetzalcoatl binomial occupies a privileged place among the unresolved issues of the Postclassic, to the extent that the solution of its multiple unknowns will continue to shed light on many of the mysteries of the entire era, not only with respect to Central Mexico, but also to many other areas of Mesoamerica. Nicholson undertook an extraordinary and meticulous research project, the results of which have come to fill a gap extant in the historiography on the subject.

News of Nicholson's dissertation spread among Mesoamericanists. Copies soon circulated among colleagues as a prelude to an edition awaited almost as much as the original. It was of such high quality that it became an essential reference tool. However, the published version never appeared, and the thesis continued circulating year after year in its original version. Those interested in the subject became accustomed to using it and citing it in our work as a fundamental, although unpublished, work. Today, when we find ourselves more than four decades away from the time the original thesis was written, Mesoamericanists will update our references, since we will be able to cite the book in such a way that our readers can have easy access to it to corroborate or find further information.

For a work to be deserving of the wide acceptance of specialists, it requires, in addition to importance of subject matter and extraordinary quality of research, a high degree of usefulness. Such is the case of *Topiltzin Quetzalcoatl of Tollan*. In the book, Nicholson consolidates disperse and contradictory sources on the life of the figure, analyzes them carefully, and provides an erudite commentary. His statements are firmly grounded from the start. He begins by situating the problem as an extension of the history initiated after the fall of Teotihuacan, which converts the Toltecs into the center of gravity of the new Mesoamerican era. The Toltecs, that people who exerted such a strong cultural and political influence over an extremely vast territory, have a history still riddled with enigma, despite an abundance of documentation. At its core is the figure of the ruler-priest who bears the name Quetzalcoatl, who is also known as the god Feathered Serpent. However, the personality of this figure is highly controversial, because as Nicholson indicates, it is very difficult to separate his identity from that of the god Ehecatl Quetzalcoatl, with whom he is intimately linked.

Nicholson dealt with a corpus that he himself described as rich, fascinating, perplexing, and contradictory, a complex blend in which historical, legendary, and frankly mythological elements are confused. The information on Topiltzin Quetzalcoatl suggested to Nicholson that the identity of the Toltec personage gradually accumulated and syncretized elements from very distinct people, languages, areas, and times, which made it extremely difficult to handle the corpus. Thus it was necessary to use a strict methodology in the study of historiographic material. Documentary sources had to be exhaustively reunited, classified, and organized into a hierarchy. Although the actual collection of material is one of the most important achievements of the thesis, the study goes far beyond that. Once the texts were grouped, Nicholson studied them one by one from the historiographic point of view; he paraphrased them, synthesized their content, and evaluated them to construct what he called "The Basic Topiltzin Quetzalcoatl of Tollan Tale." Furthermore, it was necessary to reconcile documents with archaeological information. Nicholson turned mainly to iconography, searching for testimonies of the above-mentioned "basic tale" in painting and sculpture in the two sister cities, Tollan and Chichen Itza, whose mysterious parallelisms regarding the Feathered Serpent continue to be a subject of enormous interest for specialists.

Nicholson organized his research around three fundamental purposes: (1) to reconstruct, based on the most important sources, the so-called basic tale, as it could have been among many of the Nahua peoples of Central Mexico on the eve of the Conquest; (2) to meticulously evaluate the degree of historicity of the basic tale as we know it today; and (3) to briefly discuss some of the major features of the basic tale: (a) Topiltzin Quetzalcoatl with regard to the "Toltec problem"; (b) chronological aspects of the account; (c) geographical dimensions; and (d) problems of nomenclature and etymology.

After fulfilling these aims, Nicholson followed in the footsteps of Quetzalcoatl—literally following the accounts that spoke of the impressions miraculously left by the feet of the ruler-priest in stone—and he comes to compare the account of Quetzalcoatl's life with those of Votan in Chiapas and Vucub Caquix in the highlands of Guatemala. As a result, he concludes that these figures cannot be identified with Topiltzin, although there were perhaps vague and generalized influences of the Toltec hero's feats on the specific accounts of the two Maya characters. As for individuals portrayed on the walls and stones of Tollan and Chichen Itza, Nicholson prudently negates the possibility of clearly identifying Topiltzin Quetzalcoatl and recognizes that in this field two scholars would perhaps never be in complete agreement. He concludes that based on documentary sources and iconography that the manifest importance of Feathered Serpent in Toltec culture may be confirmed, and that the existence of leaders who used the name of Quetzalcoatl or its equivalents as titles is highly probable. Finally, he offers interesting hypotheses resulting from his scrupulous analysis.

After more than four decades, Nicholson's thesis still retains the freshness of the original, as well as its scientific rigor. The subject of research, crucial in Mesoamerican studies, is far from being resolved, since many of the mysteries of the Tollan-Quetzalcoatl binomial persist to the present, both due to the difficulties of its enquiry as well as because it forms the interpretational core of many of the basic problems of the Postclassic. On the other hand, no one has duplicated the enormous task of critically analyzing the documentary corpus referring to Topiltzin Quetzalcoatl, and anyone who does research on the subject must consult this indispensable work.

We rejoice because this magnificent work can finally reach specialists as well as the general public!

—Alfredo López Austin
TEPOZTLÁN

Preface

In September 1957 I submitted my doctoral dissertation, "Topiltzin Quetzalcoatl of Tollan: A Problem in Mesoamerican Ethnohistory," to the Department of Anthropology, Harvard University. Approved by my doctoral committee, I was granted the Ph.D. in anthropology in June 1958. Two copies of the dissertation were filed at Harvard, one in the Harvard University Archives and the other in the Tozzer Library of the Peabody Museum of Archaeology and Ethnology—and later, a third copy in the library of Pre-Columbian Studies, Dumbarton Oaks, Trustees for Harvard University, Washington, D.C. In 1962, I obtained a microfilm of it, from which a hard copy was made, Xeroxes of which I made available to various scholars and to the Biblioteca Nacional de México. Others have been able to consult the copy in the Tozzer Library, and I have lent my own copy to students and colleagues. So, although it remained unpublished, the dissertation has achieved a certain dissemination over the years and has often been cited in the scholarly literature.

In September 1974, at the 41st International Congress of Americanists, Mexico City, I presented a paper entitled "The Deity 9 Wind 'Ehecatl-Quetzalcoatl' in the Mixteca Pictorials," which was published in 1978. Drawing upon the dissertation and additional research I had undertaken while preparing my article summarizing the religious/ritual system of late pre-Hispanic Central Mexico for the *Handbook of Middle American Indians* (Nicholson 1971),

I presented a paper at the 42nd International Congress of Americanists in Paris, September 1976, "Ehecatl Quetzalcoatl vs. Topiltzin Quetzalcoatl of Tollan: A Problem in Mesoamerican Religion and History," in which I compared and contrasted the wind/creator deity with the Toltec ruler/priest of the historical traditions, while recognizing their partial merger—which was published in 1979. In that same year, I presented a paper, directly derived from the dissertation, at the 43rd International Congress of Americanists, Vancouver, Canada (University of British Columbia, Simon Fraser University), entitled "Topiltzin Quetzalcoatl of Tollan: The Primary Sources Considered," an abstract of which was published in the program and abstracts of the congress. In 1987, I presented another paper, "The Comparative Iconography of Aztec Style Feathered Serpents," at the 86th Annual Meeting of the American Anthropological Society, Chicago, an abstract of which was published in the conference abstracts. I presented a somewhat fuller version of this paper at a conference at the Moses Mesoamerican Archive and Research Project, Princeton University, November 1996, and which, titled as "The Iconography of the Feathered Serpent in Late Postclassic Central Mexico," is now included in *Mesoamerica's Classic Heritage: Teotihuacan and Beyond* (Nicholson 2000). In February 1997, I presented a paper, "The 'Return of Quetzalcoatl': Did It Play a Role in the Conquest of Mexico?," at the 8th Annual Latin American Symposium, "La Conquista: Divergent Cultural Perspectives," of the San Diego Museum of Man, which is being prepared for publication. Other relevant publications include the entry "Quetzalcoatl" in the *Encylopedia of Latin American History and Culture* (Nicholson 1996b) and the entries "Feathered Serpent" and "Topiltzin Quetzalcoatl" in the *Oxford Encylopedia of Mesoamerican Cultures* (Nicholson 2001 a/b). Thus, my research concerning what can be called the "Quetzalcoatl problem" has continued throughout my career—and my interest is as strong as ever.

I had always hoped to be able to prepare a version of the dissertation for publication, but, for various reasons, until now this has not been possible. Finally, Davíd Carrasco, who has long shared my interest in Topiltzin Quetzalcoatl (hereafter abbreviated TQ) and is general editor, with Eduardo Matos Moctezuma, of the *Mesoamerican Worlds* series of the University Press of Colorado, on whose editorial board I also serve, convinced me that, in spite of the many years that have elapsed since its composition, the publication of my thesis—if accompanied by an introduction specifying and commenting on new editions published since 1957 of the primary sources concerning TQ that I had summarized and discussed—would constitute a useful contribution to Mesoamerican studies. Accordingly, he recommended its publication to Luther Wilson, then director of the University Press of Colorado, and the latter agreed. My gratitude to them, and to Scott Sessions, who copied on the computer the text of the dissertation, for their aid and support is profound.

My interest in the subject of the dissertation emerged very early. An initial fascination with the pre-Hispanic cultures of Mexico, particularly Maya and Aztec, was initially stimulated by my visits to San Diego's beautiful Balboa Park, located only a half-hour's walk from my home in San Diego's Hillcrest district. The most impressive of the Hispanic-style buildings flanking El Prado Avenue, built for the Panama-California Exposition of 1915–1916, was the California Building in colonial Churrigueresque style, featuring a tower over two hundred feet high and a large tiled dome—which became San Diego's symbol. An ambitious exhibit, focusing on New World archaeology and physical anthropology, entitled "The Story of Man Through the Ages," was organized for the exposition by Edgar Lee Hewett, director of the School of American Archaeology of the Archaeological Institute of America, in collaboration with the leading American physical anthropologist, Ales Hrdlicka, of the U.S. National Museum, Smithsonian Institution, Washington, D.C. It especially featured, displayed in the great rotunda, the finest casts of Classic Lowland Maya monumental stone carvings that had been made up to that time, stelae, giant zoomorphs, and altars from Quirigua, Guatemala, where Hewett had directed four seasons of archaeological excavations. He also commissioned a talented artist of Santa Fe, New Mexico, Carlos Vierra, to paint murals of six major Lowland Maya sites: Copan, Quirigua, Tikal, Palenque, Uxmal, and Chichen Itza. Incorporated as a permanent museum in the California Building after the close of the exposition, when I became old enough I began to visit it regularly, first with my mother, then with my neighborhood pals, especially during the second exposition in the park, the California-Pacific International Exposition of 1935–1936. I marveled particularly at the monumental casts, with their long hieroglyphic inscriptions chronicling the reigns of the lords of Quirigua (although still largely undeciphered at that time), and the murals of the six great Lowland Maya ruins.

More directly relevant to the theme of this book was my attendance at a lecture, instigated by my grandmother who was visiting us from Oregon in the summer of 1936, in the auditorium of the House of Hospitality, five minutes' walk from the museum. As I described it in an article reminiscing about the role Balboa Park and the San Diego Museum of Man had played in arousing my interest in ancient Mexico (Nicholson 1993):

> It [the lecture] was presented by an earnest young man whose thesis, in my best recollection, was that the legendary "fair god" of pre-Hispanic Middle America, Quetzalcoatl, was actually Jesus Christ, who, after His apostolic ministry in the Old World, came to the New World to undertake a similar mission. I can still recall some of the lantern slides that illustrated his talk, including the relief of the Temple of the Cross of Palenque with which I was familiar through the cast of it that [was]

> mounted on the east wall of the entrance vestibule of [the] museum. I have always been curious as to who this lecturer was (I was too young to really note his name). My grandmother must have seen an announcement of his talk in the newspaper, most likely the *San Diego Union*, to which we subscribed. A few years ago, while on a visit to my old hometown, I actually went to the San Diego Public Library and combed the back files of the *Union*, hoping to discover, in the daily schedule of events routinely published in this paper during the Exposition, the title of the lecture and the name of the speaker. I failed, and to this day I am ignorant of his identity. However, I am convinced that it was during this youthful experience . . . that the seed was planted that many years later grew into my Harvard doctoral dissertation: concerning Quetzalcoatl.

Other significant influences were my reading, while in junior high school, Lew Wallace's 1873 romance *The Fair God*, based on the conquest of Mexico and incorporating the "return of Quetzalcoatl" theme, and later, in high school, D. H. Lawrence's 1926 novel of postrevolutionary Mexico revolving around the same basic motif, *The Plumed Serpent*. As I continued to read more widely in the Mesoamerican field, particularly after I began my graduate studies in anthropology at Harvard, I became convinced, in the face of the almost chaotic plethora of theories concerning TQ, that a thorough, systematic summary and critical analysis of the extant primary documentary sources concerning this enigmatic figure, if it would not "solve" all of the many problems connected with him, would at least provide an organized body of data of considerable value to all students of the subject. The chair of my doctoral committee, the eminent New World archaeologist Gordon R. Willey, approved my project and, as indicated, after its completion approved the dissertation. And here, at long last, it is—virtually as it was when I submitted it in the fall of 1957 but frequently rephrased and occasionally corrected, in the interests of improved accuracy and precision. I offer it now for the consideration of my fellow Mesoamericanists, in the hope they will agree that, even after these many years, it still constitutes a useful contribution to our field.

—H. B. Nicholson

1957 Introduction

It is becoming increasingly clear that the culture pattern which prevailed in Central Mexico at the time of the Conquest represented only the final phase of a tradition that had crystallized during the still poorly understood period immediately following the breakdown of the Teotihuacan configuration, or, in current terminology, the earliest phase of the Early Postclassic. At this time also, the vague outlines of genuine history begin to loom into view from out of the mythic mistiness which enshrouds the Classic and Preclassic periods, in the form of systematically dated pictorial records of which a few post-Conquest copies or verbal digests have been preserved. The native entity that figures most prominently at this quasi-historical point in the Central Mexican sequence is the no longer quite so mysterious Toltecs. And at the very core of the long-standing "Toltec problem" is the personality and culture-historical significance of the figure I shall regularly refer to as Topiltzin Quetzalcoatl, usually stated to have been the greatest of their priest/rulers. A careful analysis of the available data pertaining to Topiltzin Quetzalcoatl, who could legitimately be called the first individual in Mexican history, might add significantly to our understanding of this key stage in the evolution of Mesoamerican high culture.

Speculations concerning this preeminent ancient Mexican figure have abounded ever since the sixteenth-century Spanish missionaries first learned of the traditions clustering about his life and death. Not a few of these have been frankly absurd, even some offered by scholars of considerable reputation. As Eric Thompson (1945: 13) once commented: "Modern investigators have interpreted the quetzal-feathered serpent as a deity of almost everything under and including the sun." In spite of the gradual buildup of an extensive Quetzalcoatl literature, no study marshaling more than a fraction of the available evidence has yet appeared. The time seems ripe to attempt a more thorough treatment, if for no other reason than to assemble in one place a summary of the bulk of the important primary source information, the raw material out of which any higher-level interpretations must necessarily be built. The present study, however, is intended to be somewhat more than a mere source book on Topiltzin Quetzalcoatl.

As research concerning Mesoamerican religions, ethnohistory, and archaeology continues, it becomes more evident that the complex of ideas that surrounded the composite figure of Quetzalcoatl at the time of the Conquest represented the end product of a gradual process of accretion and syncretism over a long period of time. To successfully identify and separate out the various individual strands which have gone into the weaving of this complicated historical tapestry is a formidable undertaking, requiring both the thorough analysis of numerous documentary sources in various languages from different parts of Mesoamerica and the careful consideration of the relevant archaeological evidence. This study aims only to examine one limited aspect of this larger problem, that relating to a large corpus of documentary source material that provides a number of different versions of what can be called the Topiltzin Quetzalcoatl of Tollan Tale, or, at the least, significant allusions to its protagonist. The purely supernatural figure, whom I shall refer to as Ehecatl Quetzalcoatl, will receive only tangential consideration. With the cult and mythology of this old creator/wind/rain deity, symbolized by the feathered serpent, who clearly goes back well into the Classic period if not before, the personality and tale of Topiltzin Quetzalcoatl of Tollan seems to have become almost inextricably entwined. Separating the two is difficult, but a reasonably clear division can in most cases be made. Ideally, both aspects should be considered jointly, but this would demand a far more extensive investigation. It is the figure of historical legend, then, the man, not the god, who is the subject of this study.

The summary and analysis of the written sources will consume the bulk of the study, but consideration of the relevant archaeological evidence will be briefly taken up in a special section. The paper will be roughly organized as follows: the important available primary accounts of Topiltzin Quetzalcoatl will be grouped by area, bibliographized, paraphrased, summarized, and briefly appraised. On the basis of this data presentation, an attempt will be made to reconstruct what I shall call the Basic Topiltzin Quetzalcoatl of Tollan Tale. Following this, various related themes will be considered. The key problem of the degree of possible historicity of the tale will receive particular attention. Finally, certain tentative conclusions will be offered.

An important goal of this study is to clear away much of the speculative deadwood, usually based on consideration of a limited portion of the available data and colored by romantic preconceptions, that has accumulated over the years around Topiltzin Quetzalcoatl and which has only further confused an already highly confused problem. If the following compilation and analysis clarifies to any extent one of the most important periods in Mesoamerican prehistory and the role within it of one of the indigenous New World's most famous legendary figures, it will have succeeded in its aim.

2001 Introduction

In this introduction, I will focus on significant post-1957 editions, particularly new translations, of the many primary sources I summarized and discussed in my dissertation—as well as significant studies of these sources, especially those that have clarified their authorship and revealed new relationships between them. Each section of the dissertation will be reviewed in turn.

I: Central Mexico: Nahuatl

A. EARLIEST ACCOUNTS OF THE BASIC TOPILTZIN QUETZALCOATL OF TOLLAN TALE

In this first category, I included six accounts (probably all pre-1570) that I felt were of particular importance because they presented "a more or less coherent narrative, tracing sequentially the salient features of Topiltzin Quetzalcoatl's (TQ's) career, rather than providing mere allusions, snatches, or single brief episodes." The first was the *Historia de los Mexicanos por sus pinturas* (*HMP*). I reviewed its known history and cited the editions of it that had been published up to 1957. In 1965, Angel Ma. Garibay K. published another version of the *HMP* in his *Teogonía e historia de los Mexicanos: Tres opúsculos del siglo XVI*, in Editorial Porrúa's "Sepan Cuantos . . ." series, with numbered paragraphs and correcting the spelling of and adding a glossary of the Nahuatl words, omitting those of the deities. In 1988, a popular edition of the *HMP*, with accompanying French translation and commentary by Paule Obadia-Baudesson, was published by l'Association "Oxomoco y Cipactonal," Paris.

In the introduction to his 1965 edition, Garibay agreed with the suggestion of Francisco del Paso y Troncoso, cited by Joaquín García Icazbalceta in his introduction to his 1891 edition of the *HMP*, that it could be attributed to Fray Andrés de Olmos, the great pioneer Franciscan missionary-linguist-ethnographer, who was commissioned as early as 1533 by Sebastián Ramírez de Fuenleal, president of the Second Audiencia de Nueva España, and Fray Martín de Valencia, the Franciscan custodian, to undertake a systematic investigation of indigenous Central Mexican culture. Garibay (1953–1954, II: 32–36) had earlier considered this attribution. It was further developed by León-Portilla (1969b: 39–49) and other scholars and has been most fully developed by Baudot (1977: 190–197; 1995: 193–201). The latter believes that Olmos had compiled his substantial account of the culture of the natives of Central Mexico, which he calls *Tratado de antigüedades mexicanas*, by 1539 and that the next year he sent a copy to Ramírez de Fuenleal, who had returned to Spain in 1536—where he became Bishop of Cuenca and, in 1542, president of the Chancery of Valladolid. Baudot suggests that Ramírez de Fuenleal arranged, just before his death in 1547, to have that portion of the *Tratado* copied that constitutes the twelve leaves of the *HMP*. In any case, that it was directly derived from the lost treatise of Olmos now seems almost a certainty. This, combined with its very early date and the probabilities that it was clearly based at least in part on pre-Hispanic historical and religious/ritual pictorials and was compiled by a fluent Nahuatl speaker, lends it particular value.

The second source summarized and discussed was what I called *The Juan Cano Relaciones*, two closely similar accounts, derived from a common source, of the dynastic history of Mexico Tenochtitlan and the earlier dynasties of Tollan and Colhuacan—from which the rulers of the first named center claimed direct descent. I listed the full titles of both accounts as given by García Icazbalceta in his 1891 publication (republished in 1941 and 1991). Prepared by anonymous Franciscan friars as early as 1532, based on "libros por figuras y carácteres" and information provided by "los que más saben," this account of TQ—however incomplete and abbreviated—I would still regard as quite important. In 1978, in *Chronologies in New World Archaeology*, in my article discussing western Mesoamerica during 900–1520, focusing on the primary ethnohistorical sources, I discussed the chronological aspect of *The Juan Cano Relaciones*, proposing that TQ's reign in Tollan was dated here ca. A.D. 885–895/97. In 1971, Hermann Wagner undertook a comparative analysis of these twin sources—and in 1991 the 1891 García Icazbalceta versions were published again by Germán Vázquez in his *Relaciones de la Nueva España*, Madrid, Historia 16, Crónicas de América 65.

The third source discussed was André Thevet's French translation, in the Bibliothèque Nationale, Paris (BNP), of a portion of a lost Spanish source he called *Histoyre du Mechique*. As I noted, it was first published and discussed by Edouard de Jonghe in 1905. In 1961, Joaquín Meade published a Spanish translation of the de Jonghe version, with notes by Wigberto Jiménez Moreno. In 1965, another Spanish translation, by Ramón Rosales Munguía, also based on the de Jonghe version, was published, with introduction and notes, by Garibay in the same volume in which he republished the *HMP*.

In the dissertation, I outlined the hypotheses of de Jonghe, Meade, and Garibay concerning its authorship. Recently, Baudot (1977: 197–204; 1995: 201–208) discussed this question at some length. He agreed with de Jonghe that it was derived from the writings of Fray Andrés de Olmos but differed from the views of Meade, Rosales Munguía, and Garibay that parts of it had possibly been composed by another Franciscan, Fray Marcos de Niza, of Cibola fame. Baudot argued that the chronological and geographical references in the early chapters of the *Histoyre* that seemed to be inconsistent with their composition by Olmos could be explained if they were "attributed to the occasional manipulations of Thevet." He concluded, therefore, that the French cosmographer copied this portion of Olmos's *Tratado* between 1547 (when Mexico Tenochtitlan is referred to as the See of an Archdiocese) and 1575 (date of the publication of Thevet's *Cosmographie*). Although perhaps not all of the problems connected with the composition of the *Histoyre du Mechique* have been resolved, this view appears to be the most cogent yet proposed. In any case, the account of TQ contained in its final two chapters was almost certainly collected by Olmos and appears to provide one of the earliest and most authentic versions of the tale.

The fourth source of this section was the *Leyenda de los soles*, a Mexica "world history," in Nahuatl, dated 1558, contained in the same ex-Boturini manuscript volume, "Códice Chimalpopoca," as the *Anales de Cuauhtitlan* and the *Breve relación* of Pedro Ponce de León. I noted its many similarities to the HMP, stressing that both were clearly based on pictorial histories focusing on Mexico Tenochtitlan. Primo Feliciano Velázquez's 1945 Spanish translation, including the accompanying photographs of the pages of the original manuscript, was republished in 1975 (see below, *Anales de Cuauhtitlan*). In 1974, the 1938 Lehmann paleography and German translation of the *Leyenda*, in the same volume with the *Anales de Cuauhtitlan*, was reissued, with preface, errata, and expanded index by Gerdt Kutscher. In the same year, John Bierhorst published an English translation of the bulk of the *Leyenda*'s account of TQ (corresponding to paragraphs 1555–1587 of the

Lehmann edition)—and in 1992 he published a new paleography of the Nahuatl text of the entire *Leyenda*, with English translation, notes, concordance to proper names and titles, and subject guide (reissued in 1998, in paperback). This was its first full publication, for Bierhorst completed it with the last page of the León y Gama copy, also in the BNP, which had first (1989) been published by Peter Tschohl. The ex-Boturini manuscript lacked its final leaf, so the Paso y Troncoso, Lehmann, and Velázquez editions were all incomplete. I would again emphasize the importance of the *Leyenda*, which apparently derived from the imperial capital itself, as the earliest extant Nahuatl version of the TQ tale.

The fifth source summarized in this section was the *Historia general (universal) de las cosas de (la) Nueva España* of Fray Bernardino de Sahagún—with due recognition of the earlier versions in the *Códices Matritenses*. In 1957, only six of the twelve books (I–III, VII–VIII, XII) of the *Historia general*, in the bilingual Nahuatl/Spanish version of the *Florentine Codex*, in the Anderson and Dibble edition of the paleography of the Nahuatl text, with English translation, were available. Since then, between that year and 1982, the remaining six books and the introductory volume have been published, plus, between 1975 and 1981, revised editions of books I, II, III, and XII—while books IV–V, VI, VII, VIII, IX, X, and XI were reprinted between 1974 and 1979. In 1979, a three-volume color photoreproduction of the original manuscript of the *Florentine Codex*, in the Biblioteca Medicea Laurenziana, Florence, was published by the Giunti Barbera Press, Florence, and the Archivo General de la Nación, Mexico.

In 1982, the paleography of the Spanish text of the *Florentine Codex* was published for the first time by Fomento Cultural Banamex, with introduction, paleography, glossary, and notes by Alfredo López Austin and Josefina García Quintana. In 1988, a more available edition of this text was published by the Alianza Editorial, S.A., Madrid, and the next year in Mexico by Editorial Cien. In 1990, another edition was published in Madrid, edited by Juan Carlos Temprano (Historia 16, Crónicas de América 55). Until these recent editions of the Spanish text of the *Florentine Codex*, all previous editions had been derived mainly from the *Manuscrito de Tolosa*, a sixteenth-century version virtually identical to that of the *Florentine Codex* but whose exact relationship to it is still not entirely clear.

In 1993, the University of Oklahoma Press published the first color photographic edition of the *Primeros memoriales*, the first stage of Sahagún's great ethnographic/linguistic project, in manuscripts divided between two Madrid libraries. Four years later, in 1997, the same press published the first complete paleography of the Nahuatl text of the *Primeros memoriales*, with English translation by Thelma Sullivan, Arthur Anderson, and Charles Dibble. The volume was coordinated by myself, assisted by Wayne Ruwet. I also wrote the introduction and most of the notes, while Eloise Quiñones Keber contributed a study of the manuscript and analyzed its numerous illustrations.

Since 1957, the Sahaguntine literature, including various re-editions of the *Historia general*, has grown enormously. Most of it, up to 1987, is itemized in two general, multiauthored volumes devoted to Sahagún's works (Edmonson 1974 and Klor de Alva, Nicholson, and Quiñones Keber 1988)—and in the "Ethnohistory: Mesoamerica" section of the *Handbook of Latin American Studies*. It does not appear, however, that any significantly new or different information concerning TQ that was not available in 1957 has been provided by these many recent Sahaguntine publications.

One minor item that was available in 1957, in Paso y Troncoso's 1905 black-and-white photographic reproduction of the manuscripts of the *Primeros memoriales*, which I probably should have mentioned, was the ascription of the creation of the Chichimeca ancestors of the major peoples of Central Mexico, as well as the heavens, sun, and the earth, to "Topiltzin Quetzalcoatl" (Sahagún 1997: 223). As I noted in footnote 9 of this page, this particular binomial designation was usually reserved for the traditional Toltec ruler rather than the creator/wind deity, Ehecatl Quetzalcoatl, who was clearly intended here—but I also recognized that "at least by the time of the Conquest . . . their personas had intertwined to the extent that it is difficult to sharply differentiate them."

I still regard Sahagún's account of TQ as one of the most important extant, in spite of some confusing features (e.g., the intertwining of the TQ and Huemac tales). Somewhat frustrating is the absence of any mention of his parentage and youth, which are covered in most of the other accounts in this category. A major aspect of the Sahaguntine version of the TQ tale is the emphasis on his expected return and the significant role it played in the interaction between Cortés and Motecuhzoma II (cf. Nicholson n.d.a).

The sixth source I assigned to this initial category was the *Anales de Cuauhtitlan*. As indicated, the 1945 Velázquez Spanish translation of this key source was reissued, with the same title, in 1975, in smaller paperback format and also including the photographs of all pages of the manuscript—now of particular value, since the original manuscript appears to be lost. In 1974, as was also indicated above, the 1938 Lehmann edition was reissued, with preface, errata, and expanded index by Gerdt Kutscher. That same year, John Bierhorst published his English translation of the *Anales de Cuauhtitlan's* TQ tale (paragraphs 54–157 of the Lehmann edition), and in 1992 a new paleography of the Nahuatl text of the entire *Anales*, with direct English translation, notes, concordance to proper nouns and titles, and subject guide (which, together with the *Leyenda de los soles*, was reissued in 1998 in paperback). Unquestionably, the *Anales de Cuauhtitlan*, in spite of the uncertainty surrounding the source(s) of the tradition(s) it records, constitutes one of the most valuable and authentic accounts of the life and career of Mesoamerica's most notable pre-Hispanic personage.

B. IMPORTANT SUPPLEMENTARY ACCOUNTS

The works of the pioneer Franciscan missionary, Fray Toribio de Benavente (Paredes), Motolinía, constituted the first item in this category. I used and cited two editions of his briefer chronicle, generally known as the *Historia de los Indios de la Nueva España*: that edited by Fr. Daniel Sánchez García, published in Barcelona in 1914, and the 1941 Mexican edition of the Editorial Salvador Chávez Hayhoe, a reprint of it. I should have noted that the Sánchez García edition was a reprint of the text of the *Historia* published in Mexico in 1858 by García Icazbalceta. This edition was based on a copy of the sixteenth-century copy, known as the *Manuscrito de la Ciudad de México*, that had been sent to him by William Prescott (from a copy in the Phillips collection)—with some attention to the earliest partial publication of the *Historia*, in 1848, in the ninth volume of Kingsborough's *Antiquities of Mexico*. Kingsborough's edition had been based on the Obadiah Rich copy of another sixteenth-century copy, in the Biblioteca de El Escorial near Madrid. Other pre-1957 editions of the *Historia* that I might have cited were: (1) the Madrid edition of 1869, published in volume 53 of the *Colección de documentos inéditos para la historia de España*, based on the El Escorial copy; (2) the first English translation, that of Elisabeth Andros Foster, published by the Cortés Society, Bancroft Library, University of California, Berkeley, in 1950; (3) a second English translation, by Francis Borgia Steck, O.F.M., published the following year by the Academy of American Franciscan History, Washington, D.C.; (4) that of 1956, a reprint, by the Editora Nacional, Mexico, of the 1914 Barcelona edition; (5) a selection of passages from the *Historia*, edited in 1956 by Luis Nicolau d'Olwer, in the *Biblioteca del Estudiante Universitario* series, number 72, of the Universidad Nacional Autónoma de México (second edition, 1964).

Since 1957, various new editions of the *Historia* have been published, including: (1) Krauss, of Vaduz, Lichtenstein, 1966 (facsimile of the edition of 1869); (2) Editorial Porrúa, Colección "Sepan Cuantos . . . ," núm. 129, Mexico, 1969, edited and with a study, appendices, notes, and index by Edmundo O'Gorman (based on the unpublished paleography of J. Jesús Gil Salcedo of the *Manuscrito de la Ciudad de México*); (3) Ediciones Atlas, Biblioteca de Autores Españoles, Colección Rivadeneira, vol. 240, Madrid, 1970, edited by Fidel Lejarza (reprint of 1914 Barcelona edition); (4) Ediciones del Arq., edited by Juan Cortina Portilla for Contabilidad Ruf Mexicana S.A., Mexico, 1979, with introduction, paleography, notes, and comparisons with the other two sixteenth-century manuscripts of the *Historia* (El Escorial, The Hispanic Society of America), and photoreproduction of the manuscript, by Javier O. Aragón; (5) Clásicos Castalia, Madrid, 1985, edited, with introduction and notes, by Georges Baudot; (6) Historia 16, Crónicas de América, 16, Madrid, 1985, edited by Claudio Esteva Fabregat; (7) Alianza Editorial, Sección Clásicos del Descubrimiento, El Libro del Bolsillo, 1348, Madrid, 1988, edited, with introduction and notes, by Giuseppe Bellini.

The three most useful of these many editions are the Mexican editions of 1969 and 1979, edited, respectively, by O'Gorman and Aragón, and the Spanish edition of 1985, edited by Baudot. The Aragón edition is particularly valuable, for it includes, in addition to a photoreproduction of the *Manuscrito de la Ciudad de México*, probably the earliest surviving version of the *Historia*, a faithful transcription of its text with the variants in El Escorial and The Hispanic Society of America manuscripts indicated in footnotes.

For the *Memoriales*, I used the only publication of it available at that time, the 1903–1907 edition of Luis García Pimentel. Since 1957, four more editions have appeared: (1) Edmundo Avina Levy, Guadalajara, 1967 (facsimile of 1903–1907 edition); (2) Ediciones Atlas, Biblioteca de Autores Españoles, Colección Rivadeneira, volume 240, Madrid, 1970 (reprint of 1903 edition); (3) Universidad Nacional Autónoma de México, Instituto de Investigaciones Históricas, Serie de Historiadores y Cronistas de Indias, 2, Mexico, 1971, edited, with analytic study of the writings of Motolinía, notes, and appendices, by Edmundo O'Gorman; (4) El Colegio de México, Centro de Estudios Linguísticos y Literarios, Biblioteca Novohispana, III, Mexico, 1996, edited, with introduction, notes, and appendix, by Nancy Joe Dyer. Only the 1971 O'Gorman and 1996 Dyer editions are of real significance, the former due to the editor's analysis of the document, plus its many supplementary materials, and the latter because it is its first genuinely critical edition, with a detailed description of the original manuscript in the Benson Latin American Collection of the University of Texas, Austin.

The nature of the *Historia* and the relation between it and the *Memoriales* have posed many problems ever since the publication of the latter in 1903. These problems have been discussed by various scholars, who frequently differ in their explanations and interpretations. Based on numerous references in the works of those who utilized Motolinía in their own writings, especially the 1585 *Relación de la Nueva España* of Alonso de Zorita (1909; first complete edition, 1999), most students have concluded, as I indicated in my 1957 discussion of his writings, that late in his career Motolinía completed a "final" version of his chronicle, no copy of which apparently has survived. Both O'Gorman (Motolinía 1969a: ix–xix; 1971: xxi–xlv; 1982) and Baudot (1977: 372–382; 1985: 59–70; 1995: 381–394) have made serious efforts, which differ significantly, to reconstruct the chapter structure and the subjects covered in this vanished work. In 1989, O'Gorman, assisted by his seminar students, went considerably beyond his earlier attempts to reconstruct its chapters and their topics and, utilizing both the *Historia* and the *Memoriales*, included the actual texts, chapter by reconstructed chapter, that he hypothesized were present in what he called "El Libro Perdido."

The most controversial aspect of the post-1957 attempts by scholars to better understand the relation between the *Historia* and the *Memoriales* has been O'Gorman's hypothesis (Motolinía 1969a, 1971, 1989) that the *Historia* had been written not by Motolinía but by another friar, the Comisario General, Fray Martín Sarmiento de Hojacastro, drawing on Motolinía's writings. He suggests that it was prepared for a very particular purpose, to protest against the New Laws of 1542, which were strenuously opposed by the Franciscans of New Spain. This view has not received general acceptance and has been much criticized (e.g., Gómez Canedo 1973), especially by Baudot (1971; 1977: 356–361; 1983: 82; 1995: 365–371).

This controversy and the other contrasting views of those who have addressed the "Motolinía problem"—however interesting and important because of the great value of his writings due to their early date and the exceptional opportunities he had for gathering reliable information from the most knowledgeable native informants—is not really that germane to the "TQ problem." This is because Motolinía's material on TQ appears without significant variations in all of his surviving writings or those that can reliably be attributed to him, which I summarized and which are usefully consolidated in Motolinía 1989.

The second source I discussed in this section was a "Toltec dirge" in the *Cantares Mexicanos* collection in the Biblioteca Nacional de México. As noted, its theme is the "flight"of TQ from Tollan to Tlapallan. Since 1957, a number of new translations and discussions of it have appeared (e.g., Schultze-Jena 1957: 138–141 [Nahuatl/German]; Garibay 1961: 151–152, 235–236 [Nahuatl/Spanish], 1964: 92–95 [Spanish]; 1964–1968, III: 1–2, xxiii–xxv [Nahuatl/Spanish]; León-Portilla 1964: 121–123 [Spanish], 1969: 109–111 [English]; Seler 1973: 78–80 [Nahuatl/German]; Bierhorst 1974: 63–65, 94–96 [English], 1985a: 219–221, 447–448 [Nahuatl/English]; and Brotherston 1979: 272–273 [English]). These translations often differ considerably, owing in part to the somewhat archaic idiom employed and in part to differences of opinion concerning whether certain words and phrases are place-names or if they should be translated more literally according to their ostensible meanings. However, in spite of these translational problems, there has always been general agreement concerning the overall significance of the piece as providing references to personages and places that figure prominently in the Basic Topiltzin Quetzalcoatl of Tollan Tale.

The third source discussed was the account of TQ of Fray Andrés de Olmos in his *Suma* that was utilized by both Fray Bartolomé de Las Casas, in his *Apologética historia*, and Fray Gerónimo de Mendieta, in his *Historia eclesiástica indiana.* As indicated above, Baudot (1977: 109–240; 1995: 121–245) has made the most comprehensive study of Olmos's missionary career in New Spain and his writings. He dates the *Tratado* to ca. 1533–1539, and the *Suma* to ca. 1546—and he attempted to reconstruct the topics covered in both. Since 1957, three new editions of Mendieta have been published in Mexico, in the Biblioteca Porrúa series, 46 (1971, 1980, 1987). These are facsimiles of the 1870 García Icazbalceta edition and include for the first time the ten engravings contained in the original manuscript in the Benson Latin American Collection of the University of Texas, Austin.

Two complete and one partial edition of Fray Bartolomé de Las Casas's *Apologética historia* have also appeared since 1957. The first, in 1957–1958, was published in Madrid, in the Biblioteca de Autores Españoles series, volumes 105–106, Obras Escogidas de Fray Bartolomé de Las Casas, edited, with a preliminary critical study and an Indice Onomástica y Toponómico by Juan Pérez de Tudela Bueso. The partial edition was published in 1966 by the Editorial Porrúa, Mexico, "Los Indios de México y Nueva España: Antología," in their "Sepan cuantos . . ." series, number 57, edited, with prologue, appendices, and notes, by Edmundo O'Gorman, with the collaboration of Jorge Alberto Manrique. The second complete edition, the most important, was published in 1967 by the Universidad Nacional Autónoma de México, Instituto de Investigaciones Históricas, Serie de Historiadores y Cronistas de Indias, 1–2, "Apologética Historia Sumaria," edited, with preliminary study, appendices, and notes, by Edmundo O'Gorman. Again, it is worth emphasizing that this Olmos account of TQ appears to be the earliest, by a significant margin, of those that describe him as a bearded white man.

The fourth source treated in this section was the combined account of the *Codex Telleriano-Remensis* (*TR*) and *Codex Vaticanus* A (*VA*), which contain, between them, one of the most important versions, however incomplete, of the TQ tale. Since 1957, various new editions and studies of both of these key sources have appeared. Beginning with the *Telleriano-Remensis*, in 1964 the Secretaria de Hacienda y Crédito Público, Mexico, included, in the first volume of their partial "republication" of Kingsborough's *Antiquities of Mexico*, photographs of the illustrated pages of the 1899 Loubat/Hamy color lithographic edition, with paleography of the Spanish text and commentary by José Corona Nuñez. In 1995, the University of Texas Press published by far the best edition of the *TR*, in color photographs from the original manuscript, edited, with a comprehensive commentary and analysis by Eloise Quiñones Keber. This edition includes an English translation of the Spanish texts, many appendices, detailed comparisons with the Italian text and cognate images of the *VA*, numerous line drawings by Michel Besson, and extensive notes. In the same year, Quiñones Keber also published a new transcription of the annotations of the *TR* in diskette and printed form in the SUP-INFOR series, supervised by Marc Thouvenot, which makes available to scholars important examples of the extensive Mesoamerican manuscript collection of the Bibliothèque Nationale, Paris.

Quiñones Keber (e.g., 1979, 1984a, 1984b, 1987b, 1990, 1995a), in this and other studies, suggested that the *TR* was probably prepared between 1553 and 1555, utilizing two native artists who copied earlier ritual/divinatory and historical/dynastic native tradition pictorials. After being annotated by two native informants and Spanish Dominicans (she identified six different hands), the annotations were most likely completed in 1563, in Puebla, by the Dominican lay brother, Pedro de los Ríos, mentioned in the *VA*, who had earlier been stationed in both Mexico City and Oaxaca. In her view, the original historical/dynastic chronicle might have originated in Mexico Tlatelolco—and, possibly, the *tonalamatl* and the sequence of *veintena* ceremonies as well—while the migration account (Barlow's *Codex Huitzilopochtli*) more likely derived from Puebla.

She believes that the images of the *VA* were probably copied, sometimes with slight modifications, in Mexico by a native artist directly from those in the *TR*, while its Spanish annotations were translated into Italian, consolidated, trimmed, and sometimes enhanced, probably by fellow Dominicans of Pedro de los Ríos, for presentation to a prelate in Italy. She recognized the likelihood of an intermediate stage, for consolidation and textual rearranging, of this Italian translation, but she (Quiñones Keber 1987b) explicitly rejected Thompson's view that *VA*'s drawings were copied not directly from those in the *TR* but from a common prototype.

Donald Robertson, in his *Mexican Manuscript Painting of the Early Colonial Period: The Metropolitan Schools* (1959: 107–115 [reissued, 1994]), had earlier undertaken a description and analysis of the *TR*. He appeared to tentatively accept Thompson's hypothesis that both the *TR* and the *VA* had been copied from a lost prototype, but he did not include the *VA* in his coverage. He assigned the *TR* to "The School of Mexico-Tenochtitlan: the Second Stage," dating the native tradition pictorials it derived from as pre-1550, while recognizing that it had been annotated as late as 1563. He believed that the migration portion of the historical/dynastic chronicle had been copied and rearranged from a *tira*, the layout of which he reconstructed in a drawing.

In 1973, Leon Abrams, who had been a student of Robert Barlow, published the first detailed commentary on the colonial section of *TR*'s historical/dynastic chronicle—which has been largely superseded by Quiñones Keber 1995. In this same year, Howard Cline published a study of the calendric data in the *TR*, comparing them with relevant information contained in Sahagún, while Nicholson, in his article on phoneticism in the late pre-Hispanic Central Mexican writing system, discussed the place signs of the *TR*, suggesting that some of them contained syllabic phonetic elements.

Another significant study of the *TR* was the extensive entry (number 308) on this source by Glass and Robertson (1975: 202–203) in their "Census of Native Middle American Pictorial Manuscripts" in volume 14 of the *Handbook of Middle American Indians* (*Guide to Ethnohistorical Sources: Part Three*). They (Glass and Robertson 1975: 136–139) also included a special entry, entitled the "Huitzilopochtli Group," in which they discussed in detail the relationship between *TR* and *VA*, including a table presenting a simplified concordance of the two documents. As Robertson did in his 1959 book, they assumed that Barlow had applied his term "*Codex Huitzilopochtli*" to the entire pictorial document that Thompson had hypothesized had served as the prototype from which both *TR* and *VA* had been copied. However, as Quiñones Keber (1995c: 203–204) pointed out, this was based on a misunderstanding, for Barlow had clearly intended this designation to apply only to the migration section of the historical/dynastic chronicle that commences with a depiction of the Mexica patron deity.

Three new editions and various studies of the *VA* have appeared since 1957. In 1967, in the same series that had republished the *TR* in 1964, the partial re-edition of Kingsborough's *Antiquities of Mexico*, issued by the Secretaria de Hacienda y Crédito Público, Mexico, volume 3, included the first published color photographs of the original manuscript, somewhat reduced in size, pages rearranged in correct sequence, with commentary and Spanish translation of the Italian text by José Corona Nuñez. In 1979, the Akademische Druck und Verlagsanstalt, Graz, published, with only a brief introduction, another edition of the *VA*, in slightly reduced color photographs from the original manuscript, with the pages not rearranged in correct sequence. In 1996, a third new edition was published jointly by the Akademische Druck und Verlagsanstalt, Graz, and the Fondo de Cultura Económica, Mexico, in slightly reduced color photographs of the pages, rearranged in proper sequence, with paleography of the Italian text and Spanish translation, an extensive commentary and analysis by Maarten Jansen and Ferdinand Anders—plus notes, appendices, and line drawings of the illustrations and those shared with those in the *TR*. The authors agree, with Quiñones Keber, that the *VA* was copied, adding other native tradition pictorials, probably in 1562 in Puebla by a native artist. In their view, the Italian translation of the *TR*'s Spanish annotations was undertaken by Dominican clerics, also in Puebla, for presentation to an ecclesiastical notable in Italy, arriving in the Vatican by 1565/66.

Earlier, in 1984, most of these views had already been expressed by Jansen in an article that focused on the role Pedro de los Ríos had played in the compilation, copying, and annotating of both the *TR* and the *VA*—although here he had preferred Mexico City rather than Puebla as the place where the *VA* had been copied by a native artist. Glass and Robertson had also included, in their 1975 census of Mesoamerican native tradition pictorials in volume 14 of the *Handbook of Middle American Indians*, a bibliographic entry (number 270) on *Codex Ríos*, in which they appeared to approve of Thompson's hypothesis of a lost prototype from which both *TR* and *VA* were derived. They also stated that the *VA* "is believed to have been copied by a non-Indian (?) artist in Italy." Quiñones Keber, in addition to her discussions of the *VA* in its relation to the *TR*, mentioned above, published a general discussion of the *VA* as well as special studies of sections in it, including the TQ tale (Quiñones Keber 1987a, 1995b, 1995c, 1996).

Although these recent editions and studies have significantly enhanced our knowledge and understanding of these two important Indo-Hispanic documents and their relationship, I do not believe that the summary and analysis of the material they contain concerning TQ that I undertook in 1957 requires significant alteration. In any case, I remain convinced that these *TR/VA* accounts of TQ, however fragmented, diverse, and frequently tinctured with strong biblical colorings, as a whole constitute some of the most valuable traditions relating to our hero that have survived.

The fifth source discussed in this category I denominated, adopting Barlow's term, the *Crónica X*. Since 1957, various studies concerned with the problems connected with this hypothesized source, as well as new editions of the key chronicles involved, have appeared. Beginning with Durán, a new, noncommercial edition of the Spanish text, based on the Ramírez/Mendoza edition of 1867–1880, was published in 1990–1991 by the Banco Santander, Ediciones El Equilibrista, Mexico City, and Turner Libros, Madrid, with a prologue by Rosa Carmelo and José Rubén Romero, transcription by Francisco González Varela, revised by Javier Portús. It featured color photographs of the illustrations (from the original manuscript in the Biblioteca Nacional de Madrid, correctly positioned in the text) by Rafael Doniz. In 1995, a reprint of this edition, in paperback, including the same prologue and with the illustrations grouped at the end of each volume, was published by Cien de México, Consejo Nacional para la Cultura y las Artes, Mexico City. In 1990, under the title *Códice Durán*, Arrendadora Internacional, Mexico City, reprinted the color lithographs of Durán's illustrations, which had been gathered into an "Atlas" in the second volume of the 1869–1880 Ramírez/Mendoza edition, with introduction and illustration captions by Electra and Tonatiuh Gutiérrez.

Three English translations of portions of Durán have also been published since 1957. In the first, under the title *Aztecs: The History of the Indies of New Spain*, Orion Press, New York, 1964, Doris Heyden and Fernando Horcasitas translated an abridged version of Durán's historical chronicle, with an introduction by Ignacio Bernal that focused on the *Crónica X*. Also included were black-and-white versions of some of the lithographs of the 1867–1880 Ramírez/Mendoza edition and an index. In the second, published in 1971 by the University of Oklahoma Press, entitled *Book of the Gods and Rites and the Ancient Calendar*, the same pair translated and edited the other two sections of Durán, with foreword by Miguel León-Portilla, black-and-white photographs of the copies of the illustrations made for Ramírez in 1854, and an index. In the third, published by the University of Oklahoma Press in 1994 under the title *The History of the Indies of New Spain*, Doris Heyden translated an unabridged version of the Durán historical chronicle. It included an introduction, annotations, glossary, an index, a reprint of Bernal's introduction to the 1964 Orion Press translation, and black-and-white photographs of the illustrations in the original manuscrpt.

Various studies of Durán, in addition to the often useful discussions in the introductions and prologues of the new editions and translations of his *Historia* listed above, also appeared during this period. Of special significance were the studies of Stephen Colston (1973a, 1973b, 1974, 1977, 1980, 1985, 1988). Because of the numerous differences in the accounts of Durán and Alvarado Tezozomoc, he defined the *Crónica X*, not as a single source but a detailed history of Mexico Tenochtitlan, in Nahuatl, probably composed by a descendant of Tlacaelel, the famed Cihuacoatl and half-brother of Motecuhzoma I. In his view, two somewhat variant versions of his Nahuatl chronicle were utilized by Durán and Alvarado Tezozomoc in their Spanish translations. This seems the most cogent view of the *Crónica X* and is close to the position I took in my dissertation. In any case, my treatment of it there as essentially a single basic tradition still seems justified. It should also be noted that the paste-on illustrations of the original Durán manuscript in Madrid, which were apparently cut out from an earlier version of the *Historia*, have been studied by Robertson (1968), Couch (1983), and Boone (1988).

New editions and a study of the other source that contains another important version of the *Crónica X* tradition relating to TQ, complementary to that of Durán, the *Crónica Mexicana* of Hernando Alvarado Tezozomoc, have also appeared since 1957. In 1975, the 1878 Orozco y Berra edition, which also contained the *Códice Ramírez*, was reprinted by the Editorial Porrúa, Mexico City, in their Biblioteca Porrúa series, number 61 (reissued in 1980 and 1987). In 1970, Ursula Dyckerhoff published her doctoral dissertation at the University of Hamburg, "Die 'Crónica Mexicana' des Hernando Alvarado Tezozomoc: Quellenkritische Untersuchungen." This constitutes the most thorough scholarly analysis of this key chronicle that has yet appeared.

In my dissertation, I should have mentioned that, in 1954, D. W. McPheeters had published an article describing and discussing the appearance of the Boturini copy of the *Crónica Mexicana* in a corpus of documents that had belonged to the family of the Conde de Revillagigedo in Spain, then owned by the book dealer H. P. Kraus of New York City. Now in the Library of Congress, Washington, D.C., this earliest extant version of Alvarado Tezozomoc's chronicle is still unpublished. Also worth noting was the entry (number 1012) concerning this copy of the *Crónica mexicana* in the Gibson and Glass census of Mesoamerican native tradition histories in volume 15 of the *Handbook of Middle American Indians* (Gibson and Glass 1975: 326–327).

The holograph manuscript of Juan de Tovar's *Relación del origen de los Yndios que habitan en esta Nueva España según sus historias*, which was essentially, as indicated, a digest of Durán, with some additions and modifications, was fully published in 1971 for the first time by the Akademische Druck und Verlagsanstalt, Graz. It was arranged and annotated by Jacques Lafaye, who also wrote the introduction, with color photographs of the illustrations, paleography of the Spanish text, French translation by Constantino Aznar de Acevedo, and an index. The Orozco y Berra edition (in Alvarado Tezozomoc 1878) of the other, nearly identical text of Tovar (but with only uncolored line drawings of the illustrations), the *Códice Ramírez*, was reprinted in 1975 (1980, 1987) by Editorial Porrúa, Mexico City, in their reprint edition of Alvarado Tezozomoc's *Crónica Mexicana*. It was also republished in 1975 by the Secretaria de Educación Pública, Dirección General de Educación Primaria en el D.F. Núm. 2, Mexico City, in the Colección de Documentos Commemorativos del DCL Aniversario de la Fundación de Tenochtitlan series (Document Núm. 2), and, in 1987, in the Historia 16 series, Crónicas de América, 32, Madrid, edited and with an introduction by Germán Vázquez. Useful entries on the two versions of Tovar's *Relación* were also included in the Glass and Robertson census of Mesoamerican pictorials (entries 365 and 366), *Handbook of Middle American Indians*, volume 14 (Glass and Robertson 1975: 224–225).

As I pointed out in the dissertation, the Jesuit chronicler José de Acosta, in his 1590 *Historia natural y moral de las Indias*, included an account of Tenochca history that was directly copied from Tovar's *Historia* (the John Carter Brown Library manuscript), which his fellow Jesuit had sent to him. Although containing nothing original, this account was of some significance as being the first published account of the history of Mexico Tenochtitlan, derived from the *Crónica X*, which was copied and/or paraphrased by various later writers. Consequently, I should have cited the first, Seville edition of this influential chronicle (Acosta 1590) and mentioned that it had been published in many later editions in different languages. I also should have cited the edition that I had consulted, the second, revised edition (1962) of the Fondo de Cultura Económica, in their Biblioteca Americana, Serie de Cronistas de Indias—which included a valuable prologue, discussing the *Crónica X* problem in some detail, by Edmundo O'Gorman, as well as appendices and an index. The following year, O'Gorman also edited, with a prologue, selections from Acosta's *Historia* in the Universidad Nacional Autónoma de México's Biblioteca del Estudiante Universitario series, 83. Two more recent editions also worth citing are that published by Valencia Cultural, 1977, in their Hispaniae Scientia series, edited by Barbara G. Beddall; and the edition published in 1987 by Historia 16, Crónicas de América series, 34, Madrid, edited by José Alcina Franch.

The sixth source in this category was the *Historia de Tlaxcala* of Diego Muñoz Camargo. It contained two quite distinct passages concerning TQ, only the second of which was relevant to this section. The publication in 1981 (photoreproduction of the manuscript, plus introduction) and 1984 (paleography of text, introduction, and all illustrations) by René Acuña of the 1585 *relación geográfica* (*RG*) of Tlaxcallan, written by Muñoz Camargo and quite similar to the *Historia*, has provided more reliable versions of both passages. Although it was described in a catalogue of the manuscript collection in the library of the Hunterian Museum of the University of Glasgow, Scotland, published early in this century (Young and Aitken 1908: 192–194), the existence of this *RG* had been overlooked by scholars until 1976, when it was first reported by the German Mesoamericanist Klaus Jaecklin. Acquired by the prominent Scottish doctor and bibliophile William Hunter (1718–1783) from an unknown party, probably sometime in the eighth decade of the eighteenth century, it was willed to Glasgow University and acquired by them in 1807. It had been presented to Phillip II during the visit to the Spanish court by the Tlaxcalteca delegation of 1583–1585 (which included Muñoz Camargo) and had been deposited in the Royal Library, where it was seen and used by Herrera, among others. In contrast to the fragmentary *Historia*, which is missing many leaves at the beginning and at the end, it is complete, signed by the author, and contains numerous pen-and-ink drawings, the majority cognate with those of the earlier *Lienzo de Tlaxcala* (see Brotherston and Gallegos 1990; Martínez 1990).

New editions of the *Historia* include that of the Editorial Innovación, Mexico City, 1978, a facsimile of the 1892 Chavero edition, and the 1986 Historia 16, Crónicas de América, 26, Madrid edition, edited by Germán Vázquez. The first edition based directly on the BNP 210 manuscript was published in 1998 by the Gobierno del Estado de Tlaxcala, Centro de Investigaciones y Estudios Superiores en Antropología Social, Universidad Autónoma de Tlaxcala, Colección Historia, Serie Historia de Tlaxcala, 5, edited by Luis Reyes García, with the collaboration of Javier Lira Toledo. Divided into numbered paragraphs and collated with the *RG*, it includes a useful introduction, notes, appendices, and indices. This edition supersedes all earlier versions.

The relevant passage concerning TQ appears to be part of a year-by-year dated pictorial history, a *xiuhpohualli*, as Reyes García designated it. Its text in the 1947–1948 edition that I summarized and discussed in the dissertation is virtually identical to that of the Glasgow *RG* and its cognate in the 1998 edition of the *Historia*. One minor alteration might be suggested: the name Iztactotli in the *Historia* is instead rendered Iztactlotli, "Obsidian Hawk," in the *RG*—which is more likely what was intended. Otherwise, I would stand by my discussion and analysis of this passage, which, since it was undoubtedly derived from a Tlaxcalteca source, is of considerable significance. I should, however, probably have more explicitly recognized that this account of the birth and parentage of TQ overlaps significantly, in personal (e.g., Itzpapalotl, Mixcoatl, Coatlicue/Coacueye, Xiuhnel, Mimich) and place (Chicomoztoc, Colhuacan, Comallan, [Teo]Huitznahuac) names, with those that are featured in the accounts of the "Chichimec period" in the early history of Cuauhtitlan in the *Anales de Cuauhtitlan* and in the pre-Mexica episodes of the *Leyenda de los soles*.

C. SOURCES SUPPLYING IMPORTANT FRAGMENTS OF INFORMATION

The first item in this category, among those in the subcategory of fragmentary sources, was the two long speeches, summarized by Fernando Cortés in his second *Carta de relación*, allegedly made by Motecuhzoma II to him, offering his submission. Since 1957, numerous new editions of the Cortesian *Cartas de relación* have appeared, including, in 1971, a significant new English translation by A. R. Pagden, with an introduction by J. H. Elliott. Useful new Spanish editions were those published in Mexico in 1960 and 1963 (plus later editions) by the Editorial Porrúa, with introductions, respectively, by Manuel Alcalá and Mario Hernández Sánchez-Barba—and, in 1985, the Historia 16, Crónicas de América, 10, Madrid, edition, edited by Mario Hernández. However, I do not believe that my discussion of these two passages requires any significant alteration. I would only stress the importance of these speeches in relation to the question of the role the expectation of TQ's return might have played in influencing the conduct of the Tenochca ruler vis-à-vis the Spanish commander—the subject, as noted, of an article of mine (Nicholson n.d.c).

The second source summarized in this category was the *Relación de la conquista de México* of Andrés de Tapia, a principal lieutenant of Cortés. Recent new editions of Tapia include the English translation of Patricia de Fuentes, in her *The Conquistadors*, Orion Press, New York, 1963, and another Spanish version in *La conquista de Tenochtitlan*, Madrid, 1988, Historia 16, Crónicas de América, 40, edited by Germán Vázquez. Again, it is worth reiterating that this account of TQ by Tapia, however brief, might possess special value because he had earlier been the *encomendero* of Cholollan.

The third item was Viceroy Antonio de Mendoza's 1540 letter to his brother, Diego, Spanish ambassador to Venice, which, if reported accurately, contained a strange, aberrant account of Mexica history, possibly relevant to the TQ tale. In my dissertation, I used the 1851–1855 first complete edition of Oviedo's *Historia general y natural de las Indias*, which included this letter. A more accessible edition of Oviedo's chronicle was that of the Editorial Guaranía, Asunción, Paraguay, 1944–1945, with prologue by J. Natalicio González and notes by José Amador de los Ríos. A more recent edition is that published in 1959 by Ediciones Atlas, Madrid, in their Biblioteca de Autores Españoles, 117–121, edited, with a preliminary study, by Juan Pérez de Tudela Bueso. Although I continue to regard this letter as a particularly puzzling item, in my view its early date and the care with which the first official Cronista de las Indias usually handled his sources entitle it to some degree of consideration. And the same can be said for the fourth source discussed, Mendoza's October 6, 1541, letter to the chronicler, because it is one of the earliest documentary sources to mention Quetzalcoatl by name and to hint at his "flight" to the Gulf Coast region (Coatzacoalco).

The fifth source summarized was the *Historia Tolteca-Chichimeca*, the most important surviving pictorial history, with accompanying Nahuatl text, of a major indigenous polity, Cuauhtinchan, of the Basin of Puebla. Athough quite brief, the references it contains to TQ are of considerable significance because of the somewhat different perspective that this source, from an *altepetl* located at some distance from the principal power center of western Mesoamerica, provides of late pre-Hispanic Central Mexican history. In 1976, the most satisfactory edition of this important document, superseding all earlier versions, was published by the Instituto Nacional de Antropología e Historia, Mexico, with paleography of the Nahuatl text and Spanish translation, color photoreproduction of the manuscript, and scholarly analysis, edited by Paul Kirchhoff, Lina Odena Güemes, and Luis Reyes García. A 1993 doctoral dissertation in the Department of Art, University of California, Los Angeles, by Dana Leibsohn, "The Historia Tolteca-Chichimeca: Recollecting Identity in a Nahua Manuscript," includes an English translation of the Nahuatl text, plus an analysis and interpretation of this important Pueblan chronicle.

The sixth item in this category was the 1581 *RG* of Cholula of Gabriel de Rojas. As with the account of Tapia, it may be of special value because, according to his own statement, the author had access to knowledgeable elders of the community where TQ was held in special veneration. In 1985, a much more satisfactory edition of this *RG* was published in by René Acuña in the same series as the Muñoz Camargo *RG* of Tlaxcala, cited above.

D. SOURCES PROVIDING ONLY SCRAPS OF INFORMATION

The first item treated in the next subcategory of those sources possessing mere scraps of information was the so-called Anonymous Conqueror, the

1556 Italian version of a brief account of Mexico by a still not securely identified member of the Cortesian army. Although, as noted, only a corrupted form of Quetzalcoatl was named as the principal deity of what was clearly intended to be Chalollan, it was one of the earliest printed sources, together with that of López de Gómara's 1552 account of the Conquest, to name this deity and to link him with Chalollan. In 1963, another English translation of this source was published by Patricia de Fuentes in her *The Conquistadors*. In 1967, a new edition in Spanish was published in Mexico by José Porrúa e Hijos, Sucs., translated from the Italian by Francisco de la Maza, with an introduction and notes by Jorge Gurría Estrada. The Institut Francais d'Amérique Latine, Mexico, in 1970 published a new French translation, with a useful introduction and notes by Jean Rose.

The second source discussed was Francisco de Villacastín and Cristóbal de Salazar's 1579 *RG* of Coatepec Chalco, in the southeast Basin of Mexico, which included a reference to some markings on a rocky cliff southeast of the town that were believed to have been left there by Quetzalcoatl—who often had appeared to the natives in both his feathered-serpent and human forms. I suggested that this belief could be related to an incident during the "flight" of TQ, recounted by Sahagún. This *RG*, including its maps, was republished in 1985 by René Acuña in the first volume devoted to the *RG*s of the Archdiocese of Mexico in the series containing all of the 1579–1585 *RG*s of New Spain published by the Universidad Nacional Autónoma de México.

The third item was the specification, in Salvador de Cárdenas's 1581 *RG* of Ahuatlan y su Partido, in the southern Basin of Puebla, of the chief deities of the community of Texalocan: Quetzalcoatl and his mother Cihuacoatl. This is of some relevance concerning the parentage of TQ. In 1985, this *RG* was republished by René Acuña in the second volume devoted to the *RG*s of the Archdiocese of Tlaxcala, in the same series noted for the preceding item.

The fourth source considered was Juan Bautista Pomar's 1582 *RG* of Tetzcoco, which I included because he stated that Quetzalcoatl was the title of the high priest of this city, another indication of the importance of the titular employment of his name. Three post-1957 editions of Pomar's *RG* have been published, two in Mexico—the first, in 1964, by Garibay as an appendix to his edition of Pomar's *Romances de los Señores de la Nueva España*, a collection of Nahuatl poetry in a manuscript accompanying the *RG*, with an introduction and numbered paragraphs, and the second, in 1986, by René Acuña, in the third volume of the *RG*s of the Archdiocese of Mexico in the same UNAM series that contains the two preceding items. Another was published by Germán Vázquez, in *Relaciones de la Nueva España*, Madrid, 1991, Historia 16, Crónicas de América, 65.

The fifth item discussed was the *Crónica Mexicayotl*, seemingly authored in part by Alvarado Tezozomoc, in part by Chimalpahin. It was included because it connected a locality in the lake of the Basin of Mexico, where TQ rested on his "flight," with an incident precedent to the founding of Mexico Tenochtitlan—thus, in effect, legitimizing the future rise to power of the Tenochca whose dynasty claimed direct descent from him. In 1975, a paperback reissue, reduced in size, of Adrián León's 1949 edition of the paleography of the Nahuatl text and Spanish translation of this chronicle was published by the Instituto de Investigaciones Históricas of the Universidad Nacional Autónoma de México.

A paleography of the Nahuatl text and its English translation, by Arthur J. O. Anderson and Susan Schroeder, of an earlier, slightly variant version of the *Crónica Mexicayotl*, a holograph of Chimalpahin, was published in 1997. It was included in the third volume of a collection of manuscripts, in Spanish and Nahuatl (one in Tarascan), that had been collected by the seventeenth-century Mexican savant Carlos de Sigüenza y Góngora—which had been donated in 1827 to the British and Foreign Bible Society, London, by the Mexican bibliophile Father José Mora. In 1982, Wayne Ruwet (College Library, UCLA), attempting to track down all extant manuscripts connected with Sahagún, spotted an entry in a 1903–1911 catalogue that mentioned a manuscript in the Bible Society's library that contained liturgical material similar to that contained in a putatively Sahaguntine devotional work published by Biondelli in 1858. With the aid of Alan Jesson, the society's librarian, Ruwet confirmed that this manuscript was indeed the three-volume Sigüenza y Góngora collection (Ruwet 1994). He secured a microfilm of it and apprised various of his Mesoamericanist colleagues, including Anderson and Schroeder. In addition to the Chimalpahin manuscript in volume 3, Schroeder is editing and translating all of the latter's known works (see below), while Ruwet is working on the manuscripts of volumes 1–2, most of which appear to comprise the earliest extant writings of Fernando de Alva Ixtlilxochitl (see below), hoping to arrange for their publication.

E. LATE, PROBABLY DISTORTED VERSIONS OF THE TALE

The first item summarized in this category was the account of Topiltzin/Hueymac in the first chapter of the 1581 second treatise of Fray Diego Durán's *Historia de las Indias de Nueva España e islas de tierra firme*. Recent editions of this important chronicle were discussed above. The same holds for the next item considered, the related *Historia* of Juan de Tovar, which also provides an account of this personage, clearly derived from that of Durán, with a few additions and modifications.

The third was the first account of Quetzalcoatl in Muñoz Camargo's *Historia de Tlaxcala*, most of which was missing in its one surviving manuscript (BNP 210) but had been copied virtually in its entirety by Torquemada and included in his 1615 *Monarchía indiana*. As indicated above, this account was also contained in Muñoz Camargo's 1585 *RG* of Tlaxcala, the original manuscript of which is in the library of the Hunterian Museum of the University of Glasgow and was published in 1981 and 1984. It is almost identical to Torquemada's version but adds some interesting details (Muñoz Camargo 1984: 129–133). After praising the artistic abilities and wisdom of "las naciones de gentes" led by Quetzalcoatl, called "Tultecas," who had come to Tollan from Panuco and moved on to Chololllan, Muñoz Camargo adds a substantial section emphasizing their wealth and skill as merchants. He also provides a somewhat dubious etymology of "Onoalco," to where, to escape his great enemy Huemac Tezcatlipuca, Quetzalcoatl fled with a large contingent of his followers: "en la habitación o morada de muchas gentes" or "en el lugar de gran población, donde hay gran habitación de gentes . . . lo cual es Yucatan y Tabasco y Campech, todas a tierra que está cercana a la mar, que se llama las partes de Onoalco" (129–133).

He also gives here another dubious etymology, for Huemac Tezcatlipuca: " 'el dios espejo,' o 'el dios de la luz,' y pucah quiere decir 'dios negro,' en lengua de los otomis. Dios Tezcatl, en la lengua mexicana, quiere decir 'espejo'; que compuesto destos dos verbos en estos dos lenguajes, quiere decir 'espejo dios negro' o 'luz dios.' Lo llamaron los mexicanos y tlaxcaltecas 'dios de las batallas,' y a éste atribuían que daba las victorias. Y ansí, en sus grandes trabajos y peligros, invocaban su nombre. Llamándole Tezcatl y Pucah Huemac" (129–133).

Muñoz Camargo then describes how Quetzalcoatl, as he departed, implored those that remained to abide by the good customs and laws that he had preached and not to forget him, promising them that he would not allow them to be conquered. He adds that "en aquellas provincias de Yucatán," structures "que se atribuyen a edificios romanos porque son muy fuertes y muy de ver," are presumed to have been built by "gentes que de por acá se llevó Quetzalcoatl." He goes on to relate that those of Chololllan and Cuauhquechollan, whose god was Quetzalcoatl, claimed that he had not died but "se metió en la mar y que se convirtió, del hombre mortal, en dios." The Chololteca believed that he had ascended into the sky, joining the other gods—and he was held in great veneration in Chololllan, Tollan, and Cuauhquechollan and propitiated in annual rituals. He goes on to state that the truth, however, was that Quetzalcoatl, "como hombre mortal," had died in "la provincia de Nonohualco Teotlixco," where he was cremated and his blood mixed with that of two female and two male sacrificed infants. Precious stones were added to this mixture "por corazón," and it was placed in vessels that were carried to Chololllan. There it was deposited as a sacred relic in the temple of Quetzalcoatl and highly venerated until the arrival of Cortés (129–133).

Muñoz Camargo's account of Quetzalcoatl ends, as in Torquemada's version, with the triumph of HuemacTezcatlipuca. Before that, however, he adds that Quetzalcoatl, as well as Camaxtli, the national deity of the Tlaxcalteca, was born "de linaje de los Tlaxcalteca" but had crossed "de la Mar del Sur a la del norte, y que después vino de salir por las partes de Panuco." He finally concludes by stating that Huemac Tezcatlipuca, not only in the Pueblan towns enumerated in Torquemada but also in Tlaxcallan, "se hizo temer y adorar por dios," as well as in "la mayor parte desta Nueva España" (129–133).

In discussing the fourth item of this section, I summarized the accounts of three personages (in any case, at least two) that I suggested could be related to TQ in the writings of the mestizo descendant of Tetzcocan royalty, Fernando de Alva Ixtlilxochitl. I utilized the 1952 Mexican reprint of the 1891–1892 Chavero/Ramírez edition of his works, the best available at the time. In 1965, this reprint was republished, and in 1975 the Instituto de Investigaciones Históricas of the Universidad Nacional Autónoma de México published the entire available corpus of Alva Ixtlilxochitl's writings, edited by Edmundo O'Gorman, with an introduction devoted to a critical analysis of his oeuvre, plus appendices, indices, and bibliography. The versions of the texts chosen in this edition were based on O'Gorman's detailed scrutiny of the many surviving copies of Alva Ixtlilxochitl's manuscript, a full list of which was included. Alva Ixtlilxochitl's sources were also discussed and all references to them were tabulated. However, with the possible exception of the *Codex Xolotl* or a similar pictorial history, the Tetzcocan chroniclers' typical generalized references to native *historias* and/or *pinturas* did not permit O'Gorman to establish specific identifications. In any case, the differences between the texts of the O'Gorman edition and those of the 1848 Kingsborough and 1891–1892 Chavero/Ramírez editions are not substantial enough, in my view, to necessitate significant modifications of my 1957 summaries and comments.

O'Gorman does severely criticize the Chavero/Ramírez edition for rearranging the texts of the *Relaciones*, a rearrangement that had been largely based on the chronological notions of Ramírez. The texts of the four *Relaciones* that O'Gorman identifies, discusses, and names (sometimes differing from the titles I adopted, based on the Chavero/Ramírez edition) are each presented as an integrated whole. He also proposed tentative dates for them, somewhat different from those of Chavero. He agrees that the first six on my list were composed before November 18, 1608, when the native authorities of Otumba and San Salvador Quatlacinco certified their authenticity. He suggests that the *Sumaria relación de todas las cosas que han sucedido en esta Nueva España*, which includes the two *Relaciones* that (following Chavero) I designated *Relacion sumaria . . . de los Tultecas* and *Historia de los señores Chichimecas*, was the earliest of Alva Ixtlilxochitl's writings, followed by the *Relación sucinta*, then the *Compendio histórico del reino de Texcoco*, his title for the *Noticia de los pobladores*. The *Sumaria relación de la historia general*, his title for what I called the *Relación sumaria*, essentially a summary of the *Historia Chichimeca* (O'Gorman's *Historia de la nación Chichimeca*), he prefers to date earlier than the latter. Since it is dedicated to a prelate, he suggests that it might have been presented to Archbishop Pérez de la Serna (1613–1625), perhaps in his final year. In his view, as has been generally agreed, the *Historia Chichimeca* was the latest of Alva Ixtlilxochitl's works, almost certainly, because of his mention of Torquemada, post-1615 and probably somewhat later; in 1985, Germán Vázquez republished it under the title *Historia de la nación Chichimeca*, Madrid, Historia 16, Crónicas de América.

The fifth source summarized was Chimalpahin's *Memorial breve de la fundación de la ciudad de Colhuacan*. Three new editions of this Nahuatl chronicle have been published since 1957: Lehmann and Kutscher 1958 (Nahuatl/German), Zimmermann 1963 (Nahuatl only), and Castillo 1991 (Nahuatl/Spanish). Although both the Lehmann/Kutscher German and the Castillo Spanish translations differ slightly from the unpublished Spanish translation of Barrios that I utilized in my dissertation, I do not believe that the differences are substantial enough to require any significant alterations in my summary and comments concerning the account of TQ in this source. In 1995, the Nahuatl text, with English translation, of another Chimalpahin chronicle, contained in volume 3 of the British and Foreign Bible Society corpus, the "History or Chronicle with Its Calendar of the Mexica Years," was published in the first volume of Schroeder's *Codex Chimalpahin*. It includes one brief reference (pp. 180–181) to TQ and his expected return but supplies nothing significantly new except a single addition to his nomenclatural repertoire, Tlilpotonqui, "Feathered in Black."

II. Central Mexico: Non-Nahuatl

At the beginning of this section, I briefly explored the possibility of recollections of TQ in the traditional histories of various Central and West Mexican linguistic groups other than the Nahua-speakers. Agreeing with a suggestion made by Pedro Carrasco in his 1950 monograph on the pre-Hispanic Central Mexican Otomi-speakers, I concluded that one possibility might be an Otomi term meaning "feathered serpent" for a "ministro del ídolo de las ciencias" that was listed in a colonial Spanish-Otomi dictionary. The mention in the 1582 *Relación de Querétaro* of Ramos de Cárdenas—published in a more satisfactory new edition in 1981 by Acuña—of an idol worshipped by the Otomi of Xilotepec, called *eday* (*edahi* = "wind"), indicated the presence here of at least a version of Ehecatl Quetzalcoatl. These slight notices constituted the only tidbits possibly relevant to our inquiry that I had discovered—and I am not aware of any further significant evidence that has since come to light that would change the picture.

III. Oaxaca

A. THE MIXTECA

In my summary of the ethnohistorical sources from the culturally and politically important Mixteca subregion of western Mesoamerica, I discussed the evidence for the presence here of a deity who clearly was cognate with the Central Mexican Ehecatl Quetzalcoatl (EQ) and who possibly also reflected some aspects of the Toltec priest/ruler with whom we are concerned. This last possibility was based, above all, on the fragment of the cosmogony of the Mixtec-speaking outpost of Yuta(ti)caha/Coyolapan (Cuilapan) in the Valley of Oaxaca, recorded by Fray Gregorio García in his early-seventeenth-century chronicle—plus the reconstructions of Alfonso Caso of the genealogies in different pre-Hispanic and early colonial pictorial histories of a number of the leading dynasties of the Postclassic Mixteca. Caso had based his suggestion of a likely connection between TQ and the EQ cognate 9 Wind on his identification of the former as a fundamental ancestral figure and dynastic founder of various Mixteca polities. Because Caso's researches were still in progress, I did not investigate the primary Mixteca source material, especially the pictorial histories, as thoroughly as I otherwise would have done.

After 1957, Caso did publish additional papers and monographs interpreting the Mixteca pictorial histories, including material relevant to our topic (e.g., Caso 1960, 1961, 1965, 1977–1979). Various new reproductions of those that I cited, usually accompanied by commentaries—including those by Caso—have also been issued (e.g., codices *Vindobonensis* 1963, 1967, 1974, 1992; *Zouche-Nuttall* 1974, 1975, 1987, 1992; *Bodley* 1960a and b, 1964; and *Colombino-Becker I* 1961, 1964, 1997; *Selden Roll* 1964; *Lienzo Antonio de León* [Caso 1961]). A possibly relevant Mixteca pictorial that was not available in 1957 has since been published: the *Lienzo de Ihuitlan* (Caso 1961, 1965), a member of the "Tocuijñuhu" or "Coixtlahuaca Group." As Caso (1961: 242; cf. Smith 1973: 65) suggested, the depiction of a sacred bundle labeled 9 Wind, in a stone enclosure or cave above the place sign of the Chocho/Mixtec center of Inguinche/Yodzocoo/Coaixtlahuacan, probably designated this deity—although the head atop the bundle appears to be that of the Rain God. Also, in 1981, a facsimile of the 1729 Madrid edition of Fray Gregorio García's *Origen de los Indios de el Nuevo Mundo*, with its important fragment of the Cuilapan cosmogony, was published in Mexico by the Fondo de Cultura Económica.

A plethora of new studies and interpretations of the Mixteca pictorial and documentary corpus have appeared during this period (see, especially, Caso 1965, 1977–1979; Smith 1973; Troike 1978; Jansen 1992; Pohl 1994; Pohl and Byland 1994), much too numerous to itemize here. Nearly all have been listed in the annual/biannual "Mesoamerica: Ethnohistory" sections of the *Handbook of Latin American Studies*, which I initiated in 1960. A reprint of Barbro Dahlgren's classic 1954 synthesis of pre-Hispanic Mixteca culture history was published by the state government of Oaxaca in 1979. Significant new interpretive studies of the *Codex Vindobonensis*—apart from the commentaries to the new reproductions—have also appeared (e.g., Furst 1978; Melgarejo Vivanco 1980; Jansen 1982; Hochleitner, Paula, and Krumbach 1987). All of these studies and commentaries recognize the importance of the deity/personage 9 Wind but differ somewhat in their specific interpretations.

In 1974, as noted above, I presented a paper—"The Deity 9 Wind 'Ehecatl Quetzalcoatl' in the Mixteca Pictorials," in the session "Mixtec Codices: Problems and Progress," organized by Nancy Troike, at the XLI International Congress of Americanists, Mexico City, September 2–7, 1974—which was published in 1978. It was the first study to focus specifically on 9 Wind. I tried to specify and comment on all of his significant appearances in the Mixteca pictorial corpus (cf. Caso 1977–1979, II: 60–67). I also discussed the Caso hypothesis—which he had further developed in some of his post-1957 publications—of 9 Wind's role as divine ancestor of Mixteca royalty, and I constructed a detailed genealogical chart to illustrate it. I concluded that, in spite of its somewhat hypothetical nature due principally to alternative interpretations of some of the marital and genealogical relationships depicted in the relevant pictorials, the chart might well indicate that 9 Wind "Stone Skull," the founder of the First Dynasty of Ñuutnoo/Tlillantonco (Tilantongo), the most important Mixteca Alta political center, was considered to have been the direct lineal descendant, in the fourth generation, of the first 9 Wind. As for the latter's possible relationship with TQ of Tollan, I left that somewhat open, suggesting that it deserved further investigation. Recently, Maarten Jansen (1996, 1997a, 1997b, 1998) has advanced quite a different hypothesis, one that places TQ squarely in the Mixteca. He identifies him with a personage with the calendric name 4 Jaguar, who plays a prominent role in the codices *Bodley*, *Zouche-Nuttall*, and *Colombino-Becker I*. I have criticized Jansen's hypothesis in a forthcoming paper (Nicholson n.d.a).

B. ZAPOTECAPAN

Although considerable time has elapsed, I am not aware of the emergence of new evidence that would necessitate any significant modification of my discussion of the Oaxacan Zapotecapan section of the dissertation. Concerning the wall paintings of Mitla that feature various depictions of a deity that is iconographically close to the Central Mexican EQ ((Nicholson 1957a: 208), I would stand by my view that the priesthood of this great shrine "simply had adopted this variant of the widespread Mixteca-Puebla style, along with certain Central Mexican/Mixteca religious conceptions" (cf. Pohl 1999). Since

1957, I have published various papers focusing on the Mixteca-Puebla stylistic/iconographic tradition and the various problems connected with it (e.g., Nicholson 1960 [reprinted 1966, 1977, 1981], 1961, 1982, 1996; Nicholson and Quiñones Keber 1994a and b). Also, it is worth noting that two new editions of Burgoa's *Geográfica descripción* were published in Mexico, the first, in 1989, by the Editorial Porrúa (Biblioteca Porrúa, 97–98), with a brief introduction by Barbro Dahlgren, and the second, in 1997, a facsimile of the 1674 edition, by the Grupo Editorial Miguel Angel Porrúa.

IV. Chiapas

My discussion in this section focused on the Tzeltal/Tzotzil Votan legend of Highland Chiapas, as recorded, quite imperfectly, in two versions. One was a brief paraphrase in Spanish, supposedly based in a manuscript in Tzeltal (?), by the seventeenth-century Dominican Fray Francisco Nuñez de la Vega in his 1702 ecclesiastical chronicle. The other, also putatively derived from a version in Tzeltal, was somewhat diversely paraphrased, based on different copies, by two late-eighteenth-century writers, Pablo Félix Cabrera and Ramón de Ordoñez y Aguiar—and, later, by Brasseur de Bourbourg. As I emphasized in my discussion, the romantic, mystical approach of those who recorded the Votanic legend has created serious difficulties for modern scholars in their attempt to evaluate its authenticity and possible relevance to the Topiltzin Quetzalcoatl of Tollan Tale. A reappraisal of the "Votan problem" by a scholar thoroughly conversant with Tzeltal/Tzotzil ethnohistory/ethnography would be very much in order. In the meantime, it should be noted that a new edition of Nuñez de la Vega's 1702 *Constituciones Diocesanas del Obispado de Chiapa*, the prime source on Votan, prepared by María del Carmen León Cazares and Mario Humberto Ruz, was published in 1988 by the Instituto de Investigaciones Filológicas, Centro de Estudios Mayas, Universidad Nacional Autónoma de México.

V. Highland Guatemala

In this section I summarized and discussed various colonial texts that contain significant references to pre-Hispanic personages putatively related to the subject of this study. The two most important are the *Popol Vuh* and *The Annals of the Cakchiquels*, the former in Quiche and the latter in the closely related Cakchiquel. A number of new editions and translations of the former have appeared since 1957. Before mentioning these, however, I would like to point out that in my thesis I should have cited, among the significant *Popol Vuh* translations that had been published up to that year, Burgess and Xec 1955. They utilized the 1944 Schultze Jena paleography of the Quiche text in Newberry Ayer MS 1515, checked against the original manuscript. Dora

M. de Burgess, fluent in Quiche, collaborated with Patricio Xec, a native speaker and teacher at the Instituto Bíblico Quiché near San Cristóbal Totonicapan, in producing this important translation of the indigenous New World's most famous mythological epic.

In addition to a steady stream of interpretational and analytical studies, numerous new translations of the *Popol Vuh* have appeared in recent years; most include commentary and annotatory materials. The most important are: Villacorta 1962 (Spanish), Edmonson 1971 (Quiche/English), Estrada Monroy 1973a (Spanish) and 1973b (facsimile of Ayer MS 1515/Quiche/Spanish), Seler and Kutscher 1975 (German), Chávez 1979 (Quiche/Spanish), Tedlock 1996 (English), Rolando de León Valdés and López Pérez 1985 (Spanish), Sáenz de Santa María 1989, and Saravía and Guarchaj 1996 (Quiche/Spanish). Although these translations frequently differ, they basically agree in the passages that refer to Gucumatz and Nacxit and do not, in my opinion, necessitate significant revision of my quotations and discussions concerning these personages.

Concerning the *Título de los señores de Totonicapan*, a major event connected with it was the discovery in 1973 by Robert Carmack, in the possession of the *parcialidad* Xec of San Cristóbal Totonicapan, of what is apparently the very manuscript in Quiche translated by Padre Dionisio José Chonay in 1834 (Carmack 1981a). In 1983, Carmack and Mondloch published it in facsimile, with a paleography of the Quiche text and a new Spanish translation, plus extensive notes. Although they corrected and improved on Chonay's somewhat imperfect version, the passages concerning Nacxit do not appear to require significant correction or modification.

The third source I summarized and discussed in this section was republished, entitled "Títulos de la Casa Izquin-Nehaib, Señora del Territorio de Oztoyá," with useful clarificatory notes, by Adrián Recinos in 1957. The fourth, "Papel del Origen de los Señores," was republished, by René Acuña in his monumental series comprising all of the 1579–1585 *relaciones geográficas* of New Spain, with the 1579 *Relación de Zapotitlan* (Estrada and Niebla 1982). The seventh, the *Historia de los Xpantzay*, was also republished, slightly revised, in Recinos 1957, with the paleography of the Cakchiquel text and numerous clarificatory notes.

Recinos 1957 also contained the Quiche text and Spanish translation of an early-nineteenth-century copy of a previously unpublished 1580 *título* in the Robert Garrett Collection of Middle American Manuscripts in the Princeton University Library, *Historia Quiche de Don Juan de Torres* (Carmack's [1973] *Título Tamub*). It chronicles the history and genealogy of the Tamub, one of the three principal branches of the Quiche. Although covering, more cursorily, many of the principal events of Quiche history, including the journey to the east to obtain the insignia and symbols of supreme political authority, Nacxit is not named. Significantly, however, Ah Nacxit is listed as one of the *calpules* of the Tamub.

Other sixteenth-century *títulos* and similar documents, in Quiche, Cakchiquel, and Spanish, containing significant historical and ethnographic data, have been located and published since 1957. Carmack 1973 contains a useful list and discussion, up to that year. He also included the Quiche text and English translation of what he called the *Título C'oyoi*, dated 1550–1570, also in the Garrett Collection at Princeton, which provides significant historical data concerning the C'oyoi Sakcorowach of the Quenay branch of the Quiche (also, published separately by him, in 1993, with Spanish translation by Alfonso Efra Tzaquitzal Zapeta). However, Nacxit is not mentioned, nor is he in other Quiche *títulos*, such as the *Título de los señores de Sacapulas*, published by Acuña in 1968.

Of the relevant Spanish sources, post-1957 editions include a new version of Ximénez's *Historia de la provincia de San Vicente de Chiapa y Guatemala de la orden de predicadores*, from the original manuscript, edited by Francis Gall, paleographized and annotated by Carmela Sáenz de Santa María, prologue by David Vela, published by the Sociedad de Geografía e Historia de Guatemala in 1971. The same society republished Ximénez's *Escolios* to the *Popol Vuh* in 1967. Fuentes y Guzmán's *Historia de Guatemala o Recordación florida* was republished in 1969 by Ediciones Atlas, Madrid, in the Biblioteca de Autores Españoles series, edited and with a preliminary study by Carmela Sáenz de Santa María. The first and second books of the first part of the *Recordación florida* were also republished in 1995 by the Editorial Artemis-Edinter for the Fundación Guatemalteca para las Letras.

Overall knowledge of late pre-Hispanic Quiche history and culture has been significantly enhanced by the recent researches of Robert Carmack and his students and collaborators. Their findings have been usefully summarized in numerous publications (e.g., Carmack 1973, 1979a, 1979b, 1981b; Carmack, Fox, and Stewart 1975; Wallace and Carmack 1977) and in various more specialized studies, including Carmack 1966, an analysis of Gucumatz, whom he originally considered to have been the seventh Quiche paramount ruler and, later (1981b), the eighth. He agreed with my suggestion that accounts of Gucumatz's life and reign might have been influenced to some degree by the Topiltzin Quetzalcoatl of Tollan Tale.

Carmack had earlier published, in 1968, a study of Quiche origins, in which he assembled considerable data in support of the hypothesis, adumbrated in my dissertation, that the ancestors of the ruling elite of the Quiche had originally been a militaristic group of Toltec-connected Nahua-speakers who, after establishing themselves in the key mercantile zone of Gulf Coast Tabasco-Campeche, had moved into Highland Guatemala, probably in the thirteenth century. There, while becoming linguistically Mayanized, they achieved political control over the local inhabitants of the region. At Contact, their culture was a complex amalgam of Central Mexican/Gulf Coast/indigenous Highland Guatemala patterns. This was well reflected in their historical traditions that apparently included some recollection of the great priest/ruler of Tollan, or successors who bore his name and/or title, the fountainhead of "legitimate" political and sacerdotal authority in much of Late Postclassic Mesoamerica. And in his 1981 general account of Quiche history, Carmack reiterated his basic thesis, including a discussion of Eric Thompson's well-known "Late/Epi-Classic Putun migrations hypothesis," concluding that the particular migration of the Quiche ancestors from the Gulf Coast region was probably subsequent to the earlier movements of the Putun suggested by Thompson.

Various studies and interpretations of the *Popol Vuh* have also appeared during this period, including a volume of interesting essays edited by Carmack and Morales Santos (1983). An iconoclastic study by René Acuña also appeared in 1975, in which he seriously questioned the *Popol Vuh*'s authenticity as an indigenous production, advancing various arguments that it had been composed by a Dominican missionary, Fray Domingo de Vico, to aid in the Spanish conversion effort. This view, however, has not, in general, been favorably received (see, especially, Bruce 1976–1977 and Himmelblau 1989 for significant critiques).

VI. The Pipil

In this section I discussed the scanty ethnohistorical material available on the Nahua-speaking groups of Guatemala, Honduras, and El Salvador, collectively referred to as the Pipil. In 1989, William R. Fowler published the first comprehensive monograph, utilizing all available primary sources, concerning the culture and history of the Pipil and their linguistic cousins in Nicaragua and Costa Rica, known as the Nicarao (for the latter, see also Chapman 1960 and León-Portilla 1971). He did not discern any mention in the few recorded Pipil/Nicarao traditions of a personage corresponding to Topiltzin Quetzalcoatl of Tollan. This is perhaps not too surprising in view of the absence of any clear evidence of an explicit Tollan connection for these Central American Nahua-speakers.

VII. Nicaragua

Post-1957 editions of the relevant primary sources concerning the Pipil/Nicarao include the 1959 republication, mentioned above, by Ediciones Atlas, Madrid, of Oviedo's *Historia general y natural de las Indias*. García de Palacio's 1576 *Carta de relación*, containing valuable information on the Pipil of Guatemala, has also been republished twice. In 1983, it was issued by the

Universidad Nacional Autónoma de México, Centro de Estudios Maya, Instituto de Investigaciones Filológicas, Fuentes para el Estudio de la Cultura Maya, 2, in a facsimile edition, paleographized, in a modern orthography, by María del Carmen León Cazares, with a preliminary study, glossary, analytical index, and map by María del Carmen León Cazares, Martha Ilia Nájera C., and Tolita Figueroa. In the same year, Ephraim G. Squier's 1860 English translation was republished by Labyrinthos, Culver City, California, with additional notes by Alexander von Frantzius and Frank E. Comparato.

VIII. Tabasco-Campeche

In this section I focused my discussion on the early-seventeenth-century *Paxbolon-Maldonaldo Papers* that revealed that the deity "Cukulchan" was worshipped by the ruler of Izamkanac, capital of the Chontal/Putun-speaking province of Acalan (southern Campeche). These papers, first published in 1948 by the Division of Historical Research of the Carnegie Institution of Washington in a classic scholarly monograph by France Scholes and Ralph Roys, were republished in 1968 by the University of Oklahoma Press.

IX. Yucatan

This section opened with a concise summary and discussion of Francisco Hernández's circa 1542 *Relación*, with a "Catechism" containing the names of Yucatecan Maya deities and personages, including Kukulcan, that had been sent to Fray Bartolomé de Las Casas, who incorporated it in his *Apologética historia de las Indias*. As indicated above, two complete and one partial re-editions of this work have appeared since 1957, in 1957–1958, 1966, and 1967.

I next summarized and discussed the material on Kukulcan/Quetzalcoatl in Fray Diego de Landa's *Relación de las cosas de Yucatan*. Fresh editions of Landa's classic work continue to appear. Tozzer's copiously annotated 1941 edition, in English translation, was republished in 1966, 1975, and 1978. In 1978, a paperback edition of William Gates's 1937 English version appeared—and in 1975, a new English version, edited and translated by A. R. Pagden. In Mexico, in 1959 the Editorial Porrúa published (Biblioteca Porrúa, 13) another edition (cf. Pérez Martínez 1938), with an introduction by Angel María Garibay K., that was reissued in 1966 and 1978. Another Mexican edition, edited by María del Carmen León Cázares, was published in 1994 by the Consejo Nacional para la Cultura y las Artes, in the Cien de México series. In Spain, in 1985 Miguel de Rivera edited yet another version (Historia 16, Crónicas de América, 7).

I then summarized the relevant material in the *Historical Recollections* of Gaspar Antonio Chi, contained in the Yucatecan *relaciones geográficas* of

New Spain of the 1579–1585 series, particularly utilizing the useful 1952 analysis and summary of them by M. Wells Jakeman. All of the Yucatecan *relaciones geográficas*, including reproductions of the original manuscripts in the Archivo de las Indias, Seville, were republished in 1983 by the Instituto de Investigaciones Filológicas, Centro de Estudios Mayas, Universidad Nacional Autónoma de México, edited and annotated by Mercedes de la Garza and others. Other ethnohistorical sources that contain information concerning Yucatecan Maya history and culture were also briefly reviewed. I concluded that, except for Torquemada's assertion that the Cocom dynasts claimed descent from Quetzalcoatl, they contained little or no primary additional information pertinent to our theme.

Relevant data in the *Books of Chilam Balam* were next summarized and discussed. Many re-editions and new versions of these native Yucatecan sources have appeared since 1957. Among the latter, worth particular mention (listing them by the names of their editors, annotators, and translators) are: Alvarez Lomeli 1969, 1974 (Chumayel; Spanish); Edmonson 1986 (Chumayel; English), 1982 (Tizimin; English); Craine and Reindorp 1979 (Pérez and Mani; English); Mercedes de la Garza 1983 (Chumayel; Spanish); Rivera 1968 (Chumayel; Spanish); Bricker 1990a (Chumayel; English), 1990b (Tizimin; English); and Gordon 1993 (Chumayel; English). The English translations of these recent editions often differ to some extent from those that were available to me in 1957, but I do not believe that they necessitate any significant revisions of the conclusions I arrived at in this section. And the same consideration applies to the final section that was devoted to the Yucatecan sources that contain information concerning the important deity Itzamna, whose myths sometimes contain elements that are vaguely reminiscent of some in the Topiltzin Quetzalcoatl of Tollan Tale.

Archaeological Evidence Possibly Relevant to the Topiltzin Quetzalcoatl of Tollan Tale

In this section I summarized the archaeological evidence available in 1957 that might have been connected with the personage(s) under discusssion in the dissertation. I particularly focused on representations of elite personages at the sites of Tula, Hidalgo, and Chichen Itza, Yucatan, that were associated with feathered-serpent imagery and/or were depicted wearing prominent beards. Unquestionably, portrayals—usually quite stylized—of actual historical individuals, identified by name signs and/or costume and insignia, were relatively common in many pre-Hispanic Mesoamerican cultural traditions, particularly Olmec/Izapan, Lowland Maya, Monte Albán, Tajín, Xochicalco, Toltec, and Mixteca-Puebla/Aztec. However, I concluded that, while recognizing the possible connection of these relevant Tula and Chichen Itza depictions with "the" TQ, it was more likely that they were representations of later personages invested with his symbols and accouterments, conceivably including the full beard. Considerable additional archaeological work has been undertaken at both Tula and Chichen Itza since 1957, much of it published, which has added considerably to our knowledge of these two key sites—but I am not aware of any significant discoveries during these projects that would substantially alter the views I expressed in this section regarding the relevance of the archaeological evidence vis-à-vis the problems surrounding TQ of Tollan.

Some Interpretations of the Basic Data Presented

I. THE BASIC TOPILTZIN QUETZALCOATL OF TOLLAN TALE

In this section, relying particularly on the six sources I assigned to the first category, I attempted to reconstruct the versions of the history of TQ closest to those that might have been taught in the priestly schools, the *calmecac*, of the leading communities of the Basin of Mexico and adjoining territory at Contact. This reconstruction was, of course, quite hypothetical—but, hopefully, about the best that could be done with the scattered, uneven, and often contradictory sources that are available to us. It must be considered only a working hypothesis, a tool of analysis to be appropriately modified whenever relevant new data appear.

II. THE POSSIBLE HISTORICITY OF THE TOPILTZIN QUETZALCOATL OF TOLLAN TALE

Even if my proposed reconstruction of the Contact-period basic tale was essentially accurate, it does not necessarily mean, of course, that it can be regarded as recounting the life and career of a real person who lived several centuries before the Conquest. Clearly, it was accepted as genuine history in Central Mexico at the advent of Cortés, above all by the rulers of the paramount polity of western Mesoamerica, Mexico Tenochtitlan, who claimed direct descent from this great Toltec lord. While it could be regarded as a politically motivated tradition of dubious historical validity, I still believe, considering all of the available evidence, both archaeological and ethnohistorical, that a case can be made for some degree of genuine historicity in the basic tale. I would, however, tend to be somewhat more cautious in speculating along these lines than I was in 1957. Perhaps only fresh archaeological discoveries could provide the kind of evidence necessary to determine whether at least some of the events recounted in the basic tale actually occurred. Certainly, the recovery of any amount of evidence that would throw additional light on Mesoamerica's most famous ruler, whether legendary or real, would be highly welcome. Further work at the site of Tula, particularly, might someday provide more satisfactory answers to the many questions that still surround this enigmatic figure.

III. SUPPLEMENTARY ASPECTS OF THE TALE

In these four sections I discussed TQ in relation to the "Toltec problem" and discussed various chronological, geographical, and nomenclatural aspects of the tale. Although, as indicated, since 1957 considerable additional archaeological work has been pursued at Tula and other Toltec-period sites in Central Mexico—as well as at Chichen Itza and other sites in Northern Yucatan—that has added substantially to our knowledge of Early Postclassic Mesoamerican civilization, apparently no significant new information specifically relating to Topiltzin Quetzalcoatl of Tollan has emerged. Regarding the chronological aspect, many more radiocarbon dates are now available, but it does not appear that they greatly alter the overall schemes of Jiménez Moreno and others that were current in 1957. In my 1978 article discussing the chronology of the Postclassic as revealed in western Mesoamerican ethnohistorical records, I again concluded that the case for positioning TQ near the beginning of the Toltec period rather than at its end appears to have the most evidence in its favor. I also recognized that establishing exact dates for TQ is extremely difficult because of the chronological disparities in even the earliest and putatively most reliable key primary sources. As for my discussions of the geographical and nomenclatural aspects of the tale, I would only add that I entered into a more extended discussion of the meaning and significance of Nacxit(l) in my article in the forthcoming Mary Elizabeth Smith Festschrift (Nicholson n.d.a).

Finally, in reviewing the "Conclusions" section, I would still stand by most of them, in spite of the appearance, since 1957, of a plethora of articles and books on Quetzalcoatl by many authors and in many languages, some of them advancing interpretations and hypotheses quite different from those I adumbrated in my dissertation. A thorough critical review and discussion of these recent discussions of the "Quetzalcoatl problem" would constitute a valuable contribution to Mesoamerican studies—but I must leave this task to a younger generation of scholars.

I would only like to reiterate my view that while a certain degree of historicity is probably conveyed by the earliest and ostensibly most authentic versions of the Basic Topiltzin Quetzalcoatl of Tollan Tale, today I more clearly recognize—without invoking the ghost of Lord Raglan and other hyper-skeptical students of all traditional "hero tales"—the hazards in pushing this view too vigorously. In any case, concerning one aspect of the tale there can be no doubt. Versions of it, accepted as genuine history, were widespread throughout late pre-Hispanic Mesoamerica—and it may well have played a significant role in influencing the initial reaction of the most powerful ruler of its western portion to the arrival of the European invaders. And, undeniably, the remarkable Lord of the Feathered Serpent has exerted a powerful fascination on all those interested in ancient Mexico since the time of the Conquest—and I venture to predict that he will continue to do so for a long time to come.

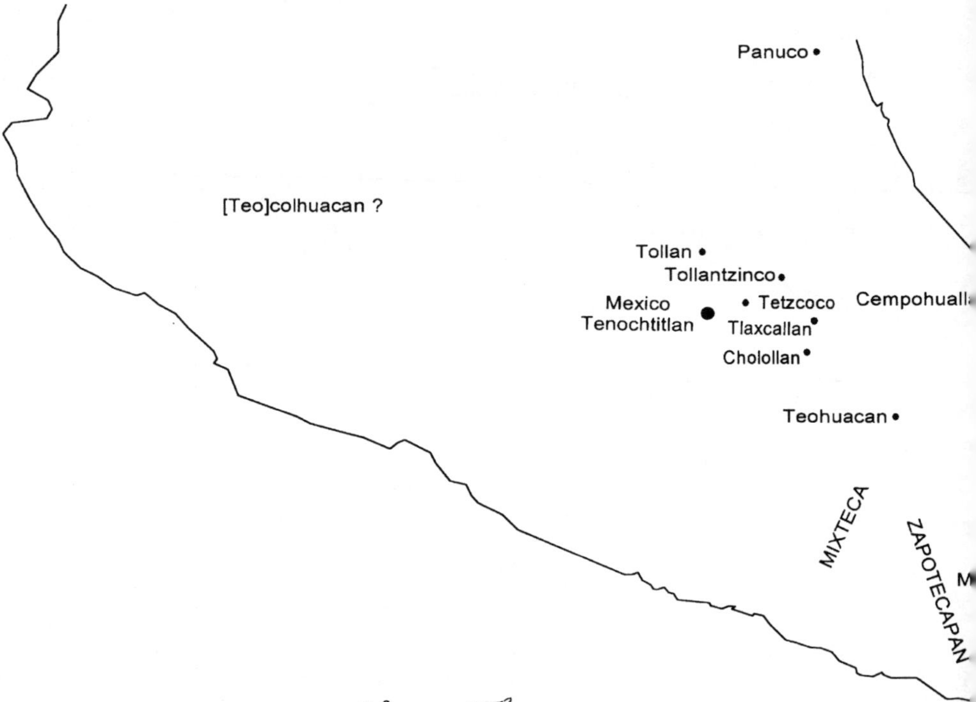

Postclassic Mesoamerica

Places associated with Topiltzin Quetzalcoatl

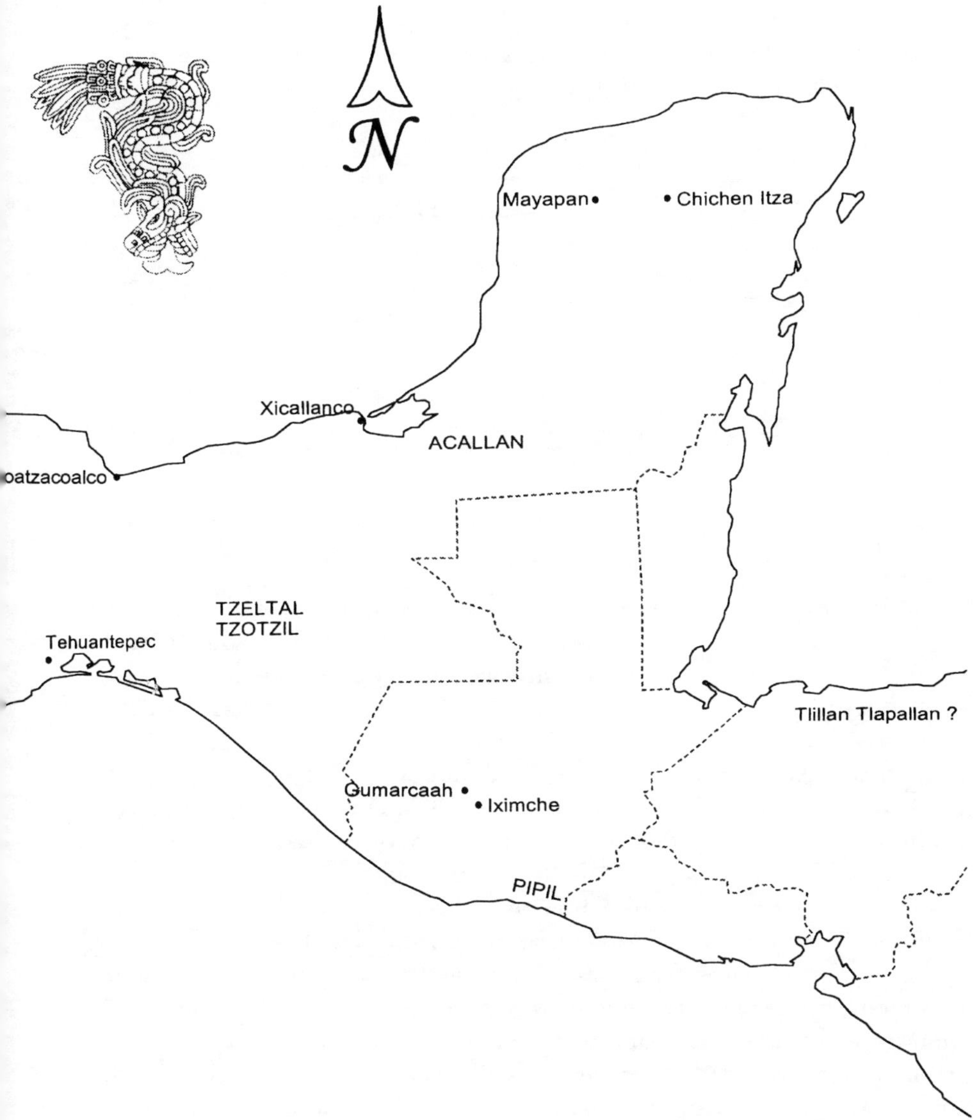

Map by Michel Besson

Note on Organization

In this section, a compromise between a strictly chronological and categorical presentation scheme will be employed. The sources that naturally belong together are roughly grouped into certain broad categories and within its category each source will be taken up in turn by date. Occasionally, a single source is "broken up," i.e., different passages relating to Topiltzin Quetzalcoatl are placed in different categories depending on their nature. Treating each source as a kind of literary lump, to be placed wholly within one particular classificatory pigeonhole, would defeat the analytical approach that I hope to employ in this book.

The general presentation technique will be as follows: First, the source itself and its author, where known, are discussed. The relevant Topiltzin Quetzalcoatl material is then presented, sometimes at considerable length, an attempt being made to omit no significant information. A condensed summary of the most essential facts it contains follows, arranged numerically to facilitate reference. This, in turn, is followed by a brief appraisal of the account as a whole, with particular emphasis on relating it to others in its category.

I. Central Mexico: Nahuatl

A. Earliest Accounts of the Basic Topiltzin Quetzalcoatl of Tollan Tale

This first category includes six sources. Five hang together unusually well and provide a reasonably coherent account of the birth, rise, downfall, death or disappearance—and, in some cases, subsequent apotheosis and/or stellar transformation—of a great Toltec priest/ruler who goes under various names but who is obviously the same figure and, as explained in the introductions, will invariably be referred to in this study as Topiltzin Quetzalcoatl (TQ). The sixth source, although ostensibly not in chronological agreement with the others and only covering the latter half of TQ's career, otherwise clearly belongs with this group. All of these accounts are particularly distinguished by their presenting more or less coherent *narratives*, tracing sequentially the salient features of TQ's career, rather than providing mere allusions, snatches, or single brief episodes.

They all probably date from before 1570, thus falling into the half century following the Conquest, a period during which much of the indigenous culture was preserved intact and informants were still living who had grown to adulthood and had been educated in the priestly schools, the *calmecac*, before the Conquest. As to provenience, three almost certainly record the authentic tradition of Mexico Tenochtitlan, while another was probably compiled in Mexico Tlatelolco. The provenience of the other two is uncertain, but they doubtless represent versions current in other important centers of the Basin of Mexico or immediately surrounding territory, if not the imperial capital itself.

All, with one partial exception, are anonymous, i.e., the identity of the informants who provided the information is unknown. And with only one exception, the names of the Spanish, mestizo, or native compilers, as the case may be, are also unknown. Two were originally written in Spanish, one exists only in a sixteenth-century French translation of a lost Spanish original, three are in Nahuatl, and for one of these three we have a contemporary translation into Spanish, made by the compiler.

Three were clearly based directly on pictorial histories, one of which is explicitly stated to have been pre-Hispanic. The ultimate sources of the others were also probably pictorial records, supplemented by the usual oral narrations. One is accompanied by a few illustrations, although in a partially Europeanized style. These probably provide some notion of the type of representations that were characteristic of these pictorial histories.

To anticipate slightly, in my judgment this group of six key sources provides the most reliable version of what was actually taught at the time of the Conquest in the *calmecac(s)* of the leading Basin of Mexico communities concerning the life and death of Topiltzin Quetzalcoatl of Tollan.

1. The *Historia de los Mexicanos por sus pinturas*

THE SOURCE

This was the title given by Joaquín García Icazbalceta (following the lead of one of its previous possessors) to an anonymous Spanish document, part of a manuscript volume known as *Libro de oro y tesoro indico*, that contains various unrelated pieces, all in script of the sixteenth century, including the *Memoriales* of Motolinía (Benson Latin American Collection, University of Texas, Austin, JGI 31). José M. Andrade purchased it for García Icazbalceta in Spain in 1860/61, and, in 1891, the latter (Garciá Icazbalceta 1891: 228–262) published most of the individual documents in it, including that under consideration. Previously, he had published it elsewhere (*Historia de los Mexicanos por sus pinturas* 1882), although in a slightly imperfect form. A year later, an English translation was made by Henry Phillips, from this edition, and published under the misleading title "Notes Upon the *Codex Ramírez*" (Phillips 1884). Paul Radin (1920) also translated the latter portion into English.

There have been many speculations as to its authorship. The names of both Sahagún and Olmos have been suggested, the former with very little foundation, the latter with somewhat more cogency (see discussion in García Icazbalceta 1891: xxxix–xli). Lacking a title, it only contains a note, in a hand identical to that of the text, stating that it was copied from "la pintura" that was brought by "ramírez obispo de Cuenca presidente de la chancillería." Sebastián Ramírez de Fuenleal, later Bishop of Cuenca, was the president of the Second Audiencia de Nueva España and apparently returned to Spain early in 1536, at which time he seems to have carried with him the original of which this document is a copy (probably post-1542, since Fuenleal did not become Bishop of Cuenca until that year). García Icazbalceta surmised that "la pintura" referred to a pictorial history that accompanied the written text. This is supported by the first sentence of that text, in which the compiler describes the sources upon which he is basing his account (*Historia de los Mexicanos por sus pinturas* 1891: 228):

> Por los carácteres y escrituras de que usan, y por relación de los que en tiempo de su infidelidad eran sacerdotes y papas, y por dicho de los señores y principales a quién se enseñaba la ley y criaban en los templos para que la deprendiesen, juntados ante mi y traídos sus libros y figuras que según lo que demostaban eran antiguas, y muchas dellas teñidas, la mayor parte untadas con sangre humana.

As to date, the year count of the principal narrative ends abruptly in 1529, but a reference to the native governor of Mexico Tenochtitlan, Don Pablo Xochiquen, who seems not to have taken office until 1531 (or 1532, according to other sources), makes it probable that this was the actual date of completion. A *terminus ante quem* seems to be provided by the date of Ramírez de Fuenleal's departure for Spain, 1536. In any case, the pictorial history upon which the principal narrative was clearly based was undoubtedly pre-Hispanic, with the year count being continued after the Conquest to the year 1529.

With the possible exception of the next source to be considered, this is the earliest version of the Basic Topiltzin Quetzalcoatl of Tollan Tale that has been preserved. This early date, plus the unquestionably authentic indigenous flavor of the account as a whole, lends it a special importance.

THE TOPILTZIN QUETZALCOATL MATERIAL

As is true of others in this group, Quetzalcoatl appears in this source in two entirely different guises—first, under that name, as one of the first gods, who participates actively in the creation of the earth and man, and second, much later, under a different name, as a great ruler of the Toltecs. This account makes unusually clear, then, the basic distinction between Ehecatl Quetzalcoatl (EQ) and Topiltzin Quetzalcoatl. In line with the primary focus of this study, it is only the material relating to the latter figure that will be considered here.

The relevant narrative begins after the creation of the sun in the year 13 Acatl (Reed) with a series of adventures involving the god Camaxtli/Mixcoatl, who creates four men and one woman, together with four hundred Chichimeca, with the object of setting them against each other to provide the new sun with his sustenance, human hearts and blood. This is finally accomplished, the former annihilating the latter, with the exception of three individuals: Xiuhnel, Mimich, and Camaxtli/Mixcoatl, the god himself who has metamorphosed into a Chichimec. Camaxtli/Mixcoatl now pursues a warlike terrestrial career, undertaking a series of conquests with the aid of a kind of sacred fetish or standard, a two-headed deer, that had fallen from heaven—and which was taken by the inhabitants of Cuitlahuac for a god. Finally, in the year 1 Acatl, Camaxtli/Mixcoatl is defeated and his potent deer charm taken from him by his Chichimec enemies. The text is not completely clear at this point, but his loss and defeat seem to have been caused in some way by the fact that he had encountered "en el campo" a woman (unnamed), descended from five who had been created by Tezcatlipoca at the time the gods first wished to create war. This woman bore him a son, Ce Acatl (1 Reed).

Camaxtli/Mixcoatl disappears from the narrative at this point, which now focuses on the career of his son. Ce Acatl, after achieving young manhood, performs seven years of penance alone in the mountains, offering his blood to the gods while seeking their aid in making him a great warrior. He then begins a martial career and becomes the first ruler of Tollan, whose inhabitants select him "por ser valiente." The date is ambiguous. The text states that he began to make war "en el treceno sexto después del diluvio" (beginning 1 Acatl, his apparent birth year), but this may be a mistake for "septo," for it is clear that he was adult at this time. In any case, Ce Acatl rules Tollan until "el segundo año del noveno trece," which would be 2 Acatl, forty-two years after his birth. Four years before this, he had constructed a great temple in Tollan. While engaged in this project, Tezcatlipoca had come to him and informed him that in the direction of Honduras, in a place that "hoy día" was called "Tlapalla," a house was prepared for him. There he was to go to die, abandoning Tollan, where he was now held to be a god. Ce Acatl responded that the heavens and the stars had told him that he must go within four years. At the end of that time, Ce Acatl left Tollan, taking with him all of the *macehuales* (common people). On his journey, he left some in Cholollan, from whom were descended its later inhabitants, others in Cozcatlan, and others in Cempohuallan. Arriving at Tlapallan, the same day he fell sick, and the next day he died. Then Tollan was depopulated and without a ruler for nine years (*Historia de los Mexicanos por sus pinturas* 1891: 236–238).

The narrative next switches abruptly to the migration of the ancestors of the Mexica from Aztlan. The further history of the Toltecs is completely omitted in this otherwise reasonably full account, although the last sentence implies that after nine years a new ruler was chosen, who continued the dynasty. Tollan reappears briefly in a later connection with the Mexica migration, when we find it "poblado de los naturales de la tierra, que eran

Chichimecas." The Mexica erect their usual temple to Huitzilopochtli there, following which the god appears to the natives "en figura de negro" and is later heard crying under the earth. When they asked why the god of the Mexica was crying, it replied: because all those of Tollan had to die. Four years later, an old woman, native of Tollan, went about handing out paper banners to each inhabitant, warning them to be prepared, since they had to die. Following this, the entire population is sacrificed by the Mexica, who become lords of Tollan, soon after continuing their migration (*Historia de los Mexicanos por sus pinturas* 1891: 242).

SUMMARY

This obviously quite sketchy narrative can be summarized as follows: (1) Ce Acatl is born, apparently in the year 1 Acatl, to Camaxtli/Mixcoatl, a god transformed into an earthly "Chichimec" and an unnamed woman encountered by him during his conquests, a relative of Tezcatlipoca descended from a group of five women created by this god, along with four hundred men, to wage war to provide the sun with sustenance; (2) his father meets his downfall at this time, somehow connected with his encounter with Ce Acatl's mother; (3) Ce Acatl, coming of age, performs penance for seven years to become a great warrior; (4) he begins to make war and is taken by the people of Tollan for their first ruler; (5) he rules, apparently peacefully, in Tollan until, in his thirty-eighth year, Tezcatlipoca comes to him as he is constructing a great temple and informs him that a kind of "rest home" is awaiting him in Tlapallan, toward Honduras, where he is to die; (6) replying that the heavens and stars have told him that he must leave within four years, at the end of that period, in his forty-second year (2 Acatl), he departs with all of the common people of Tollan; (7) on his journey, he leaves part of his band in Chollollan, some in Cozcatlan, and some in Cempohuallan, from which the inhabitants of those centers, all important at the time of the Conquest, were descended; (8) he arrives in Tlapallan, falls sick, and the next day dies; (9) back in Tollan, this center was depopulated and without a ruler for nine years; (10) somewhat later (seventy-eight years, to be exact, in the continuous year count of the chronicle, in 2 Calli), the migrating Mexica reach Tollan, now inhabited by "Chichimeca," sacrifice all of its population, and become its lords, soon after continuing their wanderings.

COMMENT

This terse account is basically straightforward and presents no particularly difficult problems. Its extreme brevity, however, is frustrating. The Spanish compiler obviously recorded (or, perhaps, was only told) just the barest bones of the full tale. Certain important incidents are related so sketchily as to be almost meaningless, above all, Ce Acatl's encounter with Tezcatlipoca, which, as we shall see, in some other accounts is narrated with a colorful wealth of detail. Fortunately, this cryptic skeletal framework can be fleshed out with material from the more complete versions of the tale considered below.

It is interesting that no linkage is made between the god Quetzalcoatl, who appears extensively in the opening cosmogonical portion of the work, and the first ruler of Tollan, who bears only the calendric name Ce Acatl. Except that he is the son of a transformed god and a woman related to a god and descended from a group created under special circumstances, he is essentially a human figure. His adoration as a god by his people of Tollan does not deprive him of his fundamentally mundane role.

Again, as possibly the earliest extant version of the Basic Topiltzin Quetzalcoatl of Tollan Tale, this account, however truncated, is of special importance. This is particularly true in view of the likelihood that the *Historia de los Mexicanos por sus pinturas* constituted an excellent example of an "official" Mexica history of the world, from earliest times to 1531. The loss of the pictorial history from which this Spanish digest was derived is one of the keenest that the vicissitudes of fortune have inflicted on ancient Mexican studies. We should be grateful, however, that this abbreviated verbal derivative fortuitously survived to provide us with one of the most authentic accounts of Mexica history—in which the Topiltzin Quetzalcoatl of Tollan Tale was significantly incorporated.

2. The *Juan Caño Relaciones*

THE SOURCE

I have given this name to two important early accounts of the dynastic history of Mexico Tenochtitlan and the earlier dynasties of Colhuacan and Tollan from which that of the first named center claimed direct descent. Separately, they are known under the titles: (1) *Relación de la genealogía y linaje de los señores que han señoreado esta tierra de la Nueva España, después que le acuerdan haber gentes en estas partes*; and (2) *Origen de los Mexicanos*. They are both contained in the same manuscript volume as the preceding piece, the *Libro de oro y tesoro indico*. Although García Icazbalceta, who in 1891 published them in the third volume of his *Nueva colección de documentos para la historia de México*, practically implied that the *Origen de los Mexicanos* is a copy of the other document, a careful examination of both texts reveals that neither is a copy of the other but that both apparently derive, with significant variants, from a lost prototype. Both texts, according to their editor, are studded with copyists' errors, particularly that of the *Origen*, which was so corrupt that he nearly despaired of successfully preparing it for the press. It is fortunate that he did, for the *Origen* occasionally contains important details that are absent in the *Relación*.

From internal evidence, it is known that the account was prepared in 1532 by unnamed Franciscan friars at the petition of Juan Cano, one of the *primeros conquistadores*, to legitimatize, by tracing her pedigree back to the Creation, the claim of his wife, Doña Isabel (Tecuichpo, the famed, oft-wed daughter of Motecuhzoma II), to what he considered her lawful patrimony. From a remark in the *Origen*, it was apparently intended that Bishop Zumárraga should carry it to Spain on his trip there in May 1532 (it was being written in April), which probably occurred. Its compilers stated that it was based principally on what was written "en sus libros por figuras y carácteres" (those that survived the burnings, which they righteously describe in some detail), supplemented by the testimony of "los que más saben." Although compiled by Spaniards who obviously only imperfectly understood the material with which they were dealing, it displays a conscientious attempt to arrive at one version of the facts, which, combined with its very early date, lends it particular value.

THE TOPILTZIN QUETZALCOATL MATERIAL

The narrative begins with a brief reference to the creation of man at Teotihuacan, following which two groups, or "linages de gente," emerged, one of which, the rustic Chichimeca, remained behind, while the second group, "que era de más capacedad," after eleven years migrated to a place called Teocolhuacan, of whose location even the natives themselves were ignorant. There, this group, now called Colhua from their city, rapidly acquired the arts of civilization. After seventeen years, they chose their first lord, Totepeuh (*Relación*: "Toteheb"; *Origen*: "Totepez"). After a long reign of fifty-six years, Totepeuh was assassinated by his brother-in-law, Atecpanecatl (*Relación*: "Atepanecate"; *Origen*: "Apanecate"), who usurped the throne—and whose image was found, according to the compilers, by the Spaniards in the "Culhuacan el desta tierra," in five pieces, four of which were made into pillars supporting the arches of the altars of the church of San Juan Evangelista in that town. Totepeuh left a son, Topiltzin (*Relación*: "Topilci"; *Origen*: "Topilce"), who, to honor his dead father, took his bones, buried them, and erected to his memory a temple pyramid, "e le tenía en mucha veneración como a otro Niño hijo de Bel." Upon learning this, his uncle-in-law, angered, sought to kill Topiltzin. Finding him in the temple dedicated to his father, he rushed furiously up the stairs at his intended victim. But Topiltzin met his would-be assassin at the summit, gave him a violent push, and sent him tumbling down the stairway, from which fall he died. Topiltzin then assumed the rulership of Teocolhuacan, reigning in peace and tranquillity for sixteen years, "que le querían mucho los de Culhua, que era muy buena persona."

At the end of this time, Topiltzin and his people determined to leave and migrate to other parts, apparently on the advice of the gods. After a journey lasting ten years, they established themselves at Tollantzinco. Their residence there only lasted four years, during which time they constructed some small houses. They then moved to Tollan. According to the *Relación* version, it was the "primera población que fué en esta tierra," since the aborigines, the Chichimeca, had not yet founded any towns. The *Origen* version, on the other hand, states that, according to some, there was already a settlement at Tollan when Topiltzin and his followers arrived. Then follows the strange remark, "los que dicen esto no lo muestran por escrituras, e pienso que se engañaban, e piensan que es el Tolpice de los mexicanos que vinieron a la postre." The compiler also expresses the view that by this time, "los más avisados a los que eran Señores" among the Chichimeca had founded some settlements, "aunque poca cosa": Azcapotzalco, Tenanyocan, Tepechpan, Coatlinchan, Colhuacan, Coyoacan, and Tlacopan (Tacuba).

Topiltzin ruled peacefully for a time (*Relación*: ten years; *Origen*: twelve years) over a Tollan, which was "cabeza de señorío como lo era Mexico al tiempo que a el vinieron los españoles," but finally a religious controversy forced him to leave. Under his benevolent rule no human sacrifice was permitted, only that of quail, butterflies, snakes, and large grasshoppers. Threatened by the gods Huitzilopochtli and Tezcatlipoca (or their human partisans), who demanded human victims, Topiltzin, refusing to change his policy, departed Tollan, accompanied by many of his people, including all of the craftsmen, who, although not ordered to do so, insisted on following him, so great was their affection for him. He proceeded to a place called Tlapallan ("Tlapala") where, after two years, he died. The compiler of the *Relación* finishes his account thus: "tienen mucha memoria los indios desta ciudad y sus comarcas deste Topici, y hay grande historia del. Dicen que sus vestidos eran a manera de los de España."

The narrative then goes on to state that his vassals remained very sad after Topiltzin's departure. The gods were so angered that they did not permit another ruler to reign over Tollan for ninety-seven years. Finally, the gods somewhat appeased, a ruler was elected from the lineage of Topiltzin, named Huemac (*Origen*: "Vemac"), who ruled in prosperity for sixty-two years. At the end of that time, disaster overtook Tollan: a fantastic monster appeared that frightened its inhabitants so terribly that many of them abandoned the city. Huemac himself led a group to Chapoltepec, in the Basin of Mexico, where, after six years, "vióse muy afligido, y desesperó," he hung himself. According to the *Origen*, others said that he entered a cave in Atlcuihuayan ("Atlacoyoaya" = Tacubaya) and disappeared. Those who remained in Tollan elected another ruler, Nauhyotzin (*Relación*: "Nahuinci"; *Origen*: "Naviunci"), apparently a near relative of Huemac, who, after sixteen years, led the final abandonment of the great center (García Icazbalceta 1891: 265–268, 284–290).

SUMMARY

(1) Topiltzin was the son of the first ruler of Teocolhuacan, a distant, legendary place to which "los de Culhua" had migrated after the Creation in Teotihuacan; (2) his father, Totepeuh, was murdered by his brother-in-law, Atecpanecatl, who usurped the throne; (3) Topiltzin, after reverentially burying his father's bones and erecting a temple over them, avenged his death by killing the usurper in self-defense; (4) Topiltzin becomes ruler; (5) after a few years he leads his people, by whom he is greatly loved, to new lands, settling for a short time at Tollantzinco, then moving on to Tollan; (6) Topiltzin rules peacefully in Tollan for about a decade, until a religious controversy arises involving a demand for human sacrifice, which he refuses to allow; (7) he leaves Tollan, accompanied by a number of his subjects, including all of the craftsmen, and arrives at a place called Tlapallan, where he dies after two years.

COMMENT

The basic outlines of this narrative are clear, and, like the preceding, it poses few difficulties. From statements in both versions, it is evident that the compiler omitted considerable detail ("dejo de decir lo que es fábula"), especially that relating to Topiltzin's downfall in Tollan, but seems to have preserved the basic structure of the tale. Since the Tenochca ruling dynasty in this account is tracing its descent directly from Topiltzin, it is obvious that he is being regarded as an historical personage. Significantly, there is no hint here of his possessing supernatural powers, nor is he apotheosized after his death. He is presented as a completely human figure. The only suggestion of anything particularly unusual connected with him is the enigmatic statement in the *Relación*, quoted above, that his clothing was like that of Spain.

It is clear that the tradition in question is essentially that of Colhuacan, the important center of the southern Basin of Mexico that provided the key cultural and political link between Tollan and Mexico Tenochtitlan. This is highlighted at one point in the *Relación* (1891: 270), when the compiler states that to further clarify a point he would need to consult "los de Culhuacan." The Colhuaque tradition of their past history, particularly that portion relating to the dynasty of Tollan, from whom their rulers claimed direct descent, was apparently taken over entirely by the Tenochca, whose own dynasty had been initiated by Acamapichtli, connected with the Colhuaque royal line. This fact, among others, clearly led the Mexica aristocracy to conceive of themselves as the latter-day representatives of the Co[u]lhua[que]. Thus, the Tenochca ruler was, according to Alva Ixtlilxochitl, referred to as Culhua Tecuhtli, Lord of the Culhua; the inhabitants of Mexico Tenochtitlan were often called the Culhua Mexica, and to nearly all of the peoples outside the Basin of Mexico they seem to have been most frequently referred to as the Culhua. Since the Colhuaque seem to have maintained their continuity with their Toltec cultural ancestors with particular success, this historical tradition relating to Tollan is particularly important, however disappointing—and puzzling—the failure to include the names of any ruler between Topiltzin and Huemac.

3. The *Histoyre du Mechique*

THE SOURCE

This important early account of pre-Hispanic Central Mexican customs, history, religion, and mythology is a copy, by André Thevet, the sixteenth-century French royal cosmographer, of a lost Spanish source. It is preserved in the Bibliothèque National, Paris (MSS Francais 19031) and was published with an introduction and notes by Édouard de Jonghe (*Histoyre du Mechique* 1905). It served Thevet for over half of the material he incorporated in the section on Mexico in his most important work, the *Cosmographie Universelle* (Paris, 1575): book XXII, chapters 15, 16, and 17 (for a detailed collation of the two texts, see Jonghe 1906: 228–231).

De Jonghe (1906) concluded, after a careful study, that it was undoubtedly based on a portion of the famous lost work of Fray Andrés de Olmos, the most important predecessor of Sahagún in compiling data on native culture. He pointed out a number of passages in Mendieta (1945, I, book II: passim), clearly based, by explicit statement, on Olmos, which parallel some of the material in the *Histoyre* so closely that some intimate connection must have existed between them. He concluded, therefore, that by some unknown means (possibly pirate capture, as with the *Codex Mendoza*, which also came into his possession) Thevet had obtained one of the Olmos manuscripts that he partially translated, the Spanish original subsequently disappearing. De Jonghe also examined the problem of the date of composition of the original Spanish version. He interpreted a rather confused passage (*Histoyre du Mechique* 1905: 20) as indicating that it was 1543.

De Jonghe's hypotheses concerning the nature of the lost prototype were generally accepted for some time, but eventually two students challenged his thesis. Joaquín Meade (1950: 385) pointed out that the author (*Histoyre du Mechique* 1905: 15) stated that he had seen the province of Culiacan. Since Olmos is not known to have visited this area at any time during his missionary career, Meade concluded that he could not possibly have been the direct author of the lost original manuscript. Garibay (1953–1954, II: 24, 47–48) seized on the same passage to suggest, following Rosales Mungía, that the author of the first portion of the work (chapters I–V) might have been Fray Marcos de Niza, the Franciscan who led Coronado into what became the U.S. Southwest. He proposed, therefore, that only the last portion (chapters VI–XI) might be derived from the lost Olmos.

As it stands now, the problem is far from solution. Certainly the strikingly parallel passages in the *Histoyre* and the Olmos-based sections in

Mendieta indicate that at least some of the information found in the former must derive, directly or indirectly, from Olmos. The problem of the passage written by the eyewitness of Culiacan must be recognized, however, and might support Garibay's composite authorship suggestion—without providing specific evidence in favor of the Marcos de Niza hypothesis. Whoever was its original compiler, this source, particularly its last six chapters, is one of great value. This is exactly what one would expect if Olmos had had a hand in it, which I think is highly likely. Most importantly for our purposes, its version of the Basic Topiltzin Quetzalcoatl of Tollan Tale, in spite of some anomalous features, is one of the fullest and earliest extant.

THE TOPILTZIN QUETZALCOATL MATERIAL

The last two chapters of this fragment (X and XI) are entirely devoted to the TQ tale. The first, entitled "De ung idole, nomé Quetzalcoatl, de son origine, oeuvres et temps qui régna," begins with the god Camaxtli ("Comachtli") taking for a wife a goddess named Chimalma. She bore him some children, among whom was one called Quetzalcoatl, who was born in Michatlauhco ("Nichatlanco"). When his mother died in childbirth, he was taken to his grandfather and grandmother (unnamed), who raised him. After coming of age, he was taken to his father, but, because Quetzalcoatl was greatly loved by him, his brothers jealously hated him and began to plot his death. They led him by trickery to a great rock, called Tlachinoltepetl ("Chalchonoltepetl"), "qui veult dire roche où l'on faict brusler." There they left him and, descending, "mirent le feu à l'entour de la roche." But Quetzalcoatl hid himself in a hole in the rock, and the brothers left thinking they had effectively disposed of him. Whereupon Quetzalcoatl emerged from his hiding place with a bow and arrows and shot and killed a deer. Taking it on his shoulders, he carried it to his father, reaching him before his brothers. The latter, arriving, were amazed on seeing him still alive, but they immediately began to plot his death in another fashion. This time they took him under a tree, and, after telling him that he would be able to shoot birds from there, they began shooting arrows at him. But, "comme il estoit discret," he fell to the ground, only feigning death. Seeing this, his brothers again left for home. Then Quetzalcoatl got up and killed a rabbit, once more taking it to his father before his brothers arrived. His father, suspecting what his brothers were up to, asked him where they were. He replied that they were coming and went with his father to another house. Meanwhile, his brothers arrived. When their father asked them where their brother was, they replied that he was coming. He then accused them of wanting to kill their brother. Angered, the brothers decided to commit patricide, taking him to a mountain. The deed committed, they went to Quetzalcoatl and induced him to believe that his father had been transformed into a rock. They also persuaded him to make sacrifices and offerings to the rock, "comme lions, tigres, aigles, biches et papillons," in order to create the opportunity of killing him—since they knew that he would be unable to find these creatures. Upon his refusal to obey, they again attempted to dispose of him, but he escaped, fleeing under a tree, "ou, qui est plus veresemblable, sus la mesme roche, et à coups de flèches les tua touts." His malevolent brothers accounted for, Quetzalcoatl's vassals, "qui l'aimoynt fort, le vindrent quérir honorablement," extracted the brains from his brothers' skulls, made drinking cups from the skulls, and proceeded to get very drunk.

From there they migrated "à terre de Mechique." After residing for a few days in Tollantzinco, they continued on to Tollan. They did not yet know, however, what it was to sacrifice, and, "comme il [Quetzalcoatl] aporta l'usaige du sacrifice, fut tenu pour dieu, aux quels il enseigna beaucoup de bonnes choses, temples pour luy et aultres choses, et dura 160 ans pour dieu en ce païs."

Chapter XI is titled "De la venue de Tezcatlipuca à Tula et de comme fit fuir Queçalcoatl." Quetzalcoatl had been living very comfortably in Tollan, adored as a god. Then, "comme la vérité no se peult long temps tenir cachée," it happened that another god arrived in Tollan, Tezcatlipoca. Envious of Quetzalcoatl, he tried to do harm to the people of the city, who adored him along with Quetzalcoatl. He entered Tollan disguised as a pauper and constantly transformed himself into different shapes, frightening the inhabitants and Quetzalcoatl, who feared Tezcatlipoca because he possessed superior power. One day, Tezcatlipoca came to the temple of Quetzalcoatl, where a number of attendants guarded an altar with an effigy of the latter and a mirror, "que les Indiens estimoynt beaucoup; car, selon que Queçalcoatl leur avoyt faict croire par le moien de ce mirouer, toutes les foys qu'ils auroint à faire de pluie, et luy demanderoynt avec ce mirouer, il leur baillaroynt." Tezcatlipoca entered the temple and, finding the attendants asleep, he went straight to the altar, stole the mirror, hiding it beneath "une pallace" where they were sleeping, and departed unawares. The guards awakened, discovered their loss, and searched in vain for the mirror. Then Tezcatlipoca encountered an old woman on the road and told her to go to the temple and inform the guards that what they were searching for was under their mat, "et tu seras bien aimée d'eux," which the old woman did.

Meanwhile, Tezcatlipoca transformed himself into several different animals and monsters, attempting to frighten the people. He also had his hair cut, "ce que les Indiens n'avoynt jamais veu." He went again to the temple of Quetzalcoatl, where he destroyed his effigy, smashing it and hurling it to the ground. Still transforming himself into various shapes, he struck the attendants, "et touts ceux de Tula, qui voiant cela se en fuirent et laissèrent la vile, et Queçalcoatl voiant ceci oust pour et se enfuit aussi avecques quelques unga serviteurs," which greatly pleased his adversary.

Quetzalcoatl fled to Tenanyocan ("Tenacuia"), where he lived for some time. From there he went to Colhuacan ("Cullinacan"), where he also resided a long time, but how long was not known. He then passed over the mountains and came to Cuauhquechollan ("Quantiquechula"), where he raised up a temple and "ung haustel pour soy," and was adored as the sole god, living there 290 years. He left a lord there, named Mactlacxochitl ("Maclalchochitl"), and continued on to Chololian ("Acholula"), where he stayed 160 years. There they built him a very magnificent temple, "du quel il y a encore grand partie; car estoyt bien basti et beau, le qual les géans avoyt faict." From there he went to Cempohuallan, "vile principale en la mer de Espaigne, où premier arriva le marquis Don Cortès, quand il alla en ce païs; mais, à présant est toute desmolie, comme les Espaignols ont facit à beaucoup de aultres." Here he lived for 260 years. Finally, Tezcatlipoca pursued him even to here. Seeing himself so persecuted by his old rival, he fled into a desert. There he "tirat un coup de flèche à ung arbre, et se mit de dans le partuis de la flèche, et ainsi mourut." His attendants cremated him, "et de là demeura la coustume de brusler les corps morts." From the smoke that issued from his body was created "une grande estoyle que se appelle Hesper." Then it is stated, as a postscript, that Quetzalcoatl "n'eust jamais femme ni enfens," and a variant account of his disappearance is mentioned: "Aultres disent que quand il devoyt mourir sen alla en ung lieu . . ." This final last sentence is unfinished, for here the manuscript ends. Perhaps "nomée Tlapala," or some such, completed it, but this is only speculation (*Histoyre du Mechique* 1905: 34–38). Earlier, in chapter IV (19), is a passage concerned with the origin of the Colhuaque, which, although Quetzalcoatl is not specifically named, is relevant to our theme:

> Mais tournant au poinct que avions oublié de la venue de ceux de Culhua qui est à deux lieues du Mechique. Ceux disent avoyr esté du costé des Mechiquiens, les quels demeurant à Culiacan (du quel nous avons ici desus parlé). Une compaignie de eux estoyt sortie combatre contre quelques aultres et quand ils furent de retour, leur seigneur ne se contentant pas de ce qu'ils avoynt faict ne les voulut pas recevoir, par quoy estant contraincts de chercher lieu où demeurer se en alèrent à Tula qui est à douze lieues de Mechique, et aiant demeuré là quelque temps, leur seigneur mourut et fut eslu en son lieu ung aultre nomé Vamac, le quel estant seigneur appareut une vision en le peuple de ung homme qui sembloyt toucher le ciel de sa teste, de quoi ce seigneur et tout ce peuple espouvantés s'en sortirent du lieu, et vindrent à Culhua qui est à deux lieues de Mechique.

"Vamac," of course, is Huemac; while the unnamed "seigneur" might well be Topiltzin Quetzalcoatl.

SUMMARY

(1) Quetzalcoatl is born at Michatlauhco to Camaxtli and Chimalma, who dies in childbirth; (2) he is taken to his (maternal?) grandparents, who raise him; (3) when of age, he joins his father and brothers, but the latter, envious of the special love his father bears him, plot to kill him; (4) after two unsuccessful attempts, Camaxtli, his suspicions aroused, accuses them of nefarious intent, whereupon they commit patricide; (5) a third attempt on Quetzalcoatl is also frustrated, and he kills his attackers; (6) his vassals render him homage and celebrate the demise of his brothers by drinking to excess from cups manufactured from their skulls; (7) Quetzalcoatl then leads his people to "the land of Mexico," stopping over briefly at Tollantzinco, then proceeding on to Tollan, where, after he has instructed them in the ritual of sacrifice, he is worshipped as a god, remaining celibate throughout his life; (8) Quetzalcoatl's happy reign of 160 years is interrupted by the appearance of a rival, the god Tezcatlipoca, who is bent on mischief; (9) after disguising himself as a pauper, transforming himself into various fearful shapes, stealing and hiding Quetzalcoatl's powerful rain-producing magic mirror, and destroying his effigy in the temple dedicated to him, Tezcatlipoca succeeds in his goal of driving Quetzalcoatl and his people from Tollan; (10) the latter and a few attendants travel to Tenanyocan, where they reside for some time, then to Colhuacan for an even longer time, then over the mountains to Cuauhquechollan, where Quetzalcoatl successfully establishes himself, adored as their sole god, for 290 years; (11) leaving behind a lord named Matlacxochitl, Quetzalcoatl moves on to Chololllan, where the great pyramid, built by the giants, is raised in his honor; (12) after 160 years in Chololllan, he flees to Cempohuallan, where he resides 260 years before his old antagonist, Tezcatlipoca, arrives to further persecute him; (13) in despair, he flees into the desert and, apparently, dies after shooting himself with an arrow; (14) his servitors cremate his body, which establishes this custom ever after; (15) from the smoke that pours from his body the planet Venus is created; (16) according to another version, he went to a place (called Tlapallan?); (17) in an earlier passage, a figure who probably corresponds to Topiltzin Quetzalcoatl is succeeded as ruler by Huemac, who, terrified by a phantasm, abandons Tollan and travels to Colhuacan (of the Basin of Mexico), with his people.

COMMENT

This account of the birth, life, and death of our hero is one of the most comprehensive that has survived, in spite of gaps and a certain sketchiness in some places in the narrative. For the most part, the French translation appears to have been essentially faithful, at least in catching the sense, although many of the Nahuatl words are quite corrupted. On the whole, it lines up fairly well with the other accounts in this section but does present some interesting variants. Of Camaxtli's earlier deeds and the nature of his encounter with Chimalma, we are told nothing. The place of Quetzalcoatl's birth, Michatlauhco, is only found in this source. Also unique to it are his misadventures with *his* brothers, the slayers of his father, rather than his father's brothers, which is standard. Since it seems unlikely that a translation slip was involved (*tio* versus *hermano*), we are probably confronted here with a genuine variant. Its general resemblance to the biblical Joseph and his brothers' tale is interesting and perhaps significant. Anything that has come down to us through the intermediation of the early missionaries must always be critically examined for possible Christian influence—and this may well apply to this case.

The skull cup incident after the killing of the evil brothers is also unique to this source. But it is told so tersely that its significance, assuming it has any over and above the obvious, is difficult to gauge. Although Quetzalcoatl is nowhere explicitly named *ruler* of Tollan, this must be assumed. Actually, the emphasis is more on his deification and his being worshipped during his lifetime, before his flight from the city. However, his role as leader of a migrating group who first reached Tollantzinco, then Tollan, is also highlighted. His persecution by Tezcatlipoca basically follows the standard pattern, but a number of interesting new incidents are introduced, particularly that involving the magic, rain-making mirror. Quetzalcoatl's "flight" also roughly follows the usual route, but his incredibly long residences at each place are unique. Gross chronological exaggeration is generally characteristic of this account. His terminus at Cempohuallan is also unique to this source, as well as the special, apparently self-inflicted manner of his demise.

It is difficult, if not impossible, to pinpoint the source of this version. Assuming it is derived from Olmos, it could have originated in various centers within a wide area of Central Mexico. "Mexico, Tezcuco, Tlaxcala, Huexotzinco, Cholula, Tepeaca, Tlalmanalco y las demás cabeceras" are specifically named by Mendieta (1945, I: 83) as towns where Olmos gathered information. The use of the sole name, Camaxtli, for Quetzalcoatl's father might point to Tlaxcallan or some Pueblan center, but a Basin of Mexico provenience can probably be supported by more cogent arguments. As we saw, even in a source as genuinely Mexica as the *Historia de los Mexicanos por sus pinturas*, Camaxtli is employed in addition to Mixcoatl. All we can be certain of is that it certainly derives from the tradition of some important Nahuatl-speaking community of Central Mexico. If the original Spanish manuscript translated by Thevet, or, better, the lost Olmos itself is ever discovered, perhaps the matter can be resolved.

4. The *Leyenda de los soles*

THE SOURCE

This important Nahuatl document, given this title by its first publisher and translator, was contained in the same manuscript volume, the *Códice Chimalpopoca*, that also contained the *Anales de Cuauhtitlan* and the *Breve Relación de los dioses y ritos de la gentilidad* of Pedro Ponce (Colección Antigua, no. 159, Archivo Histórico, Instituto Nacional de Antropología e Historia [Museo Nacional Antropología, Mexico City]). From internal evidence, it dated from 1558. It was almost certainly composed by a Spanish-educated native (or, less likely, a mestizo) whose mother tongue was Nahuatl. From a statement made during the narrative of the Mexica migration, the author would appear to have been of this affiliation, which probably means in this case specifically Tenochca. In any case, the viewpoint throughout the account does seem eminently Tenochca. Velázquez (1945: x) suggested that the author might have been one of the most important native assistants of Sahagún, Martín Jacobita from Tlatelolco, whose people also considered themselves Mexica—but there is no concrete evidence to support this hypothesis.

As in the case of the *Historia de los Mexicanos por sus pinturas*, but even more clearly here, this narrative was compiled with a pictorial history, or histories, as its immediate source. Occasionally, the text is nothing more than an explanation of images and symbols that were before the eyes of the writer. In one instance, a rough sketch diagram is intercalated in the text, undoubtedly copied directly from the original pictorial source.

Four complete translations, plus portions of a fifth, of the Nahuatl text of the *Leyenda* have been published: (1) Paso y Troncoso (1903; Nahuatl in phonetic transcription, and Spanish); (2) Lehmann (1906; Nahuatl, from León y Gama copy, and Latin); (3) Lehmann (1938: 322–388; Nahuatl, from original manuscript, and German; best edition of Nahuatl text); (4) Velázquez (1945: 119–142; Spanish, plus photoreproduction of manuscript); and (5) Garibay (1953–1954: passim; passages only in Spanish). These translations differ considerably in detail, due primarily to the obscurities of the archaic idiom of the text. These linguistic difficulties, however, do not seriously affect the purpose for which the document is utilized in this study.

The great importance of this early source in the original language is evident. Garibay (1953–1954, I: 292–293), who believed that nearly three-quarters of the text was based on poetic fragments of epic character, saw in them "los únicos restos del naufragio de la mina de temas sagrados que se cantaban en los institutos de educación, que sobreviven en su lengua original y dan la seguridad de hallarse en metro." Although later than the *Historia de los Mexicanos por sus pinturas*, to which it bears many similarities, the fact that it is preserved in Nahuatl lends to this source in certain respects an even greater value. Again, we are provided with a Mexica "panoramic" history of the world, commencing with the four previous Suns and proceeding on to the creation of man, the birth of the fifth Sun, the adventures of Mixcoatl and the four hundred Chichimeca or Mixcohua, the Topiltzin Quetzalcoatl of Tollan Tale, Huemac, the Toltec downfall, the Mexica migration, the Chapoltepec defeat, the foundation of Mexico Tenochtitlan, and the rise to power of this center, with the "official" list of its principal conquests.

THE TOPILTZIN QUETZALCOATL MATERIAL

The tale proper begins, as did that of the *Historia de los Mexicanos por sus pinturas*, with the adventures of Mixcoatl and the four hundred Chichimeca (here called Mixcohua). These latter are engendered in the year 1 Tecpatl by Iztac Chalchihuitlicue (an aspect of the water goddess). Immediately thereafter they enter a cave, whereupon the same goddess gives birth to five more—among whom is Mixcoatl—who, after entering and emerging from the water, are nourished by Mexitli, identified here with Tlaltecuhtli, Lord of the Earth.

The Sun next presents the four hundred Mixcohua with arrows and shields and instructs them to feed both him and the earth with human hearts and blood. But the latter prefer to amuse themselves by hunting birds, adorning themselves with feathers, pursuing women, and imbibing to intoxication. The Sun then turns to the other five Mixcohua, giving them arms and ordering them to slay the others who have failed in their duty. Appearing to the four hundred Mixcohua upon a mesquite bush, the latter attempt to capture the five with a net, but they leap out from various hiding places, conquer their errant brothers, and offer them in sacrifice to the Sun. A few survivors plead for mercy and surrender their home, Chicomoztoc, the Seven Caves, to the victorious five.

Then follows a long, somewhat obscure series of incidents involving two two-headed deer who descend to earth and are hunted by two of the Mixcohua, Xiuhnel and Mimich. It ends with the burning of one of them, who has been transformed into the goddess Itzpapalotl. As she burns, she periodically explodes, at which times variously colored sacrificial knives issue forth: blue, white, yellow, red, and black. The white sacrificial knife (*iztac tecpatl*), wrapped in a mantle, is taken by Mixcoatl, who adores it as a god and carries it on his shoulders when he sets forth to conquer. He advances on a place called Comallan, carrying his Itzpapalotl stone knife war fetish, and the inhabitants bring him food as a peace offering. Moving on, he receives the same reception at Tecanman. He continues his march of conquest through Cocyama, Huehuetocan, and Pochtlan. Finally, advancing on Huitznahuac, he encounters a woman named Chimalman, who stands before him, defenseless and entirely naked. He hurls a dart at her, which merely passes over her head as she inclines it. He hurls a second, which strikes her side, merely bending itself. He hurls a third, which she catches in her hand. He hurls a fourth, which she takes out from between her legs. Mixcoatl then departs, and the woman flees to a cave. Later he returns, searching in vain for her. Determined to locate her again, he maltreats the other women of Huitznahuac, who consent to fetch her. Again Chimalman stands before Mixcoatl, defenseless and naked. Again he hurls four darts at her with the same results as before. Then he goes to her and lies with her.

From this union a son is born, Ce Acatl. After four days of anguish, Chimalman delivers her child but dies immediately thereafter. Ce Acatl is brought up by Quilaztli/Cihuacoatl. When of age, he accompanies his father in his conquests, first proving himself at Xiuhuacan, where he takes captives. But Mixcoatl is killed at this point by his brothers the Mixcohua, the uncles of Ce Acatl, who bury their victim in Xaltitlan (or in the sand). Ce Acatl then searches for his father, asking after him. Cozcacuauhtli tells him that he has been killed and points out his burial spot. Ce Acatl disinters his father's bones and places them in a temple, the Mixcoatepetl (Hill of Mixcoatl). His uncles, the murderers of his father—Apanecatl, Zolton, and Cuilton—not satisfied with Ce Acatl's sacrifice of a rabbit and a snake to dedicate the temple, demand a jaguar, an eagle, and a wolf. Ce Acatl agrees and goes to the latter three creatures, informing them of his plan, which is not to sacrifice them but rather his uncles, upon whom they will have the pleasure of feeding. Then he calls to the moles, requesting them to bore a tunnel into the substructure of the temple, through which he enters the shrine above.

The uncles next intend to produce fire with fire sticks, but Ce Acatl creates a fire first. Enraged, the uncles start up after their nephew, with Apanecatl at their head. But Ce Acatl, in readiness, cleaves his uncle's skull with a smooth vessel (*tetzcaltecomatica*). He then seizes the other two, who are slowly tortured to death by the animals, their hearts finally being torn out in the usual manner.

At this point there seems to be a gap in the narrative, which should go on to tell of Ce Acatl's reign in Tollan. This is partly filled by his designation elsewhere (Lehmann 1938: § 1455) as "Topiltzin of Tollan, Quetzalcoatl," but, most importantly, by the previously mentioned sketch on folio 40, verso. Here, in the upper central portion, a standard conventionalized hill symbol (*tepetl*) bearing the inscription "Xicococ" (a hill near Tollan, the modern Jicuco) is represented. Below this is a child in a cradle, with the inscriptions "ce acatl" and "topiltzin." The cradle is connected by lines (resembling link chains) on either side of little blobs that represent, from their accompanying labels, Mixcoatl on the right and Chimalman on the left. Directly below the cradle is a figure, apparently seated on a throne and wearing a feather headdress, denominated "topiltzin." To the right is the name sign of Tollan, a nest of reeds. Further to the right and left of the Topiltzin figure are squares with doorways representing houses, two on each side, labeled: "cohuacalli" (serpent house; upper left); "teocuitlacalli" (gold house; lower left); "chalchiuhcalli" (jade house; upper right); and "xiuhcalli" (turquoise house; lower right). In addition, there are two little squares, one just to the left of the seated Topiltzin, with the label: "52 años ce acatl," and the other to the right of Mixcoatl, with the inscription: "39 (años) ce tecpatl."

Most of this little sketch is self-explanatory; it is interesting that it contains some important information not mentioned in the text. It would seem to indicate that Xicococ was Ce Acatl's birthplace (not clearly specified in the text, although Huitznahuac is probably implied). The four houses, of the serpent, gold, jade, and turquoise, receive no mention in the text. Their significance will become clear when the *Anales de Cuauhtitlan* and other accounts are examined below. The two year dates are explained by the text: 1 Tecpatl is the year of the birth of Mixcoatl and the other Mixcohua, and in one place in the text (Lehmann 1938: § 1492a) it is stated that the former lived thirty-nine years—1 Tecpatl to 1 Acatl, 3 *trecenas* of the 52-year cycle, *xiuhmolpilli*, although the narrative would indicate that Mixcoatl lived longer than this. The other date is that of both the birth of Ce Acatl and the year in which he abandons Tollan, thus constituting fifty-two years, one full cycle. The text statement (§ 1587a), that he died in the year 4 Tochtli, in Tlapallan, at the age of fifty-six, is not indicated in any way on the sketch.

The narrative completely omits that portion of Ce Acatl's career during which he rules over Tollan, nor is any reason given for his abandoning it. His "flight" is represented as a series of "conquests," in order: Ayotlan, Chalco, Xico, Cuixcoc, Zacanco, Tzonmolco, Mazatzonco, Tzapotlan, Acallan, and, finally, Tlapallan. In this last place he becomes sick. After five days be dies, following which he is cremated. Although it is stated that Tollan "was deserted," four names of individuals who succeeded Ce Acatl (in succession?) are given: Huemac, Nequametl, Tlalchicatzin, and Huitzilpopoca (in the original manuscript this passage was almost entirely obscured by a large ink blot, but Lehmann [1938: 373] was able to substantially restore it, aided by the León y Gama copy). A fifth person, Huetzin, is named as ruler of Nonohualco. Although Huemac is named first, if these four really did rule in succession, which is by no means clear, he must be considered to have been the last of the successors of Topiltzin Ce Acatl.

The downfall of Tollan is next described, involving four principal incidents: (1) the appearance of a gigantic man-eating demon (*tlacnexquimilli*), who, killed by the Toltecs, nevertheless causes many deaths; (2) a ball game between Huemac and the rain gods, which, although the former is victorious, results in a great four-year drought due to his refusal to accept the prize offered him, the *chalchihuitl(s)* (young green maize ears) and quetzal feathers (the green leaves sheltering the ear) of the Tlaloque; (3) an incident, similar to that in the *Historia de los Mexicanos por sus pinturas*, involving an old woman, at Chapoltepecuitlapilco, and the handing out of sacrificial banners; and (4) the sacrifice of Quetzalxotzin, daughter of Tozcuecuex, leader of the Mexica then resident at Xicococ, to the rain gods at Pantitlan, a whirlpool in the Lake of Mexico. This latter incident ends the drought but does not really aid the Toltecs, who in the year 1 Tecpatl are destroyed and dispersed, Huemac disappearing into the cave, Cincalco.

The account then switches to Mexica history proper, beginning with the migration from Aztlan/Colhuacan.

SUMMARY

(1) Ce Acatl Topiltzin Quetzalcoatl is the fruit of the union of the conqueror, Mixcoatl (one of the five Mixcohua engendered by an aspect of Chalchiuhtlicue, the water goddess, after the birth of the original four hundred), and a woman of Huitznahuac, Chimalman, who is taken by Mixcoatl after two ritualized dart-hurling encounters; (2) Chimalman dies in childbirth (at Xicococ? Huitznahuac?), and Ce Acatl is raised by Quilaztli/Cihuacoatl (the earth goddess); (3) when of age, he accompanies his father in his conquests, beginning at Xiuhuacan; (4) Mixcoatl is killed (another passage implies that he is killed in the same year of Ce Acatl's birth) by three other Mixcohua—Apanecatli, Zolton, and Cuilton—who bury his body; (5) Ce Acatl, after a search, disinters his father's bones and places them in a temple raised in his honor, the Mixcoatepetl; (6) after a complicated incident involving the dedication by Ce Acatl of the temple with the sacrifice of various animals, he avenges his father's murder by killing his three uncles; (7) although the narrative proper does not mention it, from brief glosses explaining a set of pictorial representations, it is clear that Ce Acatl becomes ruler of Tollan; (8) Ce Acatl abandons Tollan in the year 1 Acatl, "conquering" a series of places: Ayotlan, Xico/Chalco, Cuixcoc, Zacanco, Tzonmolco, Mazatzonco, Tzapotlan, and Acallan, finally reaching Tlapallan, where he sickens and dies in the year 4 Tochtli, at the age of fifty-six, and is cremated; (9) back in Tollan, although the city (temporarily?) is deserted, other rulers succeed, until the Toltecs are destroyed and dispersed in the year 1 Tecpatl during the rule of Huemac.

COMMENT

This invaluable account is more difficult to follow in some of its details than the three hitherto considered. This seems due to both the obscurity of the archaically formalized Nahuatl text and the general sketchiness of the narrative. Its overall similarity to the *Historia de los Mexicanos por sus pinturas* is striking—but with numerous differences in details. Fortunately, unlike this latter source, it carries the narrative through to the end of the Toltec period, although portions of this section, because of its terseness, are among the most difficult to understand. If the *Leyenda* generally appears to exhibit a more primitive, "supernaturalistic" quality than those previously examined, this may be at least partly explained by invoking Garibay's theory that most of the text is based on sacred narrative chants, strung together to form the explanation of a pictorial manuscript.

Topiltzin Quetzalcoatl appears here again as a fundamentally human figure, although the paternal offspring of a divinely engendered personage. It is noteworthy that Tezcatlipoca does not appear in any guise. This may be due to the fact that all of that portion of the tale relating to the former's downfall and abandonment of Tollan is missing. Neither is TQ specifically apotheosized or transformed upon his death. It is regrettable that this account, otherwise so important, is so brief and incomplete. Its principal value lies in the information it provides concerning Topiltzin Quetzalcoatl's origins and early life—which is precisely what is missing in the next account to be considered.

5. The *Historia general (universal) de las cosas de (la) Nueva España* of Fray Bernardino de Sahagún

THE SOURCE

It is unnecessary to discuss at length the monumental collection of priceless ethnographic information assembled by the Franciscan friar who has been called, with some justification, "the first modern ethnographer." Thanks to the investigations of Ramírez, García Icazbalceta, Paso y Troncoso, Jiménez Moreno, Nicolau d'Olwer, and Garibay, among others, we now have a reasonably accurate picture of the methods and stages by which Sahagún compiled his data, although some significant gaps and obscurities remain and perhaps will always remain. Sahagún was particularly interested and competent in the Nahuatl language; this led to his remarkably modern method of gathering nearly all of his information through carefully recorded texts in the native tongue. He was also perceptive enough to realize the great value of utilizing the pictorial techniques of recordation of the pre-Hispanic culture. Furthermore, his informants seem to have been chosen with special care. All of these factors, plus the display of a degree of objectivity rare for a sixteenth-century cleric, combine to make his work the most important single source on those aspects of Conquest-period Basin of Mexico indigenous culture to which Sahagún devoted his attention. Except for an occasional prologue, introduction, interpolated explanatory passage, or "advertencia al sincero lector," the ethnographic material assembled by Fray Bernardino was essentially the work of the natives themselves, speaking in their own language.

Different portions of the massive compilation date from different periods. Their chronology has been tentatively worked out, based almost entirely on internal evidence, most fully by Jiménez Moreno (1938) and

Nicolau d'Olwer (1952). Book VI (Rhetoric, etc.) apparently dates from around 1547, Book XII (the Conquest) from around 1550–1555 (with a later revision dating from 1585). The remainder falls into the period 1558–1569, and can be further broken down into material gathered at Tepepolco (an important dependency of Tetzcoco), Tlatelolco, and Mexico Tenochtitlan. The bulk of the information was clearly supplied by Sahagún's Tepepolco and Tlatelolco informants. A much smaller portion appears to have collected in Tenochtitlan, although the final copy was prepared there.

The surviving manuscripts of what Sahagún finally came to call the *Historia general (universal) de las cosas de (la) Nueva España* have been divided into: (1) the *Primeros memoriales*, the material gathered at Tepepolco, 1558/59–1560/61; (2) the hypothetical *Segundos memoriales* (Jiménez Moreno 1938: 37); (3) the *Memoriales con escolios*, apparently compiled in Tlatelolco, 1561–1562; (4) the *Manuscrito de Tlatelolco*, including all but Books VI and XII of the final work, assigned to Tlatelolco, 1563–1565; (5) the *Memoriales en español*, comprising Books I and V only, possibly prepared around 1568 in Tenochtitlan; (6) the *Manuscrito de Tenochtitlan*, the entire work, in Nahuatl only, finished in 1569 in Tenochtitlan; (7) the *Manuscrito de Sequera*, again the entire work, in both Spanish and Nahuatl, copied 1575–1577—possibly the so-called *Florentine Codex*, the complete work, in Spanish and Nahuatl, with copious illustrations, preserved in Florence; (8) the *Manuscrito de Tolosa* (also called the *Códice Castellano de Madrid*), of unknown sixteenth-century date, Spanish only, originally in the Franciscan convent of Tolosa and now in Madrid (very similar to the Spanish text of the *Florentine Codex*); (9) a summary of the first two books and portions of Books III, IV, VII, and IX, in Spanish, sent by Sahagún to Europe in 1570 (published by Schmidt in 1906); now in Rome; and (10) the 1585 revised version of Book XII (Bustamante 1840). The most important original Sahagún manuscripts that have survived, the *Florentine Codex* and the Madrid manuscripts, *Códices Matritenses*, have been partially published (Paso y Troncoso 1905–1907), the latter in black and white photoreproduction (see Jiménez Moreno 1938: 64–65, for a detailed assignment of the manuscripts mentioned in the above list to the pagination of the Paso y Troncoso photoreproduction volumes [only the illustrations, in color lithographic copies, of the *Florentine Codex* were published, taking up all of volume V]). A number of lesser works have been ascribed to Sahagún, but, since they seem to contain no material relevant to our theme, they will not be considered.

Most printed versions of the complete work, until the recent Anderson and Dibble edition of the *Florentine Codex*, were derived from the *Manuscrito de Tolosa*, whose own source is still not completely clear, although, as mentioned, its text is very close to the Spanish text of the *Florentine Codex*. So far (1957) six books (I–II, VII–VIII, and XII) of the Nahuatl of this manuscript, with English translation, have appeared (Sahagún 1950–1982). Earlier, all of Book XII and portions of others were published, with German translation by Seler, in 1927. Material relevant to Topiltzin Quetzalcoatl is scattered throughout the twelve books of the *Historia*, but the most important section is the long version of the latter portion of the TQ tale, possibly originally in verse (see Cornyn 1931; Garibay 1953–1954, I: 1303–1306), which is contained in Book III, Chapters III–XIV. In addition, Cornyn (1931) published a free English translation, in meter, of the *Manuscrito de Tlatelolco* version. Fragments, in Spanish, have also been published by Garibay (1945; 1953–1954, I, passim). My summary is based on a comparison of all of these translations, which do not differ except in relatively unimportant details. All direct quotes are from the Anderson and Dibble translation of the *Florentine Codex*, de-biblicized. The source from which I have derived the remaining material in Sahagún that relates to Topiltzin Quetzalcoatl is indicated in each case.

THE TOPILTZIN QUETZALCOATL MATERIAL

As stated above, the latter portion of the complete Basic Topiltzin Quetzalcoatl of Tollan Tale is found in Book III, Chapters III–XIV. The first is titled "Third Chapter, which tells the story of Quetzalcoatl, who was a great wizard [*naualli*] and of the place where be ruled, and of what he did when he went away." It begins by stating that Quetzalcoatl was considered to be a god and adored as such in Tollan, to whom prayers were offered. His temple is described as towering and lofty, with many very narrow steps. There his image lay with its face covered, for his countenance was monstrous, with a very long, heavy beard. His vassals, the Toltecs, were highly skilled in lapidary work, goldworking, featherworking, and other crafts, which, together with "wisdom," all began with Quetzalcoatl. He had houses of jade (*chalchiuhcalli*), gold (*teocuitlacalli*), red shell (*tapachcalli*), white shell (*teccizcalli*), wooden beams (*huapalcalli*), turquoise (*xiuhcalli*), and quetzal feathers (*quetzalcalli*).

The Toltecs were remarkably fleet-footed, and no distance was too great for them. On a hill called Tzatzitepetl ("just so is it named today"), a crier would station himself and deliver the edicts of Quetzalcoatl, which could be heard as far away as the coastlands (Anahuac), whereupon all would gather to hear what Quetzalcoatl had commanded. The Toltecs were also very rich. Food was practically valueless, it was so plentiful. The squashes were huge and round, the maize ears as large as the *manos* used in grinding, and could hardly be embraced in one's arms. The amaranth (*huauhtli*) plants were so large they could be climbed like trees. Cotton grew naturally in all colors: red, yellow, rose, violet, blue-green, blue, green, orange, brown, gray, dark yellow, and tawny. All varieties of birds of precious plumage abounded in Tollan: *xiuhtototl*, *quetzaltototl*, *zaquan*, and *tlauhquechol*, as well as the sweet singing birds. The Toltecs owned fabulous amounts of gold and jade. There was a great abundance of cacao, including a variety of many colors, *xochicacahuatl.* So wealthy were the Toltecs that they lacked nothing; there was never any scarcity. They were so contemptuous of small maize ears that they used them as fuel to heat the sweat baths.

Quetzalcoatl was a great penitent, staining thorns with blood drawn from his legs and bathing at midnight in a place called Xippacoyan. In this regime of austerity he was imitated by all of the other priests, who took their mode of conduct from his example, which set the pattern ever after followed in Mexico.

The fourth chapter describes how Quetzalcoatl's glory ended. He and the Toltecs becoming slothful; three sorcerers came against them—Huitzilopochtli, Titlacahuan, and Tlacahuepan—plotting the ruin of Tollan. Titlacahuan, by magic, transformed himself into a little old man, very bent, with silvery white hair. Going to the house of Quetzalcoatl, he asked permission of the attendants to see him. They refused, telling him that their master was sick. Upon his insistence, they informed Quetzalcoatl, who ordered them to permit the old man to enter, saying that he had been waiting for him for some time. The disguised Titlacahuan enters, inquires after Quetzalcoatl's health, and offers him a potion. Quetzalcoatl greets him in turn, saying that he has been awaiting him. Titlacahuan again asks about his health, and Quetzalcoatl replies that he ails in all parts: "nowhere am I well—my hands, my feet, in truth, my body is tired, as if it were undone." Titlacahuan explains that his potion is soothing and intoxicating and will heal him. It will also cause him to cry and become troubled, to think upon his death and the place where he must go. Quetzalcoatl inquires concerning where he must go, and Titlacahuan answers: Tollan Tlapallan (*sic*), where an aged man awaits him, with whom he shall consult, following which he will return as a young boy. Quetzalcoatl is much moved by this. Titlacahuan again offers him the potion, but he refuses it. Urged to merely sample it, he complies and, enjoying it, drinks heartily, whereupon he finds himself restored to health. Titlacahuan presses him to drink more, for it will strengthen him. Quetzalcoatl agrees, soon becoming intoxicated. Greatly moved, he weeps, aroused by what has occurred, unable to forget it, realizing now that he has been tricked by the sorcerer. The potion, it is then explained, was white *octli* (pulque), made from the variety of maguey called *teometl* (sacred maguey or maguey of the gods).

The next seven chapters are concerned with a long series of tricks, deceits, and enchantments inflicted on the Toltecs. Quetzalcoatl himself, however, does not appear, except in one brief reference. Instead, he is replaced by Huemac, who receives the brunt of the attack of Titlacahuan and his malevolent companions. As will be seen when the difficult problem of the relation between Huemac and Topiltzin Quetzalcoatl is discussed, there are grounds for believing that these chapters do not properly belong to the Topiltzin Quetzalcoatl of Tollan Tale but to a similar cycle involving Huemac, last ruler of Tollan, and the final downfall and dispersion of the Toltecs. Since the question is still moot, a capsule resumé of the events in these chapters follows. It should first be stated that in the Nahuatl version of these chapters no explanation is given for the sudden shift from Quetzalcoatl to Huemac as the victim of the sorcerers' machinations. In Sahagún's Spanish translation, on the other hand, Huemac is identified as "señor de los Toltecas en los temporal," while "Quetzalcoatl era como sacerdote y no tenía hijos." Torquemada (1943–1944, II: 48), possibly basing himself on another Sahagún manuscript, now lost, states that "aunque en lo temporal era el que governaba vn Señor, llamado Huemac; en lo espiritual, y Eclesiástico este Quetzalcohuatl era supremo, y como Pontífice Máximo."

In Chapter V, it is related that Huemac's daughter (unnamed) became inflamed with desire and sickened when she saw a naked stranger, called Tohueyo (= Huaxtec; really Titlacahuan in disguise), before the palace, selling green chili peppers. After a long search, Tohueyo was found and brought before Huemac. After repeated urgings, he went to the ruler's daughter, cured her by lying with her, and later married her.

In Chapter VI, the Toltecs, angered because of this marriage, persuade Huemac to dispose of his son-in-law by abandoning him to the enemy while fighting the towns of Zacatepec and Coatepec. But Tohueyo, with only the aid of the dwarfs and hunchbacks, left to die with him, slaughters his foes and is received back in Tollan in triumph.

In Chapter VII, Tohueyo organizes a dance for all the young people of Tollan at Texcalpan. Dancing madly to the beat of his drum, they fall from rocky crags at a canyon called Texcalatlauhco, as well as from a stone bridge, which the disguised Titlacahuan causes to break, and are turned into rocks.

In Chapter VIII, Titlacahuan transforms himself into a powerful warrior. He orders all of the men to come to the garden of Xochitlan (explained as the flower field [*xochimilca*] of Quetzalcoatl) to harvest the *chinampas*. When they gather there, he slaughters them all.

In Chapter IX, the "demon," calling himself Tlacahuepan, or Cuexcoch, seats himself in the marketplace and causes a little figure ("they say it was Huitzilopochtli") to dance on his hand. In pressing forward to watch him, countless Toltecs are trampled to death. At the instigation of the sorcerer himself, they stone Tlacahuepan to death. From the body a frightful stench arises, which also causes many Toltecs to die. When they try to drag the body away, they find it so heavy that it cannot be moved. Tying it with stout ropes, these repeatedly break, each time causing many deaths. Finally successful in dragging the dangerous cadaver away, the survivors who return are like drunken men and have forgotten what has occurred.

In Chapter X, Titlacahuan causes three ominous events to take place: a white kite, his head pierced by an arrow, flies to and fro over the city; the mountain of Zacatepetl burns at night and the Toltecs, regarding it as an evil omen, are filled with despair; and at a place called Chapoltepeccuitlapilco, or Huetzinco, a great rain of stones falls on the Toltecs, including a sacrificial stone (*techcatl*)—following which a little old woman goes about selling paper (sacrificial) banners to a number of Toltecs, who die on the sacrificial stone, all as if in a trance.

In Chapter XI, all the food sours and cannot be eaten. Then an old woman (another transformation of Titlacahuan) roasts maize at Xochitlan. When the Toltecs smell the fragrance, they come from all parts to where the woman is. Whereupon she kills them all, making sport of them.

In the twelfth chapter, we finally return to Quetzalcoatl. Referring to the disasters that Titlacahuan has inflicted on the Toltecs, it is related that Quetzalcoatl was so saddened by all this that he resolves to abandon Tollan. He first has everything burned, including his house of gold and house of red shell—and all of his costly treasures he buries and hides within the mountains and canyons. The cacao trees he changes into mesquite bushes. He sends away all of the birds of precious plumage, which fly before him toward the coastal lowlands (Anahuac). Then he himself sets forth. Arriving in Cuauhtitlan, where a very tall tree is growing, he peers at himself in a mirror, saying, "I am an old man," and names the place Huehuecuauhtitlan (Old Cuauhtitlan). Before he leaves, he hurls stones at the tree, which remain encrusted in the trunk—and which were still to be seen there. Continuing on his journey, his attendants go before him, blowing their flutes. At another place he rests on a stone, supporting himself on it with his hands. Looking back toward Tollan, he sheds copious tears, which fall on the stone and leave their marks.

In Chapter XIII, it is told that where he rested his hands and buttocks, impressions were left on the stone, as if on mud, which were still visible. This place he called Temacpalco (Where Are Found Hand Marks). Next, he crosses a broad river by building a stone bridge, for which the place was called Tepanohuayan (Place of the Stone Bridge). Reaching another place, Coaapan (Serpent River), the "demons" seek to force him to turn back, asking him who will now perform the penances. But Quetzalcoatl insists he must continue. When asked where he is going, he replies, to Tlapallan, to learn his fate. Asked what he will do there, he answers that the sun has called him hence. They finally agree to his continuing, but they force from him all of the arts and crafts: goldworking, the cutting of precious stones, wood carving, stone carving, writing (i.e., pictorial writing, *tlacuilocayotl*), and featherworking. Then Quetzalcoatl casts all of his jewels into a spring, which he names Cozcaapan (River, or Water, of the Jewels), "which is now called Coappan." Moving on to a place called Cochtocan, he is accosted by another "demon," who also seeks to know his destination. Quetzalcoatl again replies that he is going to Tlapallan, to learn his fate. The demon then insists that he drink the *octli* that he has brought him. At first refusing, Quetzalcoatl is finally persuaded to accept it, falling immediately into a heavy sleep in the road. While he sleeps, his snoring resounds a great distance. When he awakes, he looks about, arranges his hair, and names the place Cochtocan (Place of Sleep).

In Chapter XIV, he climbs the pass between Popocatepetl and Iztaccihuatl (here called Iztactepetl), where his attendants, the dwarfs and hunchbacks, all freeze to death, which greatly grieves Quetzalcoatl and causes him to weep. From there he looks out to another mountain, Poyauhtecatl (Mt. Orizaba), then sets forth again, passing through many villages and leaving "many of his signs, by which he is known." At one place he "took his pleasure on a mountain," sliding and bouncing down it to its foot. Elsewhere, he planted maguey fibers. At another place he built a ball court (*tlachtli*) of stone; in the midst of it, where a line (*tlecotl*) was customarily drawn, was a deep barranca. At a different spot, he shot one ceiba tree, like an arrow, at a second ceiba, piercing the one with the other (Spanish text: "hecha una cruz"). "And elsewhere he built a house entirely underground at a place named Mictlan" (Spanish text: "Mictlancalco"). At another place he set up a great rock, which could easily be teetered with the little finger, but when many men would try to move it, it could not be budged.

Quetzalcoatl did many more remarkable things in many towns, as well as naming all the mountains and other places. Finally, he reached the seashore. There he ordered a raft of serpents (*coatlapechtli*) constructed. Entering it as if it were a boat, he sailed across the sea. "No one knows how he came to arrive there at Tlapallan."

Interspersed among the text of the Topiltzin Quetzalcoatl of Tollan Tale proper (Chapters III–IV, XII–XIV) in the *Florentine Codex* are four drawings that, although highly Europeanized, clearly preserve the major elements in the costume of the deity (Ehecatl) Quetzalcoatl (e.g., Color Plate 1) and provide some notion of how an indigenous pictorial illustrating the tale must have appeared. They illustrate: (1) Quetzalcoatl, in characteristic attire, seated on a mat, drawing blood with a maguey spine from his leg; (2) Quetzalcoatl, seated naked on the edge of the river, the three most important elements of his insignia lying nearby (headdress, baton, and shield), pouring water over himself from a bowl; a number of stars in the sky indicate that it is night; (3) Titlacahuan, disguised as the old man, holding a bowl filled with *octli*, speaking (indicated by speech scrolls) to Quetzalcoatl, who stands before him in full costume, holding aloft his distinctive baton; (4) Quetzalcoatl, again in full array, lying sprawled on the road in his drunken sleep (see Color Plates 2, 3, 4, and 5).

Other passages in various sections of Sahagún's great work that contain material relating to Topiltzin Quetzalcoatl will now be briefly summarized. The first of these is found in the Spanish prologue to Book I (Sahagún 1946, I: 12), first composed, apparently, in 1569. The author, discussing "lo que toca a la antigüedad de esta gente," states that it has been ascertained that the natives have inhabited the land now called New Spain for over two thousand years. This he bases on the fact that, "por sus pinturas antiguas," Tollan was destroyed about a thousand years before he writes, while before Tollan was founded, "estuvieron muchos poblados en Tulantzinco donde dejaron muchos edificios muy notables." Since the time it took to construct Tollan, together with the time during which it flourished, totaled over another thousand years, it resulted that "por los menos quinientos años antes de la Encarnación de nuestro Redentor, esta tierra era poblada." He then goes on to compare the fate of "esta celebre y gran ciudad de Tula, muy rica y decente, muy sabia y muy esforzada," with that of Troy. The Chololteca, "que son los que de ella se escaparon," he compares to the Romans, the Great Pyramid to the Capitol of Rome. Although Quetzalcoatl himself is not named in this brief passage, its relevance to our theme is obvious.

The appendix to Book I is a long confutation of all the beliefs of the natives concerning their gods. The passage relating to Quetzalcoatl presents an excellent capsule summary of some of the principal elements of the Topiltzin Quetzalcoatl of Tollan Tale. It is worth quoting almost in its entirety (Sahagún 1950–1982, part II: 39–40; cf. Sahagún 1946, I: 84):

> These, the ancients, worshipped an idol called Quetzalcoatl, who was ruler at Tula. And you named him Topiltzin. He was a man. He was mortal, for he died; for his body corrupted. He is no god. And though a man of saintly life, who performed penances, he was not to be worshipped as a god. The things which he did which were like miracles, we know he did only through the command of the devil. He is a friend of devils. Therefore he must needs be accursed and abominated; for our Lord God has caused him to be thrust into the land of the dead. The ancients held that Quetzalcoatl went to Tlapallan; that yet he will return. He is still expected. This is not true; it is falsehood. For his body died, here on earth it became dust.

This passage is particularly significant in its emphasis on Topiltzin Quetzalcoatl's humanity and the persistence of the belief that he was someday to return. In the ninth chapter to Book III (Sahagún 1950–1982, part IV: 67–68; Sahagún 1946, I: 330–331), the dual office of high priest of Mexico Tenochtitlan is described. These pontiffs were called "Quequetzalcoa," which the Spanish text explains as "sucesores de Quetzalcoatl." One, dedicated to the service of Huitzilopochtli, was called "Quetzalcoatl Totec Tlamacazqui"; the other, dedicated to Tlaloc, bore the title "Quetzalcoatl Tlaloc Tlamacazqui." The use of

Quetzalcoatl as a sacerdotal title and the notion that he was the archetype of the Mexica priesthood is nowhere more clearly stated than here.

In the Introduction to Book IV (Sahagún 1946, I: 335), Sahagún, discussing the *tonalpohualli*, the 260-day divinatory cycle, and the prognostications that were based on it, states: "Estos adivinos no se regían por los signos ni planetas del cielo, sino una instrucción que según ellos dicen, se las dejó Quetzalcoatl." At the end of Book VII, a drawing of a calendar wheel, representing the 52-year cycle, is accompanied by a brief explanatory text in Spanish (Sahagún 1950–1982, part VIII: fig. 20 and facing; Sahagún 1946, II: 30), where this statement appears: "Dizen, que el inuenter della, fué Quetzalcoatl." Thus, in two different passages, Sahagún names Topiltzin Quetzalcoatl as inventor of both the 260-day count and the 365-day year count. This is to be added to the other arts and skills that in the Topiltzin Quetzalcoatl of Tollan Tale he is credited with introducing.

In Chapter XLI of Book VI, "De algunos adagios que esta gente Mexicana usaba," an anecdote is related to explain the phrase "mensajero del cuervo," applied to a person sent with a message who does not return with the reply (Sahagún 1946, I: 643–644). The story went that Quetzalcoatl, "rey de Tula," saw from his quarters two women bathing in his own private bath and sent one of his hunchback attendants to find out who they might be. His envoy did not return, so he sent out another, with the same result. Finally, he sent out a third. None returned, so entranced were they with the bathing beauties who had invaded the privacy of one of Quetzalcoatl's sanctuaries. Thus the origin of the phrase "moxoxolotitlan, que quiere decir, fué y no volviá más." This semihumorous anecdote is significant in that it reveals that incidents of Topiltzin Quetzalcoatl's career had passed into popular folklore.

In the prologue to Book VIII (Sahagún 1946, II: 35–36), Sahagún, again summarizing what is known of the origins of the natives of New Spain, "según que afirman los viejos en cuyo poder estaban las pinturas memorias de las cosas antiguas," mentions the search by "los primeros pobladores" for Tamoanchan, "el paraíso terrenal," a tradition that he gives in full in part 32 of Chapter XXII, Book X. These same "gente robustísima, sapientísima, y belicosísima" were the builders of Tollan, which is explained as meaning "lugar de fertilidad y abundancia," adding "y aún ahora se llama así." Then follows another important synopsis of the tale, which, although essentially an expanded version of that previously quoted from the appendix to Book I, again summarizes the fundamentals of the latter portion of the tale so neatly it is worth presenting in full (Sahagún 1946, II: 35–36):

> En esta ciudad reinó muchos años un rey llamado Quetzalcoatl, gran nigromántico, e inventor de la nigromancia, y la dejó a sus descendientes, hoy día la usan; fué extremado en las virtudes morales. Está el negocio de este rey entre estos naturales, como el del rey Arthus

> entre los ingleses. Fué esta ciudad destruída, y este rey ahuyentado; dicen que caminó hacia el oriente, y que se fué hacia la ciudad del sol llamada Tlapallan, y fué llamado del sol. Dicen que es vivo, y que ha de volver a reinar y, a reedificar aquella ciudad que le destruyeron, y así hoy le esperan. Y cuando vino Don Fernando Cortés pensaron que era él, y por tal le recibieron y tuvieron, hasta que su conversación y la de los que con él venían los desengañó.

In Chapter V of this same book (Sahagún 1950–1982, part IX: 15; Sahagún 1946, II: 48), Sahagún gives a more precise date for the fall of Tollan than that quoted above. The Spanish text gives an almost certainly erroneous 1,890 years before 1571. The Nahuatl text gives 1,110 years before 1565 (which would place the date at A.D. 455), which is a figure close to the thousand years that was given as a round number in the introduction to Book I. As will become evident when the problem of the chronology of TQ is discussed below, this date seems far too early, on both the basis of the dates that are given by Sahagún himself immediately following (for the arrival of the Chichimec of Tetzcoco: twenty-two years later; the enthronement of their first leader: A.D. 1246; the accession of Tezozomoc of Azcapotzalco: 1348, etc.) as well as the testimony of other sources and the archaeology. As is evident throughout his work, chronology was not the good friar's forte, although his informants may have been largely responsible.

In Chapter VII, a resumé of the Conquest and its immediate aftermath, it is again stated that Cortés was thought to be the returning Quetzalcoatl, and the Spanish text reiterates: "hasta hoy le esperan" (Sahagún 1950–1982, part IX: 21; Sahagún 1946, II: 51).

Skipping to Book XII, which is devoted entirely to a long narration of the Conquest supplied by some Tlatelolca who had been active participants in it, in Chapter II it is told how Motecuhzoma's officials on the coast of Veracruz, meeting Grijalva's fleet in 1518, kissed the prows of his ships "en señal de adoración," for they believed Quetzalcoatl had returned (Sahagún 1950–1982, part XIII: 5; Sahagún 1946, III: 18). In the third chapter, the same officials notify Motecuhzoma that the Spaniards have reappeared (i.e., the Cortés expedition of 1519). Immediately, Motecuhzoma dispatches envoys to greet him with rich presents, again thinking that Quetzalcoatl has come to reclaim his throne, "porque pensó que era el que venía porque cada día le estaban esperando, y como tenía relación que Quetzalcoatl había ido por la mar hacia el oriente, y los navios venían de hacia el oriente, por esto pensaron que era él." And Motecuhzoma spoke to his ambassadors: "Come, intrepid warriors, come! It is said that our lord has at last arrived. Receive him. Listen, sharply; lend your ears well to what he will say. You will bring back what is well heard. Behold wherewith you will arrive before our lord." Then the four magnificent feather costumes ("los atavíos sacerdotales que a él convienen"), which they are to present to him, are described (of Tezcatlipoca, Tlaloc, and two aspects of Quetzalcoatl; see analysis in Seler 1902–1903: 37–39). Arriving at the ships of Cortés, the envoys are taken aboard and proceed to dress the Spanish leader in the principal costume, spreading the other three out before him. This act of ritual generosity so completely failed to impress the Spaniards that they responded by terrorizing and threatening the hapless gift-bearers (Sahagún 1950–1982, part XIII: 9–13; Sahagún 1946, III: 19–25).

Another clear reference to Topiltzin Quetzalcoatl in this connection, although he is not named, is contained in the remarkable speech that Motecuhzoma is supposed to have made to Cortés, shortly after meeting him in Mexico Tenochtitlan and apparently still under the impression that he is the returning Toltec ruler/priest (Sahagún 1950–1982, part XIII: 42; Sahagún 1946, III: 41–42):

> Oh our lord, you have suffered fatigue; you have spent yourself. You have arrived on earth; you have come to your noble city of Mexico. You have come to occupy your noble mat and seat, which for a little time I have guarded and watched for you. For your governors of times past have gone—the rulers Itzcoatl, Motecuhzoma the Elder, Axayacatl, Tizoc, Ahuitzotl—who, not very long ago, came to guard your mat and seat for you and to govern the city of Mexico. . . . Oh, that one of them might be a witness to marvel that to me now has befallen what I see, who am the only descendant of our lords. For I dream not, nor start from my sleep, nor see this as in a trance. I do not dream that I see you and look into your face. Lo, I have been troubled for a long time. I have gazed into the unknown whence you have come—the place of mystery. For the rulers of old have gone, saying that you would come to instruct your city, that you would descend to your mat and seat; that you would return. And now it is fulfilled: you have returned; you have suffered fatigue; you have spent yourself. Arrive now in your land. Rest, lord; visit your palace that you may rest your body. Let our lords arrive in the land!

In Chapter 29 of Book X, which is an ethnographic survey of Central and Southern Mexico from the indigenous perspective, there are data relevant to Topiltzin Quetzalcoatl that significantly supplement the information contained in the tale itself in Book III. The *Florentine Codex* Nahuatl version of this chapter has been translated into German by Seler and Lehmann (Seler 1927: 387–398); for my summary, I have compared their version with the Spanish text of Sahagún (1946, II: 275–315).

Part 1 is dedicated to a long, quite informative description of the Toltecs, one of the most valuable that has come down to us in any primary source. Of their origins, unfortunately, little is said (cf. part XII, where they migrate from Chicomoztoc), but they are called "los primeros pobladores de esta tierra." After settling for some time at Tollantzinco, building there the famous *huapalcalli* and other structures, they settle at Tollan Xicocotitlan. A description of this center at its height is given, in which the feathered-serpent columns, *coatlaquetzalli*, are mentioned. It is stated that the Toltecs were called Chichimeca and that the name Tolteca signified "oficiales pulidos y curiosos," from their skill in all the arts.

Next follows a description of the houses of adoration of their priest, Quetzalcoatl. Although very similar to that contained in Chapter III of Book III, it presents the data more fully and systematically. The four *aposentos* of his principal house are named, in order: in the east, the House of Gold (Teocuitlacalli; "en lugar del encalado tenía oro en planchas"); in the west, the Houses of Jade and Turquoise (Chalchihuicalli, Teoxiuhcalli); in the south, the Houses of White Shell and Silver (Teccizcalli, Iztac Teocuitlacalli); and in the north, the Houses of Red Shell and Red Stone (Tapachcalli, Tezontlicalli). In addition, a similar house is described, also with four chambers, "en la que por dentro estaba la pluma en lugar de encalado": to the east, the House of Yellow Feathers (Toztlicalli); to the west, the Houses of Blue and Green Feathers (Xiuhtotocalli, Quetzalcalli); to the south, the House of White Feathers (Aztatzoncalli); to the north, the Houses of Red Feathers (Tlauhquecholcalli, Cuezalicalli). It is also pointed out that, apart from these, the Toltecs constructed "otras muchas muy curiosas, y de gran valor."

"La casa u oratorio de Quetzalcoatl" was in the middle of a great river that flowed by Tollan, and there he had his *lavatorio*, called Chalchiuhapan. There were also underground houses there, where the Tolteca left many things buried, not only in Tollan but everywhere throughout New Spain, since "por todas partes estuvieron derramados los dichos Toltecas." Then the great skill in the arts and the great wisdom of the Toltecs are described, particularly their knowledge of useful herbs and precious stones.

The invention of the calendar is also ascribed to them. They were great observers of the movements of the stars, "y les tenían puestos nombres y sabían sus influencias y calidades." Their knowledge of the twelve heavens is next described, above which dwelled the great god Ometecuhtli and his female counterpart, Omecihuatl, rulers of the universe, from whom descended to their mothers' wombs the souls of unborn children. An enumeration of some of the other characteristics and customs of the Toltecs follows, including their food, dress, physical makeup, and ability as singers.

Finally, it is stated that they adored only one god, Quetzalcoatl, whose priest bore the same name. The latter was so pious and devoted to the cult of his god that all of his commands were strictly obeyed by the other priests and all of the people. He would often explain to them that there was but one god, Quetzalcoatl, who demanded as sacrifices only serpents and butterflies, which edict they strictly followed. Eventually, however, Quetzalcoatl commanded that all of the Toltecs should join him in abandoning Tollan. Although they had lived there a long time and had constructed many sumptuous edifices in Tollan and in other places where they had settled, with great effort they assembled their wives and children, their sick and their aged, and set forth under Quetzalcoatl's guidance, abandoning their homes, their lands, their city, and their wealth, much of which they left buried. They followed Quetzalcoatl to Tlapallan, where, entering the waters, he disappeared and was never seen again.

Then follows the important, oft-quoted statement: "Estos dichos Toltecas eran ladinos en la lengua mexicana, aunque no la hablaban tan perfectamente como ahora se usa." Their skill and energy quickly enabled them to amass great wealth, "que decían les daba su dios y señor Quetzalcoatl, y así se decía entre ellos que el que en breve tiempo se enriquecía que era hijo de Quetzalcoatl." After describing their mode of wearing their hair, the description ends by stating that "todos los que hablan claro la lengua mexicana que los llaman nahuas" were descended from the Toltecs who remained behind, those unable to follow Quetzalcoatl because of age, sickness, approaching motherhood, or because they simply chose to stay.

Part 3 is dedicated entirely to these "nahuas," where they are again described as proceeding from "la generación de los Toltecas" who remained behind when the others abandoned their city, when Quetzalcoatl went to Tlapallan Tlatlayan. Their god is named Yohualli Ehecatl, "que quiere decir noche y aire," which term, in its more specific application, was often assigned to Tezcatlipoca. It seems to have been regularly employed as a generic appellation of deity, and in one case is even applied specifically to Ehecatl Quetzalcoatl (*Historia de los Mexicanos por sus pinturas* 1891: 228; Sahagún 1946, II: 288–289).

In part 10, describing the "Olmecas, Uixtotin, y Mixtecas" of the east coast littoral, it is stated that, although they spoke a barbarous (i.e., non-Nahua) language, "dicen son Toltecas, . . . y que son descendientes de los Toltecas de que arriba se ha hecho mención." Their fertile lands and great wealth are then described, as well as some of their principal customs. It is pointed out that because of this wealth they were called "hijos de Quetzalcoatl," for "así creían los antiguos, que el que era rico y bien afortunado que era conocido, y amigo del dicho Quetzalcoatl."

Lastly, it should be pointed out that in Book VI (Sahagún 1946, I: 523), "de la retórica y filosofía moral y teología de la gente mexicana," there is one clear reference to Topiltzin Quetzalcoatl in Chapter XVI, which consists of the reply on the part of "un viejo principal y sabio en el arte de bien hablar" to a moral exhortation delivered by a recently elected lord, in which are mentioned:

> . . . todos los principales, nobles y generosos caballeros que están aquí presentes, y son tan estimables como piedras preciosas, y los hijos y descendientes de señores, reyes, senadores, hijos y criados de nuestro señor e hijo Quetzalcoatl los cuales en los tiempos pasados rigieron y gobernaron el imperio y señoríos, y para ello nacieron señalados, y elegidos de nuestro señor e hijo Quetzalcoatl.

Actually, a double reference may be involved here, to Topiltzin Quetzalcoatl as fountainhead of all legitimate political authority and to Ehecatl Quetzalcoatl as creator. References to this latter, specifically in his role as creator, are found in other parts of Book VI, and he is occasionally called Topiltzin Quetzalcoatl (translated as "nuestro hijo," "nuestro señor," or "nuestro señor e hijo" [e.g., Sahagún 1946, I: 609, 611, 629]). This well illustrates the fusion, or perhaps better, confusion, that had taken place between these two fundamentally distinct figures, the great ruler/priest of the Toltecs and the old fertility/creator god whose name he bore.

SUMMARY

These extensive Sahaguntine notices on Topiltzin Quetzalcoatl can, at the risk of a certain artificiality, be summarized as follows:

(1) Quetzalcoatl, an ugly bearded person, is priest/ruler of Tollan, which was founded by his vassals, the Toltecs, after emigrating from Chicomoztoc and stopping over for many years at Tollantzinco, where they constructed many important edifices; (2) the Toltecs are the possessors of remarkable wealth in gold, jade, precious feathers, cacao, etc.; (3) they are also highly skilled craftsmen, extraordinary runners and travelers, and are distinguished for their great wisdom; (4) food is fabulously plentiful: squash and maize ears are huge in size, amaranth plants are as large as trees, cotton grows naturally in all colors, and cacao flourishes in great abundance; (5) Topiltzin Quetzalcoatl is the special devotee of a god, Quetzalcoatl, from whom he took his name, or title, and who, he instructs his people, only desires sacrifices of serpents and butterflies; (6) Topiltzin Quetzalcoatl is himself adored as a god; (7) he is also a great wizard (*nahualli*) and a devout penitent, drawing blood from his body and ritually bathing at midnight at a place called Xippacoyan (variant: Chalchiuapan), being later imitated in his observances by the priesthood of Mexico Tenochtitlan, the two supreme pontiffs of which bore his name as a title; (8) he initiates all of the crafts and is also inventor of both the 260-day divinatory cycle and the 365-day secular year count; (9) he has a lofty temple in Tollan; (10) he builds two great houses, or adoratories, each with four chambers or divisions, one of various precious materials (Gold [E]; Jade/Turquoise [W]; White Shell/Silver [S]; Red Shell/Red Stone [N]), the other with walls of precious feathers (Yellow [E]; Blue/Green [W]; White [S]; and Red [N]); (11) Quetzalcoatl's glory ends through the evil

machinations of three wizards—Titlacahuan/Tezcatlipoca, Huitzilopochtli, and Tlacahuepan—especially the first named, who, disguised as an old man, tricks Quetzalcoatl into becoming drunk on white *octli*, which the latter has accepted as a medicine to cure himself of an illness; (12) a series of disasters is inflicted on the Toltecs by the malevolent trio, in which Quetzalcoatl does not appear and which may have originally belonged to another cycle of tales concerning the final downfall of Tollan during the reign of its last ruler, Huemac; (13) Quetzalcoatl, in the face of this persecution, resolves to abandon Tollan, taking with him nearly all of the inhabitants; (14) he first burns his precious houses, buries his treasures, changes the cacao trees into mesquite bushes, and sends the birds of precious plumage to the coastal lowlands; (15) he passes through the following places on his journey: (a) Cuauhtitlan, which he names Huehue Cuauhtitlan after observing his aged visage in a mirror, and also hurls stones at a great tree, which remain encrusted in the trunk; (b) Temacpalco, where he leaves the impression of his buttocks, hands, and tears in solid rock; (c) Tepanohuayan, where he constructs a stone bridge across a river; (d) Coaapan, where his enemies, the sorcerers, importune him to return to Tollan and, failing in this, manage to force from him all of the arts and crafts, after which Quetzalcoatl throws all of his jewels into a spring, naming it Cozaapan ("now Coaapan"); (e) Cochtocan, where another sorcerer causes him to fall into a drunken sleep, after inducing him to imbibe too freely of *octli*; (f) the pass between Popocatepetl and Iztaccihuatl, where all of his attendants, the dwarfs and hunchbacks, freeze to death; (16) following this, his itinerary becomes vague, while he passes through many villages, applying names to them and performing various feats; (17) at different places he: sportively slides down a mountain; plants maguey fibers; builds a stone ball court, with a deep canyon where its center line is supposed to be; shoots one ceiba tree into another, forming a cross; builds an underground house at Mictlan (Mitla, Oaxaca?); and sets up a great teetering rock; (18) he finally reaches the shore of the Gulf Coast, where, mounting a raft of serpents, he sails across the eastern sea to Tlapallan Tlatlayan (or simply disappears); (19) he is expected to return, to reclaim his dominion; (20) when Grijalva, in 1518, and Cortés, in 1519, arrive, they are thought to be the returning Topiltzin Quetzalcoatl; (21) Motecuhzoma sends down a number of costly gifts to Cortés, including four elaborate costumes of gods (two aspects of Quetzalcoatl, Tezcatlipoca, and Tlaloc); (22) when Cortés enters Mexico Tenochtitlan, Motecuhzoma invites him, as the returning Topiltzin Quetzalcoatl, to reoccupy his "seat and mat," which has been guarded for him; (23) the natives are finally undeceived about Cortés and the Spaniards, but they still (in Sahagún's time) expect that Topiltzin Quetzalcoatl will eventually return.

COMMENT

The information provided Sahagún by his various informants concerning Topiltzin Quetzalcoatl, particularly the long narrative of Book III, perhaps originally in verse, will always constitute one of our most fundamental sources concerning him. The provenience of both the Book III narrative and the material on the Toltecs in section I, Chapter XXIX, Book X, which contain the bulk of Sahagún's TQ data, was probably Tlatelolco. Both sections appear in the *Manuscrito de Tlatelolco* and are lacking in the *Primeros Memoriales*, gathered in Tepepolco. The remaining scattered notices were also probably derived from Tlatelolca informants, for the Tenochca do not seem to have provided Sahagún with any great amount of material at any time. It is likely that the traditions surrounding TQ that were current in Tlatelolco were similar, if not substantially identical, to those current in Tenochtitlan. On the other hand, it is possible that the Tepanec origin of the ruling dynasty of Tlatelolco might have led to certain differences from the Tenochca version, which was clearly based on the tradition of Colhuacan.

This is the first account so far considered that seems, on the face of it, to make Topiltzin Quetzalcoatl the last ruler of Tollan, or its last high priest, ruling jointly with Huemac. Deferring further discussion of this apparent anomaly to a later section, I would only like to reiterate here an earlier suggestion, that this placing of him at the end rather than near the beginning of the Toltec period may have been the result of a fusion of two originally distinct cycles of tales involving Topiltzin Quetzalcoatl's downfall, on the one hand, and the final downfall of the Toltecs under its last ruler, Huemac, on the other. The *trait d'union* would be, of course, the similar machinations of Titlacahuan/Tezcatlipoca and his fellow sorcerers, which were exerted against the hapless Toltecs in somewhat similar fashion in both cases.

Another noteworthy feature of this account is its complete lack of information concerning the origin and early career of Topiltzin Quetzalcoatl, although general Toltec origins are sketchily indicated. Mixcoatl/Camaxtli does not appear in any connection—nor does Chimalman. These absences are perhaps to be at least partially explained by the fact that nowhere does Sahagún present a systematically dated historical chronicle such as those in such sources as the *Historia de los Mexicanos por sus pinturas* and the *Anales de Cuauhtitlan*. If he had collected and recorded such an account, covering the immediately pre-Toltec and Toltec periods, it seems likely that all, or most, of the important incidents of Topiltzin's origin and early career would have appeared. In any case, that portion of his career that *is* covered is generally congruent with the other versions considered in this section, particularly with that of the *Anales de Cuauhtitlan*, to be examined next. In detail, of course, all of these accounts offer considerable variety.

No account of Topiltzin Quetzalcoatl more clearly emphasizes the prevalence of the belief that he was expected to return, nor does any other version state more clearly that Cortés was thought to be he. The "culture hero" aspect of TQ is also particularly highlighted in Sahagún's version of the tale.

Another interesting absence, in this otherwise extended account of his journey to the east and disappearance, is any connection with or transformation into the planet Venus. Garibay (1953–1954, I: 305) noted that the Topiltzin Quetzalcoatl of Tollan Tale in the *Manuscrito de Tlatelolco* (139r–151v) ends abruptly in the middle of the page and hinted that the final portion might be missing. If so, his transformation into the Morning Star might have appeared here. Sahagún's failure to mention it elsewhere, however, especially in his capsule summaries of the tale, probably indicates that it simply was not an element of the tale as it was narrated to him.

The lack of specificity in the "flight" itinerary after Topiltzin Quetzalcoatl's departure from the Basin of Mexico is also noteworthy. Particularly striking is the omission of Chololla n. Only one definite place-name is mentioned, Mictlan, which, as suggested above, might well be a reference to the famous structures and tombs of Mitla, Oaxaca. As will be seen below, this is not the only account to connect Topiltzin Quetzalcoatl with the construction of the edifices there, an association that was undoubtedly both late and completely lacking in historicity.

6. The *Anales de Cuauhtitlan*

THE SOURCE

This important Nahuatl document is an unusually rich compilation of a large number of local histories of various important centers in the Basin of Mexico and the Basin of Puebla. Unfortunately, the anonymous compiler(s) tried to force all these independent traditions into a continuous chronological framework, thereby producing a highly artificial and distorted account. Each separate history must be at least tentatively distinguished before the compilation, a mine of precious information, much of it found nowhere else, can be effectively utilized. Although the necessity for this has been recognized for some time by critical scholars, it has yet to be done in a thorough fashion. Fortunately, the portion of the *Anales* that interests us here can be rather readily separated and distinguished, of which more below.

A *terminus post quem* for the compilation is provided by the mention in the Cuauhtitlan source proper of the date 1570 (Lehmann 1938: 131). A date of 1545–1555 can also be calculated from a statement in the Cuitlahuac source (248). The dates of the other original sources probably differ considerably among themselves. From the inordinate amount of space allotted to the history of Cuauhtitlan, the compilers probably were connected with that center. As suggested by Velázquez (1945: ix–xi), they may have been Pedro de San Buenaventura and Alonso Vegerano, named by Sahagún as two of his most important assistants, both natives of Cuauhtitlan. The bibliography of the *Anales* has been worked out in detail by Lehmann (1938: 11–24) and will not be repeated here. All modern editions have been based on the same manuscript copy, in seventeenth-century script, in the Archivo Histórico of the Instituto Nacional de Antropología e Historia, Museo Nacional de Antropología, Mexico—the *Códice Chimalpopoca,* which, as mentioned earlier, also contains a work, in Spanish, on indigenous religion by Pedro Ponce and the *Leyenda de los soles*.

Four translations of the *Anales* have been published. The first and second Spanish versions (Mendoza, Sánchez Solís, and Galicia Chimalpopoca 1885) are incomplete and have been superseded by those of Lehmann (1938; Nahuatl/German) and Velázquez (1945; Spanish). The former includes a critical edition of the Nahuatl text. The latter includes a photoreproduction of the original manuscript. Also, Garibay (1953–1954, I: 310–317, passim) translated a number of passages from the section devoted to Topiltzin Quetzalcoatl. Although the three modern translations of the tale do not agree in all details, since, as Garibay (1953–1954, I: 314) pointed out, "el texto está mal transmitido, y es muy oscuro," its basic structure is clear.

THE TOPILTZIN QUETZALCOATL MATERIAL

The Topiltzin Quetzalcoatl of Tollan Tale here, although frequently broken into by interpolations from the Cuauhtitlan source, can be reassembled as a continuous narrative without great difficulty (Lehmann 1938: §§ 52–157, passim). Garibay (1953–1954, I: 284) believed that it consists of a long series of poetic fragments, "mutilado, y mal conservado." Certainly, this version of the tale is either an independent piece, standing by itself, or a portion of a longer source providing a consecutive history of the dynasty of Tollan from Mixcoamazatzin to Huemac—a distinct possibility, for the Topiltzin Quetzalcoatl episode fits neatly into the early portion of this longer history. Conceivably, it could even be part of an even more extensive chronicle of the dynasty of Colhuacan, which was a direct continuation of that of Tollan and whose history is presented in this source in considerable detail.

The beginning of the tale here is confused and puzzling; copyists' omissions may be responsible. After some introductory material involving the migration of the Chichimec ancestors of the people of Cuauhtitlan, probably misplaced chronologically, there follows an important cosmogonical section describing the creation of the earth, the sun, and man, including a résumé of the five Suns. One Tochtli (Rabbit) is named as both the first year of the Fifth Sun, when the present earth and the heavens were established, as well as the beginning of the Toltec era and their year count. After referring to the earlier four Suns, the creation of mankind from the ashes of former humanity by Quetzalcoatl (= Ehecatl Quetzalcoatl) is described. The next year involving the Toltecs is 1 Tecpatl (Stone Knife) which, as arranged in these annals, follows immediately upon the 13 Acatl year in which the Fifth Sun was created. In this year, the Toltecs took as their first ruler Mixcoamazatzin. Sixty-six years later, in 1 Calli (House), he dies and is succeeded in Tollan by Huetzin. Then, without further mention of Huetzin or his death, it is stated that in the year 6 Acatl (eighteen years later), Totepeuh, identified specifically as the father of Quetzalcoatl, dies and is succeeded as ruler in Tollan by Ihuitimal.

Eight years later, in 1 Acatl, Topiltzin Quetzalcoatl ("Topiltzin Tlamacazqui Ce Acatl Quetzalcoatl") is miraculously born to Chima(l)man, after she swallows a *chalchihuitl*. Chimalman does not reappear in the tale. When her son is nine years old, in 9 Acatl, he inquires after his father, expressing a desire to see his face. He is told that his progenitor is dead, and his burial place is pointed out. Topiltzin Quetzalcoatl immediately disinters his bones and reburies them in the palace (or temple) of Quilaztli (the earth goddess). Eighteen years later, in 2 Tochtli, Topiltzin Quetzalcoatl arrives in Tollantzinco, where he resides for four years, building his House of Fasting (*nezahualcalli*), his Turquoise House of Wooden Beams (*xiuhhuapalcalli*). From there he passes to Cuextlan (the Huaxteca), where at a certain place he crosses the river (the Panuco?), leaving there a stone bridge, which still existed. In 5 Calli, according to a marginal gloss in Spanish omitted in the Nahuatl text, Ihuitimal dies. In the same year, Topiltzin Quetzalcoatl is taken by the Toltecs to be their ruler and priest in Tollan, after which the text informs us that his history is written elsewhere.

Next, there is an entry at the year 2 Acatl, ten years later, which states that, according to the tradition of Tetzcoco, "Quetzalcoatl Topiltzin" of "Tollan Colhuacan" (or at this place?) died; a Spanish gloss, however, reads: "no valen acá." The text goes on to relate that, in this year 2 Acatl, Topiltzin Ce Acatl Quetzalcoatl constructed his four houses of fasting and devotion: (1) Turquoise Wooden Beam House (*xiuhhuapalcalli*); (2) Red Shell House (*tapachcalli*); (3) White Shell House (*teccizcalli*); and (4) Quetzal Feather House (*quetzalcalli*), where he prayed, performed penance, and fasted. At midnight, he would descend to the river for ritual ablutions to a place called Atecpanamochco. The spines with which he drew penitential blood he would deposit on the tops of the hills of Xicocotl, Huitzco, Tzincoc, and Nonoaltepec. These spines were made of *chalchihuitl*, and the fir branches (*acxoyatl*) upon which he laid them, of quetzal feathers. He made burnt offerings of turquoise, *chalchihuitl*, and red shells, and sacrificed serpents, birds, and butterflies.

He prayed to the innermost heaven, invoking Citlalinicue, Citlallatonac, Tonacacihuatl, Tonacatecuhtli, Tecolliquenqui, Eztlaquenqui, Tlallamanac, and Tlallichcatl. And he cried out unto Omeyocan, above the Nine Heavens, humbly invoking the gods who dwelt there.

He discovered great riches: *chalchihuitl*, turquoise, gold, silver, precious red and white shells, quetzal feathers, and the valuable feathers of the birds *xiuhtototl*, *tlauhquechol*, *zaquan*, *tzinitzcan*, and *ayoquan*. He also discovered multicolored cacao and cotton. He was a great craftsman in all his works: his pottery vessels for food and drink, painted blue, green, white, yellow, and red, and many other things. He began the construction of his temple, with pillars in the form of feathered serpents (*coatlaquetzalli*), but did not complete it. He never showed himself publicly. He always remained, guarded by many attendants, within a dark and remote chamber in the midst of his dwelling quarters, which contained mats of *chalchihuitl*, quetzal feathers, and gold.

While Topiltzin Quetzalcoatl reigned, the "demons" or "sorcerers" (*tlatlacatecollo*, "man-owls") repeatedly tried to deceive him, to persuade him to sacrifice human beings. But Quetzalcoatl resolutely refused, for he greatly loved his vassals, the Toltecs; he would only sacrifice serpents, birds, and butterflies. Whereupon the sorcerers became angry and began to mock and ridicule him in order to cause him misery and drive him away. The three called Tezcatlipoca, Ihuimecatl, and Toltecatl consulted among themselves and agreed that his departure was necessary, so that they would live in Tollan. At first they proposed making *octli*, causing him to become drunk and to neglect his penitential observances, but Tezcatlipoca suggests that they first "give him his body (flesh)," i.e., show him his image in a mirror. Accordingly, Tezcatlipoca takes a two-faced mirror, half a foot broad, wraps it up, and goes to Topiltzin Quetzalcoatl's quarters.

Arriving there, he asks the guards to inform their master that he has come to show and to give him his body. When the guard carries this message to Topiltzin Quetzalcoatl, he refuses to permit the stranger to enter, ordering his attendant to see what it is that he has brought. But Tezcatlipoca will not show it to anyone but Topiltzin Quetzalcoatl, in person. When informed of this reply by the guard, TQ agrees to see Tezcatlipoca. The latter enters, salutes him as "my lord (*nopiltzin*), Tlamacazqui Ce Acatl Quetzalcoatl," and informs him that he is going to show him his body. Topiltzin Quetzalcoatl greets him in turn and asks him from where he comes and about this matter of his body, finally expressing a desire to see it. Tezcatlipoca, replying that he is a vassal from the foot of Nonoalcatepetl, hands him the mirror, requesting that he gaze into it and behold himself. When Quetzalcoatl complies, he is greatly alarmed, remarking that if his vassals should see him they would flee from him. For his eyelids were very bulging, his eyes sunken, and his face covered with swellings, quite unlike a normal person. He then declares his resolve that his people will never see him as he is, that he is determined to remain there permanently in seclusion.

Tezcatlipoca departs, satisfied, and later consults with Ihuimecatl to plan more tricks and deceits directed at Topiltzin Quetzalcoatl. At Ihuimecatl's instigation, they send Coyotlinahual, the featherworker (*amantecatl*), to the object of their enmity. Coyotlinahual insists that TQ leave his sanctuary so that his subjects can see him. To this end he offers to make for him a disguise. Topiltzin Quetzalcoatl then agrees. Coyotlinahual proceeds to prepare the feather adornment of Quetzalcoatl (*apanecayotl*), then a turquoise mask (*xiuhxayac*) with red lips, yellow forehead decorations, serpentine teeth, and a beard of blue and red feathers. When it is finished, TQ tries it on and views himself in the mirror. Pleased with its beauty, he immediately issues forth from his retreat.

Coyotlinahual then goes to inform Ihuimecatl of his success. The latter and his fellow sorcerer, Toltecatl, remove to a place called Xonacapacoyan, where they sit down with the laborer Maxtlaton, the guardian of the Hill of the Toltecs, Toltecatepec. There they prepare a number of different foods: edible herbs, tomatoes, chiles, young maize ears, and string beans. They next ask Maxtlaton for some maguey plants, from which, in four days, they manufacture *octli*, collecting it in little honey jars.

They then go to Tollan, to the house of Topiltzin Quetzalcoatl, carrying all the food and drink they had prepared. The attendants, however, turn them away. Twice more they return, equally without success. Finally, when, in reply to a question concerning their origins, they state that they hail from Tlamacazcatepec and Toltecatepec, TQ permits them to enter. They salute him and present him with the food, which he consents to eat. When offered the *octli*, however, he refuses, explaining that he is in the midst of a fast, and expresses his suspicion that it is intoxicating or even poisonous. They insist that he at least sample it with his little finger, since it is a potent beverage. He follows their suggestion, enjoying it so much that he informs them that he intends drinking three portions more. They reply that he must drink not three, but four. Then they press on him a fifth, explaining that it is his "libation" (*tlatoyahualli*). He finishes this, and they give five cups to each of his attendants—who proceed to drink to complete intoxication.

Next the sorcerers prevail on Topiltzin Quetzalcoatl to sing. Ihuimecatl first sings him a song, which he is to repeat. In this song, Quetzalcoatl describes his houses of quetzal feathers, zaquan feathers, and red shell, which he must abandon. Now deep in his cups, he orders his attendants to bring his elder sister, Quetzalpetlatl, to share in his revel. In obedience to his command, they go to Nonoalcatepec, where she is fasting and performing penance. They explain their mission; she acquiesces and is brought into the presence of Topiltzin Quetzalcoatl. Seating herself next to him, she accepts four cups of *octli* and later the fifth, her "libation." Both now thoroughly drunk, Ihuimecatl and Toltecatl direct a snatch of song to Quetzalpetlatl.

All of the roistering pair's penitential duties are forgotten and neglected. Then comes the dawn. Now fully aware of what they have done, they are distraught with grief. Topiltzin Quetzalcoatl begins a song of farewell, expressing his deep anguish. In the second part he makes reference to his mother, here called Coacueye (= Coatlicue). As he sings, all of his attendants are similarly filled with anguish and weep. They then proceed to sing their own song of woe. All of these songs, as is common, are filled with obscure references, which has resulted in considerable differences between the modern translations. For our purposes, however, the specific content of these difficult verses is not especially important.

When they have finished their song, Topiltzin Quetzalcoatl informs his attendants that he is planning to leave and orders them to have prepared for him a stone box (*tepetlacalli*). This is quickly done, and TQ lies down within it. After four days, feeling in bad health, he informs his attendants that the time has come for his departure. He orders them to close down everything and to hide what they have discovered: the happiness, the wealth, all their goods and possessions. The attendants promptly execute this order, concealing everything in the "bath that belonged to Quetzalcoatl," Atecpanamochco.

Topiltzin Quetzalcoatl arises, calls all his attendants to him, once more weeps with them, and starts off on his journey in the year 1 Acatl, his goal being Tlillan Tlapallan, Tlatlayan. Throughout his wanderings, he can find no place that pleases him. Eventually he reaches his destination. Overwhelmed by grief, there on the seashore (*teoapan ilhuicaatenco*) he weeps for the last time, arrays himself with the *apanecayotl*, the turquoise mosaic mask, and his other adornments, and proceeds to cremate himself. Immediately his ashes fly upwards and are transformed into all of the birds of beautiful plumage: *tlauhquechol*, *xiuhtototl*, *tzinitzcan*, *ayoquan*, *toznene*, *alo*, and *cocho*. When the fire has completely consumed itself, the heart of Topiltzin Quetzalcoatl rises into heaven and becomes the Morning Star. For this reason he was also called Tlahuizcalpanteuctli, Lord of the House of the Dawn. After he died, he was invisible for four days, while he dwelt in the underworld, in Mictlan, then for four more days he was bone (*auh no nahuilhuitl momiti*). After eight days, the great star, Quetzalcoatl, appeared. Then he was enthroned as Lord.

The account goes on to list the various influences cast by the light of Venus on different days of the *tonalpohualli*. Following this, there is a reiteration of the birth and death years of Topiltzin Quetzalcoatl, both 1 Acatl, thus making him exactly fifty-two years old at death, one complete cycle, *xiuhmolpilli*. It is then stated that his successor on the throne of Tollan was Matlacxochitl—and the dynasty of Tollan is continued thus: Matlacxochitl: 1 Acatl–10 Tochtli; Nauhyotzin: 10 Tochtli–12 Calli; Matlaccoatzin: 12 Calli–1 Calli; Tlilcoatzin: 1 Calli–9 Tochtli; Huemac: 9 Tochtli–7 Tochtli.

No events are recorded during the reigns of these successors of Topiltzin Quetzalcoatl until that of Huemac. Then a quite detailed account is presented of the downfall of Tollan, in which Huemac plays a major role. His royal title (*tlatocatoca*) is given as Atecpanecatl. Until marrying Coacueye, a *mocihuaquetzqui* ("mujer valiente," a name applied to the women who had died in childbirth), and consorting with the "demons" Yaotl and Tezcatlipoca, who had come to deceive and mock him by transforming themselves into women, Huemac had also been Quetzalcoatl, i.e., had borne that title as high priest. After his involvement with the demons, Huemac, as Quetzalcoatl, was replaced by a lesser priest named Cuauhtli, who is brought from Xicoco and seated on the throne of Quetzalcoatl, as his image and likeness.

There follows a series of disasters that result in the collapse and abandonment of Tollan. In 7 Tochtli, a great famine ensues, to alleviate which the Toltecs, at the instigation of the malevolent demons, commence human sacrifice on a major scale. In 8 Tochtli (forty years later), the earth goddesses, the Ixcuinanme, come from Cuextlan, the Huaxteca, to introduce the *tlacacaliliztli*, the arrow sacrifice. Four years later, in 13 Acatl, during a war with Nextlalpan, Yaotl (= Tezcatlipoca) stirs up the Toltecs to intensify their human sacrifices, to massacre all their captives in this way. At the same time, the flaying sacrifice of Xipe is introduced. Then the narration harks back to the time of the "first Quetzalcoatl, " Ce Acatl, recalling that he never permitted any human sacrifices, noting that they only began during the reign of Huemac, at the instigation of the "demons." The next year, 1 Tecpatl, the collapse is complete, and the Toltecs begin their migration to other parts. Before they have proceeded far, Yaotl/Tezcatlipoca gathers together a band of his partisans. A Cuauhtli is named among them; whether this is the same person who became the last "Quetzalcoatl" is not clear. Tezcatlipoca also mentions another Cuauhtli, "guardian of Atzompan," whom he had persecuted, among the Toltec leaders, whom he settles near Xaltocan. The rest move southward through the Basins of Mexico and Puebla and on to western Oaxaca, finally dispersing throughout the tropical lowlands (*anahuacatlalli*) on both coasts. Seven years later, in 7 Tochtli, Huemac, in despair, seeing his vassals scattered in all directions, hangs himself in the cave of Cincalco, in Chapoltepec (Lehmann 1938: 69–110, passim; Velázquez 1945: 5–15, passim).

SUMMARY

The basic events of this long, complex version of the tale can be summarized as follows: (1) Topiltzin Tlamacazqui Ce Acatl Quetzalcoatl is the son of Totepeuh, one of the earliest rulers of Tollan, probably the first (his probable identification with Mixcoamazatzin will be discussed below); (2) he is born miraculously to Chimalman, after she swallows a *chalchihuitl*, in the year 1 Acatl, eight years after the death of Totepeuh is recorded, in 6 Tochtli; (3)

when TQ is nine years old, in 9 Acatl, he searches for his father, is directed to his bones, and buries them at the palace, or temple, of Quilaztli; (4) eighteen years later, in 2 Tochtli, TQ goes to Tollantzinco, residing there four years, during which time he builds his Fasting House, Turquoise Wooden Beam House; (5) from there, he goes to Cuextlan (the Huaxteca), crossing a river (probably the Panuco), where he constructs a stone bridge; (6) at the end of this four-year period, in 5 Calli, Ihuitimal, who had succeeded Totepeuh as ruler of Tollan, dies, and TQ becomes priest/ruler of Tollan; (7) ten years later, in 2 Acatl, he builds four houses of fasting and devotion of turquoise, red shell, white shell, and quetzal feathers, respectively, where he performs his penitential rites and worships—a regime that involves ritual bathing in the river at a place called Atecpanamochco, depositing penitential spines on four nearby mountains, making burnt offerings of turquoise, *chalchihuitl*, and red shells, sacrificing only serpents, birds, and butterflies, and praying to various celestial deities above the nine heavens; (8) he discovers many valuable things: *chalchihuitl*, turquoise, gold, silver, valuable red and white shells, the precious plumage of various birds, and multicolored cacao and cotton; (9) he is a great craftsman, his painted ceramic eating and drinking vessels being especially outstanding; (10) he begins construction of his temple, which is adorned with feathered-serpent pillars, but leaves it unfinished; (11) he is never seen publicly, remaining sequestered in a chamber in the midst of his dwelling quarters; (12) the "demons" attempt, by various deceits and mockery, to induce him to sacrifice humans, but he refuses, since he loves his people and will permit only the immolation of the creatures mentioned above; (13) angered at this rebuff, three demons—Tezcatlipoca, Ihuimecatl, and Toltecatl—plot to drive him forth, so that they may live in Tollan; (14) they propose making him drunk on *octli* (the Mexican drink "pulque"), but Tezcatlipoca suggests first shocking him by showing him his reflection in a mirror; (15) Tezcatlipoca goes to Quetzalcoatl's quarters and, after gaining admittance to his sanctum sanctorum, induces him to take the mirror; (16) Topiltzin Quetzalcoatl, on beholding his image, is frightened by his great ugliness and resolves never to leave his quarters to be seen by his people again; (17) at Ihuimecatl's instigation, the demons send Coyotlinahual, the featherworker, to Topiltzin Quetzalcoatl, who, upon being urged to emerge from his retreat, agrees after Coyotlinahual offers to manufacture a disguise for him, an elaborate feather headdress and a feather-decorated turquoise mosaic mask; (18) after observing its beauty in the mirror, TQ is so pleased with it that he comes out of his retirement; (19) then Ihuimecatl and Toltecatl, at a place called Xonacapacoyan and with the help of a laborer, Maxtlaton (the guardian of the Toltecatepetl), prepare a number of foods and a quantity of *octli*, which they take to TQ's quarters; (20) refused admittance three times, they are finally permitted to enter and succeed in inducing Quetzalcoatl to eat the food; (21) after first refusing, he is persuaded to sample the white *octli* and is so pleased with it that he consumes four cups, plus a fifth which they urge upon him; (22) the demons further supply his attendants with the same number of cups, and all quickly become inebriated; (23) the demons induce TQ to sing a song of farewell, and, now completely under the influence, he sends for "his elder sister" (= priestess), Quetzalpetlatl, fasting at Nonoalcatepec, who joins him in his revel; (24) the demons serenade the drunken pair, who completely neglect their penitential and religious duties (and commit sexual transgressions?); (25) the next morning, sober and penitent, TQ realizes that he must now depart from Tollan; (26) after intoning a song of anguish—his attendants answering with one of their own—he orders them to have a stone chest prepared for him and, upon its completion, lies in it for four days; (27) at the end of this time, feeling badly, he informs his attendants that the time has come to leave and orders them to close down everything and hide his treasures at Atecpanamochco; (28) this done, he rises, gathers his attendants, and sets off in search of Tlillan Tlapallan, Tlatlayan; (29) after long wanderings (places not specified), he reaches his goal, the seashore; (30) there, donning his feather headdress and his turquoise mosaic mask, he cremates himself; (31) all of the birds of beautiful plumage rise from his ashes, and his heart ascends into heaven and is transformed into the planet Venus; (32) back in Tollan, Matlacxochitl succeeds him, following which three other rulers reign for short periods until Huemac ascends the throne; (33) this ruler, who originally bore the priestly title Quetzalcoatl, is deprived of it after he marries and consorts with women who are really transformations of Yaotl/Tezcatlipoca, bent on mocking and destroying him and his subjects; (34) a lesser priest, Cuauhtli, is brought from Xicoco and placed on the throne of Quetzalcoatl, as his living representative; (35) after a disastrous famine and the introduction of new cults involving novel methods of human sacrifice, which now becomes standard practice, Tollan is abandoned; (36) the Toltecs migrate southward, finally dispersing as far as the coastal lowlands on both coasts; (37) Huemac, left behind, hangs himself in despair in the cave Cincalco, in Chapoltepec.

COMMENT

With the partial exception of that collected by Sahagún, this account of Topiltzin Quetzalcoatl is the longest of this earlier group of sources. Most of the detail, however, concerns the later portion of his career: his downfall, flight, and death. Although arranged, as is all the material in the *Anales*, in annalistic form, it has the appearance of a unified tale, probably—as Garibay suggested—based on a single epic narrative poem, or poems, much more detailed than the skeletal entries ordinarily encountered in the purely historical chronicles. Although the basic structure of this version of the tale generally parallels those previously considered, it presents various interesting new features, such as the miraculous birth through the swallowing of the jade jewel, the trip to Cuextlan, and the Coyotlinahual and Quetzalpetlatl incidents. Some elements are difficult to understand, e.g., the significance of the Cuextlan journey and, especially, the incident involving his four-day interment in the stone chest. From certain remarks in the text, it is clear that the tale here is not complete, which may explain the obscurity of some of the events narrated.

The "gaps" in this account are one of its most interesting features. Of Totepeuh we are told nothing except that he apparently was ruler (this is actually implied rather than specifically stated) of Tollan. The "vengeance of Topiltzin Quetzalcoatl" against his father's murderers is completely absent. Perhaps the most striking gap is the failure to mention a single place-name during his journey from Tollan to Tlillan Tlapallan, in an otherwise quite full account of his downfall and death. Some or all of these omissions may have been the work of the compiler.

No other source so clearly emphasizes the mild nature of Quetzalcoatl's ritual and his aversion to human sacrifice. Also, no other source paints him so completely as the priest, the great penitent. Judging from this account alone, his control over the secular affairs of the Toltec dominion would have been slight indeed. Furthermore, Topiltzin Quetzalcoatl's humanity here is almost complete. Only at the very end, after his death, is there any hint of deity in his character—and this is presented as a clear apotheosis.

The precise provenience of the *Anales de Cuauhtitlan* version of the tale can only be surmised. If it really does constitute part of a long, connected account of the dynasties of Tollan and Colhuacan, then it might well have originated in this latter center. It bears enough general similarity to the version preserved in the *Juan Cano Relaciones* to make this suggestion at least plausible. In any case, it almost certainly hails from some major center in the Basin of Mexico. Its exact date can also only be guessed at. It bears every indication, however, of being derived from a genuine pre-Conquest narration, quite possibly in metered verse, and must have been recorded before the last elders educated in the *calmecac* had begun their journey to the Nine Fold Stream. If 1570 is really the compilation date of the *Anales* in its entirety, this would, of course, provide the tale's *terminus ante quem*.

This will always remain one of the most fundamental of the Topiltzin Quetzalcoatl accounts, both because of its probable comparatively early date as well as for its rich detail. These details, many of which are not found elsewhere, have the authentic ring and, occasionally, strangeness, of the still imperfectly understood *Weltanschauung* of pre-Hispanic Mexico.

B. Important Supplementary Accounts of the Basic Topiltzin Quetzalcoatl of Tollan Tale

The sources of this category provide data of considerable importance concerning Topiltzin Quetzalcoatl but consist of brief summaries of, or significant snatches from, his career rather than a sustained narrative. As in the previous chapter, each source will be briefly considered in turn, beginning with the earliest.

1. Motoilnía

THE SOURCE

The writings of Motolinía, the Nahuatl nickname for Fray Toribio de Benavente, one of the original twelve Franciscans who arrived in New Spain on May 13, 1524, aged approximately thirty-four, are particularly important as a source of information on the indigenous culture. They represent the work of a vigorous personality who was intimately associated with the natives until his death in 1569, during the great outburst of proselytizing enthusiasm that swept the Mendicant orders working in New Spain in the first half of the sixteenth century (see, especially, the bio-bibliographies of Ramírez [1858], Sánchez García [1914], Foster [in Motolinía 1950], and Steck [in Motolinía 1951]). Their importance is revealed in the number of later writers who utilized them in their own works (López de Gómara, Las Casas, Cervantes de Salazar, Zorita, Suárez de Peralta, Mendieta, Dávila Padilla,

Bautista, Román y Zamora, Torquemada, Herrera, Martínez, et al.). Motolinía, however, was no Sahagún. He did not collect texts in the native tongue (although he must have spoken it well), nor did he devote anything like the same amount of time and patience to recording indigenous customs. His principal aim was to chart the progress of the early missionary endeavors of his order in New Spain; his material on the native culture was subsidiary to this larger purpose. His writings, as they have come down to us, are somewhat disorganized stylistically, and they are rarely felicitously phrased. In spite of these drawbacks, they often provide valuable information found in no other source. The best-known work of Motolinía is the chronicle that William Robertson in his *History of America* (1777) and others have called *Historia de los Indios de la Nueva España*, accompanied by an important "Epístola Proemial" to a nobleman resident in the Franciscan's town of origin, Antonio Pimentel, sixth Conde de Benavente, dated February 24, 1541. Most modern editions of this work are derived from a sixteenth-century copy of the lost original now in the library of El Escorial, near Madrid. From internal evidence, it was apparently prepared between 1536 and 1541. During most or all of this period, Motolinía seems to have been guardian of the Franciscan establishment at Tlaxcallan but also frequently made trips to nearby places (Motolinía 1950: 8; 1951: 10).

In addition, there exists another sixteenth-century work of Motolinía (also accompanied by the "Epístola Proemial"), which, although much of its material is duplicated in the *Historia*, includes considerably more information on the native culture. It is contained in the previously mentioned *Libro de oro y tesoro indico* and was published in 1903 by García Icazbalceta's son, Luis García Pimentel, under the title *Memoriales de Fray Toribio de Motolinía*. García Icazbalceta and others believed the *Memoriales* to be a rough draft for the *Historia*, but López (1931) and Ricard (1933), who made the most intensive analyses of the relationship between the two chronicles, both concluded, in the words of the latter (Ricard 1933: 151): "Les *Memoriales* representent le stade intermédiaire: ils sont en même temps la compilation d'où l'auteur à tiré l'extrait qui constitue *l'Historia* et l'ébauche du grand ouvrage disparu."

This final lost work, which was used by so many writers of the sixteenth and early seventeenth centuries, was probably completed by the middle years of the sixteenth century, no later than the 1560s.

THE TOPILTZIN QUETZALCOATL MATERIAL

In the "Epístola Proemial," Motolinía, after giving the history of the Mexico Tenochtitlan dynasty, based on the *Juan Cano Relaciones*, repeats a legend accounting for the peopling of aboriginal New Spain that he states was told to him by an unnamed and unplaced native informant, "bien habil y de buena memoria." This was the oft-quoted tale of Iztac Mixcoatl and his wife Ilancueye (or Ilancueitl) of Chicomoztoc and their six sons: Xelhua, Tenoch,

Olmecatl, Xicalancatl, Mixtecatl, and Otomitl, who were the progenitors, respectively, of: (1) the Nahuatl speakers of Itzocan, Epatlan, Teopantlan, Teohuacan, Cozcatlan, and Teotitlan; (2) the Tenochca; (3) the Olmeca Xicalanca, who originally occupied portions of the Basin of Puebla but were forced off the plateau down into the coastal lowlands; (4) the Mixtec; and (5) the Otomi. Iztac Mixcoatl also married another woman, Chimalma, who bore him Quetzalcoatl. The latter turned out to be "honesto y templado." He began to perform penance by fasting and "disciplinas," to preach "la ley natural," and to teach fasting by both example and word. From that time many in the land began to fast. He was not married, nor did he know women, but lived virtuously and chastely. He also began the practice of sacrifice and of drawing blood from the ears and tongue, not "por servir al demonio" but as a penance for the vices of the tongue and ears—"después del demonio aplícolo a su culto y servicio" (Motolinía 1903–1907: 9–13; 1941: 8–12).

A puzzling, probably somewhat garbled, anecdote follows, to the effect that a person named Chichimecatl tied a band of leather around Quetzalcoatl's arm, up near the shoulder (Nahuatl: *acolli*), for which deed he was called Acolhuatl and became the progenitor of "los de Colhua," the ancestors of Motecuhzoma, and the lords of Mexico and Colhuacan. Next follows a statement concerning Quetzalcoatl's role as wind god (Motolinía 1903–1907: 13; 1941: 12).

In a continuation of chapter 16 of the first part of the *Memoriales*, after a description of the cult rendered to, and the count kept of the appearances of, the planet Venus, the author explains that the reason so much attention was paid to this star was because the natives believed that one of their principal gods, called Topiltzin, or, by another name, Quetzalcoatl, when he died and departed from this world was transformed into that resplendent star (Motolinía 1903–1907: 56–57).

In chapter 24 of the first part of the *Memoriales*, Motolinía mentions Quetzalcoatl again, this time to identify him with the principal god of Tlaxcallan, Huexotzinco, and Cholollan, who was known by three names: Camaxtli, used most in the first two centers; Quetzalcoatl, which "se usaba mucho" in Cholollan; and Mixcoatl (Motolinía 1903–1907: 67). Another mention of Quetzalcoatl is found in chapter 27, first part, when, describing the principal Tlaxcalteca ceremony, dedicated to Camaxtli every four years, it is stated that at one point the gigantic idol of this god was attired with the vestments and insignia of Quetzalcoatl, "este decían ser hijo del mesmo Camaxtle," which were brought to Tlaxcallan by the Chalolteca especially for this ceremony. The Tlaxcalteca reciprocated and brought to Cholollan the costume and insignia of Camaxtli during the great ceremony of Quetzalcoatl at the latter center. Then it was said: "hoy sale Camaxtle como su hijo Quezalcouatl" (77; cf. Motolinía 1941: 63–67).

The last significant passage concerning Topiltzin Quetzalcoatl is at the end of chapter 30, first part, of the *Memoriales* and in chapter 12, "Tratado Primero," of the *Historia*. After describing the round temples to the "dios del aire que llamaban Quetzalcovatl," it is stated that he was the principal god of Chalollan, in which city and in Tlaxcallan and Huexotzinco there were many of these temples. This Quetzalcoatl was native of a town called "Tulla," from which he left "edificar" (Mendieta 1945, I: 92, copying this passage, has used "poblar") the provinces of Tlaxcallan, Huexotzinco, Chalollan, etc., and afterwards went toward "la costa de Covazacualco," where he disappeared. His return was always awaited, and when the ships of Cortés appeared, seeing their tall white sails, they said that it was Quetzalcoatl coming, bringing temples (*teocalli*) over the sea. But when the newcomers disembarked, they said that it was not their god, but many gods ("en su lengua dicen quiteteuh"; Zorita [1909: 144], who copied this passage, has "miequeteteuth") (Motolinía 1903–1907: 78–79; 1941: 75).

SUMMARY

(1) Quetzalcoatl was the son of Iztac Mixcoatl/Camaxtli of Chicomoztoc and his second wife, Chimalma; (2) he becomes a great penitent, fasting and drawing his own blood from the ears and tongue, living in celibacy, and preaching his penitential doctrine, which many followed; (3) he was a native of Tollan, which he left to build or populate the provinces of Tlaxcallan, Huexotzinco, and Chalollan, the last center taking him to be their principal god; (4) he went down to the coast at Coatzacoalco, where he disappeared, or died, and was transformed into the planet Venus; (5) his return was expected, and when the Spaniards arrived it was at first believed to be Quetzalcoatl, bringing his temples with him across the sea.

COMMENT

Although the data concerning Topiltzin Quetzalcoatl provided by Motolinía are quite limited, it generally squares well with the information contained in the more ample accounts described above. Most of his notices were probably gathered in the Basin of Puebla, rather than in the Basin of Mexico. The provenience of the "Epístola Proemial" tale of Iztac Mixcoatl/Ilancueitl and their seven sons might well have been Teohuacan, where the letter was written, or some other nearby center, judging from the prominence accorded Xelhua, the legendary ancestor of the peoples of this zone. The listing of peoples particularly important in the Pueblan Basin or adjacent regions, and the failure to include any of the Basin of Mexico groups other than the politically dominant Tenochca, would also support this attribution.

Consequently, Motolinía's Topiltzin Quetzalcoatl material is doubly important—first, for its early date, and, second, for its probable Pueblan provenience. Its basic similarity to certain Basin of Mexico accounts is striking.

This may indicate a substantial uniformity in the most salient features of the tale as told in the major centers of both areas, which perhaps was to be expected in view of the strong Toltec cultural background they shared.

2. A Toltec Elegy

THE SOURCE

Lehmann gave this title ("Ein Tolteken-Klagegesang") to a brief hymn, or chant, that is included in the manuscript compendium known as the *Cantares Mexicanos*. This extensive collection of old hymns is part of a larger series of manuscripts, many in Nahuatl, bound together in one volume (Biblioteca Nacional de México 97 [15–3–97]). The early history of this volume is unknown. Garibay (1953–1954, I: 153) suggested it may have reposed in "una biblioteca franciscana en su origen primario." Later, it formed part of the collection of the old Biblioteca de la Universidad de México, where Ramírez had a copy made by Faustino Galicia Chimalpopoca in 1859 (Peñafiel 1899, prologue: iii). A copy made about the same time by Brasseur de Bourbourg was later utilized by Daniel Brinton for his edition of the Nahuatl texts and English translations of twenty-seven of the hymns (Brinton 1887a). After this, the original corpus was believed lost, but José M. Vigil rediscovered it in the late 1880s in the Biblioteca Nacional de México (Vigil, in Peñafiel 1899, prologue: v). From it, Antonio Peñafiel published, first, the text of all of the *Cantares*, poorly paleographized (Peñafiel 1899), and, later, a photoreproduction of the original manuscript (Peñafiel 1904).

Garibay believed that we are dealing here with "un documento mandado hacer por el famoso Padre de Etnografía," a suggestion that has also been made by others. Both the paper and script seem to be of the sixteenth century. The dates 1536 (possibly an error for 1563), 1550, 1551, 1553, 1565, and 1597 are found in various of the poems. Garibay (1953–1954, I: 154–156) concluded that the compilation was made up in the decade 1560–1570, with the final two folios being added in 1597. In any case, this last date, or one very close to it, appears to constitute a *terminus ante quem* for the collection.

The poem that interests us here is found on folio 26, verso, and 27, recto. Brinton (1887a: 104–107) was the first to publish both the Nahuatl text (somewhat inaccurately) and a poor English translation. Lehmann (1922) published an accurate version of the Nahuatl, direct from the original, with a German translation, which was translated into Spanish by Hendrichs (Lehmann 1941) and published together with a valuable introduction and notes by Jiménez Moreno. More recently, Garibay (1952: 33–35) published a Spanish translation, direct from the original, of the entire poem. A second translation of the bulk of the poem, which differs in many respects from his first, appeared in 1953 (Garibay 1953–1954, I: 358–360). In this second version, Garibay visualized it as accompanying a ritual drama, with its various sections being spoken by different participants. Due to the archaic style of the Nahuatl employed—the best proof of its authenticity, as Jiménez Moreno (1941b: 4) pointed out—its precise translation has been difficult, which explains the considerable differences between the translations of Lehmann and Garibay (and between the two made by the latter himself). Its main outlines, however, seem clear.

THE TOPILTZIN QUETZALCOATL MATERIAL

The hymn is a dirge, apparently, from its title, *teponazcuicatl*, intended to be sung, or chanted, to the accompaniment of the *teponaztli*, the two-toned cylindrical wooden drum. Its theme is a lament over the "flight" of Nacxitl Topiltzin from Tollan. It begins by describing the *huapalcalli*, the Wooden Beam House, which stood in Tollan. Next, it is stated that the feathered-serpent columns, *coatlaquetzalli*, still remain there. These were abandoned by Nacxitl Topiltzin, when he departed for Tlapallan. Then, three place-names are mentioned: Cholollan, Poyauhtecatitlan (which might belong with Cholollan), and Acallan, through which Nacxitl Topiltzin and companions apparently passed on their journey. Next, four names of individuals appear: Ihuiquecholli, Mamaliteuctli, Ihuitimalli, and Matlacxochitl. The first, and perhaps the second, is associated with the place-name Nonoalco. It is also possible that these two names belong to the same person. The last-named person apparently laments because Ihuitimalli has abandoned him.

Then what appear to be two more place-names follow, somewhat corrupted. Jiménez Moreno (1941b: 13) interpreted them as Tepehuitonco and Xalliquehuac. There, it would seem, Matlacxochitl weeps and laments at the departure of his lord, Ihuitimalli. Tlapallan is again mentioned at this point, where someone (probably Nacxitl Topiltzin) is expected, is bidden to sleep. Ihuitimalli then reappears and has apparently been ordered to go to Xicalanco and Zacanco.

Some puzzling lines follow, which seem to mention a place called Ayanco, where something or someone no longer exists. Then someone (again, probably Nacxitl Topiltzin) is asked about or reminded of his home and his palace that was abandoned in Tollan Nonoalco; "that lord," Timalli, is mentioned as grieving.

Nacxitl Topiltzin definitely reappears in the final lines, which address him directly. His painting on stone and wood is mentioned, and it is stated that his name will never perish and that his vassals will weep for him. Finally, his Turquoise House (*xiuhcalli*) and his Serpent House (*cohuacalli*) are mentioned. The poem ends with a repetition of the reminder that his name will never die and that his subjects will weep for him.

SUMMARY

(1) Nacxitl Topiltzin, apparently ruler of Tollan, has departed; (2) he leaves behind his mourning vassals and abandons the following structures: *huapalcalli*, the Wooden Beam House; *coatlaquetzalli*, the feathered-serpent columns; *xiuhcalli*, the Turquoise House; and *coacalli*, the Serpent House; (3) the following places are seemingly either on or connected with the itinerary of his journey: Chalollan, Poyauhtecatitlan (combined with the former?), Acallan, Tepehuitonco, Xalliquehuac; Xicalanco, Zacanco, Ayanco (?), and Tlapallan (not necessarily in geographical order); (4) certain individuals appear, apparently either important leaders left behind or some of those who accompanied him: Ihuiquecholli, Mamaliteuctli (two names, or titles, for the same individual?), Ihuitimalli, and Matlacxochitl; (5) the first named, and possibly the second, if they are distinct persons, are associated with Nonoalco (or Tollan Nonoalco); (6) a fifth person possibly appears, Timalli, unless, as Lehmann suggested, he is to be identified with Ihuitimalli; (7) the dirge ends with a reminder that Nacxitl Topiltzin's name will never perish and that his vassals are mourning his departure.

COMMENT

Many details of this interesting and significant piece are obscure, but it clearly supplies valuable information on Topiltzin Quetzalcoatl, particularly his flight to Tlapallan. Another important name for him, Nacxitl, is here encountered for the first time. The absence of the term "Quetzalcoatl" itself is not too surprising, in view of its similar absence in certain previously considered sources that clearly concern him. The subject matter and the archaic quality of the Nahuatl may indicate that this elegy is actually a relic from late Toltec times, which would, of course, lend it particular value.

Most of the material presented is by now familiar, but certain new details are important, particularly what seem to be place-names on the route of Topiltzin Quetzalcoatl's journey from Tollan to Tlapallan—as well as the names of some important individuals associated with him. The most significant of these will be further discussed below.

3. Fray Andrés de Olmos

THE SOURCE

In the bibliographical section on the *Histoyre du Mechique*, the "lost Olmos" was briefly described, and the possibility indicated that at least a part of the *Histoyre* might be derived from it. Practically all that is known of this work is the brief notice contained in the prologue to Book II of Mendieta's *Historia eclesiástica indiana* (1945, I: 81–82). There we are told that in 1533 the president of the Second Audiencia of New Spain, Sebastián Ramírez de Fuenleal (who carried the *Historia de los Mexicanos por sus pinturas* to Spain), and the custodian of the Franciscans, Fray Martín de Valencia, commissioned Fray Andrés to compile a book treatment of "las antigüedades de estos naturales indios, en especial de Mexico, y Tezcuco, y Tlaxcala, para que de ello hubiese alguna memoria." Olmos was chosen because at that time he was considered the best "lengua mexicana" in the province, having come over with Fray Juan de Zumárraga in 1528, as well as being "hombre docto y discreto." He conscientiously pursued his task, gathering together and questioning the most learned old men of the leading Central Mexican communities and examining their pictorial manuscripts. All this activity resulted in the formation of "un libro muy copioso," of which three or four copies were made and sent to Spain; later, his original was also carried there. Some years later, "algunas personas de autoridad" in Spain requested the work of Olmos, who, without his original complete manuscript but aided by his "memoriales," formed an "epílogo o suma" of his treatise.

The original, its copies, and the later summary, all have disappeared, but portions of the last named account were utilized by Las Casas (1909), Zorita (1909), Mendieta (1945)—who claims to have used the holograph manuscript—and, doubtfully, Torquemada (1943–1944), and has thus been preserved. The early date of the Olmos compilation makes it particularly valuable, a value enhanced by the fact that its author covered an unusually wide territory in gathering his data.

THE TOPILTZIN QUETZALCOATL MATERIAL

The most important passage relating to Quetzalcoatl is found in a section dealing with the principal gods of pre-Hispanic Central Mexico: Huitzilopochtli of Mexico Tenochtitlan, Tezcatlipoca of Tetzcoco, Camaxtli of Tlaxcallan, Quetzalcoatl of Chollollan, and Tlaloc. Las Casas seems to have copied it almost verbatim; Mendieta omitted many portions but included the Quetzalcoatl passage almost in its entirety (Las Casas 1909, I: 326–328; Mendieta 1945, I: 98–100). In this account, Quetzalcoatl, named the patron god of Chollollan, is stated to have been, in the opinion of all, "el más celebrado y tenido por mejor y más digno sobre los otros dioses." According to their histories, he came to Chollollan from "las partes de Yucatan" (Mendieta parenthetically adds: "aunque algunos digan que de Tula"). He was a white man, large of body, with a broad forehead, large eyes, long black hair, and wore a large round beard. They canonized him as their "sumo dios," and rendered him great love, reverence, and devotion, offering him gentle, very devoted, and voluntary sacrifices for three reasons: (1) because he taught them the art of metallurgy (*platería*), which before his coming had been completely unknown and of which the natives of Chollollan greatly boasted; (2) because he never desired or permitted sacrifices of the blood of men or animals, but only of bread, flowers, and sweet odors; and (3) because he prohibited, with considerable success, war, robbery, murders, and other harmful activities. Whenever such matters were mentioned in his presence, he turned away and closed his ears, in order not to see or hear anything that pertained to those subjects. He was extremely chaste, virtuous, and temperate in many things. He was so revered and so much the subject of vows and pilgrimages that even the enemies of the Chololteca were accustomed to come there safely on pilgrimages, to fulfill their vows and devotions. The rulers of other major towns established there chapels, oratories, and idols for their worship. Only Quetzalcoatl, among all the gods, was called Lord par excellence, so that, when they swore and exclaimed "by our Lord," Quetzalcoatl was always meant—although there were many other highly esteemed gods. All this was because of the great love they bore him, for "en la verdad el señorío de aquel fué suave." He only required trifling services, teaching them the virtues and forbidding evil, demonstrating his distaste for such things. Here, Olmos parenthetically adds that this demonstrates that the natives performed human sacrifices, not because they desired to do so, but because of their fear that the gods would harm them if they failed to comply.

Quetzalcoatl lived for twenty years in Cholollan, and at the end of that time he returned whence he had come, taking with him four young virtuous leaders. From Coatzacoalco ("provincia distante de allí ciento cincuenta leguas hacia el mar"), he sent them back to their city. Among other doctrines that he gave them was an instruction to tell their people that they should hold it as certain that at some future time there would come from across the sea, where the sun rises, some white-skinned men, with beards as long as his, who would become lords of those lands and would be his brothers. Thus, when the Christians first arrived, they were called gods, sons, and brothers of Quetzalcoatl, "aunque después que conocieron y experimentaron sus obras, no los tuvieron por celestiales."

At this point Mendieta ends his chapter, probably on his own hook, but Las Casas proceeds to explain that this change in attitude was due to the great massacre that the Spaniards inflicted on the people of Chololan. Next, he interpolates a passage derived from Motolinía, already described, which also deals with the purported return of Quetzalcoatl. Then, obviously returning to Olmos, he states that the four young men sent back by Quetzalcoatl were received by the Chololteca as their lords, "dividiendo todo el señorío della en cuatro tetrarcas, quiero decir cuatro principados." From these four descended the four lords who were ruling at the time of the Conquest—and even after. The statement that follows, that the same god was worshipped in Tlaxcallan and Huexotzinco under the name of Camaxtli, Las Casas probably took from Motolinía. Finally, it is explained that Quetzalcoatl in the Mexican language signifies a certain kind of serpent, "que tiene una pluma pequeña encima de la cabeza," that was native to the province of Xicalanco ("que está en la entrada del reino de Yucatan, yendo de la de Tabasco"). The author goes on to state that, outside of this province, this type of serpent was rarely, or never, seen. The natives affirmed that at certain times those snakes were converted into birds with green feathers (probably quetzals), which were numerous in this region (Las Casas 1909, I: 328).

SUMMARY

(1) Quetzalcoatl, a bearded white man, was principal god of Cholollan, to which center he arrived from the direction of Yucatan (or Tollan, if this parenthetical note was really in Olmos and not, as is perhaps more likely, added by Mendieta); (2) he was greatly loved for three principal reasons: his teaching them the jeweler's art, his prohibition of human sacrifice, and his strong aversion to any kind of violence among men; (3) he lived chastely and virtuously and was so revered throughout the land that even the enemies of Cholollan came there on pilgrimage and maintained shrines there; (4) Quetzalcoatl was esteemed above all of the other gods, and the term "Lord" was applied peculiarly to him; (5) at the end of a twenty-year sojourn in Cholollan, Quetzalcoatl returned to the east, taking with him four young men; (6) from Coatzacoalco, he sent them back, instructing them to inform their people that at some future time white men, his brothers, bearded as he, would come from this direction and become lords of the land; (7) when the Spaniards arrived, they were at first thought to be those whom Quetzalcoatl had predicted, but the natives were soon disenchanted; (8) from the four young men were descended the rulers of the four divisions of Cholollan; (9) the name Quetzalcoatl referred to a type of snake, native to the Xicalanco district, with a small feather on the head, who had the power to transform itself into a quetzal.

COMMENT

This account was probably collected either at Cholollan itself or in the general Pueblan region. It might be legitimately queried whether we are dealing here with Topiltzin Quetzalcoatl of Tollan at all. There are so many resemblances, however, between the activities ascribed to the latter and to this Quetzalcoatl of Cholollan that it is reasonable to assume that this tradition does refer to the same figure. Additional support for this view is provided by the frequency with which Cholollan is named in different accounts as one of the places visited and/or resided in by Topiltzin Quetzalcoatl after his departure from Tollan. Perhaps the most significant single feature of this account is the description of Quetzalcoatl as "un hombre blanco." This seems to be the earliest statement to this effect in any source. This element in the TQ tradition has sometimes been denounced as a late Spanish fabrication or misinterpretation. This may be true, but its early date here is noteworthy.

Also striking is the statement that Quetzalcoatl came from the direction of Yucatan. Significantly, Tollan does not appear at all—assuming Mendieta's parenthetical note was added by him and not taken from Olmos. Quetzalcoatl is a stranger, coming to Chololtan from the outside; his birth and early life are not treated. At the end of a kind of apostolic mission, he departs in the direction from whence he had come. His promise of eventual return is prominently emphasized. In many respects this version is an anticipation of certain much later accounts that particularly feature Quetzalcoatl's foreign origin and "missionary" activities. They will be described and analyzed in a special section devoted to them below.

ADDITIONAL TOPILTZIN QUETZALCOATL MATERIAL IN OLMOS

Another important passage in Olmos that concerns Quetzalcoatl is found only in Mendieta (1945, I: 88–89). There, it is stated that Tezcatlipoca (called the chief idol of Mexico) lowered himself from the sky on a spider's thread, and, "andando por este mundo," banished Quetzalcoatl, who was for many years lord of Tollan. Playing the rubber ball game with him, he transformed himself into a jaguar, which so terrified the onlookers that they stampeded into a barranca, through which a river flowed close by, and drowned. Tezcatlipoca persecuted Quetzalcoatl from town to town, until the latter came to Chololtan, where he was held to be the principal god and where he remained for a certain number of years. Finally, however, the more powerful Tezcatlipoca also drove him from there. He went with some of his devotees down to near the sea, "donde dicen Tlillapa o Tizapan," where he died and was cremated, from which arose the custom of cremating the bodies of dead lords. The soul of Quetzalcoatl was transformed into a star, like a comet, whose appearance was considered a bad omen. Some said that Quetzalcoatl was the son of Camaxtli, who took Chimalma for a wife and by her had five sons, "y de esto contaban una historia muy larga." Others said that Chimalma, while sweeping, found a *chalchihuitl* and swallowed it, from this conceiving and later giving birth to Quetzalcoatl.

Lastly, in another obviously Olmos-derived passage describing the origin of the calendar, also found only in Mendieta (1945, I: 106–107), Quetzalcoatl again appears. The gods, aware that newly created mankind lacked a "libro por donde se rigiese," two of their number, Oxomoco and Cipactonal, husband and wife, residing in a cave in the region of Cuernavaca (Cuauhnahuac), consult concerning this matter. The latter suggests that they consult their grandson, Quetzalcoatl. He gives his blessing to their calendric scheme, and a debate ensues as to who shall name the first of the signs. Chivalrously, the two males finally accord this honor to Cipactonal. She eventually decides on a "cierta cosa llamada Cipactli, que la pintan a manera de sierpe, y dicen andar en el agua," and fixes the first sign, Ce Cipactli. Oxomoco follows with "dos cañas" (*sic*), Quetzalcoatl with "tres casas," and so on, until all twenty signs are established—following which the principles of the calendar are briefly explained.

COMMENT

These additional accounts of Topiltzin Quetzalcoatl are considerably more standard than the main one, summarized earlier. They present few new facts of importance concerning his career, with the exception of the method of Tezcatlipoca's descent from heaven and his transformation into a jaguar during an athletic contest with his victim. Quetzalcoatl's participation in the creation of the calendar is treated more fully here than elsewhere. Finally, the "conception by jewel," or virgin birth of our hero, strikingly recalls the *Anales de Cuauhtitlan* account.

4. The *Codices Telleriano-Remensis* and *Vaticanus A*

THE SOURCES

These cognate documents will be considered together, for reasons that will become obvious during the discussion. Both contain pictorial and accompanying textual annotations, on sheets of European paper. The early history of both is obscure. Beginning with the *Telleriano-Remensis* (*TR*), this manuscript first turns up in the extensive private collection of Charles Maurice Le Tellier, a prominent aristocrat of the ancien regime, brother of one of Louis XIV's chief ministers, who became the archbishop of Reims. A certain case can be made for his having obtained it in Italy in 1767, perhaps in Rome (Paso y Troncoso 1898: 333), but there is also evidence that it was in Spain at one time (Hamy 1899: 2). In 1700, Le Tellier donated all of his manuscripts, including that under discussion, to the Bibliothèque du Roi, where it has remained ever since (now Bibliothèque Nationale du France, Ms. Mexicaine No. 385). During the eighteenth century various writers confused it with the *Codex Mendoza* (then in England), but Alexander von Humboldt (1810–1813: 279–283, plates LV–LVI) finally clarified the situation, dubbed it with its present name, and was the first to publish some portions of it. In 1830, Edward King, Lord Kingsborough (1830/31–1848, I: 1–70) first published it complete, a hand-colored lithographic copy by Agostino Aglio. He also published an inaccurate and incomplete paleography of the Spanish annotations (V: 127–158), plus a poor English translation (VI: 95–153). The Aglio version was reproduced again by Leon de Rosny (1869: 190–232, plates 24–97), but it was not until 1899 that the Duc de Loubat published a more accurate version, a color lithograph of the original, accompanied by a careful paleography of the text and a commentary by Ernst Hamy (1899).

The document consists of three distinct parts, probably originally from different sources, which a compiler brought together: (1) the eighteen annual *veintena* ceremonies; (2) a *tonalamatl* (260-day divinatory cycle); and (3) a long pictorial historical/dynastic chronicle, covering the years 1195 (originally; the first sheet is missing) to 1562. All three parts bear Spanish annotations, in various hands. As José F. Ramírez, the first serious student of the document, pointed out: "formar de todas ellas un solo texto [as Kingsborough did; HBN] sin discernir las que pertenecían a cada comentador era formar una más indigesta incoherente, y, aún absurda, por la dificultad de evitar las contradicciones, y aún contrasentidos" (quoted in Paso y Troncoso 1898: 336). In his paleography, Hamy distinguished three of the handwritings by employing italics and different-sized type, but this is inadequate. A numerical system (Ramírez used colored underlinings) would have been preferable. In my comments below, I have tried to adopt such a system (with the caveat, however, that it is not always possible to be certain to which hand any given annotation belongs).

One of these hands, a particularly shaky one (my number 2), which usually is added to that which seems to have belonged to the first and principal commentator (my number 1), has been tentatively identified (Paso y Troncoso 1898: 340; Hamy, 1899: 3) as that of Pedro de los Ríos, a Dominican lay brother who is given credit in the Italian text of the *Codex Vaticanus A* (*VA*) for having assembled the bulk of the paintings found in that document. Almost nothing is known of Ríos (see Paso y Troncoso 1898: 340, 341; Jiménez Moreno 1940: 72, 76). He apparently performed the bulk of his missionary work in Oaxaca, the special province of the Dominicans. The comments in both the *TR* and the *VA* display particular familiarity with that region. If not the work of Ríos himself, they were probably written by other Dominicans who had labored in Oaxaca. As for the date of the document, the year count of the third section ends in 5 Tochtli, 1562. The last seven years, however, are obviously later additions, in handwriting 2 (Ríos?). On folio 24, recto, the year 1563 is mentioned, the latest found in the manuscript, providing its *terminus ante quem*. The watermark of the putatively Genoese paper used would support such a date (Hamy 1899: 1–2).

The *VA* (frequently called *Codex Ríos* or *Vaticanus 3738*), which contains two whole sections lacking in the *TR* and is also more complete in those sections that are cognate, first appears in the catalogue of the Vatican library, compiled 1596–1600 by the Rainaldis—but it may have been referred to earlier. The Italian text is in a script (or scripts, for there are several) that can best be dated as of that general period. According to Ehrle (1900: 11), from the watermarks of the paper it must have been composed after 1569. Reina (1925) presented cogent evidence that in its present form the text of the *VA* is a copy, by more than one scribe, of an earlier Italian translation of a Spanish text by a Spaniard whose knowledge of Italian was not perfect. As to its date, the year 1566 is mentioned on folio 4, verso (error for 1556?), providing its *terminus ante quem*, although the year count of the historical chronicle, which is cognate with that in the *TR*, likewise ends in 5 Tochtli, 1562. As mentioned above, the text in two places (folios 4, verso, and 24, recto) specifically names Pedro de los Ríos as the compiler of the bulk of the paintings.

The precise nature of the relationship between these two sources has posed a difficult problem from the beginning. An explanation was advanced as early as 1855 by Ramírez (quoted in Paso y Troncosco 1898: 337), who believed he had discovered compelling reasons for accepting the view that the *TR* (before it bore all the annotations it eventually was to display) had served as the direct model for the *VA*. Paso y Troncoso (1898: 350–351), on the other hand, suggested that the pictures, at least, of both documents had been copied from a common prototype, since lost. He did not present his evidence for this view, however, in any detail. It remained for Thompson (1941b) to do this. He believed that the *TR* was copied from the prototype in Mexico, later being carried to Europe. The prototype, meanwhile, he suggested was taken to the Vatican library, where, in the decade 1570–80, the present *VA* was copied from it, the prototype subsequently disappearing before 1600. This view has been widely accepted.

So much for the history of the two documents as we now have them. What of the indigenous sources on which they were based? Paso y Troncoso (1898: 349), based on certain phonetic peculiarities of some of the Nahuatl words employed, believed that the calendric sections of the *TR* had been compiled in the Tlaxcallan-Puebla region. He suggested that the opening cosmogonical section of the *VA* "transcribe mucho la leyenda Tolteca," pointing to specific similarities in Sahagún. On the basis of the subject matter, he felt that the historical/dynastic annals were exclusively Mexica, while the "costumbres" section of the *VA* he believed was largely based on Oaxacan data. Orozco y Berra (1880, I: 401–402), however, followed by Hamy, believed that both documents were Acolhuaque in affiliation—a view that must be very seriously questioned.

Certainly a strong case can be made for separate origins for the different sections of the two manuscripts. The historical/dynastic annals definitely seem to stem from a genuine Mexica tradition, since they focus so intensely on that group. On the basis of style alone, the calendric and cosmogonical sections can probably be safely assigned to the Basin of Mexico or immediately surrounding territory. The *VA* section on customs need not especially concern us, for it contains no Topiltzin Quetzalcoatl data. Clearly, however, some of the information here was gathered in Oaxaca.

The great value of these twin documents has long been recognized, in spite of the biblical vagaries of some of the annotations. The *tonalamatl(s)*, particularly, provided the nearest thing to a "Rosetta Stone" for the interpretation of the Central/Southern Mexican native tradition religious/

divinatory pictorials and were utilized to skillful advantage by the greatest pioneer student of this subject, Eduard Seler. The Topiltzin Quetzalcoatl data contained in these two manuscripts are also fairly extensive and of considerable importance.

THE TOPILTZIN QUETZALCOATL MATERIAL

The two documents will be considered together, although, as we have seen, there are often striking differences between them in textual content. The long introductory section describing the heavens and underworlds, the four previous ages, or Suns, and the structure of the calendar is found only in the *VA*. This section also includes an important version of the Topiltzin Quetzalcoatl of Tollan Tale. Quetzalcoatl is first mentioned, however, on folio 4, verso, as the deified ancestor of the Chichimeca ("Chishineche"), one of seven who escaped from the deluge that ended the first age.

The tale proper begins on folio 7, recto, describing the fourth age (labeled "Sochiquetzal idest essaltatione delle rose"; also called "età delli capelli negri"), during which Tollan rose to prominence and was eventually destroyed by a great famine, brought on by the vices of its inhabitants (according to folio 4, verso, however, this destruction took place at the end of the first age). Although the statement is made that the famine lasted 5,042 years, this figure, consistent with the time spans allotted to the previous ages, must refer rather to the total duration of the age (based on the numerical symbols depicted, however, it should be 5,206). The Topiltzin Quetzalcoatl Tale begins at this point and can be summarized as follows.

The god Citlallatonac (all names, except where identification is dubious, have been corrected to standard orthography), "ch' è quello segno, che si vede in cielo detto strada di Santo Iacobo ò via latea," sent an ambassador from heaven on an embassy to a virgin of Tollan, Chimalman, "che voul dire Rodella." The emissary appeared to Chimalman and her two sisters, Xochitlicue and Coatlicue, while they were alone in their house. The latter two perished from the shock, but Chimalman survived to receive the announcement that it was the will of Citlallatonac that she should conceive a son. Immediately after the departure of the messenger, this in fact occurred, "senza congiontione, di huomo." The resulting offspring, Topiltzin Quetzalcoatl, was born miraculously, possessing the use of reason. Here the commentator parenthetically adds that Quetzalcoatl was the wind god, who caused hurricanes, the destroyer of the world thereby, to whom round temples were first erected and which he had invented. This comment includes the cryptic remark "così ciò parmi che si diceva Citoladuale [*sic*]."

Topiltzin Quetzalcoatl, "che vuol dire' nostro molto caro figliuolo'," cognizant that the vices of men were the cause of the world's woes, determined to end a four-year famine by offering sacrifices to Chalchiuhtlicue, the water goddess. He was considered to have been the first who offered prayers to the gods and sacrificed to them. He was also the first who performed penance to propitiate the gods to pardon his people. This was done by drawing his own blood with thorns. He was further accustomed to burn gold, jewels, and incense as offerings, realizing that man's woes stemmed from the lack of reverence shown the gods in favor of worldly pleasures. After a considerable time, his sacrifices and offerings finally succeeded in appeasing the gods sufficiently that they sent a sign that the famine would soon cease: a lizard scratching the ground, soon followed by a period of fruitful abundance.

The commentator then goes on to state that from this event they "pigliorno quattro segni della loro superstitione, della quale usavano fin'adesso." The first sign was the deer, "depingono li huomini ingrati." The second was a stone with a withered ear of maize on it, representing sterility. The third was a lizard, symbolizing abundance of water. The fourth, denoting general fruitfulness, was a green ear of maize.

Convinced of the efficacy of TQ's penitential rites, men began to imitate them, especially ritual bloodletting. To further this observance, he invented temples, founding four in particular: one for the fasting of the rulers and nobles, Zaquancalli; one for the fasting of the common people, Nezahualcalco ("Xecaualcalco"); the "House of Fear," or, by another name, the "House of the Serpent," Coacalco ("Cauacalco"); and the "Temple of Shame," Tlaxapochcalco, where all immoral and sinful men were sent (here the commentator adds parenthetically that a common opprobrious epithet was "Go to Tlaxapochcalco!").

There follows a paragraph devoted to a consideration of the Mexica claim that they had invented temples and were the first to introduce them to New Spain. Then a new sequence begins, involving a disciple of Topiltzin Quetzalcoatl called Totec, who was particularly famous among those who imitated his penitential observances. A great sinner, he had first stood in the Tlaxapochcalco, here called "House of Sorrow," and performed penance. This completed, he climbed the thorn-covered mountain, Tzatzitepetl ("Catcitepetli"), "che vuol dire montagnetta che parla," and cried out reprovingly to the inhabitants of Tollan, upbraiding them for their neglect of the gods and their generally licentious behavior, while exhorting them to perform penance with him. Here, the commentator explains that Totec was accustomed to go about clad in a human skin. During the ceremonies dedicated to his sign, participants danced wearing human skins. He was also considered to have been the inventor of wars, and, since those who died in battle went to the highest heaven, was greatly venerated as "il principio d'aprir loro la strada del cielo."

While Totec continued in his penitential exercises, preaching from the top of Tzatzitepetl, every night he dreamt he saw a horrible figure with protruding bowels. Upon praying to the gods to reveal the significance of this phantasm, he was informed that it was "il peccato del suo populo." He was then instructed to order all of the people to assemble with thick ropes to bind the spectre, the cause of all their sins, which could be removed by dragging it away. The multitude having congregated, Totec led them, dancing and singing, to a certain place where they bound the monster. While hauling it backwards, they all fell into a ravine between two mountains, which closed together, sealing them in. None escaped from this destruction except the innocent children, who had remained in Tollan.

The two "maestri della penitenza," Topiltzin Quetzalcoatl and Totec (here for the first time also called Xipe ["Chipe"]), next led the children and "gente innocente" out of Tollan, "populando et aggregando seco altri populi, che traovavano." Arriving at a certain mountain, which presented an insurmountable barrier, they bored a tunnel into it, through which they passed. Others said that their followers were sealed up in this passage, all turning into stone.

Topiltzin Quetzalcoatl, meanwhile, continuing on his journey, finally reached the "mare rosso," called Tlapallan. Entering into it, he was never seen again nor was it known what became of him. He requested his followers at the time of his disappearance, however, to restrain their grief and to expect his return, which would occur at the appointed time. The commentator goes on to state that he was still expected even then. When the Spaniards arrived, it was believed that it was he returning. The Zapotec revolt of 1550 was caused by a report that their god, "che haveva da redimerli," had appeared. It is then pointed out that Topiltzin Quetzalcoatl was born on the sign One Cane (Acatl) and that the year of the Spanish arrival commenced on that sign—from which the belief arose that the latter were their gods, since TQ had prophesied that a bearded nation would come to subject them. He was worshipped as a god, for they held that he had ascended into heaven where he was transformed into the Morning Star, the planet Venus.

This long verbal account is actually only an extended commentary on a series of paintings, rather poorly copied from the lost originals. Aside from the running text, the illustrations themselves are often specifically labeled.

On folio 7, recto, is the representation of what should be the fourth age, "Sochiquetzal idest essaltatione delle rose." In certain respects it parallels the representations of the three previous ages, while in other respects it is quite different. The correct interpretation of the four Suns scheme of this manuscript is by no means clear. The differing theories of Chavero (1887: 85–86), Seler (1902–1923, IV: 49–53), and Imbelloni (1943) are the most serious analyses of the problem; none appears to be fully satisfactory. For our purposes, however, it is only necessary to point out that in the *VA* version, in striking contrast to other schemes, this fourth age terminated with the destruction of Tollan and the Toltecs rather than with the nearly total destruction of mankind, as in the three previous ages. Since this was associated with the sinful licentiousness of its inhabitants, it is not surprising that the goddess of flowers (a sexual symbol) and love, Xochiquetzal, serves as patroness of this era. The scene represents the goddess descending from above (against a rose-colored sky containing two sprouting seeds), grasping two long strands of intertwined flowers. Beneath her, two men and a woman are apparently dancing, each holding a paper banner and a bouquet of flowers and wearing very sketchily indicated "leis" of flowers around their necks. On the right, the symbols for the duration of this age are drawn (= 5,206 years). There is nothing in this scene that specifically links this age with Tollan and the Toltecs; we are entirely dependent on the commentary for this information.

The pictorial scenes that illustrate the Topiltzin Quetzalcoatl of Tollan Tale proper are much more important for our purposes. Unfortunately, the first two paintings seem to be missing, i.e., those that illustrated the conception and birth of our hero. The first of the surviving series portrays TQ standing on a stepped pyramid (Color Plate 6). He is garbed in the standard—if somewhat simplified—attire and insignia of Ehecatl Quetzalcoatl, including a mantle decorated with two red crosses. Before him is the usual penitential instrument, the maguey spine, *huitztli* (two smaller ones are thrust into his calves), and a handled *incensario* (*tlemaitl*). The second scene in the series depicts, just behind him, the four symbols that, according to the commentary, illustrate the account of TQ's successful "penitential campaign" to overcome the hostility of the gods toward man: a deer ("*maçatl*"); a stone ("*tetl*") with maize ear issuing from it; a lizard ("*guetzpallin*"); and a maize stalk ("*centli*").

The third scene pictorializes, just below him, in a vertical series, the four "temples" founded by Topiltzin Quetzalcoatl. They are labeled, from top to bottom: "Çaquancalli, casa di digiuno per li santi"; "Xecaualcalco, casa di digiuno comune"; "Cauacalco, casi di timore"; and "Tlaxapocalco, prigione di tristezza o pianto." These temples are represented by the standard stylized house symbols, with certain additions. The first is decorated with circular motifs, both as roof battlements and as a cornice decoration. The second has similar, but rectangular, devices; the battlements are painted red. The third displays much fancier battlements and, above them, bunches of green feathers. The lintel post is painted green. Descending from it is a green oblong element, tipped with what appears to be a red forked tongue. It apparently is a very crude representation of a serpent (feathered?). The fourth has red circular motifs on the cornice and wall; its battlements seem to be highly stylized flowers, the upper portions painted red. All of the doorposts and lintels of these houses are red, with the exception noted.

On folio 8, recto, the penitent Xipe Totec is pictured, wearing the standard attire of that deity, including the human skin. He stands on a large maguey spine, resting in turn on the usual stylized hill, in this case with mouth and teeth and speech scrolls issuing forth on either side. On folio 8, verso, the gigantic monster, labeled "Maacaxoquemiqui, Il peccato," is being hauled by a group of Toltecs with heavy ropes. Above is the place sign of Tollan (a bunch of reeds), labeled "Tolteca" and "Tulan." Folio 9, recto, displays an interesting scene that illustrates the passage describing the leading of the innocents out of Tollan by Topiltzin Quetzalcoatl and Xipe Totec (Color Plate 7). Seven figures are bundled together at the left. In front of them march, first, TQ, again in a simplified version of Ehecatl Quetzalcoatl's costume and carrying the crooklike baton (*chicoacolli* or *e(he)cahuictli*) and an incense pouch (*copalxiquipilli*), then Xipe, also in characteristic attire. Lastly, to the right of the latter is a representation of the mountain (really two hills meeting at their tops), within which their followers are apparently being trapped and turned to stone. The last scene in the series, on folio 9, verso, depicts Quetzalcoatl, again wearing standard costume, including the mantle with two crosses, one of which is painted red, standing against what is apparently a kind of place sign for Tlillan Tlapallan: a large pool of water in two colors, red on the left and dark brown to bluish on the right (= "the black and red land," its literal meaning) (Color Plate 8).

These scenes, undoubtedly based ultimately on a pre-Hispanic pictorial, are of considerable importance. They provide us with the only significant group of native-style illustrations, apart from those in the *Florentine Codex*, previously described, of the Topiltzin Quetzalcoatl of Tollan Tale that have survived. As in the case of those drawn by Sahagún's artists (see Color Plates 1–4), they demonstrate that Topiltzin Quetzalcoatl was regularly portrayed displaying the attire and insignia of Ehecatl Quetzalcoatl but without the snout-like "wind mask" that the latter regularly displays.

Topiltzin Quetzalcoatl is also mentioned a number of times in the commentaries to the *tonalamatl*, in both documents. The first in the *VA* is on folio 14, verso, in the passage accompanying the second *trecena*, beginning 1 Ocelotl and ruled over by Quetzalcoatl himself, who is portrayed in the full costume of Ehecatl Quetzalcoatl. Here his creation by Tonacatecuhtli/Citlallatonac is again described, "non per congiontione di donna, ma solo col suo fiato," after the sending of the ambassador to "qella Vergine de Tullan." It is then stated that he was believed to be the "signore delli venti," the first to whom round temples were erected, without any angles. His reformation of the world by penance is again alluded to, as well as the assignment of this mission to him by his father (the parallel to Christ's mission is duly noted at this place by the commentator). Finally, it is stated:

> Facevanli grande festa quando veniva il suo giorno, come vedremo nel segno delli quattro tremoir (4 Ollin), che è il quarto in questo ordine, perché temono, che sia destrutto il mondo in quel giorno, come lui haveva predetto, quando disparve nel mare rosso, che fú in quello

> medesimo giorno, et per haverlo per advocato celebrano solenne feste e digiunano quattro giorni.

On folio 15, recto, the right side of the double sheet dedicated to this *trecena*, under a picture of a penitent drawing blood from his ear, it is explained that the figure signifies that Quetzalcoatl was the inventor of sacrifices of human blood—following which the various types are described.

The relevant comments on the sheet (folio 8, verso and recto) devoted to the same *trecena* in the *TR* are, first, in script 3: "nació en chiuenauiecatl (*chicunahui ehecatl*) q[ue] es donde esta la mano"; and, on the recto sheet: "El que nacía en este nueve ayre sería libre dichoso q[ue] au[n]q[ue] fuese de baxo linage vendría a tener grandes cargos en la república." In script 1, "tierra" and "Queçalcoatle" are written near the figure of the god, and below:

> Este queccalcoatle fué él que dizen que hizo el mundo y así le llaman señor del viento porque dizen queste tonacatecotli quando a él le pareció [bien] sopló y engendró a este queçalcoatle ha este le hazían las higlesias rredondas sin esquina ninguna. Este dizen que fué él que hizo el primer honbre. Es señor de estos treze días questan aquí hazían fiesta. En este cuatro temblor al destruymi° que havía de ser del mundo otravez.

Then two lines follow that are nearly obliterated in the original but which can probably be reconstructed as: "Este solo tenía cuerpo humano y como los hombres, y los demás dioses no tenían [cuerpo?]." In script 2 are the comments: "Es el q[ue] nació de la virgen que se dize chimalma en el cielo. Chalchiuiztli [*sic*, for *chalchihuiztli*, jade, or precious, penitential spine] quiere dizir la piedra preciosa de la penite[n]zia o sacrificio/ sálvose e[n] el diluvio/ sería penite[n]te."

There are other valuable comments on these sheets, but, since they do not specifically concern Topiltzin Quetzalcoatl, they will not be considered here.

On *VA* folio 16, recto (right side of third *trecena*, beginning 1 Mazatl, patron Tepeyollotl), under a depiction of Ehecatl Quetzalcoatl holding a little male figure by the hair and excrement in the other, the comment is made:

> A questa figura non metteno nome, perché solo dimostra come dipoi che disparse Topiltzim Quetalcotl, compexorno li huomini sacrijficcar li putti, á fine d'honorare la sua festa, ch 'era il di delle sette canne pexis. Dicono che in quel giorno nacque, et cosi in questo giorno se faceva in Chululan, una grandissima festa, alla quale venivano de tutto il paese et portavano offerte o doni, et li signori or Papi et sacerfoti di quel tempio: et la medema festa et solennita facevano il giorno che disparse, che fu giorno d'una canna. Venivano queste solennita et feste de 52 in 52 anni.

In the *TR* (folio 10, recto), the following comments are placed near the same figure (in script 2 or a cursive version of script 1):

> tetl
> coytlatl [= *cuitlatl*, excrement]
> Q[ue]çalcoatle
> como después q[ue] cesó el diluvio empeçaron a sacrificar topilcin quecalcoatle nació el día de VII cañas y el día destas VII cañas se hazía una gra[n] fiesta en cholula y venía[n] de toda la tierra y pueblos a esta fiesta y traya[n] gra[n]des prese[n]tes a los señores y papas del te[m]plo, y lo mesmo hazía[n] el día q[ue] se fué o murió q[ue] fué el día de vna caña. Caya[n] estas fiestas de LII en LII años.

The comment is also made, in script 3, annotating the date 7 Acatl: "la q[ue] nacía en este día de 7 cañas si era muger era haze[n]dosa."

On *VA* folio 16, verso (left side, fourth *trecena*, beginning 1 Xochitl, Huehuecoyotl patron), the commentator has written, after identifying the regent: "Dicono che li sottomies tenevano questo per dio, et era signore di questi 13 giorni, in quali celebrano, la sua festa, et li quattro ultimi digiunavano in reverentia dell'altro, Quetzalcoal de Tula. Et queste chiamavan le feste della discordia." This four-day fast is explained by the fact that the next succeeding *tonalpohualli* day was that especially dedicated to Quetzalcoatl, 1 Acatl.

The corresponding annotation in the *TR* (folio 10, verso), in script 1, runs: "Este huehuecoyotl es señor destos treze días quiere dezir la rraposa viexa aqui ayunavan los cuatro días prosteros al queçalcoatli de tula ques él que tomó nonbre del primer queçalcoatli y agora le llaman una caña que es la estrella Venús de laqual se dizen las fábulas questos tienen."

On *VA* folio 17, verso (left side, fifth *trecena* beginning 1 Acatl, Chalchiuhtlicue regent), after a description of Chalchiuhtlicue and the general auguries of this period, it is stated: "et quando entrava con una canna, facevano gran festa in Chululan a Quetzalcoatl, perché dicono, che fu il primo loro papa o sacerdote." The *TR* commentary (folio 11, verso), in script 2, is nearly identical: "en esta vna caña hazían la otra gra[n] fiesta en cholula al queçalcoatle o primer papa o çacerdote."

On *VA* folio 19, verso (left side, seventh *trecena*, beginning 1 Quiahuitl, Nahui Ehecatl and Tlaloc regents), the commentary describes the principal patron, who, from his insignia, is a blend of Tlaloc and Ehecatl Quetzalcoatl. Although not directly relevant to our analysis of Topiltzin Quetzalcoatl, the calendric name that this deity bears, 4 Ehecatl, is significant, as will be seen when the names of Topiltzin Quetzalcoatl are discussed below. Also significant is the fact that the statement is made that Nahui Ehecatl received the special veneration of the merchants, who celebrated a feast in his honor. The corresponding text of the *TR* (folio 13, verso) is very similar, but here special stress is placed, in different comments (scripts 2 and 3), on the evil fortune of the day 4 Ehecatl, "y asý en veniendo este día todos los mercaderes se encerrava en casa porq[ue] dezía[n] q[ue] era causa de q[ue] se perdiesse sus hazie[n]das."

On *VA* folio 21, verso (left side, ninth *trecena* beginning 1 Coatl, Tlahuizcalpantecuhtli patron), is a long commentary, the bulk of which, rather than commenting on this deity in detail, is devoted to "proving" that the Mexican Indians had descended from the Hebrews by describing the "baptism" ceremony at some length. The corresponding commentary in the *TR* (folio 14, verso), in script 3, is more to the point: "Este Tlauizcalpanteuctli o estrella venus es el queçalcovatl . . . [three crossed-out lines follow, practically illegible] dize[n] q[ue] es aq[ue]lla estrella q[ue] llamamos luzero de la lus y así pinta[n] con vna caña q[ue] era su día [script 2 adds: cuando se fué o desapareció tomó su no[m]bre]."

On *VA* folio 26, verso (left side, fourteenth *trecena* beginning 1 Itzcuintli, Xipe Totec regent), the penitence of Xipe is described, "qell'altro Quetzalcoal" on the "montagna delle spine." On the right-hand sheet devoted to this *trecena* (folio 27, recto) is a representation of a feathered serpent swallowing a man. The commentary reads: "Quetzalcoatl . . . Questa è la figura del suo compagno Quecalcoatl. Depingonlo cosi per significare, ch'era festa de grande timore, per la cui causa mettono questo serpente, che ingiotte li huomini vivi."

The corresponding passage in the *TR* (folio 18, recto), in script 2, is quite similar: "esta era la culebra queçalcoatle para dar a ente[n]der es la fiesta de temor pinta[n] este drago[n] q[ue] se esta comiendo vn honbre."

VA folio 27, verso (left side, fifteenth *trecena* beginning 10 Calli, Itzpapalotl regent), contains a long passage describing the patron deity and an incident that resulted in the casting out of certain deities from heaven. Apart from Itzpapalotl (here considered male) himself, no other is named, but in the corresponding passage in the *TR* (folio 18, verso) six deities are named, including "queçalcoatle"; all are described as the "hijos de citlalcue y citlalatona" (script 2).

On *VA* folio 31, recto (right side, eighteenth *trecena* beginning 1 Ehecatl, Chantico patron), there is a representation of a gold enclosure—within which is a figure with 1 Acatl as a calendric name but otherwise not accoutered as Ehecatl Quetzalcoatl—holding an incense pouch. The caption reads: "Contro a questo Cantico mattevano questo Quetzalcoatl in questa casa d'oro e vestito de quije richissime, e sededno come pontefice con la sporta dell'incenso in mano, volendo dar ad intendere, che cosi come per la gula fu il altro castigato, cosi fu questo honorato per le astinentie e sacrificij."

The same caption in the *TR* (folio 22, recto) reads, in script 2: "Q[ue]cal coatle . . . casa de oro por esto corespo[n]de este sacrificio de queçalcoatle, a quel prime[o]."

SUMMARY

Pooling all of this scattered information and attempting to organize it into a more coherent narrative structure—at the risk, again, of a certain artificiality—we find:

(1) During the fourth age, or Sun, Topiltzin Quetzalcoatl, named after "the other Quetzalcoatl" (i.e., apparently the old creator/wind god, Ehecatl Quetzalcoatl), was miraculously born, with full use of reason, on the day 7 Acatl (variants: 1 Acatl; 9 Ehecatl) to a virgin of Tollan, Chimalman, after she had received an annunciation from a messenger sent down from heaven by Citlallatonac/Tonacatecuhtli, the great creator/sky god; (2) to end a four-year drought, Topiltzin Quetzalcoatl, realizing that this misfortune had been brought on by men's sins, devised a set of prayers and penitential sacrifices, stressing the drawing of one's own blood, to propitiate the gods, especially the water goddess, Chalchiuhtlicue; (3) the gods finally relented, a period of abundance followed, and mankind, perceiving the efficacy of TQ's rites, began to imitate him; (4) Topiltzin Quetzalcoatl built four houses, or temples—Zaquancalli, Nezahualcalco, Coacalco, and Tlaxapochcalco—in furtherance of his cult, dedicated to fasting and prayer, and he also invented round temples; (5) a particularly enthusiastic partisan of TQ's penitential program was an ex-sinner named Xipe Totec, the inventor of wars, who was accustomed to go about clad in a human skin; (6) from the spine-covered "talking mountain," Tzatzitepetl, he preached to the people of Tollan, exhorting them to mend their evil ways; (7) after having dreamt many times of a horrible gigantic spectre, with protruding entrails, he led the Toltecs to it, who, when they attempted to drag it away, perished by falling into a deep barranca that swallowed them up; (8) Topiltzin Quetzalcoatl and Xipe Totec then led the children and the few remaining Toltecs out from Tollan, populating and collecting others as they went, until, coming to a barrier mountain, they bored a hole for a passage, within which, according to one version, all their followers were sealed up and turned to stone; (9) Topiltzin Quetzalcoatl traveled on to Tlapallan, where he entered the sea and disappeared on the day 1 Acatl (or, in another dubious version, 4 Ollin), telling his followers to expect his return, that a bearded people would eventually come and conquer them; (10) this belief was held until the time of the Conquest, when the connection between the day on which he had been born, 1 Acatl, and the year, 1519, which began with that sign, contributed to the belief that the Spaniards were divinely sent (the Zapotec revolt of 1550 reflected this same belief); (11) Topiltzin Quetzalcoatl was deified after he ascended into heaven and became the morning star—and was expressly identified with the special deity of the planet Venus, Tlahuizcalpantecuhtli; (12) Topiltzin Quetzalcoatl is also further identified as the creator of the world and the first man, as the wind god (who caused hurricanes and destroyed the world by that means),

and the possessor of a humanlike corporeal body, in contrast to the other gods; (13) 7 and 1 Acatl, the days, in one version, of his birth and disappearance, respectively, were the occasions for great celebrations in Chalollan.

COMMENT

The account of Topiltzin Quetzalcoatl that can be reconstructed from the scattered texts in these twin pictorial manuscripts lines up fairly well with most of those in the core group. The total absence of Mixcoatl/Camaxtli/Totepeuh is noteworthy, although Chimalman—and the virgin birth—is prominently featured. The question of the degree of Christian influence in this version is pertinent, for this bias of the ecclesiastical commentators in both documents is manifest throughout. For the most part, however, the overall flavor of this version of the tale—however garnished with a biblicized overlay—smacks of authentic aboriginality. In any case, the paintings may well go back, at least indirectly, to a pre-Conquest pictorial history. While it is obvious that the commentators frequently either misunderstood what was told to them concerning the significance of its images, were misinformed, or consciously or unconsciously distorted the truth, the account is sufficiently congruent with the Basic Topiltzin Quetzalcoatl of Tollan Tale that it can be fairly assumed that a reasonably conscientious attempt was made to convey the essential facts of what was explained to them by their informants. The compilation date was early enough that many oldsters educated in the *calmecac(s)* would have been available for this explanatory task. It is unfortunate, however, that so many questions still surround the prototype source(s): its precise place of compilation; the individuals involved, on both the native and Spanish sides; the motivation, in the first instance, for the assembling of these data, etc.

Also noteworthy in this account is the lack of specificity concerning the life of our hero between his birth and his abandonment of Tollan. The prominent role ascribed to his penitential disciple, Xipe Totec, alias one of the most important Conquest-period deities, is unique to this source. Throughout, the emphasis is on Topiltzin Quetzalcoatl's religious role; his political career, to a large extent, is omitted. Tollan itself and its people, the Toltecs, are but shadowy background silhouettes—against which Topiltzin Quetzalcoatl, the arch-penitent, plays out a kind of prosyletizing mission of "redemption." Not once is he identified as founder or ruler of Tollan. A strong supernaturalistic flavor pervades the whole. In short, we seem to be in the presence here of a quasi-historical tradition in the process of transformation into legend and myth.

The variations in the dates of our hero's birth and disappearance probably reflected divergent traditions from different centers. It is clear that the traditional histories and religious/ritual systems of the leading late pre-Hispanic Central Mexican polities were far from uniform. Although they appear to have shared most of the same basic cultural patterns, each seems to have had its "official" history that strongly reflected its own political and economic interests. The local elites, operating within the political and cultural framework of the Empire of the Triple Alliance, may have been increasingly standardizing their polities' historical traditions—but this process probably still had a long way to go, when violently and unexpectedly interrupted by the Conquest.

All in all, in spite of a certain amount of Christian reinterpretation, this account is clearly one of the most valuable that has been preserved. Once it is recognized that this version of the career of Topiltzin Quetzalcoatl was probably not intended to be strictly "historical," even in native terms, then the possibly very real historical value of some aspects of it can be more fully appreciated. This matter will be more fully considered below.

5. The *Crónica X*

THE SOURCE

The complicated relationship between five works that present the most detailed history of Mexico Tenochtitlan—(1) the *Historia de las Indias de Nueva España e islas de tierra firme* of Fray Diego Durán; (2) the "*Códice Ramírez*"; (3) the "*Historia de los Yndios mexicanos*" of Juan de Tovar; (4) most of the section devoted to New Spain in the *Historia natural y moral de las Indias* of José de Acosta; and (5) the *Crónica Mexicana* of Hernando de Alvarado Tezozomoc, has long posed one of the most complex problems in Mesoamerican ethnohistorical bibliography. The studies, above all, of Ramírez, Chavero, Orozco y Berra, Bandelier, García Icazbalceta, Beauvois, Chávez Orozco, Barlow, Sandoval, Gibson, and Leal have gradually unraveled much of this unusually tangled bibliographical skein. Used in conjunction, Barlow (1945), Sandoval (1945), and Gibson (in Gibson and Kubler 1951: 10–18) provide a generally adequate tracing of the history of research on this problem and an up-to-date statement of its present status, which can be briefly summarized as follows:

It seems almost certain that the Tenochca history contained in these five sources ultimately derives from a lost work, in Nahuatl, accompanied by pictures, compiled, definitely before 1581, by an unknown native or mestizo, which was labeled by Robert Barlow (1945) the "*Crónica X*." The Dominican, Fray Diego Durán, apparently translated or paraphrased one version of this history in the first part of his *Historia*, finished in 1581, accompanying it with highly Europeanized illustrations copied from the native-style originals. Between 1582 and 1586–1587, his relative, the Jesuit Juan de Tovar, either himself made a condensation of the first and second parts of Durán's work or copied one that came into his hands—which he sent, together with another version of the illustrations, to his fellow Jesuit, José de Acosta. The latter incorporated it, nearly in its entirety, in his description of the New World, first published in 1590. Tovar's manuscript finally reached a private English collection, whose owner partially published it in 1860 (Tovar 1860). Another sixteenth-century manuscript, textually almost identical to it, was discovered by José F. Ramírez in the Franciscan convent in Mexico City in 1856 and published by Orozco y Berra in 1878 (Tovar 1878). Its precise relationship to the other, which is apparently Tovar's holograph, is still not completely clear. It is known to have been used by Torquemada, and, if Chavero's (1880: 13) statement is accurate that it was written in the latter's "puño y letra," it may have been a copy made by Torquemada either of the Tovar original or of a lost prototype from which both it and the Tovar were derived. Another, somewhat distinct version of the *Crónica X* is found in Alvarado Tezozomoc's *Crónica Mexicana*, which may have been, like the historical portion of Durán, a translation or paraphrase of the missing original. If it also contained illustrations, they have been lost.

Thus, only two *primary* versions of the *Crónica X* are extant: Durán and Alvarado Tezozomoc. Although similar in essentials, they differ enough in detail to make it unlikely that they are derived directly from a single common source. An *indirect* derivation, however, the exact nature of which remains to be worked out, is practically certain. Since the works of these two authors constitute our sole means of reconstructing the lost original, each will be briefly considered in turn.

DURÁN

Fray Diego Durán has been justly called "an enigmatic figure in Mexican bibliography" (Gibson, in Gibson and Kubler 1951: 16). Almost nothing positive is known about him, beyond the facts that he was born in Seville, ca. 1537, came to New Spain when very small, apparently grew up while living in the Tetzcoco region, professed in the Dominican establishment in Mexico City in 1556, discharged his duties as a friar in a number of places in Central and Southern Mexico, and died in 1587 or 1588 (Sandoval 1945). The reasons for the preparation of his great work are not known. Certainly, like his fellow Dominican, Las Casas, he was a strong partisan of the natives, which may explain his interest in their past history and customs. As stated above, the historical portion was finished, by his own statement, in 1581, the calendric section in 1579, and the section dealing largely with religion and ceremonialism ("libro de los ritos") probably before that time.

Only Tovar and Dorantes de Carranza seem to have made use of Durán in manuscript. The first portion of the *Historia* was finally published in Mexico in 1867 by Ramírez from a copy that he had made in 1854 of a sixteenth-century manuscript version of the work in the Biblioteca Nacional de Madrid. This does not seem to have been Durán's holograph but a copy prepared for the printer. In 1880, the remainder of the work, with an atlas of the illustrations (engravings of tracings made from the originals), was published by Gumesindo Mendoza. A second printing of this 1867–1880 edition appeared in Mexico in 1951.

ALVARADO TEZOZOMOC

Even less is known of this native author than of Durán. Until recently, not even his ethnic affiliation was certain. However, since the publication of the *Crónica Mexicayotl* (1949), a portion of which at least was apparently authored by him, it is known that he was no less than the grandson of Motecuhzoma Xocoyotzin, on his maternal side, and the great-grandson of Axayacatl, on both sides. His father, Diego de Alvarado Huanitzin, who married his first cousin, the daughter of Motecuhzoma II called Doña Francisca, was ruler of Ehecatepec in 1519 and later served as native governor of Tenochtitlan from 1539 to 1542, the year of his death. Hernando Alvarado Tezozomoc must have been born before this year; how long before, however, is not known. He was living at least as late as 1609, when be was seemingly preparing his portion of the *Crónica Mexicayotl*. The only other known fact of importance concerning his life is that he served as interpreter to the Audiencia Real de México (Mariscal 1944).

On internal evidence, the *Crónica Mexicana* was in composition in 1598 and was probably finished not long after. The manuscript was in the possession of José Sigüenza y Góngora and after his death passed with the rest of his collection to the library of the Jesuit college of San Pedro y San Pablo in Mexico City. There it was apparently seen by Francisco Clavigero, although not used by him. Lorenzo Boturini came into possession of it in the early 1740s, and it is listed as § VIII, No. 12, in his catalogue (Boturini 1746: 17). Mariano Veytia, who had access to Boturini's sequestered collection, had it copied in 1755, which copy in 1792 was itself utilized as the basis for a series of copies made in connection with the compilation, under the direction of Fray Francisco Figueroa, of the *Memorias para la historia de la América septentrional*, ordered by the Spanish government. One of these copies, in the Mexican national archive, was the source for the first impression of the work, by Lord Kingsborough (1830/31–1848, IX: 1–196). A copy sent to Spain, which came into the hands of Muñoz, was apparently the basis for the French translation of Ternaux-Compans (1844–1849). Finally, in 1878, Orozco y Berra published the first Mexican edition, based on the Archivo Nacional copy that had served Kingsborough, comparing it with two other manuscript copies in the collections of Chavero and García Icazbalceta—the latter's, at least, also made in 1792. This edition was reprinted in Mexico in 1944.

Thus, all published versions derive from the Veytia copy of 1755. The Boturini manuscript came to light again in the possession of a New York book dealer in 1951 (McPheeters 1954) and is now in the Library of Congress,

Washington, D.C. Whatever the reason, the text of the *Crónica Mexicana* as we have it is truncated and corrupt. The Durán version of the *Crónica X* seems to have better preserved all of the basic elements of the lost original, but AlvaradoTezozomoc's version frequently provides considerably more detail, particularly in native names, which in many respects lends it an even greater value.

THE PROTOTYPE

Lastly, a word concerning the lost "original." It almost certainly was the work of some educated native or mestizo, who must have been connected with the dynasty of Mexico Tenochtitlan. From the exaggerated importance assigned to the long-lived Cihuacoatl, Tlacaelel, the half-brother of Motecuhzoma I, it might be surmised that the author was some descendant of this prominent Tenochca leader. As to its own sources, it undoubtedly was based on one or more pictorial annals, historical songs and chants, and the verbal historical tradition that was apparently part of every student's education in the *calmecac*. Although known to be historically inaccurate in many instances, no other source presents a more authentic and vivid picture of imperial Mexico Tenochtitlan during its rise to power.

THE TOPILTZIN QUETZALCOATL MATERIAL

In presenting these data, both the Durán and Alvarado Tezozomoc versions will be treated as essentially one, with significant variants in either being specifically noted.

Although Quetzalcoatl, as a god, is sporadically mentioned in the early portion of the two versions of this source, it is only in the later chapters that fuller mention is made of Topiltzin Quetzalcoatl of Tollan. The first significant notice is contained in the passage describing the carving of Motecuhzoma Ilhuicamina's effigy on the cliff at Chapoltepec (Durán 1951: 251; Alvarado Tezozomoc 1944a: 170–171). The two accounts here differ more than usual, but both mention the remarks exchanged by Motecuhzoma and the Cihuacoatl, Tlacaelel, as they gaze on the newly completed statue (or statues; in Durán's account, Tlacaelel's image was also carved). According to Durán, Motecuhzoma expresses his pleasure at seeing the effigies, which will be a perpetual reminder of their greatness. Then he recalls that it was written ("escrito," significantly, is the precise term employed) of "Quetzalcoatl y de Topiltzin" (*sic*) that when they departed they too left their images sculpted in wood and stone, which were worshipped by the common people, adding parenthetically, "y sauemos que eran hombres como nosotros." In Alvarado Tezozomoc's version, it is Tlacaelel who reminds Motecuhzoma that in other times, when the Mexica had just arrived in the region, "mandaron labrar y edificar al dios Quetzalcoatl," who went to the sky, saying that he would return and would bring with him "nuestros hermanos." This image, however, was carved in wood and gradually disintegrated, "que no hay memoria de ella," which has to be restored, since he is the god whom we all are awaiting, who departed through the sea of the sky.

Quetzalcoatl is again mentioned during the description of the funeral ceremonies of Axayacatl, when it is stated that the costume of this god was one of four with which a wooden image of the dead ruler was arrayed. From its description, it is clear that it was that of Ehecatl Quetzalcoatl (Durán 1951, I: 306; Alvarado Tezozomoc 1944a: 240–241). In any case, it points up the close connection of the Tenochca ruler with Quetzalcoatl, which is strikingly brought out in the next passage.

This is the coronation oration that was made to the new ruler, Tizoc, by his fellow ruler, Nezahualpilli of Tetzcoco (Alvarado Tezozomoc mistakenly calls him Nezahualcoyotl), in which he is charged that from that day forward he will occupy the throne "que primero pusieron Zenacatl y nacxitl quetzalcoatl, la caña sola no alcanzada de la culebra de preciada plumería," in whose name came Huitzilopochtli and later the first ruler of Mexico Tenochtitlan, Acamapichtli. Then he is reminded that this throne does not belong to him, but to them, that it is only loaned to him and will not endure forever but will eventually be returned to whom it really belongs (Alvarado Tezozomoc 1944a: 247). Durán's version is much more condensed but describes the position that the new ruler has inherited in more colorful terms, as the royal dais of rich and beautiful feathers and the chamber of precious stone that was left by "el dios Quetzalcoatl y el gran Topiltzin y del marauilloso y admirable Vitzilopochtli" that has only been loaned, "no para siempre, sino por algún tiempo" (Durán 1951, I: 322).

Alvarado Tezozomoc, in describing the funeral ceremonies of Tizoc, states that the third and last costume with which the image of the deceased was attired was that of Quetzalcoatl, whose insignia is itemized (Alvarado Tezozomoc 1944a: 265). It differs substantially from the Ehecatl Quetzalcoatl costume previously described by Durán as placed on a similar image of the dead Axayacatl. Durán (1951, I: 322), in this same place, states that the "cuerpo" of Tizoc, like that of his predecessor, was dressed "en semejança de los quatro dioses," but they are not named.

One of the most intriguing references to Topiltzin Quetzalcoatl is found only in Alvarado Tezozomoc. It appears near the end of the strange tale (recounted in both sources) of Motecuhzoma Xocoyotzin's plan to flee to the underworld cave of Cincalco, ruled over by last Toltec ruler, Huemac, to escape the dark future the omens seem to be prophesying for him. The person who dissuades him from carrying out his plan, the image and representative of Tezcatlipoca, Tzoncoztli (called Texiptla by Durán), later attempts to console the melancholy ruler by stressing the inevitability of fate and reminding him (Alvarado Tezozomoc 1944a: 514):

> . . . mirad, señor a lo que se trata de el Ceteuctli, que era un señor principal este Ceteuctli, que llevó consigo Quetzacoatl ¿no fueron a morir a Tlapalan, por la mar del cielo arriba y sus principales de ellos llamados Matlacxochitl y Ozomatli y Timal, que fueron estos los mayores nigrománticos del mundo en Tula, y al cabo no vinieron a morir que los llevó su rey y señor Quetzalcoatl, ni están ahora en el mundo?

The last series of references to Topiltzin Quetzalcoatl in the *Crónica X* is in the sections (Durán 1951, II: 3–35; Alvarado Tezozomoc 1944a: 517–536) that describe, somewhat confusedly, the events surrounding the first appearance of the Spaniards on the Gulf Coast (Juan de Grijalva, June 1519). Motecuhzoma, informed of their arrival by a native of Mictlancuauhtla (a town, now disappeared, near Veracruz), sends the Teuctlamacazqui Tlilancalqui and Cuitlalpitoc to investigate. When they return, corroborating the report, he prepares a number of gifts. These he entrusts to Tlilancalqui, instructing him to present them, along with a rich banquet of food, to those who have arrived, "que entiendo que es el dios que aguardamos Quetzalcoatl." He goes on to explain that "los viejos de Tulan" held for certain that their god Quetzalcoatl told them that he, or his sons, would return to rule again in Tulan "y en toda la comarca de esto mundo." He was also returning to repossess the riches that he had left hidden in the mountains when he went to the sky "a ver al otro dios," to the place called Tlapalan, "pues este trono, silla, y majestad suyo es, que de prestado lo tengo." The food is a test, for, if accepted, it will then be certain that he is Quetzalcoatl, "pues conoce ya la comidas de esta tierra y que el las dexó y vuelve al regosto de ellas." Motecuhzoma also assures Tlilancalqui that if, as a god, he prefers human flesh and kills and eats him, his inheritance will be protected and his sons amply rewarded. He orders Tlilancalqui to beseech the god to permit him to finish out his rule, and after his death he is welcome to reassume his throne, "pues es suyo y los dexó en guarda a mis antepasados."

Tlilancalqui fulfills his mission, presents the gifts and food to the Spaniards on board their ships, delivers Motecuhzoma's message via Marina, their interpreter (*sic*), and returns, after being assured by the newcomers that they are returning home and will not come again for some time. He also brings a number of Spanish gifts for Motecuhzoma, including some biscuits and a little wine. Motecuhzoma and his hunchback pages hesitantly taste this last. Then, afraid of eating the biscuits, "que era cosa de los dioses, que no quería usar de alguna irreverencia," he orders his priests to place them in a richly adorned vessel, covered with a fine cloth. This vessel is first placed in the cup-shaped depression in the great *cuauhxicalli* of the temple of Huitzilopochtli and incensed. Then the priests carry it to Tollan, where, after placing it in a stone chest, covered with mantles, they deliver it to the priests of Tollan (the late pre-Conquest community that succeeded the old Toltec capital), ordering them to bury it "en el templo que era de Quetzalcoatl," to the accompaniment of incensing, sacrifice of quail, and the blowing of conch shell trumpets.

Following which, Motecuhzoma remarks to his emissaries: "en verdad que tenía por cierto que estos dioses os habían comido, pero pues no fué así, tampoco comerían de nuestras comidas, habránlas olvidado, que há más de trescientos años que se fué Quetzalcoatl al cielo y al infierno." Regarding the other gifts, including strings of glass beads, he says: "Verdaderamente me ha hecho mucha merced el dios Quetzalcoatl, el que estaba y residió con nosotros en Tula, y creo verdaderamente ser el Ce acatl ynacxitl, el dios de la una caña caminador." Then he orders the beads buried at the feet of Huitzilopochtli, which is done "con tanta solenidad de encensarios y sonido de caracoles y otros instrumentos, como si fuera alguna cosa divina."

Finally, a wise elder of Xochimilco, Quilaztli, is found who tells of a prophesy that almost exactly corresponds to the reality reported by Tlilancalqui, complete to pictures of the strangers who are to conquer the land. He further predicts their speedy return, and Motecuhzoma arranges to have the coastline closely watched. Much time passes, and he recovers much of his former arrogance and pride and begins to believe they will not reappear after all. Then, when three (*sic*) years have passed, a messenger arrives, sent by the governor of the coastal province, Cuetlaxtlan, where they first landed, informing him that the strangers have returned. Motecuhzoma, at first struck dumb with shock and fear, finally recovers sufficiently to arrange a rapid messenger service to keep him advised of their movements. Notified that they are disembarking, he orders Tentlil, his governor, to provide them with food and other necessities.

Then Tlilancalqui is sent again to welcome the Spaniards in Motecuhzoma's name and to learn their intent. Arriving before Cortés and Marina, he tells them that his lord has sent him to inquire whether it is their intention to visit Mexico Tenochtitlan, where Motecuhzoma is governing his empire in his name, and, if so, "será tenido por dichoso de verle, y adorarle y ponerle su persona en su lugar." Marina answers that it is the intention of the captain to visit Motecuhzoma; after arranging his affairs on the coast, for which journey he requests guides. Tlilancalqui returns to Mexico with this reply, which Motecuhzoma this time receives stoically, now resigned to the death he is convinced will soon be his lot.

There follows one last attempt on Motecuhzoma's part to escape his fate, by sending sorcerers to bewitch and destroy the newcomers. This having failed, still believing that they might be eliminated in some fashion after their arrival in his city, he sends an important leader to be their guide and to arrange for their welcoming and provisioning in all of the towns along their route. After many vicissitudes, the Spaniards finally reach Mexico Tenochtitlan. Motecuhzoma, the ruler of the most powerful native state in North America, goes forth to meet the gods at the outskirts of the city. There, near the temple of the earth goddess, Toci, just off the southern causeway (Durán 1951, II: 35):

> Montezuma, por lengua de Marina, habló al Marqués y la dió la buena venida a aquella su ciudad de cuya vista y presencia el tanto holgaba y se recreaba y que pues el abía estado en su lugar y reynado y regido el reino que su padre el Dios Quetzalcoatl abía dexado, en cuyo asiento y estrado el indinamente se abía sentado y cuyos vasallos abía regido y gobernado, que si venía a gozar de el, que allí estaba a su servicio y que él hacía dejación de él, pues en las profecías de sus antepasados y relaciones lo hallaba profetizado y escrito; que los tomase mucho de hora buena, que el se sujetaba a su servicio, y que si no abía venido más que por velle; que él se lo tenía en muy gran merced y en ello abía recibido mucho gusto y contento y suma alegría en su corazón que descansese proveería con mucha abundancia.

SUMMARY

Summarizing these scattered notices, we find: (1) Quetzalcoatl, also called Topiltzin, Ce Acatl, and Nacxitl, was ruler of Tollan, where he had a temple that was still known as such at the time of the Conquest; (2) more than three hundred years earlier he had left, taking with him the following leaders, who were also great sorcerers: Ceteuctli, Matlacxochitl, Ozomatli, and Timal; (3) on his departure, he hid great treasures in the mountains, caves, and rivers; (4) he went to Tlapallan, disappearing across the eastern sea; (5) before he left, he promised to return, with his sons, to repossess his buried riches, his throne, and his dominion; (6) he was considered to be, in a sense, the founder of the royal power of the Mexico Tenochtitlan dynasty, whose rulers were considered his vice-regents, ruling in his name and only possessing a "borrowed" throne, which he was some day to reclaim; (7) both Grijalva and Cortés (confused in the account) were thought to be the returning Topiltzin Quetzalcoatl and treated as such by Motecuhzoma—who went so far as to voluntarily relinquish his throne to Cortés upon his entrance into Mexico Tenochtitlan.

COMMENT

In general outline, the information given in this source concerning Topiltzin Quetzalcoatl squares quite well with most of the other versions so far considered. Topiltzin Quetzalcoatl is, above all, the preeminent ruler, the founder of a great kingdom. Also strongly emphasized is his eventual return to reclaim his own. No source brings out more clearly the intimate connection between the dynasty of Mexico Tenochtitlan and TQ or describes more dramatically the "borrowed throne" concept. The final passages describing Motecuhzoma's dealings with the two Spanish expeditions are basically similar to Sahagún's native-authored version of the Conquest. Since these accounts were apparently independent (one might be considered the Tlatelolca version, the other the Tenochca), they can probably be regarded as essentially faithful renderings of the native tradition surrounding the early events of the Conquest that was current in the middle years of the sixteenth century. They are historically inaccurate in numerous instances, especially the *Crónica X* version, which strikingly illustrates the rapidity of legend formation in native Mexico concerning even recent events—and which behooves us to maintain a judiciously critical attitude in considering the possible historicity of events that occurred hundreds of years before the Conquest.

6. The *Historia de Tlaxcala* of Diego Muñoz Camargo

THE SOURCE

An unusual amount of identificatory confusion has surrounded this author and his work. Now, however, owing largely to the careful researches of Charles Gibson, the picture is considerably clarified. He was the son of a conquistador, Diego Muñoz, who arrived in New Spain in 1524. His mother was apparently a Tlaxcalteca. At any rate, he seems to have been born in Tlaxcallan, where his father had economic interests, in 1528 or 1529. He married a member of the native dynasty of Ocotelolco, the most powerful of the four sixteenth-century *cabeceras* of Tlaxcallan. One of his sons, with whom he has been regularly confused since he bore the same name, served as governor of that province from 1608 to 1614. The historian himself held many important administrative posts in the local government of Tlaxcallan, including that of official interpreter (he seems to have had a full mastery of both Spanish and Nahuatl)—and, in addition, has been characterized by Gibson as "one of five or six largest entrepreneurs of sixteenth-century Tlaxcala." Although a mestizo, he "repeatedly identified himself with native interests" and served as the interpreter for the group of four Tlaxcallan leaders who visited the Spanish court in 1583, seeking special privileges from the Crown. He died in 1599 or early 1600 (Gibson 1950).

The *Historia de Tlaxcala* seems to have been composed between 1576 (Carrera Stampa 1945: 102) and sometime in the late 1590s (probably post-1596, since Mendieta is cited). A *terminus ante quem*, is provided, of course, by his death in 1599/1600. It presents a fairly detailed history of Tlaxcallan from earliest times to the late sixteenth century. The *Historia* was used extensively by Torquemada. All modern editions of the work, commencing with Ternaux-Compans's 1843 paraphrastic edition in French translation, are ultimately derived from an incomplete (lacking the beginning and end), late sixteenth- or early seventeenth-century manuscript, discovered by Boturini (catalogue § XVIII, No. 3)—which is now in the Bibliothèque Nationale, Paris (Aubin-Goupil collection, Manuscrit Mexicaine Num. 210; Gibson 1952: 238–245). I have used the Mexican edition of 1947–1948, which is based on a composite manuscript of José F. Ramírez, compared with the Cahuantzi manuscript that was apparently copied in 1836 directly from the Boturini manuscript, at that time in the library of the Universidad de México.

THE TOPILTZIN QUETZALCOATL MATERIAL

Two quite distinct Quetzalcoatls appear in the early chapters of the *Historia*. Only one will be considered in this section; the other is discussed at length below. The reasons for this split treatment will become clear as the discussion proceeds.

In chapter V, Muñoz Camargo, probably basing himself here on a Tlaxcalteca pictorial history, describes the migration of the Teochichimeca ancestors of the Tlaxcalteca from the crossing of a "pasage del agua y río o estrecho de mar" to Poyauhtlan in the Basin of Mexico, from where they later migrated to Tlaxcallan. In the year 5 Tochtli they reached the Seven Caves (Chicomoztoc). From there, they moved to Mazatepec, where they left Itztotli (Itztlotli) and Xiuhnel, "personas principales." Arriving at Tepenenec ("que quiere decir en el cerro del Eco"), they killed Itzpapalotl, Mimich shooting her with arrows. They then moved on to Comallan, "donde tuvieron grande guerra," until they conquered it, afterwards migrating to Colhuacan, Teotlacochcalco, and Teohuitznahuac. Here they intended to kill with arrows a chieftainess named Coatlicue, "Señora de esta provincia," but instead "hicieron amistades con ella"—and Mixcoatl Camaxtli took her for a wife, from which union Quetzalcoatl was born. Muñoz Camargo then refers to his other, earlier account of Quetzalcoatl, pointing out that, although *that* Quetzalcoatl came "por la parte del Norte y por Panuco," all these others (i.e., the Teochichimeca) came from the West, "e que como fuesen personas tan principales y de grandes habilidades, los tuvieron por dioses, especialmante Camaxtli, Quetzalcoatl y Tezcatlipoca, y todos los demás ídolos." He then suggests that these deified leaders must have been sorcerers who "tenían hecho pacto o conveniecia con el demonio."

Quetzalcoatl, having been born in this province of "Teohuitznahuatl," a certain Xicalan "les hizo grandes fiestas" and presented them with plentiful gifts of cotton clothing. From here they moved on to Colhuacan, and the remainder of the account concerns the genealogical background of the dynasty of Tetzcoco, their further wanderings, and their eventual establishment in the northern Basin of Puebla. Quetzalcoatl does not reappear again until the Chollollan massacre episode of the Conquest, where he is prominently mentioned as the patron god of that unfortunate city.

SUMMARY

This extremely brief and obviously truncated account can be concisely summarized thus: (1) Quetzalcoatl was born to Mixcoatl/Camaxtli, a leader of the migrating Teochichimeca ancestors of the Tlaxcalteca, and Coatlicue, a chieftainess of a province called Teohuitznahuac, who, first threatened by the Teochichimeca, later entered into friendly relations with them; (2) following Quetzalcoatl's birth, a great feast is given by a leader named Xicalan, accompanied by gifts of cotton clothing, following which the Teochichimeca move on to Collhuacan and eventually, after further wanderings and conquests, reach Tlaxcallan.

COMMENT

We are obviously dealing here with only a historical snatch, but the account of Quetzalcoatl's birth parallels that of some other versions we have examined. The designation of his mother as Coatlicue is also significant (cf. Topiltzin Quetzalcoatl's song in the *Anales de Cuauhtitlan*). Of Quetzalcoatl's later career and connection with Tollan, nothing is said. Whether this was suppressed by Muñoz Camargo or was lacking in the source he was following is impossible to determine. At any rate, this brief passage does provide us with one more account of the birth of our hero, apparently in this case derived from Tlaxcalteca sources.

C. Sources Supplying Important Fragments of Information

The information concerning Topiltzin Quetzalcoatl supplied by the sources of this group, although scanty, is often important. As usual, each will be considered in approximate chronological order.

1. The Second *Carta de relación* of Fernando Cortés

THE SOURCE

This important document is dated October 30, 1520, at Segura de la Frontera (Tepeyacac), having been composed in the period between the Spaniards' evacuation of Mexico Tenochtitlan and their reentry into the Basin of Mexico. Although often sketchy and by no means infallible, its contemporaneity with the events it describes and the fact that it was authored by no less a person than the commander himself make it the most valuable account extant of the early stages of the conquest of Mexico. Sent to Spain, probably in 1521, it was first published in November of the following year in Seville. Since then it has been republished numerous times. I have used the Buenos Aires edition of 1946 (Cortés 1946).

THE TOPILTZIN QUETZALCOATL MATERIAL

The name Quetzalcoatl, or Topiltzin, was probably unknown to Cortés when the letter was written—or to any other member of his army. But the account given of Motecuhzoma's speech to Cortés shortly after the latter's entrance into Tenochtitlan, and the same ruler's later address to the assembled subrulers of his dominion at the time of his swearing allegiance to Charles V, almost certainly contain references to Topiltzin Quetzalcoatl—perhaps merged (or confused) with Huitzilopochtli. The first, differing from the native accounts previously considered, was delivered, according to Cortés, in the palace of Axayacatl, Motecuhzoma's father, in the center of Tenochtitlan, soon after the Spaniards had occupied it. Motecuhzoma, after presenting him with a rich gift, seated himself near Cortés and, through Marina and Jerónimo de Aguilar, addressed the Spanish leader. He told him that they, "por nuestras escrituras . . . de nuestros antepasados," had known for a long time that they were not the aborigines of the land but had migrated hence from very distant parts. They also knew that they had been conducted to their destination by "un señor, cuyos vasallos todos eran," who returned to his native land. After a long time he came back, but by this time those who had remained had married the native women, produced offspring, and founded towns. When he sought to have them return with him, they refused, nor would they recognize him as lord. He departed, and they had always held that his descendants would someday come to conquer the land and his former vassals.

Motecuhzoma then explained to Cortés that, according to the direction from which he said he had come, where the sun rises, and from the things that he told about this great lord or king who sent him, he, Motecuhzoma, believed for certain that Cortés is "nuestro señor natural," especially since he told them that for some time he had known of them. He goes on to promise to obey Cortés as the representative of that great lord, without lack or deception, and to place all that he possesses at his disposal. He bids the Spaniards to rest, explaining to their commander that he has been well informed of all of their movements. He also cautions him not to place any stock in what his enemies may have told him, such as exaggerated tales concerning his fabulous riches or his divinity. To make this last point, he pulls aside his mantle and displays his naked body, saying, "Véisme aquí que soy de carne y hueso como vos y como cada uno, y que soy mortal y palpable." Finally, after offering Cortés all that he desires of "algunas cosas de oro" left him by his ancestors, he promises to keep his guests well provided and free from annoyance, since "estáis en vuestra casa y naturaleza" (Cortés 1946: 160–162).

Motecuhzoma's later "abdication speech" to his assembled subrulers (Cortés 1946: 178–180) is nearly identical, but the unnamed great lord's promise to return or to send a force "con tal poder que los pudiese costreñir y atraer a su servicio," which was implied but not explicitly stated in the first speech, is here made explicit. He also requests them, since their ancestors did not fulfill their obligations to their former lord, to now do so and to give thanks to their gods "porque en nuestros tiempos vino lo que tanto aquellos esperaban." He ends by requesting them to render all of the tributes and services they had formerly rendered to him to their new master.

SUMMARY

(1) The people of Motecuhzoma had migrated to their present homes from distant parts, led by a great lord; (2) the latter had returned to this original homeland; (3) when he returned, some time later, he found his former subjects so well settled in their new country that they refused his request to return with him, also refusing to accept him as ruler; (4) he departed, promising to return or to send those who would subject them and reestablish his dominion; (5) Cortés was considered to be the representative of this great lord, a view based principally on the direction from which the Spaniards came and Cortés's informing Motecuhzoma that his sovereign had known of him.

COMMENT

Most of the elements of these remarkable speeches, recorded so carefully, perhaps almost too carefully, by Cortés correlate fairly well with some of the other versions of the Topiltzin Quetzalcoatl of Tollan Tale previously examined. A new twist, however, is the departure and later return of the unnamed lord, followed by his departure *for the second time*, after unsuccessfully attempting to persuade his subjects to return with him.

To perhaps explain this apparent anomaly, we should keep in mind the complicated method of transmission of the discourse between Motecuhzoma and Cortés: first, Motecuhzoma to Marina in the most elegant brand of Nahuatl (which she perhaps did not fully comprehend in the first instance, since her own Coatzacoalco dialect must have been somewhat distinct from that of the imperial capital); next, Marina to Aguilar, undoubtedly in Tabasco Chontal Maya (Putun), which the latter must have had some difficulty in understanding, since the Maya he had picked up had been a variety of east coast Yucatec; and, finally, Aguilar to Cortés, in Spanish. For simple, direct ideas the system probably worked quite well, but for anything as complex as this elegant, formal speech of Motecuhzoma the chance for error creeping into this elongated, complex linguistic circuit was clearly very great. In addition, even if Aguilar's version had been close to that uttered by Motecuhzoma, Cortés, with little understanding of the culture and history of the natives at this point in time, may not have fully comprehended it. I suspect, in fact, that Cortés used the second speech for both, for this abdication proceeding, as Cortés himself tells us, was duly notarized in characteristic sixteenth-century Spanish fashion. Thus, at the time of writing he may well have had a written document to consult (it seems unlikely that all such records were lost during "La Noche Triste"). The virtual identity of the two speeches lends support to this view. In any case, although there was probably confusion concerning the supposed return and redeparture of the ancient, unnamed lord, the basic import of the speech can probably be accepted as authentic, since it fits so well with other information.

These two speeches by Motecuhzoma, as recorded by Cortés, will always remain one of our principal sources on Topiltzin Quetzalcoatl, in spite of the fact that his name nowhere appears, for both are, by quite a margin, the earliest notices putatively concerning him that have survived. In my view, they strongly support the case for the authenticity of the belief in the return of Topiltzin Quetzalcoatl and the very real part it may have played in influencing Motecuhzoma's initial responses to the arrival of the Spaniards.

It is also worth pointing out that the same general gist of one or the other of the speeches is also provided by three other Conquest participants, Andrés de Tapia, Bernal Díaz del Castillo, and Fray Francisco de Aguilar. I would not overrate their value, however, for they wrote long after the events and perhaps had access to published versions of the Cortesian letters, which they might have consulted to refresh their memories. Nearly every later chronicler of the conquest of Mexico also records one or both of these speeches, but since all or most obviously derived their versions—often with various embellishments and mild distortions—from that of Cortés, they need not be considered.

2. The *Relación sobre la conquista de México* of Andrés de Tapia

THE SOURCE

Andrés de Tapia, who played an important role in the conquest of Mexico as one of the principal captains of Cortés, wrote a *relación* of that enterprise that presents a reasonably complete narrative of the principal events up to the defeat of Pánfilo de Narváez. This important eyewitness account was used by López de Gómara (1552) in his account of the Conquest and the career of Cortés but was not itself published until 1866 by García Icazbalceta, from a manuscript in the library of El Escorial, near Madrid.

The *Relación sobre la conquista de México* bears no date. Henry Wagner (1944: xv, 190) surmised that Tapia wrote it for López de Gómara while he was in Spain with Cortés, 1539–1547, probably circa 1543. The *terminus ante quem* is provided by the date of first publication of López de Gómara's history of the Conquest, 1552. Tapia's brief but important passage relating to Topiltzin Quetzalcoatl probably possesses special value because he was *encomendero* of Chalollan for a short time after the Conquest (until 1526) and may have received his information from the town elders, with whom he most likely would have had some dealings.

THE TOPILTZIN QUETZALCOATL MATERIAL

In his account of the Spanish stay in Chollolan while en route to Mexico Tenochtitlan in the fall of 1519, Tapia states that the principal god of this great religious/mercantile center was originally a man who had lived in former times and who was called "Quezalquate." He had founded the city and had ordered them not to kill men but to erect edifices to the creator of the sun and the sky where they should sacrifice only quail and other game. He further decreed that they should not harm or hate each other. It was said that he wore a white garment like a friar's robe and over it a mantle covered with red crosses. They possessed certain green stones, one of them carved in the shape of a monkey's head, which they said had belonged to this man and which they kept as relics (Tapia 1866: 573).

COMMENT

A formal summary of this interesting little capsule is hardly necessary. Although incipient Christian influence may explain the white robe and the mantle sown with red crosses (but cf. the pictorial representation of Topiltzin Quetzalcoatl in the *Codex Vaticanus A*, Color Plate 6 [see also Beyer 1920]), nothing else seems significantly out of line with the other versions so far considered. It is worth noting that, in spite of his ascription to him of friarish garb, Tapia does not characterize Quetzalcoatl as a white man; even the ubiquitous beard is not mentioned. Nor is he connected in any way with Tollan. It is also interesting that Tapia does not associate this deified founder of Chollolan with the lord who was to return, about whom Motecuhzoma told Cortés, even though the *Relación* does contain a summary of the Tenochca ruler's second speech. Perhaps he was unaware of a prophecy of return connected with the Quetzalcoatl of Chollolan; at any rate, it is significantly absent in his account.

3. Letter of Viceroy Antonio de Mendoza to his Brother, Diego de Mendoza

THE SOURCE

A copy of this letter, sent by the viceroy of New Spain in 1540 to his brother, then Spanish ambassador to the Republic of Venice, was sent to the first official chronicler of the Indies, Gonzalo Fernández de Oviedo y Valdés, then resident in Santo Domingo, by Diego de Mendoza's secretary, Giovanni Battista Ramusio. Oviedo gave a paraphrase of it in book 14, second part, chapter 50 (1851–1855, III: 531–535) of his monumental work on the early history of the Spanish New World empire.

THE TOPILTZIN QUETZALCOATL MATERIAL

Although this letter does not actually deal with Quetzalcoatl at all, but with Huitzilopochtli, its relevance to our theme will become apparent during the following summary. It presents a strange and remarkably garbled account of the Mexica migration, the founding of Mexico Tenochtitlan, and the lives of "Guateçuma" and Motecuhzoma. It begins with the coming from the north ("hacia la provincia de Panuco") of "un capitán que llamaban Orchilobos," with four hundred well-accoutered men, bearing arms of silver and gold. "Mexico" at this time was at war with "Tascala." Orchilobos and his men successfully aid the former to defeat the latter. He then founds a settlement on an islet in the lake, building a small "torre de piedra" that afterwards becomes "templo mayor de Orchilobos consagrado a su nombre." From there he gradually subdues the surrounding territory, "hasta hacerse señor de Mexico." His settlement having grown into a substantial city, he promulgates laws, the most important of which is one decreeing that the "más valiente e mayor capitán" should be their ruler. He also gives them ceremonies, "orden de sacrificios," and laws concerning combats and duels. He finally assembled all the people of the city and delivered a long speech in which he explained that he was sent from God and desired to return to him and that they should await him, "que quando ellos más nescessidad tuviessen volvería a ellos." He then departed, going to "la parte de Guatimala," from where it is believed he left for Peru, since it was reported there that "hallan cierta orden de sacrificios e vestigios de Orchilobos."

The account goes on to relate that Mexico remained without a ruler for many years, then proceeds to give a very garbled etymology of Tenochtitlan ("Temistitan"). A ruler was finally elected, "e de uno en otro vinieron a Guateçuma," elected because of his virtue and courage, "e porque fabulosamente decían ser hijo de Orchilobos." A virgin, serving in the temple of Orchilobos, was one day cleaning the idol. A feather fell, which she took and placed in her breast, after which she slept and dreamed that Orchilobos came and slept with her. She became pregnant and gave birth to Guateçuma. "Por excusarse de la peña e por hacer mayor su hijo," she told what had happened but was not believed and was banished from the city. She went to another province, declaring "como en profecía" that her child would be king. Afterwards, Guateçuma coming of age, he turned out to be so valiant that they say he conquered twenty-five "campos por su persona." Since he was so esteemed and more handsome than the others, "dieron fee a la fábula de su madre" and made him captain against Tascala, "los quales fueron siempres perpetuos enemigos suyos." He conquered those of Tascala and died there.

Then the account switches abruptly to "Monteçuma," who, while still only twelve years old, was made captain against the surrounding provinces, which through his courage were subdued, including Tascala, following which they elected him "señor de la tierra." He was so prudent and wise that "quassi lo adoraban" and so valiant that "por su persona venció diez y ocho campos." When Cortés arrived, he was well received, since he was believed to be

Orchilobos, "el qual en su cuenta dellos avía quatrocientos años que era partido." All this and other histories they had "en sus libros de sacrificios escriptos por figuras," which the viceroy had had interpreted to send to His Majesty, with a book "que hace hacer de la descripción particular de las provincias, pueblos, e fructos de la tierra, e leyes, e costumbres e orígenes de la gente."

SUMMARY

(1) Tenochtitlan was founded by Huitzilopochtli, coming with four hundred followers from the north, near Panuco, after he had aided those of "Mexico" in a war with Tlaxcallan; (2) he conquers the surrounding territory, becomes lord of the land, and introduces various laws and customs; (3) he departs, after telling his people to expect him, for he will return when they are most in need of him; (4) he goes to Guatemala and from there possibly to Peru; (5) after an interim of some years, another ruler is selected, different ones succeeding one another until "Guateçuma" is reached, thought to be the son of Huitzilopochtli by miraculous conception; (6) his mother, a temple virgin, becomes pregnant after placing a feather in her breast and dreaming of sexual relations with Huitzilopochtli; (7) driven from Mexico Tenochtitlan after the birth of her son, she prophesies that he will become king; (8) when of age, Guateçuma, because of his valor, is chosen captain against Tlaxcallan, which he conquers, although he is killed there; (9) Motecuhzoma pursues a similar career, also conquers Tlaxcallan, and is almost adored as a god for his prudence and wisdom; (10) when Cortés arrives, he is thought to be the returning Huitzilopochtli, who was believed to have departed four hundred years before.

COMMENT

It is difficult to appraise this puzzlingly aberrant account. Apparently the legends of Topiltzin Quetzalcoatl and Huitzilopochtli, the patron god and, in some accounts, deified leader of the migrating Mexica, have been thoroughly confused and intermingled. The account of "Guateçuma" is particularly strange. It appears to be a badly garbled account of the life of the elder Motecuhzoma (*Gua* = *hue*[*hue*]; *teçuma* = [Mon]*tezuma*??), who, according to the *Crónica Mexicayotl*, was also miraculously conceived and who also, according to the *Origen de los Mexicanos*, spent a period of exile in Huexotzinco before being accepted in Mexico Tenochtitlan as ruler. The version of the miraculous conception here, on the other hand, strikingly recalls Sahagún's account of the birth of Huitzilopochtli. As we have seen, Topiltzin Quetzalcoatl in some accounts was also supernaturally conceived.

It is possible that a prophecy of return was associated with both Quetzalcoatl and Huitzilopochtli. In this connection, it is worth pointing out that the unnamed lord mentioned in Motecuhzoma's speech to Cortés would fit the latter as well, if not better, than the former. However, no other source supports this, and a confusion—and/or some blending—with Topiltzin Quetzalcoatl seems more likely.

4. Viceroy Mendoza's Letter to Oviedo

THE SOURCE

Viceroy Mendoza also wrote a letter addressed to Oviedo, dated October 6, 1541, in response to a query directed to the former by the latter concerning the origin of the Mexicans, which was quoted in the latter's chronicle (book 14, second part, chapter 52; Oviedo 1851–1855, III: 536–539).

THE TOPILTZIN QUETZALCOATL MATERIAL

In his letter, Mendoza denies having stated that the Mexicans came up from the south, and goes on to express his opinion that they came from the north, "e assi lo dicen e se muestra en edeficios antiguos, y en nombres de lugares por donde vinieron." He further states, referring to Oviedo's mention of Mexicans in Nicaragua: "E pues allegaron hasta Guacacalco con un señor que se llamaba Quetçalcoatl, no tengo a mucho que passassen otros a León [Nicaragua]."

SUMMARY

From this brief statement we learn: (1) the "Mexicans" migrated from the north; (2) they passed on as far as Coatzacoalco with a lord named Quetzalcoatl.

COMMENT

Mendoza here has either confused the later Mexica migration with the earlier Toltec movement in the direction of Coatzacoalco, or is using the term "Mexicano" in a general linguistic (= Nahua-speakers) sense. The latter seems quite probable in view of the fact that the discussion is concerned with the presence of Nahua-speakers in Nicaragua. Although only a tidbit, its clear association of Quetzalcoatl with a migration to Coatzacoalco, combined with its very early date, gives this brief statement by New Spain's first viceroy genuine pertinence.

5. The *Historia Tolteca-Chichimeca*

THE SOURCE

This anonymous native chronicle, containing both an extensive text, in Nahuatl, and accompanying illustrations, undoubtedly derived from a pre-Hispanic pictorial history, was composed, probably around 1544–1545, in Cuauhtinchan, an important Nahuatl/Popoloca-speaking polity southeast of Chollollan. It describes the last days of Tollan, the abandonment of that center by two groups, the Nonoalco Chichimeca and the Tolteca Chichimeca; their subsequent migration to the Basin of Puebla; the struggle of the latter with the Olmeca Xicallanca, whom they found established there (with their capital at Cholollan); their enlisting the aid of seven groups of Chichimeca living at Colhuatepec/Chicomoztoc; the migration of these latter into the same area; the overthrow of the Olmeca Xicallanca; and the subsequent history of the zone, with emphasis on the history of Cuauhtinchan and its immediate neighbors, down to 1544.

The manuscript, or a cognate, was apparently utilized by the compiler of the *Anales de Cuauhtitlan*. It was later part of the Boturini collection (Catalogue § I, No. 1), and, passing through the hands of León y Gama, Aubin, and Goupil, it eventually reached the Bibliothèque National, Paris, where it is now located (Manuscrit Mexicaine, Nums. 46–50, 51–53, 54–58). Although used in manuscript by various investigators during the late nineteenth and early twentieth centuries, it was not published in its entirety until 1937, with the Nahuatl text and German translation by Konrad Preuss and Ernst Mengin in parallel columns. Ten years later, a Spanish translation by Heinrich Berlin of the German translation was published in Mexico (with the Nahuatl text checked by Silvia Rendón), accompanied by a useful introduction by Paul Kirchhoff. In 1942, a facsimile of the entire manuscript was published in Copenhagen but not distributed until 1946–1947. I have used the German and Spanish editions, in conjunction. I cite by paragraphs, which are identical in both editions.

THE TOPILTZIN QUETZALCOATL MATERIAL

This chronicle actually contains very few references to Quetzalcoatl, since it deals with a period subsequent to the time during which he flourished; but the few that it does contain are of considerable interest. The first is found near the beginning, when the two factions in Tollan, the Nonoalca Chichimeca and the Tolteca Chichimeca, are in conflict (brought about by the behavior of the ruler Huemac, who had been raised by the latter group). There it is related that the Nonoalco Chichimeca, having resolved to abandon Tollan, during the night hid all the wealth, the property of Quetzalcoatl, and all guarded it (§ 32).

Quetzalcoatl is not mentioned again until paragraph 85, in connection with the "scouting expedition" of Couenan, the priest of the Tolteca Chichimeca (who, fifteen years after the departure of the Nonoalca Chichimeca, are also resolved to abandon Tollan), to the Tlalchiuhaltepetl, the Great Pyramid of Chololan, where he performs religious rites. Seeing the attractiveness of the region and the prosperity of its Olmeca Xicallanca inhabitants, he prays to Ipalnemohuani, "Through Whom All Live," requesting that he grant the Toltecs this region. And Quetzalcoatl is named as answering, consoling the sacerdotal scout and promising him that Chololan will be theirs. Couenan returns to his superiors in Tollan, where he reports what he has seen and recounts the favorable promise of "Topiltzin Quetzalcoatl." The Toltec leaders then assemble their people, telling them of the command of "Topiltzin Quetzalcoatl Nacxitl Tepeuhqui," after which theTolteca Chichimeca undertake their migration, by a somewhat circuitous route, to Cholollan.

Quetzalcoatl is only mentioned twice more: first, in paragraph 330, when, in the year 7 Acatl (1187?), it is related that Cuextlaxtlan was conquered and (afterward?), as was customary, the "chichimeca, totomiuaque, quauhtinchantlaca, texcalteca, malpantlaca, zacateca, tzauhteca, and acolchichimeca" visited again in Cholollan the house of the "demon" (*tlacatecolotl*), Quetzalcoatl, offering quail, serpents, deer, and rabbits, placing feathers on the "Coamomoztli" (serpent platform oratory). Finally (§ 337), in the year 3 Acatl (1235?), the Huexotzinca, enemies of the "Tolteca Tolteca," shot arrows at Quetzalcoatl (the face of Quetzalcoatl), i.e., wage war against Cholollan (desecrating the great shrine?), following which there is a severe famine in Cholollan.

SUMMARY

These brief references inform us that: (1) the goods and wealth of Quetzalcoatl were still in Tollan at the time of its abandonment and were hidden by the Nonoalca Chichimeca when they departed; (2) the Great Pyramid of Cholollan, Tlachiuhaltepetl, seems to have functioned as a shrine (and oracle?) to Quetzalcoatl under Olmec rule; (3) Topiltzin Quetzalcoatl and Topiltzin Quetzalcoatl Nacxitl Tepeuhqui are given as names for our hero; (4) the Quetzalcoatl shrine at Cholollan was apparently an object of pilgrimage on the part of the "Chichimec" peoples of Puebla after the establishment of the Toltecs there.

COMMENT

Although the information on Topiltzin Quetzalcoatl contained in this valuable early native-authored source is disappointingly brief, it does point up the clear preservation of at least some elements of the Topiltzin Quetzalcoatl of Tollan Tale in the Pueblan region. In addition, it provides two significant new facts: (1) Cholollan apparently contained a shrine to Quetzalcoatl (the Great Pyramid?) even before its conquest by the Tolteca Chichimeca coming from Tollan (unless the later situation was projected back into the past); and (2) the name "Tepeuhqui" was applied to our hero, in addition to his other standard epithets.

6. The *Relación de Cholula* of Gabriel de Rojas

THE SOURCE

This *relación geográfica*, one of the most informative of the 1579–1585 series (for this series of *relaciones geográphicas*, see H. Cline 1964) is dated 1581 and was compiled by Gabriel de Rojas, the *corregidor* at that time; it is accompanied by a colored map of colonial Cholula and its *barrios*. The complete *relación* was published in 1927 by Gómez de Orozco, from a copy made from the original sixteenth-century manuscript by García Icazbalceta, to whom the original belonged (now in the Benson Latin American Collection of the University of Texas, Austin).

THE TOPILTZIN QUETZALCOATL MATERIAL

In his answer to question 13, as posed in the manuscript (H. Cline 1964), Rojas explains the native name for the city, "Tullam Chollullam Tlachiuhaltepetl." After giving their etymologies, he states that the inhabitants claimed that the founders of the city came from a town called "tullam," "del qual por ser muy lejos y auer mucho tiempo no se tiene noticia," and that "de camino" they founded the Tullam, located twelve leagues from Mexico, and "Tullamtzinco," after which they founded Cholollan and also called it Tullam. In his answer to question 14, Rojas states that the two theocrats who ruled Chololllan, Aquiach and Tlalquiach, resided in the principal temple of the city, which was called "Quetçalcoatl," where the Franciscan convent was built. This temple was founded in honor of "un capitán que truxó la gente desta ciudad antiguamente a poblar en ella de Partes muy Remotas hazia el poniente que no sabe certinidad dello," whose name was "Quetçalcoatl," after whose death the temple was erected to him (Rojas 1927: 160).

Later, Rojas (1927: 161) describes the image of Quetzalcoatl in the temple as "hecha de buelto y con barba larga," which was beseeched to grant "buenos temporales salud y sociego y Paz en su República." He also states that the two high priests who ruled Chololllan regularly confirmed in their offices "todos los gouernadores y Reyes desta nueua españa," who would come to Chololllan to render "obediencia al ydolo della quetçalcoatl," to which they offered precious feathers, mantles, gold, precious stones, and other valuable things. After making this obeisance and presenting their offerings, they were placed in a little edifice set apart for this purpose, where the two high priests pierced their earlobes, nasal septums, or lower lips (for insertion of jewels) "según el señorío que tenían," which constituted a confirmation of their titles—following which they returned to their homes.

Finally, Rojas states that offerings were brought by "los indios que de toda la tierra uenían por su deboción en Romería a visitar el templo de queçalcoatl porque este era metropoli y tenido en tanta veneración como lo es Roma en la christiandad y meca en los moros" (Rojas 1927: 162).

SUMMARY

These brief remarks of Rojas inform us that: (1) Chololllan was founded by a group that came originally from a distant mythical place called Tollan, in honor of which they named the historic Tollan and Tollantzinco, and from which they had come to establish themselves at Cholollan, also called Tollan; (2) the principal temple was called Quetzalcoatl and was raised, after his death, to honor a "captain" with this name, who had conducted the founders of the city to it from the remote west; (3) the image of Quetzalcoatl stood in the temple, was large in size, with a long beard; (4) the two sacerdotal co-rulers of the city customarily confirmed in their offices the rulers of the land, who came to Chololan, made obeisance before Quetzalcoatl, and received their formal investiture by the standard ear, nasal septum, and lip-piercing ceremony; (5) Chololan was a great pilgrimage center, comparable in significance to Jerusalem for the Christians and Mecca for the Moslems.

COMMENT

Here again, as in Andrés de Tapia, we find Quetzalcoatl being named as a leader who founded Chololan, afterwards revered as a god. However, it is possible that Quetzalcoatl as founder of the historic Tollan has been confused with Quetzalcoatl as founder of Tollan Chollolan. The circumstances surrounding the establishment of the former center might well have been transferred to the latter, to enhance the prestige and antiquity of the new Toltec headquarters. Alternatively, this "founding" may only refer to the coming of Topiltzin Quetzalcoatl to Chololan during his "flight" to the Gulf Coast.

Rojas's account fully confirms the information provided by a number of other sources concerning the importance of Quetzalcoatl at Chololan. Coming from a person who was intimately associated with the town and who undoubtedly consulted its learned elders while compiling his *relación*, this confirmation has a special importance. The clear statement concerning Quetzalcoatl's original humanity is also worth noting, as well as the long beard that the image supposedly displayed. Even more significant was the ascription to the dual high priests of Quetzalcoatl at Chololan of the power to invest rulers with political office. The special significance of this will become clearer when the Highland Guatemala sources are considered in Part II.

Although none of the sources in the following group supplies substantial new information concerning the Basic Topiltzin Quetzalcoatl of Tollan Tale, the scraps they do provide often significantly corroborate or supplement the fuller data contained in the sources previously considered. As usual, each will be considered in turn—in roughly chronological order.

D. Sources Providing Only Scraps of Information

1. The Anonymous Conqueror

THE SOURCE

This interesting account of the customs of the natives of New Spain, ascribed to a "gentil'huomo del signor Fernando Cortese," was first published, in 1556, in an Italian translation by Giovanni Battista Ramusio; the Spanish original has been lost. There have been many speculations concerning its authorship. Bustamante (1840) suggested Francisco de Terrazas, Cortés's mayordomo. More recently, Wagner (1944: xv–xvi) suggested Andrés de Tapia. Gómez de Orozco (1953) even doubted that the author was a member of the Cortesian army, but this view seems extreme. The standard Spanish translation (plus a re-edition of the Italian) is that of García Icazbalceta (1858–1866, I: 568–598), but the only complete Spanish version was published by León Díaz Cárdenas in 1941. Saville (Anonymous Conqueror 1917) also published an English translation of García Icazbalceta's Spanish translation.

THE TOPILTZIN QUETZALCOATL MATERIAL

The only mention of Quetzalcoatl in this source is in the passage where the author is explaining that the principal god bore different names in different provinces, being called "Horchilobos" in Mexico and "Quecadquaal" in

"Chuennila" (Anonymous Conqueror 1941: 35). Although this scrap, of course, does not provide anything new, it does stand as one of the earliest published mentions of Quetzalcoatl by name. It also may indicate that the association of Quetzalcoatl with Chalollan was known fairly early to at least some members of the Cortesian army.

2. The *Relación de Coatepec Chalco* of Francisco de Villacastín

THE SOURCE

This *relación geográfica*, dated October 28, 1579, was written by the "escribano e intérprete" Francisco de Villacastín, acting for the *comendador* Cristóbal de Salazar, the *corregidor* at that time of this Nahuatl-speaking community, located in the southeast Basin of Mexico. It was first published in 1905 by Paso y Troncoso, from the original sixteenth-century manuscript in the Archive of the Indies, Seville.

THE TOPILTZIN QUETZALCOATL MATERIAL

In his answer to question 4, as posed in the manuscript, Salazar recounts some tales of the natives relating to a "sierra alta" south of the town, which bore the name Quetzalcoatl. This god, in ancient times, would frequently appear in both his feathered-serpent and human forms. On the rocky cliffs, "parescen oy día" the footprints and the concavity where he "estubo echada" and where he was seen in his human form climbing these cliffs on his knees, dragging a staff, "se paresce vna canaleja en la dicha peña." The account then goes on to describe the great noises that this "demonio" made, telling how he was transformed into stone, in human form, holding a staff, which effigy was later worshipped as an idol.

COMMENT

Although most of this account of the "demonio" of the mountain called Quetzalcoatl relates to the latter in his purely supernatural manifestation, the description of the footprints and other marks left in the solid rock forcibly recalls the Temacpalco incident in Sahagún's account of the Tollan to Tlapallan journey of Topiltzin Quetzalcoatl. It is probable that certain natural markings on the cliffs were taken to be the impressions of Quetzalcoatl's body and the groove worn by his staff—from which belief the hill received its name. Later, a series of marvelous tales apparently became current concerning the frequent apparition of Quetzalcoatl himself, in both human and serpentine guise, on the mountain, the original significance of the rock impressions probably having faded in importance.

3. The *Relación de Ahuatlan y su partido* of Salvador de Cárdenas

THE SOURCE

This *relación geográfica*, dated August 24, 1581, was written by Salvador de Cárdenas, the *corregidor* of four Nahuatl-speaking towns in the southern Basin of Puebla: Ahuatlan, Texalocan, Zoyatitlanapan, and Coatzinco. It was first published in 1905 by Paso y Troncoso, from the original sixteenth-century manuscript in the Archive of the Indies, Seville.

THE TOPILTZIN QUETZALCOATL MATERIAL

For two of the towns, Zoyatitlanapan and Coatzinco, Camaxtli is named as chief god, undoubtedly reflecting his importance in the religious/ritual systems of such nearby *cabeceras* as Tlaxcallan, Huexotzinco, and Tepeyacac. For Texalocan, however, the chief deities are specified as Quetzalcoatl and his mother, Cihuacoatl (whose names are accurately etymologized), to whom human victims were sacrificed.

COMMENT

The significance of this tidbit lies in the identification of Cihuacoatl as the mother of Quetzalcoatl, which should be added to the other names we have so far encountered. All will be discussed together below.

4. The *Relación de Tetzcoco* of Juan Bautista Pomar

THE SOURCE

The author of this information-packed *relación geográfica*, one of the richest for ethnographic information in the 1579–1585 series, was the mestizo son of a Spaniard and a daughter of Nezahualpilli by a concubine. The original manuscript, dated March 9, 1582, has disappeared. García Icazbalceta discovered an early seventeenth-century copy in the library of the Colegio de San Gregorio in Mexico City, from which he published his edition of 1891 (re-edited, 1941).

THE TOPILTZIN QUETZALCOATL MATERIAL

In Pomar's highly abbreviated account of the principal deities of Tetzcoco, Quetzalcoatl is not mentioned. His name appears twice, however, as the title of the high priest of the city, "a quién los demás respetaban y obedecían como a señor o más principal," and to whom it fell to rip out the heart of the victim.

COMMENT

This use of the term Quetzalcoatl as the title for the supreme priest of Tetzcoco, just as in Mexico Tenochtitlan, significantly points up the importance of

Topiltzin Quetzalcoatl as the priestly archetype in Central Mexico at the time of the Conquest. Furthermore, the considerable evidence for the frequent use of the term Quetzalcoatl as a title, to which Pomar's datum here is a significant addition, is fundamental to a sensible historical interpretation of the Topiltzin Quetzalcoatl of Tollan Tale, as will be seen below.

5. The *Crónica Mexicayotl*

THE SOURCE

This Nahuatl account of Tenochca history, seemingly composed in part by Hernando Alvarado Tezozomoc (see Kirchhoff 1951), dates, on internal evidence, from after 1609. It was in the Boturini collection and came by way of Aubin and Goupil to the Bibliothèque Nationale, Paris (Manuscrit Mexicaine, Núm. 311). The Mexican edition of 1949 was based on photostats of the original manuscript (the first six and a half pages are apparently in the hand of Chimalpahin, the remainder in that of León y Gama), with a transcription of the Nahuatl text and both a literal and an idiomatic Spanish translation by Adrián León.

THE TOPILTZIN QUETZALCOATL MATERIAL

Only one mention is made of Quetzalcoatl in this source, in paragraph 57, which involves a version of the well-known tale of Copil, the enemy of the Mexica who is killed by his uncle, the god Huitzilopochtli, before the foundation of Mexico Tenochtitlan. Afterward, the god orders the *teomama* (god-carrier) Cuauhtlequetzqui, or Cuauhcoatl, to go to the canebrake to find the woven straw mat (*tepetlatl*), upon which Quetzalcoatl rested when he departed, and his throne, colored red and black, upon which he is to stand and hurl the heart of Copil into the canebrake. This is dutifully done by Cuauhtlequetzqui/Cuauhcoatl, and from the heart of Copil eventually grew the nopal cactus upon which alighted the eagle grasping the serpent, marking the spot where Mexico Tenochtitlan was later founded.

COMMENT

The mat and throne of Quetzalcoatl, upon which he rested during his journey, are here intimately connected with the legend of the founding of Mexico Tenochtitlan. Obviously, another attempt is being made here to link the great Toltec lord, the fountainhead of all legitimate political power, with the establishment of the city that grew to achieve political dominance over a large area of Central and Southern Mexico.

E. Late, Probably Distorted, Versions of the Basic Topiltzin Quetzalcoatl of Tollan Tale

The following five accounts differ substantially from those hitherto considered, although the protagonist of each appears to be Topiltzin Quetzalcoatl. All are late sixteenth or early seventeenth century in date. One was recorded by the native chronicler Chimalpahin, two by the mestizo chroniclers Muñoz Camargo and Alva Ixtlilxochitl, and the fourth and fifth by the Dominican friar Fray Diego Durán and the Jesuit Juan de Tovar—the latter's account being largely, but not entirely, derived from that of Durán. All of them present great difficulties of interpretation. Obvious Christian influence is present in each in varying degrees, particularly in Durán's version. Here for the first time we encounter Huemac and Topiltzin Quetzalcoatl either being identified or named as contemporaries (this last, ostensibly anticipated in Sahagún). Although four of these accounts differ markedly among themselves, they are grouped together in this category because of certain anomalous qualities that they all share.

1. The *Historia de los Indios de Nueva España e islas de tierra firme* of Fray Diego Durán

THE SOURCE

This account of Topiltzin Quetzalcoatl is contained in the first chapter of Durán's second treatise: "Libro de los ritos y ceremonias en las fiestas de los dioses y celebración de ellas" (completed in 1579). Barlow (1945: 80), by implication, considered it part of the *Crónica X*, but this seems very doubtful. Certainly the chapter under consideration is derived from various sources, some of them specifically mentioned by the author. Since Durán and his work have been treated above, it is unnecessary to repeat our earlier discussion of it.

THE TOPILTZIN QUETZALCOATL MATERIAL

The title of this first chapter summarizes its contents thus: "De quién se sospecha que fué un gran barón que ubo en esta tierra, llamado Topiltzin y por otro nombre Papa, á quien los mexicanos llamaron Hueymac: residió en Tulla." The author, in the first paragraph, explains that before he treats of the gods in particular and the rites performed in their honor, he wishes to discuss this "gran barón" and the doctrine that he preached.

He begins by stating that this Topiltzin, or Papa, was a very venerable and religious person, greatly honored and esteemed, "como persona santa." Durán saw a painting of him "en un papel bien viejo y antiguo" in the city of Mexico. He was represented as an elderly man of venerable presence, with a long beard "entre cana y roja," a rather long nose "con algunas ronchas en ella, o algo comida," tall in height, with long hair, quite unadorned, and seated with considerable dignity. He spent his time retired in a cell, a place from which he rarely issued. He lived a very ascetic life, praying, fasting, and performing penance. He was accustomed to erect altars and oratories in all of the quarters of the towns, to place images on the walls above the altars, and to kneel before them, doing them reverence, kissing the earth, sometimes with the mouth, other times with the hand. He always slept "en la piana del altar, que edificaba, en el suelo." He taught his disciples to pray and to preach. These disciples were called *tolteca*, "oficiales o sabios en algún arte."

Durán then enters into a long, rambling aside, during which he rather hesitantly suggests that this Topiltzin might have been "algún apostol bendito," pointing out that since the natives of the New World "eran criaturas de Dios," they too should have received some knowledge of the Gospel. Since it was said that Topiltzin was a stone carver ("entallaba imágenes en piedra y las labraba curiosamente"), and, since St. Thomas was also an "oficial de aquel arte," as well as being "predicador de los indios," he hints at this more specific identification.

He goes on to point out that, in any case, Topiltzin "era un hombre adbenedico de tierras estrañas," and that "ninguna relación puede allar de que parte ubiese benido." After arriving, he gathered disciples together, built temples and altars, and, together with his followers, climbed the hills to preach, so effectively that their voices "se oyan de dos y tres leguas como sonido de trompeta." They also performed "algunas cosas maravillosas, que debían de ser milagros," for which they received the appellation of Tolteca.

Furthermore, they "hacían cosas por sus manos heroycas," and Durán adds that when asked such questions as who made the cleft in this hill, or opened this spring, or discovered this cave, or built this edifice, they would answer: "los toltecas discípulos del papa." All this emboldens the author to more strongly suggest that "este barón fué algún apostol de Dios" who came to Mexico and that "los demás que llamaban oficiales, o sabios" were his disciples—who, confirming his preaching with miracles, attempted to convert the people "a la ley ebangélica." However, seeing "la rudeça y dureça de sus terrestres coraçones," they abandoned the land and returned whence they had come.

He goes on to relate that a great persecution was raised against Topiltzin and his disciples ("se levantó guerra contra ellos"), because the number of converts to his teachings was very large. It was said that the chief of this persecution was Tezcatlipoca, who descended from the sky for this purpose. Performing miracles, he gathered his own band of disciples and "gente maligna" to harass "aquellos barones de buena vida" and drive them out, not allowing them to settle in any community, forcing them from place to place, until they succeeded in establishing themselves in Tollan, where they remained "por algún tiempo y años." Finally, the persecution became too great even here, and they determined to escape their tormentors and leave for good.

Topiltzin gathered together all the people of Tollan, thanked them for their hospitality, and bade them farewell. When asked the cause of his departure, which was regretted, he cited the persecutions "de aquella malvada gente," and, making a long oration, prophesied the coming of strangers from the east, "con un traxe estraño y de diferentes colores, bestidos de pies a cabeza y con coberturas en las cabeças." Their punishment would be sent to them by God for the bad treatment they had received; large and small would perish, and there could be no escape. They "pintaron en sus escrituras" that which he had prophesied concerning these strangers "para tener memoria della y esperar el suceso"—which afterwards was fulfilled with the coming of the Spaniards. He also told them that their coming would not be in their time, or in that of their children, but in the fourth or fifth generation hence. The newcomers would become their masters, whom they would have to serve, being in turn maltreated and cast from their lands, as they had done to him. Finally, turning to his disciples, he said to them, "Brothers, let us depart from where we are not wanted and go to where we will have more peace."

He began his journey, passing through most of the "pueblos de la tierra," giving to each place and hill its appropriate name, with many people following him from each town. According to one version, taking a direction toward the sea, he opened "con solo su palabra," a great mountain and disappeared inside. According to another, he cast his mantle on the waters; seating himself upon it and making a sign with his hand, "empeçó a caminar por el agua y que nunca más lo bieron." A third version duplicates the Exodus account of the Israelites' crossing of the Red Sea.

Durán then returns to the journey of Topiltzin, stating that en route he "yba entallando en las peñas cruces y ymágenes." Upon Durán's inquiring where they could be seen, he was told of various places, one in the Zapotec region, which last was confirmed by a Spaniard who claimed to have seen a crucifix there, carved on a cliff in a gorge. An old native also told Durán that, while passing through the town of Ocuituco (southwest of Popocatepetl), the *papa* left "un libro grande, de quatro dedos de alto, de unas letras." When Durán went to the town, requesting to see it, "con toda la omillad del mundo," he was told that it had been burned six years before. They told him that "la letra" was not the same as that used by the Spaniards, and Durán speculates that it might have been the gospel written in Hebrew.

Durán then describes the costume of the disciples of Topiltzin, which were long, multicolored gowns that reached to the feet, plus headgear in the form of conch shells. They wore their hair long, from which they took the name Papa. He then refers to his illustration of these disciples, stating that it was based on an ancient painting that was loaned to him by a somewhat reluctant Indian of Chiautla (north of Tetzcoco). This informant related to him the entire story of Topiltzin that Durán had narrated up to this point, explaining that all the ceremonies and rites, the building of temples and altars and the placing of idols in them, fasting and going naked and sleeping on the ground, climbing mountains "a predicar allá su ley," the custom "besar la tierra y comella con los dedos," and the ceremonial blowing of trumpets, conch shells, and flutes were all done in Topiltzin's memory—who had incensed the altars and caused instruments to be blown in the oratories that he built.

Durán, desiring to further check on the truth of these tales, also sought information from an old native of Coatepec (probably the town southeast of Tetzcoco), "letrado en su ley natural." He brought to the friar a pictorial document that related the life of the *papa* and his disciples and verbally confirmed the account of his other informant. In addition, he pointed out on the portrait of Topiltzin (Color Plate 9) the "corona de plumas" and explained that Topiltzin wore this during ceremonies, "a la manera que se ponen la mitra los obispos en la cabeza quando dicen missa."

He goes on to present more data on the disciples of Topiltzin, mentioning that they were called "hijos del sol," in addition to being called *toltecas*, and that "ay de sus hechos grandes cossas y obras memorables." They had their "principal assiento" in Chalollan, before the coming of the Chololteca, although they "discurieron por toda la tierra." They preached to the mountaineers of Tlaxcallan, called Chichimeca, and to the "giants." Their colored robes were called *xicolli*, and because of their headgear they were called *cuateccize*, "caveças con caracoles."

The rulers of the land besought Topiltzin, here for the first time in the text called "Hüeimac" (*sic*), to marry. He replied that he had determined to marry when "el roble echase manças," when the sun rose from the west, when the sea could be passed as on dry land, and when the nightingales grew beards like men. Durán saw one picture of him (here again called "Hüeímac") with a long gown and a great hat on his head, with a caption that read: "padre de los hijos de las nubes."

Durán again asked the same natives of Coatepec about the causes of his departure, to which they replied that it was due to the persecution of him by Quetzalcoatl (*sic!*) and Tezcatlipoca, who were sorcerers and wizards and could transform themselves into the forms they desired. Asked what harassments they perpetrated on him, his informant told him that the principal reason for his leaving was a trick engineered by the sorcerers that involved the secret placing in his cell of a harlot, Xochiquetzal. Publicizing this fact in order to cause him the loss of the good opinion in which he and his disciples were held, "como era tan casto y onesto Topiltzin, fué grande la afrenta que recibió y luego, propusso su salida de la tierra." Asked whether he knew or had heard where he had gone, the informant, after relating "algunas cosas fabulosas," confirmed that "acia la mar se avía ydo" and that nothing more was known of him, nor was it known where he went. They only knew that he went to inform his sons, the Spaniards, about the land and that he brought them (the Spaniards) to be avenged. Thus the Indians, with the old prophecy in mind, always were on the alert. When he received news of the arrival of the Castilians at the port of San Juan de Ulua, or at Coatzacoalco, and learning of their costume and aspect, Motecuhzoma consulted the "pinturas y libros," finally deciding that they were indeed the sons of Topiltzin. He then sent them a great gift of jewels, feathers, gold, and precious stones, together with a message requesting them to depart, since he knew from the prophecy that they came, not for any good, but to do harm. When the sentinels had relayed the news of the Spaniards' coming, saying that the "hijos de Hüeimac" had arrived, Motecuhzoma replied that they had come for the treasure that Hüeimac had left behind when he departed and which he had accumulated to build a temple. He therefore instructed his envoys to tell the newcomers to be content to take it and then depart without seeing him. Durán finally adds that he found this last item "en una pintura, que de la vida y hechos de Montezuma me mostraron."

SUMMARY

The information presented in this rambling and somewhat disjointed account can be boiled down to the following essential facts: (1) A saintly man arrived in New Spain, from parts unknown, preaching a kind of new moral doctrine, involving rigorous penance; (2) he was called Topiltzin, Papa, and Hüeimac; (3) he pursued an almost monastic existence, refusing to marry, praying, fasting, performing penances in his cell, which he rarely left, and erecting temples and altars; (4) he was represented as an old man of venerable appearance, clad in a long robe, with a long reddish-gray beard; (5) he gathered together a band of disciples, called *tolteca* and sons of the sun, who, from their principal headquarters at Chollollan (before the arrival of the historic Cholollteca), preached his doctrine throughout the land, especially to the mountaineers and giants of Tlaxcallan, at times from hilltops in voices that could be heard at great distances; (6) these disciples, who were capable of performing miracles, were dressed in long colored garments called *xicolli*, and wore over their long hair (thus the name Papas) coverings shaped like conch shells, from which they took the name *cuateccize*, "heads with conch shells"; (7) against Topiltzin and his disciples a great persecution was raised, headed by the sorcerer Tezcatlipoca (according to one version, joined also by Quetzalcoatl!), who descended from the sky and organized his own band of malevolent disciples; (8) Topiltzin and his followers, driven from town to town, finally found a temporary haven at Tollan but were eventually forced to leave after his enemies tricked him by introducing into his cell a harlot, Xochiquetzal; (9) on departing, Topiltzin prophesied the coming, four or five generations hence, of strangers who would conquer the land and avenge his ill treatment; (10) he commenced his journey, passing through countless towns, which he named as he went, drawing many people after him; (11) en route, he carved many crosses and images on rocks and cliffs, including a place in the Zapotec region, and even left behind a book in strange letters at the town of Ocuituco; (12) arriving at the seashore, he seated himself upon his mantle, made a sign with his hand, and sailed off to unknown parts (or, according to another version, magically opened a great mountain and disappeared inside); (13) when the Spaniards arrived, Motecuhzoma, consulting his records, considered them to be the sons of Topiltzin and sent them gifts, hoping to induce them to depart and escape his vengeance (in another version, he offered them the treasure that Topiltzin had left behind on his departure, having accumulated it to build a temple); (14) Durán suggests that Topiltzin may have been some Christian apostle, who came with his disciples to Mexico to convert the natives and, meeting with little success, returned to whence they had come; (15) he specifically suggests an identification with St. Thomas, on the ground that he, like Topiltzin, was a carver of images and also was known to have preached to "los indios."

COMMENT

This account of Topiltzin Quetzalcoatl is one of the strangest and most confused that has come down to us. The confusion reaches the point that, ostensibly based on the testimony of an old native of Coatepec, Quetzalcoatl is named as one of the sorcerer-persecutors of Topiltzin! Strong Christian influence is manifest throughout. The great native priest and penitent becomes a type of Christian missionary, vainly preaching an austere cult of self-denial.

Yet many features conform to the Basic Topiltzin Quetzalcoatl of Tollan Tale, making it reasonably certain that the same personage is involved. Whether Durán's informants, under the influence of Christian teachings, deliberately misled him, or whether the pro-Indian, well-meaning Dominican consciously or unconsciously distorted the authentic information conveyed to him is difficult to say. Probably both factors were operative.

Durán's identification of Topiltzin with Huemac, which will also be encountered later in Alva Ixtlilxochitl, probably reflects the same type of confusion that was so dramatically demonstrated in the separation of Topiltzin and Quetzalcoatl into two antagonistic personalities. The suggested identification of Topiltzin with the "glorioso Santo Tomás" is only the precursor of later countless romantic speculations concerning the identity of our hero.

This peculiar account is obviously a very eclectic one, derived from a number of informants in different places, which may partly explain its disjointed quality. The paintings that Durán claims to have seen, and to which he refers as authority, from his brief descriptions appear to have been synthetic colonial creations, probably composed under Christian influence. One of the most puzzling features of the account are the headdresses in the form of conch shells ascribed to the disciples of Topiltzin, a notice that is confined to this source. Whether this unique style of headgear bears some relation to the *ehecacozcatl*—the sliced conch shell pectoral that is a standard item of Ehecatl Quetzalcoatl's insignia—is unclear; it is lacking in Durán's illustration of Topiltzin (Color Plate 9).

ADDITIONAL MATERIAL IN DURÁN

The two illustrations mentioned by Durán in the text represent: (1) Topiltzin, wrapped in his mantle, seated on what seems to be a low throne or stool, resting in turn on a kind of elevated bench (or litter?) supported by low, angled legs, with two-headed serpents (feathered?) edging the two longer sides (heads projecting beyond the four corners). He wears a reasonably full beard, and on his head is a large feather headdress. Below him is a strange little image, consisting of a grotesque serpentine face with bifurcated tongue and "nose" formed by a looped two-headed snake (a form of Tlaloc?) (see Color Plate 9); (2) a portrayal of four of the disciples of Topiltzin wearing their long colored robes and their conch shell headdresses. Two are bearded. These drawings (Durán 1951, atlas, tratado 2: lámina 1), although quite Europeanized, do retain a definite native stylistic flavor, even though their iconographic detail is minimal.

For the sake of clarification, it should be mentioned that the *xicolli*, the name given for the "opas de colores" worn by Topiltzin's disciples, is the standard priestly jacket, frequently depicted in the native-tradition pictorials. The term *cuateccize* for these disciples, referring to their headdresses, was rendered, more correctly, as *quateccicèquè* by Seler (1902–1923, IV: 149), who translated it as "die Schneckengehause auf dem Kopfe haben."

In chapter VI, Durán presents data on quite a different kind of Quetzalcoatl. In the chapter heading he is called god of the Chololteca, "el padre de los tolteca y de los españoles porque anunció su uenida." In the chapter text, however, these latter features are not mentioned. He begins by explaining that each important town of New Spain had its particular patron god and that Quetzalcoatl held this position for Chalollan, which city was particularly noted for its rich merchants. He then goes on to specifically label Quetzalcoatl "el dios de los mercadores" and describes his high temple and richly adorned wooden idol there. Both from the illustration and its detailed description, it was clearly an image of Ehecatl Quetzalcoatl (see Color Plate 10).

There follows a long description of the annual ceremony dedicated to Quetzalcoatl, its high point being the sacrifice of a slave who had impersonated the god for forty days. Durán also describes the Quetzalcoatl temple in Mexico Tenochtitlan, whose substructure had seventy steps and whose shrine, entered through a low doorway, was round with a conical thatched roof. The duties of the priests, who served there in weekly shifts, are described. One of the most important of these duties was to mark the hours of sunset and sunrise by striking a great drum. During this description, "Yacatl" is given as a second name for the god. The annual ceremony to Quetzalcoatl here is also described, which featured dancing by the merchants and lords and comic impersonations of deformed and diseased individuals and animals on a large raised platform in the patio of the temple. These had serious ritualistic overtones, for Quetzalcoatl was held to be "abogado de las bubas y del mal de los ojos y del romádico y tosse." During their mimic performances, the participants uttered pleas to this god for health, while sufferers from these afflictions came to his temple with prayers and offerings. Durán also details the offerings made by the common people during this ceremony and states that everywhere, except in the Huaxteca, maize bread mixed only with water (*atamalli*) was eaten on this day. He concludes by stating that the merchants feasted this idol because "su dios era el más abentajado y rico mercader de su tiempo y por bentura el que dió entre ellos forma y reglas de tratar."

Lastly, it should be mentioned that Durán (1951, I: 160) states in one place: "Al supremo sacerdote [of Mexico Tenochtitlan] llamauan con diversos nombres; unos le llamauan Papa, otros Topiltzin, . . ."

COMMENT

The last statement is significant, for it informs us that Topiltzin, as well as Quetzalcoatl, was employed as a sacerdotal title. Durán's emphasis on the Chololteca Quetzalcoatl's role as particular patron of the powerful merchants of that great Pueblan pilgrimage mecca/commercial emporium is also quite important. It is clear that this Quetzalcoatl of Chalollan exhibits a high degree of fusion between Ehecatl Quetzalcoatl and Topiltzin Quetzalcoatl, although Durán or his source very much slights the latter in this context—for which we must rely on such sources as Tapia and Rojas, discussed in Chapter 3.

2. The *Relación del origen de los Yndios* (*Códice Ramirez*) of Juan de Tovar

THE SOURCE

As stated above, this chronicle, which exists in two slightly varying versions (Tovar 1860 [incomplete], 1878, 1944), is essentially a digest of the first two parts of Durán's *Historia.* Gibson and Kubler (1951: 12–18) reviewed the biography and bibliography of Tovar and believed this digest was composed, most probably, between 1583 and 1597.

THE TOPILTZIN QUETZALCOATL MATERIAL

Tovar briefly summarized Durán's "Tratado Segundo," Chapter 1, introducing it into his account (derived ultimately from the *Crónica X*) of the first appearance of the Spaniards on the coast of Veracruz that instigated Motecuhzoma's assumption that Quetzalcoatl had returned. Although substantially the same as Durán's version, it differs from it at certain points, for which reason it is briefly considered here. Most importantly, Tovar identifies the "hombre santísimo" straightaway with Quetzalcoatl, which, as we have seen, Durán does not. According to Tovar, he was known under three names: Topiltzin, Quetzalcoatl, and Papa. Significantly, the name Huemac does not appear. He also states that this holy man was not an idolater but abhorred the idols and "malos ritos y ceremonias" that he found current among the natives, for which reason a great persecution was raised against him. This slant is really somewhat different from that of Durán, as a careful reading of both versions makes clear. Tovar also calls him "el propio señor y emperador de toda esta tierra enviado por Dios," who introduced various ceremonies "que conforman con la ley evangélica"—for which many understood that he was "algún ministro del Santo Evangelio." This view, he goes on to state, was supported by the discovery, in an unnamed town near the coast, of "un cuero curtido muy antiguo donde estaban figurados todos los misterios de nuestra fe, sin faltar ninguno en figuras de indios, aunque con muchos yerros" (a notice lacking in Durán). Tovar (1944: 105–107) also states that "entre las pinturas que se hallan de su efigie" they portrayed the holy man with a tiara "de tres coronas," like that of the pope, a detail that is also absent from Durán's account. Finally, this statement of Tovar (1944: 101) is worth quoting: "En esto tiempo [the first appearance of the Spaniards on the coast] anunció el ídolo Quetzalcohuatl, dios de los Chulultecas la venida de gente extraña a poseer estos reinos."

COMMENT

No formal summary is necessary here. Tovar's account, which is obviously mainly derived from that of Durán, was included because he unequivocally identified the saintly missionary of his source with Quetzalcoatl, something Durán himself did not do, in addition to presenting slightly differing slants and some new details of interest. These latter may have been added from Tovar's own knowledge (he had reportedly earlier composed a significant work on indigenous Central Mexican customs, traditions, and religion, in addition to his compilation of "The Tovar Calendar") or they may have been drawn from another manuscript of Durán, now lost.

3. The Muñoz Camargo / Torquemada Account of Quetzalcoatl

THE SOURCES

Muñoz Camargo's *Historia de Tlaxcala* has already been discussed in section B above. At the beginning of that work there is an account of Quetzalcoatl of which only the conclusion is preserved, since in the one manuscript (Bibliothèque Nationale, Paris, Manuscrit Mexicaíne Num. 210) from which all of the others are ultimately derived, the beginning is missing. However, in the *Monarchía Indiana* of Fray Juan de Torquemada the account is apparently preserved in full. There it stands at the end of the chapter devoted to Tollan. The fact that Torquemada's account of the history of Tlaxcallan, clearly based on Muñoz Camargo, immediately follows is additional support that this account of Quetzalcoatl is taken from the same source. What clinches the case, however, is a town enumeration at the very end, which is identical in both.

Little is known of the Franciscan Fray Juan de Torquemada (for some limited biographical data, see García Icazbalceta 1896–1899, IV: 9–12), whose *Monarchía Indiana* was the most ambitious description of the pre-Hispanic culture of Mexico and account of the sixteenth-century Spanish missionary activities composed up to that time. Although its late date precludes it from being considered a primary source, the fact that its author copied virtually verbatim many genuinely primary sources that are now lost does, in effect, make these at least "primary" in the accepted sense of that word. In the *Monarchía Indiana*, the writings of such important sixteenth- and early seventeenth-century chroniclers as Sahagún, Mendieta, Muñoz Camargo, Alva Ixtlilxochitl, and others first saw print, although this was not always evident from the compiler's own statements. The work was seemingly completed circa 1612 and first published in 1615, in Seville. The second edition, Madrid 1723, is the one most used, especially since a facsimile of that edition was published in Mexico in 1943–1944. The accuracy of Torquemada's transcriptions of earlier sources can be ascertained in those cases where the originals are known. For the most part, he appears to have been a faithful copyist. We can probably rely, therefore, on the essential accuracy of his version of the (first) Muñoz Camargo account of Quetzalcoatl.

THE TOPILTZIN QUETZALCOATL MATERIAL

As noted above, Torquemada introduces the material that interests us here at the end of his chapter (chapter VII, book III) devoted to Tollan, "y su Señorío," the first part of which is an account ultimately derived—with slight modifications, via López de Gómara—from the *Juan Cano Relaciones*. It begins, after Tollan had been flourishing for some time, with the arrival of "ciertas Naciones de Gentes" from the north, by way of the Panuco region. These newcomers consisted of men of good carriage, dressed in long robes of black linen ("a manera de Turcas"), like priests' cassocks, open in front, without hoods, cut low in the neck, with short broad sleeves that did not reach to the elbow, which robes "el día de oi" were used by the natives in their dances. These people passed forward from Panuco, "con buena industria," without any conflict and by degrees arrived in Tollan. Here they were hospitably received with gifts, since they were very prudent and skillful in gold- and silverworking, lapidary work, and all the crafts—as well as being skilled in "otras industrias, para la sustentaxión Humana" and in cultivating the land. For their knowledge and skills and "su buen govierno," they were greatly esteemed and held in high honor. The origin of "esta Nación" was not known, beyond the fact that they "vinieron a aportar a la Provincia de Panuco." Some had suggested that they were Romans or Carthaginians, blown ashore; others that they were Irish, finding support for this view in their customs of striping their faces and eating human flesh and because of the geographical proximity of the Emerald Isle to the New World.

Since Tollan was so heavily populated that they could not be sustained, the newcomers passed on to Chalollan, where they were also very well received, mixing with the natives, and settling for a long time. They brought with them "una Persona mui principal por Caudillo," who governed them, called Quetzalcohuatl, whom the Chololteca afterwards adored as a god. He was "de mui buena disposición," white and blond, wearing a beard, "y bien acondicionado." While still in Tollan, the lords committed adultery, especially "Tezcatlipoca, Huemac." Quetzalcoatl, seeing his bad behavior, angrily left Tollan and went to Chalollan, where he lived many years with his people. From there he sent them to populate the "provincias de Huaxyacac," the Mixteca Baja and Alta and the Zapotec region, and it was said that they built "aquellos Grandes y Sumptuosísimos Edificios Romanos" of Mitla.

Quetzalcoatl's people were so proficient in all the arts that their name "Tulteca," from "Tullan," where they first settled, became applied to all "Maestros de qualquier Arte, Ingenio sutil, y delicado a nuestro entendimiento." For this reason Chololan was called Tollan Cholullan, and the Chololtecas were great metallurgists, not with the hammer or in *relievo* work, but in casting in "Moldes sutiles." They were also great lapidaries, not because they knew the properties of stones, "ni aplicarlas para ninguna virtud," but because they held them to be precious things and because they knew how to work and carve them with great skill.

After Quetzalcoatl and his Toltecs had spent considerable time in Chololan, mixing with the populace, and after many had gone as colonists to Oaxaca at his command, he received the news that his great enemy, Huemac, was approaching with a large following against him, destroying and terrorizing as he came. As Quetzalcoatl considered the "rei Huemac" to be a great warrior, he did not wish to wait for his coming and determined to leave the city. This he did, taking with him a great part of his followers, giving as the excuse for his departure that he went to visit certain provinces and peoples, the latter which he had sent to colonize the "Tierras de Onohualco," which "son las que aora llamamos Yucatan, Tabasco, y Campech."

After his departure, Quetzalcoatl, seeing that Huemac still came against him with such a mighty force, did not wish to await him, possibly because he was so old, wanted to avoid any more clashes with him, did not wish to endanger or lose "sus Glorias y Gentes," or because he wished to save what he had accomplished and colonized. Whatever the reason, it was only said that he departed, not wishing to await him. Huemac, arriving at the place where he expected to find his enemy, upon learning that he had fled, was filled with rage and committed great massacres in the land. The fear of him grew to such an intensity that he made himself adored as a god, thinking by this to destroy and obscure the fame that Quetzalcoatl had enjoyed in that city. He also made himself ruler, not only of Chololan, but also of "Quauhquechulan, Itzyucan, Atlixco, y todas las provincias de Tepeyacac, Tecamachalco, Quecholac, y Tehuacan." Over all of this region Huemac became ruler and was in fact afterwards adored as a god by its inhabitants.

Very little of this long narrative is preserved in the editions of Muñoz Camargo's *Historia,* derived from the Paris manuscript, that begins, in the middle of a sentence, at the finale of what was undoubtedly his version of it. Since it is incomplete, the first portion of it will be quoted verbatim (Muñoz Camargo 1947–1948: 21):

> . . . linaje de los Tlaxcaltecas é que pasó con ellos por aquel estrecho de que tienen noticia que vivieron ó que viniendo por el camino nacieron, el y camaxtle, Dios de los Tlaxcaltecas, sino que éste atravesó de la mar, del Sur á la del Norte e que después vino á salir por las partes

de Pánuco, como tenemos referido y adelante diremos [cf. Chavero edition (Muñoz Camargo 1892): ". . . viniendo por el camino nacieron el Camaxtle"; and ". . . este atravesó de la mar del Norte a la del sur . . ."].

Muñoz Camargo then goes on to give an account of the end of Quetzalcoatl that closely approximates, but in a more summary way, the final passages of Torquemada's version. As pointed out above, his enumeration of towns and provinces over which Huemac extended his anger and his sway is identical to that given by Torquemada.

Indicating how much has been lost, Muñoz Camargo, about to pass on to a new topic, refers back to the account just ended, saying: "hemos tratado largamente deste Tezcatlipoca y de Quetzalcohuatl." Somewhat later, after presenting his brief account of the birth of Quetzalcoatl discussed earlier, he refers again to the narration just summarized in these terms: "por cuya causa y razón dejo atrás declarado, que aunque Quetzalcohuatl dijo que vino por la parte Norte y por Panuco, y de Panuco por Tulantzinco y por Tula donde tuvo su habitación," going on to explicitly differentiate this Quetzalcoatl from the one born to Mixcoatl Camaxtli and Cohuatlicue in Teohuitznahuac during the Chichimec migration from the west. He also notes that some of their great leaders, "especialmente Camaxtli, Quetzalcohuatl y Tezcatlipuca," were afterwards held to be gods. This mention of Tollantzinco as a stop on the journey of Quetzalcoatl from Panuco to Tollan is interesting, for it is lacking in Torquemada's version.

SUMMARY

(1) Quetzalcoatl, a bearded white man, is the leader of a group of followers, dressed in long black robes like clerical vestments, who, coming from the north, from the Panuco region, slowly proceed peacefully to Tollan, where they are hospitably received; (2) because of their wisdom and skills in all kinds of crafts and the cultivation of the soil, they are held in great esteem; (3) finding the Tollan area too heavily populated to support them, they pass on to ChololIan, where they are also welcomed; (4) there they mix with the natives, and some are sent to colonize Oaxaca (constructing the buildings of Mitla) at the command of Quetzalcoatl, who has also abandoned Tollan after becoming enraged at the adultery committed by the leaders, especially Tezcatlipoca Huemac; (5) after some time in Chololلan, Quetzalcoatl, learning that his particular enemy, Tezcatlipoca Huemac, is advancing with a great host against him, abandons Chololلan with many of his followers and heads for "Onohualco," the eastern Gulf Coast region; (6) Chololلan, after his departure, adores him as a god and maintains the Toltec tradition of fine craftsmanship, particularly in metalworking and the lapidary art; (7) Quetzalcoatl, informed that Huemac is again approaching, leaves or disappears; (8) the latter, learning that his enemy has fled, vents his rage on a number of

prominent towns of central and southern Mexico, including Cholollan, Cuauhquechollan, Itzocan, Atlixco, Tepeyacac, Tecamachalco, Quecholac, and Teohuacan, dominating them and causing himself to be worshipped as a god in an effort to eradicate all memory of Quetzalcoatl; (9) it is suggested that the group that Quetzalcoatl led may have been Romans, Carthaginians, or Irish.

COMMENT

This account, in its general atmosphere, bears considerable similarity to that of Durán. Again, Quetzalcoatl is a bearded missionary leading a band of disciples who appears from parts unknown, performs a kind of apostolic mission for some time at Tollan and Cholollan, and is eventually forced by persecution to abandon the country. On the other hand, the emphasis here, in contrast to the Durán account, is on cultural proselytization rather than moral or ritual. This version is also important in two other respects: (1) the identification of Tezcatlipoca with Huemac; (2) the contemporaneity of the latter with Quetzalcoatl. An interesting absence is the "prophecy of return" element.

Assuming Muñoz Camargo is the source of this account, there still remains the problem of *his* source. Is this a faithful reporting of a genuine Tlaxcalteca tradition current in the late sixteenth century? Or did Muñoz Camargo draw from non-Tlaxcallan sources for this version of the Quetzalcoatl tale—as he obviously did for certain other portions of his *Historia*? These pertinent questions, unfortunately, may never be answered. In any case, this account, like that of Durán, clearly displays strong Christian influence and is perhaps the most typical of the group under consideration here.

4. The Writings of Fernando de Alva Ixtlilxochitl

THE SOURCES

This is not the place for an extended analysis and appraisal of the works of this very controversial mestizo author, perhaps the number-one problem child of Central Mexican ethnohistory. An up-to-date critical analysis of his writings is a very real historiographical need. Little is known of his life, beyond the fact that he was a descendant of both the royal house of Tetzcoco and of the *cacicazgo* of Teotihuacan (he was the great-grandson, on his maternal side, of an early sixteenth-century ruler of that place). The late date at which he wrote makes him necessarily largely a secondary source. The quality of his primary sources, few of which are known, seems to have been very uneven, apart from the question of how well he and his aged informants could understand them. Throughout his writings, distortion in favor of the glorious deeds of his Tetzcocan ancestors is very obvious, particularly in his accounts of the Conquest.

The original manuscripts of Alva Ixtlilxochitl have been lost, all modern editions being based on various copies. His writings have been conveniently divided into two groups: the *Relaciones* and the *Historia Chichimeca.* Only the last is a reasonably complete narrative of the pre-Hispanic history of Central Mexico from a Tetzcocan point of view. The *Relaciones* treat of various themes, often in greater detail than the *Historia Chichimeca.* Grouped broadly, they consist of: (1) *Sumaria relación . . . de los Tultecas* (five *relaciones*); (2) *Historia de los señores Chichimecas* (twelve *relaciones*; essentially an interpretation of the *Codex Xolotl* (Dibble 1951) or a cognate, plus some later material; (3) *Ordenanças de Nezahualcoyotl*; (4) *La venida de los Españoles a esta Nueva España* and the *Entrada de los Españoles en Texcuco* (a Tetzcocan account of the Conquest, possibly not authored by Alva Ixtlilxochitl but given to him by the elders of Tetzcoco); (5) *Noticia de los pobladores, etc.* (thirteen *relaciones*, the last devoted to the Conquest and its immediate aftermath); (6) the *Relación sucinta* (eleven *relaciones*); (7) the *Sumaria relación de la historia general de esta Nueva España*; (8) various fragments, some of which have probably been erroneously attributed to Alva Ixtlilxochitl. As to dates, the first six items seem definitely to have been completed before 1608 (certification of the Cabildos of Otumba and San Salvador Quatlacinco, November 18, 1608, where it is also brought out that these *relaciones* were ostensibly written originally in Nahuatl and translated into Spanish by Francisco Rodríguez, the *alguacil* of Otumba). The date of 1616 has been suggested for the *Historia Chichimeca,* but Chavero (in Alva Ixtlilxochitl 1952, II: 5) suggested that, since it seems to be unfinished, it may have been composed toward the end of his life. A *terminus post quem* of 1615 is provided by a reference (Alva Ixtlilxochitl 1952, II: 319) to Torquemada's *Monarchía Indiana.* Chavero also theorized that the *Historia Chichimeca* as we have it is only a part of a much larger work, the rest now lost.

Much of Alva Ixtlilxochitl first appeared in print, although not named as source, in the 1615 *Monarchía Indiana* of Torquemada (especially books I and II, passim), unless both derive from a common source(s). His manuscripts descended to Sigüenza y Góngora, and in the eighteenth century, copies and some originals passed into the hands of Boturini, who had further copies made. These last (which apparently eventually came into the possession of Chavero) served Veytia for his copies made in 1755 (at least of the *Historia Chichimeca*), which were utilized in the manuscript versions of Alva Ixtlilxochitl made for the Figueroa compilation of 1792, previously described. In 1829, Bustamante published the *Relación décima tercera* of the *Noticias de los pobladores*, the first of Alva Ixtlilxochitl's writings to see print in modern times (republished in Sahagún 1938, IV: 239–336). From the copy of the Figueroa compilation sent to Spain, in 1848 Lord Kingsborough (1830/31–1848, IX: 197–470) published the first nearly complete edition of the works of Alva Ixtlilxochitl. Ternaux-Compans had published in 1838 the *Relación décima tercera* of the *Noticias de los pobladores* and in 1840 the *Historia Chichimeca*, in poor French translations, also from the Madrid manuscripts. Finally, in 1891–1892, Chavero, apparently from a copy made by Ramírez of the copy of the Figueroa compilation in the Archivo General de la Nación, Mexico (compared with another manuscript copy, seemingly made by Panes from the Madrid manuscripts, in the Museo Nacional de México, and what Chavero called the original copy of Boturini, in his possession), published the entire writings, the *Relaciones* in one volume, largely grouped following the ideas of Ramírez and including his notes, and the *Historia Chichimeca* in another. This edition was reprinted in Mexico in 1952.

THE TOPILTZIN QUETZALCOATL MATERIAL

Ramírez assembled all of Alva Ixtlilxochitl's material relating to the pre-Toltec and Toltec periods together, which procedure was followed by Chavero in his 1891–1892 edition. In this convenient grouping are found almost all of Alva Ixtlilxochitl's references to our hero. The first, found only in the *Historia Chichimeca* (Alva Ixtlilxochitl 1952, II: 21), refers to Quetzalcoatl as having been the first of "los más graves autores e historiadores que hubo en la infidelidad de los antiguos."

Quetzalcoatl next appears in the same source (cf. the almost identical account in the *Sumaria relación de la historia general de esta Nueva España*, in Alva Ixtlilxochitl 1952; I: 470–471) as a missionary who comes to preach to the "Ulmecas y Xicalancas" of Chalollan during the Third Age, Ehecatonatiuh, the Wind Sun. He is also called Hueman or Huemac. He was distinguished for his great virtues (and called a "virgen" in the *Sumaria relación*) and considered "justo, santo y bueno." He taught by deed and word "el camino de la virtud y evitándoles los vicios y pecados, dando leyes y buena doctrina." In order to curb "sus deleites y deshonestidades" he instituted the custom of fasting. He was also the first who adored and set up the cross, called "Quiahuitzteotlchicahualizteotl" and "Tonacaquahuitl," the first of which Alva Ixtlilxochitl translates as "dios de las lluvias y de la salud," the second as "árbol del sustento o de la vida." After preaching in most of the cities of the Olmeca and Xicalanca, especially in Chalollan, seeing the "poco fruto que hacía con su doctrina," he returned whence he had come, disappearing at Coatzacoalco. Before departing, he prophesied that in a future year Ce Acatl he would return, his doctrine would be accepted, and his sons would be lords and would possess the land—while to his listeners and their descendants would occur many calamities and persecutions. Alva Ixtlilxochitl then explains that the name Quetzalcoatl, interpreted literally, signifies "sierpe de plumas preciosas," or, interpreted allegorically, "varón sapientísimo." The name Huemac was applied to him, according to some, because he impressed his hands upon a cliff, "como si fuese en cera muy blanda," as a testimonial that all that he had predicted would come to pass. According to others, the name signified "el de la mano grande o poderosa." A few days after his departure, the Third Age was terminated by giant winds, including the destruction of the Great Pyramid of Chollollan, "que era como otra segunda torre de Babel." Afterwards, the survivors erected a temple to Quetzalcoatl on its ruins, holding him to be "dios del aire," since the cause of their destruction was the wind, which they understood had been sent by him. Alva Ixtlilxochitl terminates the account by describing Quetzalcoatl as a man "bien dispuesto, de aspecto grave, blanco, barbado. Su vestuario era una túnica larga" (Alva Ixtlilxochitl 1952, II: 23–25).

Alva Ixtlilxochitl's account of the Toltecs in the *Sumaria relación . . . de los Tultecas* (1952, I: 11–73, passim) begins with a detailed description of the migration of the Toltecs, commencing in the year 1 Tecpatl, by a remarkably roundabout route from "Huehue Tlapallan" in the northwest to Tollan. One of the two principal leaders of this migration is called "Cecatzin" (Ce Acatltzin?). The Toltecs were also subject to the supernatural guidance of "un gran astrólogo," variously called Hueman, Huemac, and Huematzin. He advises them to continue their migration toward the east, predicting at least "un siglo dorado y dichoso" for them and their descendants to the tenth generation. After long wanderings, Tollan is finally reached, and, on the advice of Huematzin, now over 180 years old, they take as ruler Chalchiuhtlanetzin, a son of the ruler of the "Chichimecas" of the north, their old enemies. This was done both to ensure peace and because Huematzin prophesied that eventually the land was to be settled by the Chichimeca. A few years before the death of the second ruler, Ixtlilcuechahuac, Huematzin dies at an age of almost three hundred years. Before expiring, he gathered "todas las historias que tenían los Tultecas desde la creación del mundo hasta en aquel tiempo" and painted them in a great book, Teoamoxtli, "diversas cosas de Dios y libro divino," which constituted both a comprehensive history and an encyclopedic inventory of all of their knowledge and wisdom. He also prophesied that 512 years after their departure from their ancient homeland a ruler was to accede to the throne, with the consent of some and against that of others. This ruler was to be known by certain "señales en el cuerpo," particularly "cabellos crespos," which were to form "la naturaleza una tiara en su cabeza desde el vientre de su madre hasta que se muriera." In his early years this ruler was to be "muy justo, sabio y de buen gobierno," but later was to become "necio, y desventurado," for which reason the nation was to perish with great punishments from heaven. The destruction was to occur in the year Ce Tecpatl, which was always a time of evil omen for the Toltecs, and would come about through the rebellion of leaders of his own lineage who would persecute him with great wars until nearly all of his people had perished—although he himself was to escape and return whence his ancestors had come. In his last years he was to revert to his former wisdom and rectitude, and some years before the final destruction certain signs and prognostications would appear. These would include a rabbit with deer's antlers, a hummingbird growing spurs like a cock, fruit growing from rocks, and noble ladies going on pilgrimages to the temples and there entering into sexual relations with the priests who were bound to vows of chastity—for which outrage the gods would wreak destruction upon them.

Ruler followed ruler until the eighth, Tecpancaltzin, was reached. In the tenth year of his reign a beautiful girl came to his palace with her parents, nobles of the ruler's own lineage, to present a gift, a new thing they had discovered, "la miel prieta de maguey." Tecpancaltzin was highly pleased at the gift and became immediately enamored of the girl, called Xochitl. He requested more of the honey, asking that she bring it herself, accompanied only by a female servant. After a few days she returned as requested. Leaving her old nurse outside, the king's retainers ushered her alone into his presence, where he openly declared his desire for her, promising to grant her and her parents many favors. After considerable hesitation, she yielded, and the king ordered her guarded in a place outside Tollan, a hill called Palpan. He sent messengers to inform her parents that their daughter was safe in his palace and being trained by certain noble ladies, for he intended to give her as a bride to a neighboring ruler as recompense for the gift they had brought to him. He also granted them many privileges and presented them with towns and subjects, which were to pass to their descendants. Although her parents were saddened by their daughter's situation, they reluctantly acquiesced. Xochitl soon gave birth, in the year 1 Acatl, which Alva Ixtlilxochitl equates with A.D. 900, to a son, who was called Meconetzin, "niño del maguey," commemorating the discovery of the honey of this plant. This child grew up to have almost every one of the characteristics that the ruler in whose time the Toltecs were to be destroyed was to display.

All this time her parents were searching for Xochitl in vain. At the end of three years, her father, Papantzin, learning where she was sequestered, disguised himself as a worker and gained admission, discovering her in a garden with the child in her arms. Told the story, he left in anger and the next day went to the king, complaining of the dishonor inflicted on his daughter. The latter tried to soothe him, promising him many benefits, allowing him to see his daughter as often as he wished and informing him that he intended to make the child his heir, after which Papantzin departed somewhat mollified.

At the end of his "legal term" of fifty-two years, Tecpancaltzin, true to his word, wished to establish his illegitimate son, Meconetzin, also called Topiltzin, "que ya era hombre de más de cuarenta años, y muy virtuoso y gran sabio," as his successor. Worried about the reaction of "tres señores de su linaje muy propincuos herederos"—Xiuhtenancatzin, Cohuanacoxtzin, and Huehuetzin, who ruled in provinces two hundred leagues from Tollan next to the "Mar del Sur en Xalixco"—he invited two other great rulers, Cuauhtli and Maxtlatzin, to rule jointly with his son in Tollan, "aunque su hijo había de tener el más supremo lugar, como persona suya y rey de reyes como él era." This invitation accepted, Topiltzin was crowned in the year 2 Acatl, and ruled together with Cuauhtli and Maxtlatzin in prosperity for forty years. At the end of this time, the signs that Huematzin had prophesied commenced to appear. Topiltzin began to commit many serious sins, setting a bad example for his people. Noble ladies, going on pilgrimage to the temples, entered into sexual relations with the priests. A "señora de Tula, muy principal," went to Cholollan to visit the temples there ("que había setenta y ocho años que se acabaron de fundar"), particularly one dedicated to the "dios Ce Acatl," and copulated with the second of the two incumbent priests, Ezcolotli and Texpolcatl. From this union a son, Izcax, was born, "que después él y sus descendientes fueron heredando esta dignidad de falsos grandes sacerdotes o pontífices." The instigators of these sins were two brothers, "señores de diversas partes, muy valerosos y grandes nigrománticos," the elder called Tezcatlipuca and the younger, Tlatlauhquiztezcatlipuca (Red Tezcatlipuca, another name for Xipe Totec), who were later revered by the Toltecs as gods.

While this reign of sin was at its height, Topiltzin, going one day to a certain pleasure forest, encountered a rabbit with deer's antlers and a hummingbird with a very long spur. As he had frequently seen the Teoamoxtli of Huematzin, he recognized the import of these omens and was greatly disturbed. Calling together his priests, he showed them the two creatures, which had been slain with blowguns, as well as the Teoamoxtli, explaining that these were portents of their "total destrucción." Thereupon, to appease the anger of the gods, "grandes fiestas y sacrificios, ritos y ceremonias" were instituted.

The following year, 1 Calli, the disasters began, beginning with "grandísimos aguaceros, huracanes y sapos del cielo," which destroyed most of the buildings, while it rained continuously for one hundred days. The next year, 2 Tochtli, a "grandísima calor y seca" ensued, withering all of the vegetation. The third year, 3 Acatl, great snowstorms devastated the lands. The following year, 4 Tecpatl, mighty storms of hail and lightning destroyed all of the trees that had managed to survive, even the magueys, as well as the remaining buildings and walls. A brief respite was enjoyed for the next twelve years, following which, in the year 4 Calli, a great plague of "langostas, gusanos, sabandijas y aves" descended, destroying everything in their path, coupled with great, albeit unsuccessful, wars begun by the "tres propincuos herederos" angered over the influence exercised by the beautiful Xochitl, whose son now ruled. At the end of this time, all granaries of the Toltecs were destroyed by grubs and weevils. After another brief respite of four years, in the fifth year, 7 Tochtli (*sic*), a child, "muy blanco y rubio y hermoso," was found on a hill and carried to Tollan to be shown to the king. Upon seeing him, the latter ordered him taken back to the place where they had found him, since he appeared to him to be an evil omen. The head of the child then commenced to rot, and from the stench many people died. The Toltecs tried to kill him but were unable to do so; all who approached near him immediately died. This stench eventually caused "una gran peste por toda la tierra," during which 90 percent of the Toltecs perished. Many other calamities ensued, and the three enemy rulers, seeing their advantage, exerted more and more pressure on the Toltecs, gradually capturing many provinces and towns tributary to Topiltzin. Alva Ixtlilxochitl adds parenthetically here that from this time forth "alguna criatura muy blanca y rubia" was sacrificed at the age of five years, this custom lasting until the coming of the Spaniards.

Upon the cessation of the plague, Topiltzin, seeing his danger from his enemies, ordered a rich gift sent to them, of gold, mantles, and precious stones, as well as a ball court (*tlachtli*) "del tamaño de una mediana sala," constructed of emeralds, rubies, diamonds, and topaz—and, for a ball, a precious stone. He also sent a message seeking an honorable peace between them, in which all four would rule in equal majesty. These gifts were so heavy that it took 180 men to carry them, "que dentro de ciento cuarenta días hablan de estar alla adelante de Xalisco en Quiyahuitztlanxalmolan." This rich gift failed to have its desired effect, and in the year Ce Acatl the three rulers led a great army into Tollan, mocking the weakness of the Toltecs. Topiltzin greeted them, desperately trying to arrange a favorable peace, but they demanded only satisfaction on the battlefield. Since it was "ley entre ellos que antes de la batalla se avisaban algunos años antes para que de una y otra parte estuviesen avisados y prevenidos," it was agreed that the trial of combat would take place ten years hence at Toltitlan. Thereupon, the three kings returned to their lands, for their army was suffering from hunger. Their expedition had really been made for the purpose of scouting and spying on the resources that were still available to the Toltecs.

At the end of the stipulated ten-year period, in 10 Tecpatl, they returned with an even more powerful army. Topiltzin, on his part, had gathered into two large armies every able-bodied man in his dominion, even impressing the women as food carriers. He stationed one army, under command of a "gran capitán llamado Huehuetenuxcatl," almost a hundred leagues from Tollan, "hacia las últimas tierras y provincias de los Tlahuicas," and the other, with himself and all his vassal lords, at Toltitlan. The battle was joined for three years with the advanced army, which was finally overcome due to the constant reinforcements available to the three enemy kings.

Huehuetenuxcatl fled with the survivors to Toltitlan, where Topiltzin, bracing himself for the end, ordered his servants to carry his two legitimate heirs, Pochotl and Xilotzin, "a los muy altos montes y tierras de Toluca," in order that "no se acabara en ellos el linaje de los Reyes Tultecas."

Topiltzin's last stand lasted forty days, during which the battle raged furiously, day and night. Finally, seeing all was lost, Topiltzin personally entered the fight, along with his aged father, his wives "y otras matronas de las ciudades," and his mother, Xochitl, all "peleando valerosamente y haciendo todo lo que pudieron." The final slaughter of the Toltecs ensued, "y muertos viejos y mozos, mujeres y niños, no perdonado a nadie." Finally, in the year Ce Tecpatl, on the last day of the *veintena* of "Totozoztzintli," Ce Ollin, Topiltzin, and the few survivors fled from Tollan. Caught up with at "Chiuhnauhtlan," they managed to escape and fled through Xaltocan, Teotihuacan, and Totolapan. Before reaching a place called "Tulteca Xochitlalpan," the old ex-ruler Tecpancaltzin and his favorite, Xochitl, were overtaken and slain, the former by king Xiuhtenancatzin himself, the latter by his co-ruler, Cohuanacoxtzin. The third king, Huehuetzin, overtook Topiltzin's two co-rulers, Cuauhtli and Maxtla, at Totolapan, and "allí los hicieron pedazos." Topiltzin himself, however, successfully fled, hiding himself in "Xico, una cueva que está junto a Tlalmanalco." Beyond Xico, the remnants of the Toltec army, with the captain-general Huehuetunexcatl, were cornered and slaughtered to a man. Xilotzin was also overtaken and killed, but Pochotl, carried by his nurse, escaped, along with some other Toltec families, both nobles and commoners, who hid "en las lagunas y sierras." Others, from the towns of "Mallauxiuhcohuac, Mazatepec, Tzotzatepec, Tototepec, Quauhquechollan, Tepexomacotlazallan, Chapoltepec, Culhuacan y otras partes," also made good their escape.

The three victorious kings, sated with the slaughter, proceeded to loot the temples and palaces of the great Toltec cities and returned with rich booty to their homelands, not leaving a man behind, "porque estaba la tierra muy seca y enferma y sin fruto." Some days later, Topiltzin, with some of his servants, emerged from Xico. Seeing his enemies gone and "la tierra de todo punto destruída," Topiltzin addressed the Toltec survivors in Colhuacan. He explained that he was going "hacia donde el sol sale, a unos reinos y señoríos de sus pasados, muy prósperos y ricos," and that 512 years hence he would return in the year Ce Acatl and punish the descendants of his enemies. One night he departed from Xico, with some retainers, and, traveling "de noche por desiertos," arrived at Tlapallan (which Alva Ixtlilxochitl also calls "Atlapallan, provincia que cae hasta la mar del Sur"), where he lived almost thirty more years, "servido y regalado de los Tlapaltecas." He finally died at the age of 104, leaving behind many laws, which "su descendiente Netzahualcoytzin" confirmed. He also ordered that his body should be burned, "con los ritos y ceremonias que después se usaron (y él fué el primero que fué quemado)."

Alva Ixtlilxochitl then adds that many said that Topiltzin did not go to Tlapallan, but is still in Xico, with his descendants Nezahualcoyotl and Nezahualpilli of Tetzcoco, as well as Moquihuix of Tlatelolco, "porque fueron los más valerosos y de grandes hazañas que cuantos reyes han tenido los Tultecas y Chichimeca." They were to emerge from there at some future time (Alva Ixtlilxochitl compares this belief to the similar Portuguese belief that their king, Sebastian, was to return to them). He also states that others of the Toltecs who escaped migrated "por las costas del mar del Sur y Norte, como es Huatimala, Tecuantepec, Cuauhtzacualco, Campeche, Tecolotlan y los de las islas y costas de una mar y otra que después se vinieron a multiplicar." After a passage describing more Toltec customs, as well as an evil omen involving a howling deer that had occurred in Toltitlan before the Toltec defeat, Alva Ixtlilxochitl gives totals on the number of Toltecs who perished in the calamities and wars. His account ends with a listing of the important Toltec nobles who survived and certain places where they established themselves: Colhuacan, Tlaxcallan, Cuauhquechollan, "Tolzatepec," Tepexomaco, Chalollan, and Chapoltepec.

The account of the Toltecs and Topiltzin in the third *relación* of the *Noticia de los pobladores* (Alva Ixtlilxochitl 1952, I: 11–68, passim) is substantially similar, although much more abbreviated. Here the home of the three enemy/destroyer kings is more clearly indicated as "Quiahuiztlan y Anahuac." Topiltzin's flight to Tlapallan is also similar, but "según otros" it was to Hueyxalac, "antigua patria de sus pasados," where Topiltzin after his death was deified. The account in the *Relación sucinta* (Alva Ixtlilxochitl 1952, I: 11–70) is even more truncated. Its only significant deviation from the account just summarized is the *veintena* position of the day, Ce Ollin, of the Toltecs' final destruction in the year Ce Tecpatl: the impossible figure of the twenty-ninth day of Izcalli.

In the *Historia Chichimeca* (Alva Ixtlilxochitl 1952, II: 27–34) and the *Sumaria relación de la historia general de esta Nueva España* (Alva Ixtlilxochitl 1952, I: 469–474), Tecpancaltzin becomes "Iztaccaltzin" and his favorite, the mother of Topiltzin, "Quetzalxochitl." She is here not the daughter, but the wife of the noble, Papantzin. The three enemy kings are named "Coanacotzin, Huetzin, y Mixiotzin," and their provinces are specified as being on the coast of the "mar del Norte." The confusion increases when we are told that Topiltzin ordered his treasures carried to "la provincia de Quiahuixtlan, por temor de los reyes sus contrarios." The *Historia Chichimeca* version also makes it clearer that Topiltzin fulfilled one of the portents of the Toltec destruction by having "el cabello levantado desde la frente hasta la nuca, como a manera de penacho." The only other major variant in this much briefer account is the complete suppression of all details of Topiltzin's flight to Tlapallan. Just the bald statement is made that "el rey Topiltzin se perdió, que nunca más se supo de él."

Going back to the *Tercera relación* of the *Sumaria relación . . . de los Tultecas*, there is a relevant passage that was not mentioned at the time, for it seemed definitely out of place. It is found at the very end of the *relación*, immediately after describing the reign of the fifth ruler of Tollan, Nacaxoc (Alva Ixtlilxochitl 1952, I: 33). Here the statement is made that "estos reyes" were "altos de cuerpo y blancos, y barbados como los españoles." When Cortés arrived, he was believed to be Topiltzin (note the abrupt shift to the *last* ruler, who is not even introduced into the narrative until the fifth *relación*), who had promised to return at a future time "con sus vasallos antiguos de sus pasados." This "esperança incierta" was held until the coming of the Spaniards, "digo los simples y los que eran Tultecas de nación," for the lords well knew that he had gone to die in the province of Tlapallan, leaving certain laws that were afterwards enforced by the later rulers of the land.

Topiltzin also appears in the brief insert, *La orden y ceremonia para hacer un señor la cual constituyó el rey Topiltzin, señor de Tula, es la que sigue* (Alva Ixtlilxochitl 1952, I: 72–73), which in the Figueroa Compilation stands between the *Ordenanzas de Nezahualcoyotl* and the *Venida de los Españoles*. The coronation ceremony of Topiltzin is described, which involved being placed on the throne, covered with a blue mantle, and fasting in seclusion for four days. The passage then leaves the subject described in the title and goes on to tell how Topiltzin after some time as ruler announced that he desired to go "donde salía el sol," stating that within a certain time, in the year Ce Acatl ("en qual llegó gente Española a esta Nueva España"), he would return. Many people accompanied him on his departure, and at every town he passed through he left some of them, "y teníanle por ídol y por tal le adoraban." He went to die "a su pueblo, que se llama Matlapallan" (*sic*), saying again that he would return at the time he had specified and that they should await him. As the Spaniards arrived in that year and since they came from the east, they were thought to be Topiltzin returning. When Topiltzin died, he ordered that all his treasure should be burned with him. For four days it burned, at the end of which time he was cremated. His ashes were collected and placed in a pouch made from a jaguar skin, "y por esta causa a todos los Señores que en aquel tiempo morían los quemaban."

Topiltzin is also referred to in the *Décima relación* of the *Historia de los señores Chichimecas* (Alva Ixtlilxochitl 1952, I: 190–191), where, describing the last illness and death of Tezozomoc of Azcapotzalco, it is stated that the custom of placing a veil over the face of the idol of Tezcatlipoca during the illness of the supreme ruler (over Huitzilopochtli's face for the sickness of lesser rulers or other idols to which they might be especially devoted) had been originally instituted by Topiltzin of Tula.

In the *Relación cuarta* of the *Noticia de los pobladores* titled "De los antiguos Reyes Monarcas Chichimecas," Alva Ixtlilxochitl (1952, I: 263–264) presents some information on the "Chichimec" rulers who preceded Xolotl. After giving the details on the reigns of the immediate ancestors of the latter, he states that, "por haberles quemado las historias a estos naturales," no more information concerning the Chichimec rulers was available. But he does go on to say that there were many predecessors of those named, who succeeded the first ruler, the eponymous "Chichimecatl," giving the following list: "Mixcohuatl, Huitzilopochtli, Huemac, Nauhyotl, Cuauhtexpetla, No[no]hualca, Huetzin, Cuauhtonal, Mazatzin, Quetzal, y otros muchos." This list is actually the early portion of the Tollan/Colhuacan dynasty first presented in the *Juan Cano Relaciones*, with one significant substitution, that of "Huitzilopochtli" for Topiltzin Quetzalcoatl, and the omission of the eighth ruler, Achitometl. This is one of the most striking examples of the extreme confusion into which Alva Ixtlilxochitl, perhaps misled by his informants, could fall.

In the *Historia Chichimeca* (Alva Ixtlilxochitl 1952, II: 207–208), Quetzalcoatl is named, by inference, the god of Chololłan, in a passage explaining the institution of the "flowery war" between the Triple Alliance of Mexico Tenochtitlan, Tetzcoco, and Tlacopan and "los enemigos de casa," Tlaxcallan, Huexotzinco, and Cholollan. Lastly, in the final chapters of the same work, which describe the events leading up to and the events of the Conquest, the return-of-Quetzalcoatl concept plays an important role (see, especially, Alva Ixtlilxochitl 1952, II: 302, 313, 347, and 387). Interestingly, in these passages he is always called Quetzalcoatl, never Topiltzin. In Alva Ixtlilxochitl's other account of the Conquest, the *Décima tercera relación* of the *Noticia de los pobladores*, although there is one reference to the prophecy of the coming of the "hijos del sol" associated with the Spanish arrival, neither Quetzalcoatl nor Topiltzin is named.

SUMMARY

Alva Ixtlilxochitl provides somewhat confused data on three distinct figures, two of which at least appear to be aspects of Topiltzin Quetzalcoatl. The first can be summarized as follows: (1) during the Third Age, the Wind Sun, Ehecatonatiuh, a virtuous white-bearded missionary, wearing a long tunic, called Quetzalcoatl and also Hueman or Huemac, comes from the east in the year 1 Acatl to preach to the Olmeca and Xicalanca, particularly at Cholollan; (2) he preaches a highly moral doctrine, instituting the custom of fasting and introducing the adoration of the "cross"; (3) discouraged at his lack of success in propagating his creed, he departs in the direction from which he had come, prophesying great calamities and promising that he will return in a future year Ce Acatl, with his sons; (4) he disappears at Coatzacoalco, and, soon after, the Third Age is terminated by great winds, which also destroy the Great Pyramid of Chalollan; (5) on its ruins, the survivors build a temple to Quetzalcoatl (also called Ce Acatl, after the year of his arrival) as Wind God, believing that it was he who had sent the destructive hurricane.

Whether the "spiritual" guidance of the "gran astrólogo," Huematzin, during the Toltec migration and the early years of their establishment in Tollan is really a confused recollection of the leading of the Toltecs to Tollan by Topiltzin Quetzalcoatl, as recounted in other sources we have examined, is difficult to say, as is the case with so many of the variant versions of pre-Hispanic history found only in Alva Ixtlilxochitl. Some support for such a view lies in his statement that the "missionary" Quetzalcoatl, whose activities were just summarized, was also called Huemac. The name of one of the principal migration leaders, "Cecatzin," is also significant. Finally, Huematzin's office as seer, prophet, and priest jibes well with Topiltzin Quetzalcoatl's sacerdotal role. Since the question is highly confused, however, rather than further discuss the problem of the identity of Huematzin, I would prefer to examine a figure who, in spite of the striking deviancy of the account from any other, seems definitely to qualify as Alva Ixtlilxochitl's version of the Topiltzin Quetzalcoatl of Tollan Tale.

This long, discursive narrative can be briefly summarized as follows: (1) Topiltzin, by another name Meconetzin, is the son, born in the year 1 Acatl, of the next-to-last Toltec ruler, Tecpancaltzin (or Iztaccaltzin), by a beautiful girl, Xochitl (or Quetzalxochitl), whom he takes as concubine after seeing her for the first time when she came with her parents to present to him as a gift a new discovery, the honey of the maguey; (2) Topiltzin turns out to exhibit the characteristics predicted by the prophet Huematzin for the last ruler of Tollan, especially his hair in the form of a *penacho*; (3) acceding to the throne of Tollan at the expiration of his father's fifty-two-year term and reigning with two only slightly subordinate co-rulers, Cuauhtli and Maxtla, he finally fulfills the prophecy by becoming, after forty years, a dissolute and immoral ruler, bringing on a series of great calamities and disasters; (4) one of the gravest sins is committed by a noble lady of Tollan with one of the high priests of the Ce Acatl temple of Chalollan; (5) instrumental in inciting the Toltecs to further sin are two sorcerer-rulers, Tezcatlipoca and Tlatlauhqui Tezcatlipoca (= Xipe Totec), later deified; (6) after the appearance of other portents of the Toltec destruction prophesied by Huematzin, a series of disasters ensues, including great storms, droughts, insect plagues, and wars; (7) the greatest calamity is caused by an albino child, found on a hill near Tollan, the stench from whose rotting head results in a pestilence that carries off 90 percent of the Toltecs; (8) hard-pressed by his enemies—three rulers of the provinces of Quiahuitztlan Anahuac (Xalixco?), Xiuhtenancatzin (or Mixiotzin), Cohuanacoxtzin, and Huetzin—Topiltzin sends to them, along with a peace proposal, a rich gift that included a ball court and ball fashioned from precious gems; (9) this overture is rejected, and the three rulers lead an army into Tollan, where Topiltzin induces them to leave by agreeing to the test of combat ten years hence at Toltitlan; (10) at the appointed time, the battle is joined and the Toltecs are crushingly defeated, both on the borders of the Tlalhuica country and at Toltitlan; (11) in the year Ce Tecpatl, day 1 Ollin (the *veintena* varies between "Totozoztzintli" and Izcalli), Topiltzin, his co-rulers, his family, and the surviving Toltecs abandon Tollan, fleeing through Chiuhnauhtlan, Xaltocan, Teotihuacan, and Totolapan, during which flight all are killed but Topiltzin himself and a small band of Toltecs who successfully hide around the lake and the mountains of the Basin of Mexico; (12) after the departure of the three victorious enemy rulers with their army and their booty, Topiltzin emerges from his hiding place, a cave called Xico, near Tlalmanalco, and explains to an assembly of Toltec survivors at Colhuacan that he is leaving for some rich kingdoms of his ancestors, in the east, and will return in the year 1 Acatl; (13) he then travels to Tlapallan, where he lives for thirty more years; (14) dying, he orders his cremation, which initiated this custom, later general in Central Mexico; (15) at his death, he is deified and leaves behind many laws and ordinances that the later rulers attempted to enforce; (16) groups of surviving Toltecs establish themselves at various places, some migrating to the coasts of eastern and southern Mexico and continuing on to Guatemala and Campeche; (17) when the Spaniards arrive in the year Ce Acatl they are believed to be the returning Topiltzin.

COMMENT

Alva Ixtlilxochitl's account or, better, accounts of Topiltzin Quetzalcoatl are very difficult to evaluate. As stated above, three, possibly more, distinct figures seem to be described. Only one of them is specifically labeled Quetzalcoatl. Alva Ixtlilxochitl's account of him, although his chronology differs, is basically similar to the others in the category under consideration. Again, he is a virtuous bearded white stranger who comes to Mexico from parts unknown, from the east, and carries out an unsuccessful apostolic mission, especially at Cholollan, following which he departs again to the east, promising to return, which leads to his confusion with the Spaniards. Significantly, there is no association here of Quetzalcoatl with Tollan and the Toltecs, who are entirely replaced by the Olmeca and Xicalanca of ChololIan. His coming is placed in the third of Alva Ixtlilxochitl's four Suns, long before the entrance of the Toltecs onto the historical stage. As in Durán, he is identified with Huemac. How the prophet and early Toltec leader who bears this same name fits into this picture is unclear.

Alva Ixtlilxochitl's account of the third figure, Topiltzin, the last Toltec ruler, is the most difficult to assess. In the following elements, his version coincides with most accounts of the Basic Topiltzin Quetzalcoatl of Tollan Tale as previously reconstructed: (1) the name; (2) birth in year Ce Acatl; (3) ruler of Tollan; (4) forced to emigrate after series of calamities associated (very cursorily) with Tezcatlipoca; (5) death and subsequent cremation at Tlapallan; (6) prophecy of return and confusion with the Spaniards. In most other particulars it is quite unique.

What was it based on? Alva Ixtlilxochitl (1952, I: 60), himself, states, at its end: "Esta es la verdadera historia de los Tultecas, según yo la he podido interpretar, y los viejos principales con quienes lo he comunicado me lo han declarado, y otros memoriales escritos de los primeros que supieron escribir me lo han dado, así de esto como de los Chichimecas."

He then gives the name of six aged natives from different towns in Central Mexico, calling them "los principales que me han declarado memoriales de esto y de otras cosas." Without their original works it is, of course, impossible to evaluate the validity of the information they supposedly supplied our author. Alva Ixtlilxochitl occasionally refers in his account of the Toltecs to "la historia," as if he were basing it on a single fundamental document. He does this much more clearly in his account of "Chichimec" history. In this case, we know for certain that his source for its earlier portion was the *Codex Xolotl* or a very similar pictorial history. Did Alva Ixtlilxochitl also have a pictorial history interpreted for him for his account of Toltec history? Some support for this view might be found in the testimonial of the *cabildos* of Otumba and San Salvador Quatlacinco, which speaks of "cinco historias y crónicas . . . antiquísimas, escritas en pinturas y carácteres." The language is not completely clear, but *La historia y crónica de los Tultecas* seems to be named as one of them. In any case, of this chronicle and *La crónica de los reyes Chichimecas*, it is stated (Alva Ixtlilxochitl 1952, I: 461): "Estas dos Crónicas referidas hay mucho tiempo que fueron escritas o pintadas."

If this Toltec pictorial history ever existed, nothing remotely similar has ever come to light. Assuming for the moment that it did and that Alva Ixtlilxochitl's informants interpreted it more or less accurately, it can be said that it presents a most unusual version of Toltec history and of Topiltzin Quetzalcoatl's role in it, only agreeing in the most general way with any other known account. The wealth of detail it provides, even to dates in the native year count, makes it unlikely that it was the product of Alva Ixtlilxochitl's imagination, although various embellishments—many of which have a noteworthy "unindigenous" aspect—might well be ascribed to him.

This brings us to one of the most striking characteristics of Alva Ixtlilxochitl's writings as a whole—their markedly European flavor. This in spite of his much-touted native ancestry (he actually does not seem to have been more than one-quarter "Indian") and the possibility that at least the *relaciones* were originally composed in Nahuatl, which he certainly spoke well. In general, his writings display a distinctly more "rational" flavor, in the Western sense, than those accounts of Toltec history and Topiltzin Quetzalcoatl that we have reason to believe more or less faithfully record the authentic native tradition. The frankly supernatural is, of course, also present in Alva Ixtlilxochitl but is very much played down compared to these other, more genuinely indigenous versions. In short, one very definitely gets the impression that most of Alva Ixtlilxochitl's data have been strained through a basically late Renaissance European mind—the voice of the priest in the *calmecac* has faded to a whisper.

We will probably never know how much of Alva Ixtlilxochitl's confusion was due to himself and how much to that of his informants. In the case that can best be checked, his utilization of the *Codex Xolotl* or a cognate, his account appears to provide a substantially accurate rendering of the main facts presented in this detailed pictorial history. It is doubtful, however, whether we can extrapolate from this particular case and assume that his rendering of the unknown source or sources of his account of the pre-Toltec and Toltec periods is to be relied upon to an equal degree.

It is worth mentioning that one document has been claimed (Jiménez Moreno 1938: 575–576) as a source for Alva Ixtlilxochitl's account of Toltec history, the so-called *Anónimo Mexicano*, an apparently early seventeenth-century Nahuatl history (*Anónimo Mexicano* 1903; original manscript in the Bibliotèque Nationale, Paris, Manuscrit Mexicaine Núm. 254). This has yet to be demonstrated, however. Actually, in its version of Toltec history (Topiltzin Quetzalcoatl is completely omitted, even from the dynastic list, which otherwise duplicates that of Alva Ixtlilxochitl) the *Anónimo Mexicano* is much closer to the account of Torquemada (book III, chapter VI; 1943–1944, I: 252–254), the first portion of which in turn seems to be essentially a digest of the relevant portions of Alva Ixtlilxochitl's *Sumaria relación de la historia general de esta Nueva España*.

One of our chief problems in evaluating Alva Ixtlilxochitl's account of the Toltecs is the lack of other Tetzcocan accounts covering the same period. We have virtually nothing with which to compare it that would help us ascertain whether it might really constitute an authentic Tetzcocan version of Toltec history, as contrasted with those of the Colhuaque, Mexica, Cuauhtinchantlaca, and others. In addition, the task of appraising the reliability of Alva Ixtlilxochitl's chronicles is rendered more difficult by the fact, made obvious in our bibliographical discussion, that the only texts we possess are obviously somewhat corrupt copies, his original manuscripts having disappeared.

Concerning Alva Ixtlilxochitl's notoriously confused chronology little need be said. His dates for Topiltzin Quetzalcoatl are no exception, some of them being internally contradictory. Certainly his correlations with the Christian calendar are probably not to be taken very seriously. Even his geography at times seems as confused as his chronology. In certain instances, e.g., (Huehue) Tlapallan, in different passages he situates a certain place in widely separated regions.

The possibility was mentioned above that in Alva Ixtlilxochitl we may be confronted with a number of distinct figures that relate to Topiltzin Quetzalcoatl. Three have been mentioned. A fourth possibility might be the Topiltzin of *La orden y ceremonia para hacer un señor*. Although his name equates with Topiltzin Meconetzin, last ruler of Tollan, and their identification in Alva Ixtlilxochitl's mind is probable, it is noteworthy that the description of his "flight" is quite different from that in the *Relación quinta* of the *Sumaria relación . . . de los Tultecas* and corresponds more closely to the accounts of the tale that we assigned to the first, core category. Here, his departure is not occasioned by disasters at the time of the end of Tollan but appears more in the nature of a voluntary act. Many followers accompany him on his journey, in contrast to the other account where he flees by night with only a handful of retainers—and he leaves some behind at every town through which he passes, being adored as a god. There is no mention of a residence in Tlapallan, only of his cremation and the burning of his treasures. It could be argued that this brief passage is just an abbreviated version of the longer ones, with some variants, but these latter are at times considerable. In any case, the possibility remains that here Alva Ixtlilxochitl was recording a distinct tradition that corresponded more closely to the usual accounts of Topiltzin Quetzalcoatl's flight to Tlapallan.

One of the most significant aspects of Alva Ixtlilxochitl's account of Topiltzin is his chronological position as last ruler of Tollan—and in an obviously secular more than a sacerdotal capacity. This turnabout is accompanied by another even more interesting: the placement of Huemac (Huematzin) at the *beginning* of the Toltec era. The identification of Huemac with Quetzalcoatl, the white bearded missionary who preached to the Olmeca and Xicalanca, only increases this typical Alva Ixtlilxochitlian confusion. To top it off, in one passage, mentioned above, a white skin and beard are given to *all* of the Toltec rulers, including Topiltzin. Working with Alva Ixtlilxochitl is not recommended for scholars with low thresholds of frustration.

In sum, I must admit that I view much of Alva Ixtlilxochitl's data on the Toltecs and Topiltzin Quetzalcoatl with a somewhat jaundiced eye—without, by any means, rejecting them as valueless. As noted, many of the individual elements in his accounts find clear corroboration in sources that are earlier and exhibit much more of an authentic indigenous flavor. However, it cannot be without significance that most of these accounts, while differing among themselves in many respects, generally hang together rather well in opposition to Alva Ixtlilxochitl's versions, which often stand by themselves in a kind of lonely variancy. Although the information they contain should definitely be taken into consideration, in my view their relatively late date and the manifest internal confusion they display relegate Alva Ixtlilxochiitl's versions to a position of secondary value for our knowledge of the Basic Topiltzin Quetzalcoatl of Tollan Tale as it was current in the major centers of Central Mexico at the time of the Conquest.

5. The *Memorial Breve acerca de la fundación de la Ciudad de Colhuacan* of Domingo Francisco de San Antón Muñón Chimalpahin Cuauhtlehuanitzin

THE SOURCE

As is the case with most of the native and mestizo chroniclers, little is known of the life of this important author who, in the interests of spatial economy, we shall call simply Chimalpahin. On internal evidence, all that we know is that he was born in Amaquemecan on May 27, 1579, and was educated in the Convento de San Antonio Abad in Mexico City, where he seems later to have performed certain sacerdotal administrative functions (Siméon, in Chimalpahin 1889: xii–xiii; Rendón 1949: 199). The year of his death is not known, but a *terminus post quem* is provided by the probable year of the composition of the seventh *relación*, 1629 (see Chimalpahin 1889: 37). From his own statements, his impressive genealogy can be worked out in some detail (Siméon, in Chimalpahin 1889: 196; Rendón 1949: 200). He was a direct descendant of members of the most powerful royal dynasties of the province of Chalco, in the southeast Basin of Mexico.

Of his writings, eight separate but closely related works, called *relaciones*, have come down to us. Passing through the successive hands of Sigüenza y Góngora, Boturini (Catalogue § VIII, 12), Aubin, and Goupil, they are now the property of the Bibliothèque Nationale, Paris (Manuscrit Mexicaine Núm. 74), have been best described by Boban (1891, I: 27–31) and Jiménez Moreno (1938: 563–568), and have been published in sumptuous facsimile (Chimalpahin 1949). Whether these manuscripts are the holographs of Chimalpahin is not clear; their many mistakes make it more likely that they are seventeenth-century copies.

Of the eight *relaciones*, apart from the unpaleographized and untranslated facsimile versions, only three have been published. Siméon (Chimalpahin 1889) published the sixth and seventh, with Nahuatl and French translation in parallel columns, and Rendón (1949) has published the fourth, with Spanish translation. The *relación* that interests us here, the second, is unedited; its latter portion (folios 15–67) constitutes the *Memorial breve acerca de la fundación de la ciudad de Colhuacan*. At least two unpublished direct translations from the Nahuatl are extant, one in German by Walter Lehmann (see Kutscher 1948: 408–409), and one in Spanish by Miguel Barrios (Chimalpahin, n.d.). Kutscher has summarized the contents of the *Memorial breve* in a brief article (1948), based on the former translation. I have used the Barrios translation.

Chimalpahin was an annalist whose methods were similar to those employed by the anonymous compiler, or compilers, of the *Anales de Cuauhtitlan*. He utilized independent chronicles (apparently based ultimately on pre-Hispanic pictorial histories) from different places in the Basin of Mexico and attempted to fit them into a coherent, continuous chronological scheme—which resulted in the same kind of artificiality and distortion. As with the *Anales de Cuauhtitlan*, it is necessary to carefully distinguish his various sources before his writings can be critically utilized.

The *Memorial breve* has a somewhat misleading title (inserted in Spanish in the original manuscript); it is neither particularly brief nor is it dedicated solely, or even principally, to the history of Colhuacan. Many more of its fifty-two folios are devoted to a detailed account of the earliest history of the various separate groups that coalesced to form the province of Chalco, the history of the migrating ancestors of the Mexica, up to the "Babylonian Captivity" in Colhuacan, and a few brief snatches of Tetzcocan history. The history of the Colhuacan dynasty is only sketched out in the briefest and most laconic terms—but it is here that nearly all of the Topiltzin Quetzalcoatl material is found.

The *Memorial breve*, which is quite panoramic in its historical scope, may actually be only the first portion of a much more ambitious work, of which the latter part was left unfinished or has been lost. Its date is uncertain. It ends with a testimonial on land boundaries by one Miguel Quetzalmazatzin, which is dated 1607, but it is not certain that this can be also considered the date of the preceding *Memorial breve*.

THE TOPILTZIN QUETZALCOATL MATERIAL

The *Memorial breve* begins with the establishment of the "Chichimeca culhuaque" at Colhuacan in the year 10 Tochtli, which Chimalpahin equates with A.D. 670. No data are presented concerning their point of origin or their migration. It is also stated that the Xochimilca and those of Atlacuihuayan (Tacubaya) were already established upon their arrival. The Colhuaque soon became the overlords of Xochimilco, Cuitlahuac, Mizquic, Coyoacan, Ocuillan, and Malinalco. Forty-seven years later, in 5 Calli, Topiltzin Nauhyotzin becomes the first official ruler of Colhuacan (his birth is assigned to 2 Acatl, A.D. 675 in Chimalpahin's computation). Before that time, the Colhuaque had only been governed by war captains. Nauhyotzin is succeeded in 3 Acatl (A.D. 767) by Nonohualcatl, who in turn is succeeded, in 3 Calli, A.D. 845, by Yohuallatonac. In the twelfth year of the latter's reign, 1 Tecpatl (A.D. 857), a "triple alliance" is set up, with Colhuacan, Tollan, "on the right," and Otompan, "on the left," as the participating members (this is the first mention of Tollan). After a seventy-year reign, Yohuallatonac is succeeded by Quetzalacxoyatzin, who in turn is followed, in 7 Calli (A.D. 953), by Chalchiuhtlatonac. In 4 Acatl (A.D. 963), Hueymac is born to the prince Totepeuh, son of Chalchiuhtlatonac. Totepeuh becomes ruler twenty-two years later, in 13 Calli (A.D. 985). In the New Fire year, 2 Acatl (A.D. 987), Hueymac takes a bride, Maxio, in "Tototepec Metztitlan," and in 8 Calli (A.D. 993), he is placed on the throne of Tollan.

In 4 Tochtli (A.D. 1002), it is stated that "Topiltzin Acxitl Quetzalcohuatl" is born in Tollan. There follows a somewhat obscure statement, however, that indicates that according to another version he was brought to Tollan from parts unknown (Barrios's translation: "Pero no es verdad que vino del pecado (de los de Tullan) para que allí haya vencido a aparecer. ¿De dónde vino? Justamente no se sabe. Así van diciendo los viejos"). Back in Colhuacan, Totepeuh is succeeded in 2 Tochtli (A.D. 1026) by Nauhyotzin II.

In 5 Calli (A.D. 1029), it is stated that, according to one version, Hueymac died in this year and Topiltzin Acxitl Quetzalcohuatl succeeded to the throne of Tollan. Seven years later, in 12 Tecpatl (A.D. 1036), the evil omens of the coming destruction of the city commence. In 3 Tecpatl (A.D. 1040), Tollan cracks up and the dispersion of the Toltecs follows, with the consequent founding of new towns (only Chalollan is specifically named). Topiltzin Acxitl Quetzalcohuatl, however, remains eleven more years in Tollan before abandoning it. In the year 1 Acatl (A.D. 1051), he journeys toward the eastern seacoast to "Poctlan Tlapallan," saying that he would return to reestablish his kingdom. Chimalpahin parenthetically adds that the later rulers of Tenochtitlan were all cognizant of this prophecy, especially the second Motecuhzoma, who extended his hospitality to Cortés, believed to be the returning Quetzalcoatl.

He further states here that one of the causes of the abandonment of Tollan was a comet that appeared over the city, frightening its inhabitants. He also makes the important declaration that, upon Topiltzin Acxitl Quetzalcohuatl's departure from Tollan, 342 years had passed since its foundation, which would take that event back to 3 Calli (A.D. 689) (it was not mentioned, however, in its proper chronological position in the account). The author then states that, after Quetzalcohuatl's departure, the Toltecs (indicating that a substantial group of survivors remained) made Matlacxochitzin the new ruler of Tollan, adding that nothing was known of his subsequent fate.

A variant account is next presented, in which Hueymac, in this same year, 1 Acatl (A.D. 1051), comes from Tollan in pursuit of his enemy, Quetzalcohuatl. After failing to discover him anywhere, he enters "Cincalco

Chapultepec." Chimalpahin seems to express his preference for this version, which would give Hueymac a continuous reign of forty-nine years up to the time of his disappearance and would further necessitate some kind of joint rule with Quetzalcoatl for a long portion of this period.

In 10 Acatl (A.D. 1047), Tollan and Otompan having been destroyed, a new "triple alliance" is organized, Coatlinchan substituting for Tollan, Azcapotzalco replacing Otompan, and with Colhuacan playing the dominant role. The narrative then shifts abruptly to the migration of the ancestors of the Mexica from Aztlan/Chicomoztoc but continues throughout to present the chronology of the subsequent rulers of Colhuacan, whose names (but not dates) agree almost exactly with those in the *Juan Cano Relaciones* and the *Anales de Cuauhtitlan* (see complete lists in Lehmann 1938: 38–39).

Topiltzin Acxitl Quetzalcohuatl reappears somewhat later in the narrative in an entry under the year 3 Calli (A.D. 1209). In this year the ancestors of one of the Chalcan groups, the "Eztlapictin Teochichimeca," established themselves at Tizatepec, near Xochimilco. Chimalpahin takes this opportunity to employ one of his favorite devices, the flashback, this time to the period of the residence of this group in "Teotenanco Cuixcoc Temimilolco Yhuipan Zacanco," where they remained for perhaps as long as three hundred years while on their migration from Aztlan/Chicomoztoc to the Basin of Mexico. The Toltecs were established in Tollan at this time. During the reign of Topiltzin Acxitl Quetzalcohuatl, the envy of the latter was aroused by the sumptuous temple that the Eztlapictin Teochichimeca had raised to their god, Nauhyoteuhctli, and the rich offerings brought to it. This shrine was almost identical to those erected by Topiltzin Quetzalcoatl himself in Tollan, with four edifices constructed of jade, precious feathers, turquoise, and red shell. Topiltzin Acxitl Quetzalcohuatl's war against these devotees of Nauhyoteuhctli, in an attempt to capture the shrine and the richly attired idol, failed, however, and later the Eztlapictin Teochichimeca continued their migration, carrying the image of their god and oracle.

Topiltzin Acxitl Quetzalcohuatl occasionally reappears in Chimalpahin's frequent chronological flashbacks, but only the last of these supplies any significant new information. This is found at the very end of the narrative (just before the inserted testimonial of Miguel Quetzalmazatzin), as part of a long recapitulation of various periods, beginning with the creation of the world (biblical), that had elapsed up to the time of the entrance of the migrating Mexica into Tizapan Colhuacan following the Chapoltepec defeat. Here it is indicated that the cause of the Toltec destruction was their great sins, leading to the appearance of the comet for eleven years. This was in the time of the ruler Topiltzin Acxitl Quetzalcohuatl, who was feared and respected throughout New Spain. The cognizance of this by the nine rulers of Mexico Tenochtitlan is again mentioned, and a statement of Motecuhzoma

Xocoyotzin, the "superstitious," is quoted to the effect that they (the rulers) were only the representatives, the lieutenants, of this great sorcerer and seer. Again, Chimalpahin states that eleven years after the abandonment of Tollan, Topiltzin Acxitl Quetzalcohuatl departed for the east, for the "towns of the sun," to Tlapallan, where he was called by the sun. And the wise ancients still said, "He lives yet, he has not died. And he will come again to rule."

SUMMARY

(1) Topiltzin Acxitl Quetzalcohuatl is either born in Tollan or brought there from unknown parts in the year 4 Tochtli, A.D. 1002, while Hueymac, son of the incumbent ruler of Colhuacan, Totepeuh, is reigning; (2) according to one version, Hueymac dies in 5 Calli, A.D. 1029, and is succeeded by Topiltzin Quetzalcoatl, a great sorcerer and seer; according to another, Hueymac continues his rule, but the former also succeeded to the throne; (3) while ruler, Topiltzin Quetzalcoatl wages an unsuccessful war against the "Eztlapictin Teochichimeca," then established in Teotenanco Cuixcoc Temimilolco Yhuipan Zacanco, in an attempt to capture the richly adorned idol Nauhyoteuhctli and his sumptuous temple; (4) in 12 Tecpatl, A.D. 1036, the portents of Tollan's approaching destruction begin, and in 3 Tecpatl, A.D. 1040, the Toltec dispersion commences; (5) Topiltzin Quetzalcoatl remains in Tollan for eleven more years, then departs in the year 1 Acatl, A.D. 1051, journeying to the east to Poctlan Tlapallan, where he has been called by the sun; (6) before he disappears, he promises to return to reclaim his kingdom; (7) this prophecy was always recalled by the nine rulers of Tenochtitlan, especially Motecuhzoma II, who considered himself only the deputy of the departed ruler and who greeted Cortés as the returning lord of Tollan; (8) in the variant version of Hueymac's end, he and Topiltzin Quetzalcoatl are great enemies, and, in the same year that the latter abandons Tollan, Hueymac also departs in pursuit of him; (9) failing in his aim of overtaking him, he disappears in "Cincalco Chapultepec."

COMMENT

Although not quite as difficult as the accounts of Alva Ixtlilxochitl to work with, this version of his contemporary, Chimalpahin, presents some genuinely challenging problems. Parallels for nearly all of the individual elements in Chimalpahin's account of Topiltzin Quetzalcoatl can also be found in the sources we assigned to our first category, but they have been juggled and rearranged in a somewhat disconcerting fashion. Although we encounter here again the names of the three standard preeminent figures of Toltec history, Totepeuh (-Mixcoatl), Topiltzin Quetzalcoatl, and Huemac, they stand in an entirely new relationship with one another. The first has become a Colhuaque ruler who is the father of the third, not the second, and Huemac is named as acceding to the throne of Tollan before Topiltzin Quetzalcoatl himself. The latter's own antecedents are obscure. He and Huemac are contemporaries and enemies, and Huemac leaves Tollan in his pursuit. Tezcatlipoca's persecutions of Topiltzin Quetzalcoatl, Huemac, and the Toltecs in general are not mentioned. The account of Topiltzin Quetzalcoatl's flight is sketchy but fairly standard. Only the place-name Poctlan, linked with that of Tlapallan, is new. Chimalpahin's chronology of the Colhuaque and Toltec dynasties, especially the great antiquity he attributes to the former, will not be commented upon here, being reserved for a later discussion.

Explaining the anomalous features of this version of the tale is difficult. Can we detect the hand of Chimalpahin himself here—or are we dealing with an authentic pre-Hispanic variant of the history of Colhuacan and Tollan? Unless some new information comes to light concerning the source (or, better, sources, since, by his own statement, he was drawing from at least two distinct traditions) upon which Chimalpahin based his account, it is doubtful that this question can ever be satisfactorily answered. Its similarity, in three important points—(1) the coming, in one version, of Topiltzin Quetzalcoatl from parts unknown to Tollan; (2) his contemporaneity with Huemac; and (3) his persecution by the latter—with another late sixteenth-century account, that of Muñoz Camargo (via Torquemada), is perhaps significant. On the other hand, the lack of the white skin, beard, and proselytizing activities usually ascribed to Quetzalcoatl in the longer later accounts is also noteworthy (explained by the extreme sketchiness of Chimalpahin's treatment of our hero?).

As will be brought out below, the great antiquity assigned in the *Memorial breve* to the dynasty of the Colhuacan of the Basin of Mexico agrees with no other source. Some distortion, therefore, might also be expected in Chimalpahin's account of Topiltzin Quetzalcoatl. The best clue, I believe, is provided by the obscurity of his origin. As we have seen, in the most reliable early accounts there is nothing really obscure about either his parentage or place of origin, however much these may differ from source to source. With the exception of Olmos, an unknown or "foreign" origin for our hero is only encountered in the sources of the category now under consideration, all dating from the later sixteenth and early seventeenth centuries (Sahagún's silence is a special case). Obvious Christian influence has been at work in all of these accounts. The same influence is probably present, to a somewhat lesser degree, in this *Memorial breve* account of Topiltzin Quetzalcoatl—certainly not surprising in view of the compiler's known education and later career, as well as his manifest interest in and knowledge of biblical matters. Again, however, whether this presumed distortion was due to Chimalpahin himself is uncertain; he may only have been faithfully copying his sources.

Chimalpahin was undoubtedly utilizing a valid source for his account of the later history of the Toltec-Colhuaque dynasty, since, from the time of the fall of Tollan, it agrees so closely with both the *Juan Cano Relaciones* and the *Anales de Cuauhtitlan*. I am inclined to be quite skeptical, however, of the validity of its early part, especially that involving the chronology and familial relations of Totepeuh, Topiltzin Quetzalcoatl, and Huemac. It stands strikingly apart from the (probably separately compiled) accounts in these two earlier sources, whose general reliability is supported by many lines of evidence. This, at least, would be my somewhat negative hypothesis until fresh evidence appears. For this reason, together with its late date, I have placed Chimalpahin's version of the Topiltzin Quetzalcoatl of Tollan Tale in this category of later accounts possessing secondary value.

This completes the survey of the most important sources from the Nahuatl-speaking area of Central Mexico that contain relevant data concerning our hero. Since most of the ruling dynasties of the leading polities of this region at the time of the Conquest claimed Toltec descent, it is not surprising that the rich body of traditional lore surrounding Tollan and its past glories, which seems to have usually included the Topiltzin Quetzalcoatl of Tollan Tale, was preserved in various versions throughout this wide area. It also follows that not only in Central Mexico but wherever in Mesoamerica the stamp of Toltec influence is clearly apparent, some reminiscences of their great priest/ruler are likely to be present. The remainder of the basic data presentation section, therefore, will consist largely of following out "the tracks of the Toltecs" into those areas of Mesoamerica where linguistic, ethnohistorical, and archaeological evidence makes it probable that Toltecs and Toltec-connected dynasts—and/or their strong influence—must have penetrated.

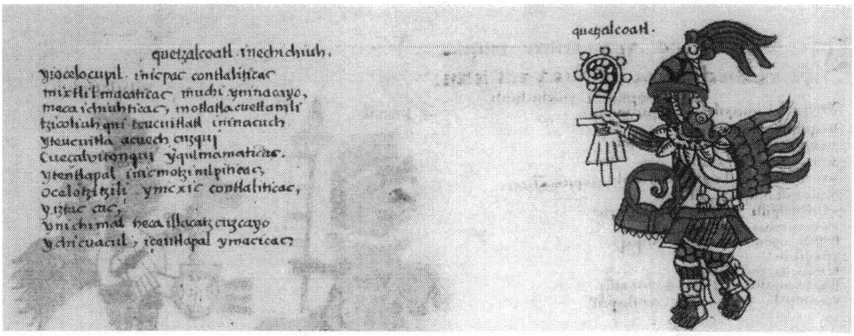

Color Plate 1. *The deity Quetzalcoatl, with itemization of the Nahuatl terms for all significant elements of his costume and insignia. Fray Bernardino de Sahagún,* Primeros Memoriales, *folio 261 verso. From Sahagún 1993. Courtesy of the Palacio Real de Madrid.*

Color Plate 2. *First depiction of Topiltzin Quetzalcoatl illustrating the narrative of his tale in the Sahaguntine* Florentine Codex. *He is attired as the deity Quetzalcoatl (see caption to* Color Plate 6*) and is seated on a mat seat while drawing blood from his leg with a maguey spine. Before him are the* chicoacolli *and a feather-trimmed shield bearing the* ehecacozcatl *("wind jewel") motif.* Florentine Codex, *fol. 211 recto. From Sahagún 1979.*

Color Plate 3. Topiltzin Quetzalcoatl, seated in a pool bathing, surrounded by his chicoacolli, *his headpiece, and his feathered shield.* Florentine Codex, *211 verso. From Sahagún 1979.*

Color Plate 4. *Topiltzin Quetzalcoatl, in standard garb, confronting Titlacahuan (Tezcatlipoca) disguised as an old man, who offers him a cup of* octli *(pulque)*. Florentine Codex, *213 recto. From Sahagún 1979.*

Color Plate 5. *Topiltzin Quetzalcoatl, in a drunken sleep, with his* chicoacolli *and feathered shield*. Florentine Codex, *folio 223 recto. From Sahagún 1979.*

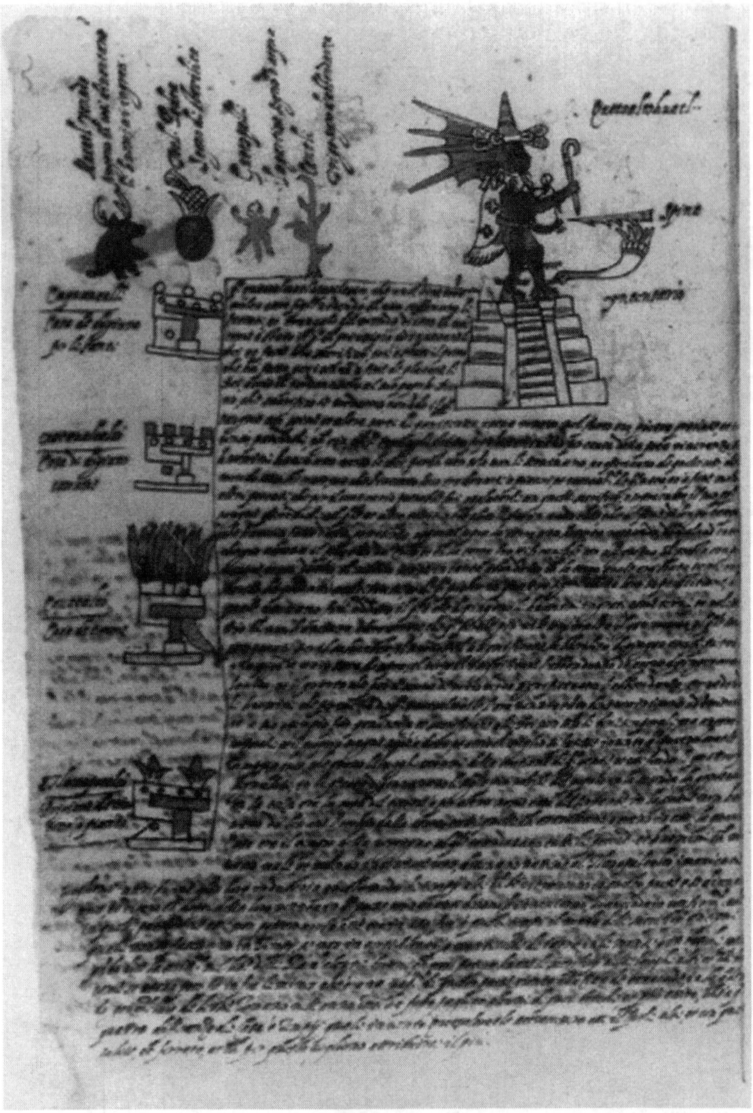

Color Plate 6. *Account, in the Italian* Codex Vaticanus A, *fol. 7 verso, of the Topiltzin Quetzalcoatl of Tollan Tale. TQ, painted the sacerdotal black and attired as the deity Quetzalcoatl, wearing his usual headpiece,* ocelocopilli, *the black and red feather neck fan,* cuezahuiltoncatl, *and wearing a white cloak decorated with crosses (= stylized knots?), is depicted standing on a pyramid temple, brandishing his curved baton,* chicoacolli *or* e(he)cahuictli. *Before him is a maguey spine and a handled* incensario (tlemaitl). *Other maguey spines puncture his legs. Also depicted, in addition to the four icons that symbolized the cessation of the drought that occasioned the collapse of Tollan, are the four "penitential houses" of TQ—Zaquancalli, Nezahualcalco, Coacalco, and Tlaxapochcalco. From Kingsborough 1964–1967: III.*

Color Plate 7. Second depiction of TQ illustrating the narrative of his tale in the Codex Vaticanus A, *folio 9 recto. He is shown, holding the* chicoacolli *and an incense pouch,* copalxiquipilli, *leading a multitude from Tollan, accompanied by his "disciple," the penitent Xipe Totec, and approaching twin mountains, where most of his followers turned to stone. From Kingsborough 1964–1967: III.*

Color Plate 8. Topiltzin Quetzalcoatl, again brandishing the chicoacolli *and holding an incense pouch, at the end of his "flight" to Tlillan Tlapallan, "The Black and Red Place," in the* Codex Vaticanus A, *folio 9 verso. From Kingsborough 1964–1967: III.*

Color Plate 9. A bearded personage, ostensibly Fray Diego Durán's version of Topiltzin Quetzalcoatl, seated on a stool on a stand, or litter, with serpentine handles, wearing what appears to be a variant of the quetzalapanecayotl *feather headdress. Before him is what appears to be his serpent mask,* coaxayacatl. *Durán,* Historia de las Indias de Nueva España y islas de tierra firme, *folio 228 recto. From Durán 1967. Courtesy of Courtesy of Editorial Porrúa (Mexico).*

Color Plate 10. *Ehecatl Quetzalcoatl. Durán,* Historia de las Indias de Nueva España y islas de tierra firme, *folio 251 verso. From Durán 1967. Courtesy of Editorial Porrúa (Mexico).*

Color Plate 11. Ignacio Marquina's reconstruction drawing of the upper portion of Pyramid B, Tula, Hidalgo. From Marquina 1964: lámina 46. Courtesy of the Instituto Nacional de Antropología e Historia (Mexico).

II. Central Mexico: Non-Nahuatl

Before leaving Central Mexico, however, some brief attention to possible Topiltzin Quetzalcoatl reminiscences among other linguistic groups of this area—significant portions of which were probably subject at one time to Toltec political authority—is in order. Next to the Nahuatl-speakers, the Otomi were numerically the most important group in the area. It is to them we first turn. Since the data are so scanty, rather than considering each source in turn, the information concerning this group will be discussed in general terms. Practically all of the available data on the pre-Hispanic culture of the Otomi-speakers of Central Mexico were conveniently summarized by Pedro Carrasco (1950). He noted that the Otomi of Xilotepec, not too far from Tollan (Ramos de Cárdenas 1897: 34), "reverenciaban en gran manera un ídolo de piedra de la figura de hombre al cual llamaban eday que quiere decir dios de los vientos, el cual creía que había criado todo lo universo. Tenía dos bocas una encima de otra."

Carrasco (1950: 147), with justice, corrected *eday* to *edahi*, which translates as "wind." This passage is clearly a description of an Otomi version of Ehecatl Quetzalcoatl. However, the anonymous Spanish-Otomi dictionary of the Biblioteca Nacional de México (whose *terminus post quem* is 1640 but which is probably a later copy of a much earlier document that may have been compiled in the Xilotepec area) gives, among other names, *ek'çmaxi* or *k'çmaxi* (= feathered serpent) for "ministro del ídolo de las ciencias" (Carrasco

1950: 147–148). Carrasco suggested that this personage, judging from the way he is described, might have been a version of Topiltzin Quetzalcoatl. This seems a distinct possibility, although no traditions concerning this figure appear to have survived.

Whether other linguistic groups of Central Mexico (Huaxtec, Totonac, Tepehua, Mazahua, Matlatzinca, Ocuilteca, etc.), some communities of which had almost surely been subjected at one time to Toltec control or strong influence, also possessed at Contact some version of the Topiltzin Quetzalcoatl of Tollan Tale is difficult to judge, since so little primary source material on these groups has been preserved. It has long been recognized that Ehecatl Quetzalcoatl—and possibly Topiltzin Quetzalcoatl as well—displays some obvious links to the Huaxteca, but the skimpy sixteenth-century sources on this important northern Gulf Coast region provide nothing definite concerning the presence of recollections of the latter among Huaxtec-speaking groups at the time of the Conquest. As for the Totonac, it has been suggested (Krickeberg 1933: 80–81; Dahlgren 1953: 155) that the third member of the "trinity" of major deities reported from that group (Las Casas 1909, I: 311–312; Mendieta 1945, I: 96–97 [apparently derived from Olmos]) might bear a relationship to Topiltzin Quetzalcoatl, but, if so, obviously only in a very general and nonspecific way. With certain of the other groups, deities have been reported that conceivably shared some features with Ehecatl Quetzalcoatl, but no clear-cut Topiltzin Quetzalcoatl recollections have so far been discerned in the surviving ethnohistorical sources.

There appears to be no positive trace of the presence of the tale in western Mexico, among the Tarascans, their neighbors of archaic Nahua affiliation, and some other little-known linguistic groups—in spite of a certain amount of archaeological and ethnohistorical evidence for Toltec influence in this region. Corona Núñez (1946, 1948) believed that some of the Tarascan deities described in the *Relación de Michoacán* are related to Quetzalcoatl. Even assuming this to be the case, however, their relationship would probably be much closer to Ehecatl Quetzalcoatl than to the Toltec priest/ruler with whom we are concerned. There are scattered traces throughout western Mexico in colonial works (e.g., in Tello 1891–1945 and the *Relación de Ameca* [Antonio de Leiva 1878]) of missionary-like prophets that somewhat resemble the way our hero is featured in certain late Central Mexican versions of the tale, previously examined. Whether they contain any genuine reminiscence of Topiltzin Quetzalcoatl of Tollan, however, seems unlikely.

III. Oaxaca

It is now south and east that our trail leads, along the route that is known to have been followed by various émigré Toltec groups probably before, during, and shortly after the crack-up of the Toltec *Reich*. The first major region to be especially examined will be Oaxaca, where the Mixtec- and Zapotec-speakers were, by a considerable margin, in the numerical ascendancy over a medley of other tongues, the majority related in varying degrees of closeness to one another and belonging to the so-called Macro-Otomangue stock (Popoloca, Chocho, Mazatec, Ichcatec, Cuicatec, Chinantec, Tlapanec, Tequistlatec, Trique, Amuzgo, Chatino, Huave, Mixe, et al.). The Mixtec will be considered first, among whom Toltec influence seems to have been especially evident and in parts of whose region Toltec and/or Toltec-connected dynasts appear to have settled. In this and succeeding sections, the presentation scheme will frequently be straightforwardly discursive unless the importance of the source(s) warrants a return to the outline method employed in the previous chapters.

A. La Mixteca

As mentioned, Toltec influence in this particular region of Oaxaca is especially apparent (Dahlgren 1954: 54–56, 78–86, 380), an influence that must have been significantly intensified by actual settlement of some Toltec or Toltec-connected groups along the northern frontier of the Mixteca (Acatlan, Piaztlan, etc.) and even well into Mixtec/Chocho territory (Coixtlahuacan, Tamazolapan, Tequixtepec, etc.) (Velázquez 1945: 15; Lehmann 1938: §§ 215–222; Alva Ixtlilxochitl 1952, I: 89). Earlier, the possible presence of "un substrato o cultura base común a los grupos del Valle de México, de Puebla, Tlaxcala, Mixteca, Tula y otros," which Dahlgren (1954: 379–380) suggested might be called "olmeca, pretolteca o cultura base," would have provided significant links between the Toltec cultural configuration and that which developed in western Oaxaca with its focus among the Mixtec-speakers. Some recollections of Topiltzin Quetzalcoatl, therefore, might be expected in this area.

Primary documentation on the Mixteca, however, is not nearly as extensive as for Central Mexico, in spite of the region's importance as a key secondary cultural and political center in Postclassic Mesoamerica. Apart from what is chronicled in the numerous native-tradition pictorials, only a few fragments of local traditional history have been preserved—especially in certain of the 1579–1585 *relaciones geográficas*, the Fray Antonio de los Reyes *Arte en lengua Mixteca*, and the chronicles of Fray Francisco de Burgoa (quoted and discussed in Dahlgren 1954: 51–54). No mention of a figure clearly corresponding to Topiltzin Quetzalcoatl seems to be contained in this material, but the extreme sketchiness of much of it must be emphasized.

A statement in the 1674 *Descripción geográfica* of the seventeenth-century Dominican Fray Francisco de Burgoa (1934, I: 332), describing the important local god of Achiotlan (Achiutla), whose cult extended throughout a large area of the Mixteca, indicates that a form of Quetzalcoatl might have been known. This deity, called "Corazón del Pueblo," was venerated in the shape of "una esmeralda tan grande como un grueso pimiento de esta tierra," which "tenía labrado encima una avecita, o pajarillo, con grandísimo primor, y de arriba abajo enroscada una culebrilla con el mesmo arte." Although the name given by Burgoa would seem to connect this god more with the Central Mexican Tepeyollotl, "Hill-Heart," the iconography of the image carved on this "esmeralda," as Seler, Dahlgren, and others have pointed out, rather suggests an association with Quetzalcoatl, the bird-snake.

The sketch of the cosmogony of the important Valley of Oaxaca Mixtec-speaking outpost of Coyolapan (Cuilapan), preserved in the 1607 *Origen de los Indios de el Nuevo Mundo* (second edition, 1729: 327–328) of the early-seventeenth-century Dominican Fray Gregorio García, appears to indicate that a form of Ehecatl Quetzalcoatl was also known, with possible overtones of Topiltzin Quetzalcoatl. This interesting fragment, based on a lost pictorial history, recounts how the two primal creator gods, "un Ciervo, Culebra de León" and "un Ciervo, Culebra de Tigre," residing in a palace on the summit of a magically raised cliff near Apohuallan (Apoala) in the Mixteca Alta, give birth to two sons, "mui hermosos, discretos, i sabios en todas las Artes," called "Viento de nueve Culebras" and "Viento de nueve Cavernas," from their natal days. After being "criados en mucho regalo," the pair possessed the power to transform themselves into various shapes. The elder, when he wished to amuse himself, turned into an eagle and flew over the mountaintops. The other could change himself into "vn Animal pequeño, figura de Serpiente, que tenía alas, con que volaba por los Aires con tanta agilidad, i sutileza, que entraba por las Peñas, i paredes, i se hacia invisible."

The brothers undertook to offer sacrifices to their parents, utilizing clay *incensarios*, "sobre las quales echaron cierta cantidad de veleño molido," which was the first offering made in the world. They next proceeded to create a recreative garden, after which they made "oración, votos, i promesas" to their parents, beseeching them to create the heavens, to permit light to appear, to form the earth, "o . . . aparciese, i las aguas se congregasen, pues no havía otra cosa para su descano, sino aquel pequeño vergel." To aid their cause, they drew blood from their ears and tongues, sprinkling it on the trees and plants with a willow branch, "como cosa santa y bendita." García, wishing to avoid prolixity, skips certain succeeding details, concluding his account with a reference to further sons and daughters engendered by the creators, a great deluge in which many of the gods perish, followed by the creation of the earth and the heavens by a deity called "Criador de todas las cosas." Humanity is soon restored, and "de aquesta manera se pobló aquel reino Mixteco."

As Seler (1904b: 290), Dahlgren (1954: 297–298), and others have noted, the hero brothers, both of whom probably originally bore the calendric name 9 Ehecatl, the first with the additional name of serpent and the second with that of cave, or earth monster, obviously bear a close relation to Ehecatl Quetzalcoatl (plus Xolotl?)—and possibly Topiltzin Quetzalcoatl as well. The name 9 Ehecatl, the flying serpent, the magical transformative powers, the instituting of sacrifice and ritual bloodletting—all these elements suggest a conception in which both aspects of Quetzalcoatl have been fused.

In addition to these sketchy notices of figures that perhaps are related to both versions of Quetzalcoatl in the documentary sources, in the Mixteca pictorial histories (especially the codices *Vindobonensis*, *Zouche-Nuttall*, and *Bodley*, the *Selden Roll*, and the *Lienzo Antonio de León*) numerous references to either or both have been identified. Alfonso Caso has for some years been engaged in an exhaustive analysis of these documents, but only some of his findings have been published (e.g., Caso 1949, 1950, 1951, 1954; cf. Burland 1947, 1955; Nowotny 1948a, 1948b). In view of this research in progress, I will limit my consideration of Quetzalcoatl in the Mixteca pictorials to a brief summary.

A figure displaying the costume and insignia similar to that of Ehecatl Quetzalcoatl in the Central Mexican pictorials, with or without his distinctive snouted "wind mask," is frequently depicted in these documents. He often bears the calendric name 9 Wind (1 Reed is also occasionally associated with him). Most importantly for our purposes, Caso (1949: 23; 1950: genealogical chart) and others have interpreted certain scenes as indicating that many of the ruling dynasties of the leading polities of the Mixteca traced their descent from him. The most striking are those that illustrate "the descent of Quetzalcoatl" from heaven to earth (e.g., *Codex Vindobonensis* 1929: 48; *Selden Roll* [Burland 1955]), after apparently being engendered and receiving his instructions from the creator pair, both of whom bear the calendric name, 1 Deer (= Central Mexican Ometecuhtli and Omecihuatl). The relevance of these scenes to the Coyolapan cosmogony is obvious. In another scene (*Codex Vindobonensis*: 1929: 49), 9 Wind is issuing from a giant stone knife (cf. birth of 1,600 gods from a similar implement in the Olmos/Mendieta cosmogony, mentioned above). In the following *Codex Vindobonensis* 48 scene, above the small naked 9 Wind who is surrounded by his insignia, four small houses, or temples, are depicted. As Burland (1953: 18; his specific identifications must be questioned, however) suggested, these may be the Mixteca version of the four houses, or oratories, of Topiltzin Quetzalcoatl, different versions of which in the Central Mexican sources were described above.

Again, in these passages we are possibly dealing with a personage who represented a fusion of Ehecatl Quetzalcoatl and Topiltzin Quetzalcoatl, the latter primarily in his role as the fountainhead of legitimate political power. These scenes in the pictorials, combined with the statement of Fray Antonio de los Reyes (1889: i–iii) in his 1593 Mixtec grammar, that the lords of Apohuallan were originally outsiders who moved in and set up their rule over "los naturales mixtecos que habitaban en esta tierra antes y la poseían y tenían por suya," bolster the evidence from Central Mexican sources, previously cited, that various of the leading dynasties of this region—like those in northern Yucatan and Highland Guatemala—possessed a Toltec background. Some of these putatively Toltec-connected Mixteca dynasts, as seems to have been the case with some of those in the Mayance-speaking areas, may well have borne a version of the name Quetzalcoatl or related denominations, including his calendric name, as a *title*. And the Mixteca ancestral figure 9 Wind, iconographically so similar to the Central Mexican Ehecatl Quetzalcoatl, could possibly hark back to Toltec conquests of—and/or dispersions to—parts of western Oaxaca.

COMMENT

Caso's definitive study may clarify the problem of the possible presence of traditions relating to Topiltzin Quetzalcoatl in the Mixteca, particularly in the pictorial histories. Again, enough evidence has been adduced to indicate that wandering Toltec dynasts, at least in some parts of the Mixteca, might have carried with them recollections of their great priest/ruler, resulting in an ancestral figure that combined aspects of this personage with the old creator/wind god, Ehecatl Quetzalcoatl. There is also some evidence for more generalized Toltec—or at least archaic Nahua—influence on the cosmogony, early legendary history, and religion of the Mixteca. Examples are the importance of Chicomoztoc, the Seven Caves, as primeval homeland (especially in the *Selden Roll* and *Lienzo Antonio de León*), the investiture of Mixteca dynasts by ostensibly Toltec or Toltec-connected rulers (Caso 1949: 26), and the near identity, in costume and insignia, of numerous Mixteca deities with their Central Mexican counterparts (e.g., Tlaloc, Tonatiuh, Ehecatl Quetzalcoatl, Xolotl, Xipe Totec, Xochiquetzal, et al.). Stressing the importance of Quetzalcoatl's appearance in the Mixteca pictorial histories, Caso (1941b: 51) went so far as to characterize him as "el héroe tribal de esta nación, como Huitzilopochtli lo fué de los aztecas." This may be somewhat of an exaggeration, but his importance in one form or another in the region can hardly be denied.

B. Zapotecapan

In spite of the considerable cultural and political importance of this region of eastern Oaxaca, dominated by the Zapotec-speakers, primary documentation on its pre-Hispanic polities is frustratingly scanty. The somewhat scattered 1579–1585 *relaciones geográficas* and Burgoa constitute the chief sources of ethnographic and historical information, although the *Codex Vaticanus* A contains a few tidbits of value. The rich religious and ceremonial aspect of Conquest-period Zapotec culture is very imperfectly known; traditional history with substantial time depth is nearly lacking. The situation here is much less satisfactory than in the case of the Mixteca, where the rich corpus of historical/genealogical pictorials, both pre- and post-Conquest, supplies a copious amount of information. Not a single Conquest-period pictorial history with time depth reaching as far back as the Early Postclassic has yet been identified as originating in a Zapotec-speaking community.

There is much less evidence for clear-cut Toltec influence in Zapotecapan than in the Mixteca. As Seler (1904b: 258) pointed out, for the Central Mexican Nahua-speakers it was somewhat beyond their more immediate ethnic horizon, the great Toltec trade and migration routes seemingly having bypassed much of their territory. There should be less cause, therefore, to expect any very clear reminiscences of Topiltzin Quetzalcoatl of Tollan in eastern Oaxaca.

Nevertheless, Seler (1904b: 276) believed that the Zapotec high priests, particularly those at Mitla (Lyobaa), "were considered as the living images of the priest god of the Toltecs, as the incarnation of Quetzalcoatl." He based this view on the similarity of the Quetzalpetlatl incident in the *Anales de Cuauhtitlan*, described above, to Burgoa's (1934, II: 125) description of the method of the transmission of the office of high priest at Mitla:

> . . . nunca se casaban estos sacerdotes, ni comunicaban a mujeres, sólo en ciertas solemnidades que celebran con muchas bebidas y embriagueces les traían señoras solteras y si alguna había concebido, la apartaban hasta el parto, porque si naciese varón se criase para la sucesión del sacerdocio, que tocaba al hijo o pariente más cercan, y nunca elegía.

I would regard this suggested connection as quite dubious. Even assuming a sexual connotation for the Quetzalpetlatl incident, there can be no certainty that this practical expedient of the Mitleños for furthering their sacerdotal line was intended to be a reminiscence of this particular incident in the Topiltzin Quetzalcoatl of Tollan Tale.

Seler (1904b: 284–286) also saw a connection between certain of the appellatives given in Fray Juan de Córdova's 1578 Spanish-Zapotec dictionary for the great creator god (especially Coqui-Xee and Coqui-Cilla) and the name of Topiltzin Quetzalcoatl after his transformation into the planet Venus, Tlahuitzcalpantecuhtli. The latter certainly and probably the former can be translated: "Lord of the (House of) Morning, or the Dawn." However, a connection with Ehecatl Quetzalcoatl also seems likely, for the additional appellations, Pije-Tào and Pij-Xòo, can probably be translated as "the strong or great wind" and "the great, the strong, powerful spirit."

Finally, Quetzalcoatl in some form was certainly known to the Zapotecs of Mitla, for nine representations of a deity iconographically cognate with Ehecatl Quetzalcoatl are present on the fragmentary Mixteca-Puebla–style wall paintings of the structures there (Seler 1904b: 306–324, passim). One of these (fragment 4, plate XXXIX) displays the year 1 Reed, accompanied by the "Mixtec" year symbol, next to the head. The style of these paintings is closely related to that which in late pre-Hispanic times prevailed in the Mixteca, and the suggestion has been made that these paintings were added by Mixtec-speakers after their political rise in late pre-Hispanic times in the Valley of Oaxaca. However, in my view (Nicholson 1957b) it seems more likely that the Zapotec-speaking priesthood of one of the greatest shrines in Zapotecapan had adopted or inherited this variant of the widespread Late Postclassic Mesoamerican Mixteca-Puebla style, along with certain Central Mexican/Mixteca deities and religious conceptions.

There is another figure of Zapotec myth or legend, concerning whom only vague allusions have been preserved in Burgoa, that has been claimed to have been analogous to Topiltzin Quetzalcoatl in his late "foreign missionary" guise. Brasseur de Bourbourg (1851: 69–70; 1857–1859, III: 9–11), followed by Bancroft (1882–1883, III: 454, 457), called this figure "Wixepecocha" or "Guixipecocha." However, the original relevant passage in Burgoa (1934, I: 351–352) reads:

> . . . está en distancia de cuatro leguas de este sitio de Tehuantepeque, otro que llamaron Guixipecocha, en su lengua, y hoy es pueblo de La Magdalena en el campo, cerca de un arroyo un peñasco de hasta quince o veinte estados de alto y cerca de la cumbre, una prodigiosa figura de tiempo inmemorable de su antigüedad y entre la peñas a distancia de docientos pasos se ve una estatua de un religioso, con hábito blanco como el nuestro, sentado en una silla de espaldar, la capilla puesta, la mano en la mejilla, vuelto el rostro al lado derecho y al izquierdo una india con el traje y vestido, que hoy usan de cobija, o manto blanco, cubierta hasta la cabeza, hincada de rodillas, como cuando en este tiempo se confiesan . . .

Burgoa goes on to say that, since they did not understand its significance nor did consulting the gods help explain it, they held it to be a "cosa misteriosa y de gran prognóstico, que algún tiempo lo sabrían para daño suyo." When Cosijopij became the paramount Zapotec ruler, they prevailed upon him to sacrifice to the gods and again seek information as to its significance. He complied and conducted sacrifices to the "ídolo mayor, que llamaban Corazón del Reino," whose seat was a great cave on an islet in "la grande laguna de San Dionisio." Returning sadly to his people, he announced that the god had told him that their days of freedom were numbered and that soon white strangers would appear from the east against whom they would be powerless and who would subject them. After them would come others dressed like the rock-hewn figure, their priests, who would take confession of sins such as was represented in the sculpted scene. Later, when Cosijopij heard of Cortés's conquest of the Mexica, realizing that the prophecy had been fulfilled and that resistance was useless, he voluntarily submitted to the Spaniards and embraced Christianity.

It is clear from the quoted passage that Brasseur de Bourbourg confused a place-name with a personal name; the "religioso" is actually unnamed by Burgoa. The French scholar also combined this with other passages in Burgoa to create an artificial, connected account of this mysterious missionary. One of these passages (Burgoa 1934, II: 293) concerns the famous miraculous cross of Huatulco (cf. Torquemada 1943–1944, III: 205–206; Veytia 1944, I: 120–121), which Thomas Cavendish, an English corsair, supposedly unsuccessfully tried to destroy during a raid in 1587: ". . . una muy descollada y hermosa cruz de más de mil quinientos años de antigüedad, que sin conocer sus altísimos ministerios, adoraban estos gentiles como cosa divina, como oficina general del remedio de todas sus necesidades y botica universal de todas sus enfermidades."

This cross had been brought to the natives "al tiempo de los apóstoles" by an aged bearded white man, coming from the direction of Peru, dressed in a long robe and mantle. When he appeared on the beach, embracing the cross, the natives flocked to see him. He addressed them in their native tongue (Mixtec) and attempted to expound his doctrines. Before his departure, he explained that he was leaving the cross for them, "la señal de todo su remedio," which they should venerate, and the time would come when they should learn of the true God.

Finally, a third passage (Burgoa 1934, II: 201) tells how a certain Fray Juan de Ojeda climbed to the top of Mount Cempoaltepec "y vido aquella cima que descuella sobre las nubes y tocó con sus manos la piedra memorable de un peñasco con lo raso de una mesa que hace, y en él esculpidas dos plantas como si las esculpieran a cincel con todos los músculos y forma de los dedos como si se imprimieran en cera."

The tradition of the natives concerning this prodigy, which had been handed down from their forefathers and "escrita en sus pieles y carácteres," was that an aged white man had come from the Pacific Ocean, "con el hábito que pintan a los apóstoles." He entered the Mixteca and began to preach concerning the true God to them in their own language. When they sought to kill him, he climbed up to that cliff, left the marks impressed there, and disappeared. Burgoa links this apostle with the one who brought the cross of Huatulco, whom he suggests might be Saint Thomas, pointing out that "esta muy recibido" that the latter, after entering Peru, came to Mexico over the waters.

COMMENT

Extended comment on these passages in Burgoa is hardly necessary. Their close resemblance to those Central Mexican sources summarized and discussed in the last category devoted to that area is evident. This unnamed visitor to Oaxaca is again a bearded white missionary who enters the region from unknown parts, undertakes a proselytizing mission, and departs. Later the appearance of the Spaniards is connected with his alleged prophecies. His association with the cross is reminiscent of a similar mention in Alva Ixtlilxochitl, cited above, and the suggestion of a connection with Saint Thomas harks back to Durán, another Dominican. The Peruvian tie is intriguing; some allusion to Viracocha is perhaps involved, although he is not named. The handprints in the solid rock recall the mention in the *Anales de Cuauhtitlan* and the *Relación de Coatepec Chalco* of a similar phenomenon connected with Topiltzin Quetzalcoatl, also cited above.

Whether these vague Oaxacan tales collected by Burgoa in the late seventeenth century actually represent a genuine survival, however garbled, of a

Zapotec version of the Topiltzin Quetzalcoatl of Tollan Tale is extremely difficult to determine. By this time, tales of Christian apostles who had visited New Spain and left behind certain traces of their mission were obviously commonplace and certainly lost nothing in their constant retelling. The friars had always been intensely interested in what seemed to them close parallels between their own faith and that of the natives; and their active sacerdotal imaginations were obviously often fanned by these intriguing similarities. The later versions of the Topiltzin Quetzalcoatl of Tollan Tale undoubtedly proved to be an especially fertile speculative seedbed. As knowledge of them grew, they apparently spread, with increasing embellishments, over a wide area of the Spanish colony. Burgoa's tales, quoted above, seem to be fairly typical versions. Their relationship to the genuine Topiltzin Quetzalcoatl of Tollan Tale of Central Mexico was probably very indirect—if connected at all. In themselves, they hardly constitute cogent evidence for his existence in the traditional history and cult of Zapotecapan and adjoining territory at the time of the Conquest—although some version of this figure had perhaps filtered in through Mixteca sources.

IV. Chiapas

This area of Mesoamerica constitutes an important cultural and ethnic boundary zone. Ecologically, the highland and lowland strips are essentially western extensions of the corresponding zones of Guatemala, immediately to the east, and there has clearly always been close contact between the two regions. Linguistically, the northern and eastern part of Chiapas is Mayance (Chol, Tzotzil/Tzeltal, Toholabal, Mototzintlec, Chicomultec, Mam, etc.). The center was held by the politically powerful Chiapanec (now extinct), belonging to the Macro-Otomangue linguistic family. In the west and south (Soconusco) prevailed the closely related Zoque and Tapachultec—groups that, together with the Mixe and Popoluca of Veracruz, were possibly related very distantly to the Mayance-speakers. In addition, particularly in the latter region, certain Nahua-speaking groups had established themselves, probably as part of the same general movement that brought the Pipil to Guatemala. The presence of these Nahua, with possible Toltec (and pre-Toltec?) connections, might have resulted in the survival of some reminiscences of Topiltzin Quetzalcoatl of Tollan.

Knowledge of the Conquest-period Chiapas indigenes, however, is not extensive, particularly for Soconusco (Xoconochco). This is all the more regrettable for our purposes, since there is one significant legendary figure of the highland Tzeltal/Tzotzil groups concerning whom fragmentary information is extant, who can possibly be somewhat vaguely related to Topiltzin

Quetzalcoatl of Tollan. This is the famous Votan (or Uotan), apropos of whom Daniel Brinton (1882b: 212) justly remarked: "Few of our hero-myths have given occasion for wilder speculation than that of Votan." This speculative, romantic approach to Votan was initiated by the first writer to mention him in print, Fray Francisco Núñez de la Vega, and reached a climax with the absurd theories of Ramón de Ordóñez y Aguiar and Pablo Félix Cabrera in the late eighteenth century. The more romantic nineteenth-century students, including Brasseur de Bourbourg, Müller, Charencey, and Chavero, as might be expected, did little to tone down this mystic approach—and even otherwise fairly sober scholars such as Humboldt (who suggested possible identifications with Odin and Buddha) and Orozco y Berra (who elaborated on the Buddhistic theory) were ensnared in this typically Votanic speculative tradition. On the other hand, Bancroft (1882–1883, III: 450–454, V: 159–165) and Brinton (1882b: 212–217) provide more factual résumés of the Votan legend.

On the primary source level, only two accounts supply any significant original information about Votan: that of Núñez de la Vega, ostensibly based, at least in part, on a *quadernillo* written after the Conquest in Tzeltal or Tzotzil by an educated native, and, either the same manuscript in Tzeltal, or, perhaps more likely, another similar in content, which was described and briefly paraphrased by Cabrera and Ordóñez y Aguiar. Each will be considered in turn.

1. Fray Francisco Núñez de la Vega

The author of the *Constituciones diocesanas del obispado de Chiapas*, published in Rome in 1702, was born in Colombia, and, after entering the Dominican order and serving in various capacities in his native country, Santo Domingo, and Spain, was appointed in 1683 to the bishopric of Chiapas and Soconusco, where he vigorously labored until his death. His work is devoted almost entirely to ecclesiastical matters of the laboriously repetitious type that seventeenth-century divines in the Spanish New World empire were so fond of composing, but contains a few tidbits of precious information on the culture of the surviving indigenous groups with which he had some familiarity.

Núñez de la Vega's all too brief description of the legends clustering about the personality of Votan is found in the preamble, number 34, XXX (1702: 9–10):

> Votan es el tercero Gentil, que está puesto en el Calendario, y en Quadernillo Histórico escrito en Idioma de Indio va nombrando todos los parages, y pueblos, donde estuuo, y hasta estos tiempos en el de Teopisca ha hauido generación que llaman de Votanos: dice más, que es el Señor de *Palo hueco* (que llaman Tepanaguaste), que vió la pared grande (que es la Torre de Babel), que por mandado de Noè su abuelo

> se hizo desde la tierra hasta el Cielo, y que él es el primer hombre, que embió Dios a diuidir, y repartir esta tierra de las Indias, y que allí donde vió la pared grande se le dió a cada pueblo su differente idioma: dice que en Huehueta, (que es Pueblo de Soconusco) estuuo, y allí puso dantas, y vn thesoro grande en vna casa lobrega, que fabricó a Soplos, y nombró Señora, con tapianes, que le guardasen. Este thesoro era de vnas tinajas tapadas con el mismo barro, y de vna pieza donde estauan grauadas en piedra las figuras de los Indios gentiles antiguos que están en el Calendario con chalchihuites, (que son vnas piedrecitas verdes mazicas,) y otras figuras supersticiosas, que todo se sacó de vna cueva, y lo entrego la misma India Señora, y los tapianes, o guardas de ella, y en la plaza de Huehuetan se quemaron publicamente quando hicimos la visita de dicha Prouincia por el año de 1691, a este Votan lo veneran mucho todos los Indios, y alguna Prouincia le tienen por el Corazón de los Pueblos.

In the following paragraph he again mentions the "Quadernillo Histórico en idioma Indio" and briefly describes material concerning other "heroes" (actually *tonalpohualli* day names). The paragraph ends with a listing of these "veinto generaciones de Señores," the third of which is Votan. This Tzeltal list of the twenty days is very close to lists compiled somewhat later, where again Votan is named as the third day (e.g., Emeterio Pineda 1845; Vincente Pineda 1888; Lara vocabulary, in Brinton 1893). As Seler (1904b: 294) suggested, it probably represented a nomenclatural transfer from its patron god (Akbal, or variants thereof, is the standard designation for the third day in most other Mayance lists). This is all the information that the bishop provides concerning this important Chiapas hero/god.

2. Pablo Félix Cabrera

About a hundred years later, an enthusiastic Italian anti-quary, Pablo Félix Cabrera, became interested in the traditions of the natives of Chiapas. In Guatemala he became acquainted with a *vecino* of San Cristóbal (Ciudad Real), then the capital of that province, who had long been working on the same problem, Ramón de Ordóñez y Aguiar. The latter lent him a "memoir" consisting of "five or six folios of common quarto paper, written in ordinary characters in the Tzendal language," which Cabrera believed had been "copied from the original in hieroglyphics, shortly after the conquest." He goes on to describe it as follows (Cabrera 1822 [English translation]: 33–34):

> At the top of the first leaf, the two continents are painted in different colours, in two small squares, placed parallel to each other in the angles; the one representing Europe, Asia, and Africa is marked with two large SS; upon the upper arms of two bars drawn from the opposite angle of each square, forming the point of union in the centre, that which

> indicates America has two SS placed horizontally on the bars, but I am not certain whether upon the upper or lower bars, but I believe upon the latter. When speaking of the places he had visited on the old continent, he marks them on the margin of each chapter with an upright S, and those of America with an horizontal S. Between these squares stands the title of his history, "Proof that I am Culebra" (a snake), which title he proves in the body of his work, by saying that he is Culebra, because he is Chivim. He states that he conducted seven families from Valum Votan to this continent and assigned lands to them; that he is the third of the Votans; that having determined to travel until he arrived at the root of heaven, in order to discover his relations the Culebras, and make himself known to them, he made four voyages to Chivim (which is expressed by repeating four times from Valum Votan to Valum Chivim, from Valum Chivim to Valum Votan); that he arrived in Spain, and that he went to Rome; that he saw the great house of God building; that he went by the road which his brethren the Culebras had bored; that he marked it, and that he passed by the houses of the thirteen Culebras.

He further relates that, in returning from one of his voyages, he found seven other families of the Tzequil nation, who had joined the first inhabitants, and recognized in them the same origin as his own, that is, of the Culebras. He speaks of the place where they built their first town, which, from its founders, received the name of Tzequil. He affirms that having taught them refinement of manners in the use of the table, tablecloth, dishes, basins, cups, and napkins, in return for these they taught him the knowledge of God and of his worship; his first ideas of a king and obedience to him; and that he was chosen captain of all these united families.

This sketchy, obscure paraphrase is the best available account of the mysterious Tzeltal manuscript purportedly based on a tradition rendered by Votan himself. Cabrera goes on to discuss the difficulties of translation, pointing out that it was written "in a laconic and figurative style." The remainder of his treatise is taken up with an attempt to link the Votanites with the Phoenicians.

3. Ramón de Ordóñez y Aguiar

Ordóñez y Aguiar, who eventually broke bitterly with Cabrera and deeply regretted ever having lent him the manuscript, claims to have received it from the Indians. He obviously knew some Tzeltal and attempted a translation (which is what was actually paraphrased by Cabrera, since the latter obviously did not know any Tzeltal). In his *Historia de la creación del cielo y de la tierra* (about 1794), he purportedly devoted part II to an analysis of this account of Votan. Nicolás León, however, who published two versions of

Ordóñez y Aguiar's work (León 1907 is the best known), did not succeed in obtaining a manuscript that included more than the opening passages of this second portion. Another, somewhat more complete manuscript, unpublished, is in the Bancroft Library, University of California, Berkeley (ex-Ramírez collection; Smisor 1943)—and another, much longer version, also unpublished, is in the library of the Middle American Research Institute, Tulane University, New Orleans (Gropp 1933: 249–250). Brasseur de Bourbourg (1851, 1857–1859, 1861), who in 1848–1849 copied a different manuscript (in the Museo Nacional de México) from that which served as the basis for the two León editions, provided tidbits from "Fragmentos" of book II, which are not found in the published versions of León and which were apparently lacking in the (Brühl) manuscript that served as their basis.

In the first part of his work, which is a copious paraphrase and "analysis" of Ximénez's Spanish translation of the *Popol Vuh*, Ordóñez y Aguiar occasionally refers to his "cuadernillo historial" or "Probanza de Votan," which he was convinced was the same as that utilized by Núñez de la Vega, "el mismo que he ofrecido traducir y esplanar; y lo haré . . . en el segundo libro de esta historia." His few remarks concerning it do not add very much to Cabrera's account. A sample (Ordóñez y Aguiar in León 1907: 134) reads:

> Este nombre Votan . . . quiere decir corazón. Fué Votan, como de su pluma veremos en su Provania [*sic*], . . . originario de la Isla de Havanna (que en el lenguage figurado de los Culebras se dice Valunvotan) tercero de los de su linage, nacidos en aquella Isla, y noveno nieto de un Tripolitano, llamado también Votan, de quien, con la sangre, heredó el bastón y el nombre.

He traces Votan, by way of the Laguna de Terminos and the Río Usumacinta, to Palenque, which he names Na-Chan, House of the Serpent. (Ordóñez y Aguiar was one of the first to describe this Classic-period Lowland Maya ruin, visited by his brother in 1773.) Later, "(sin olvidar su primitivo nombre) llamaron los Culebras, en su lenguage figurado, a la Isla Havana, Valunvotan; nombre compuesto, de Votan, syncopa de Valuneb, que en su idioma, quiere decir Nueva, y Votan, que es el corazón" (elsewhere he translates Valun Votan as "Land of Votan"). He then claims that Valun Votan was represented pictorially by nine hearts, "cuya letra, gramaticamente, o bien en el sentido ideal interpretada, quiere decir: El noveno de los Votanes ([footnote]: Este geroglyphico se verá en la Estampa del Caudillo Votan, cuyo examen será materia de uno de los capítulos del segundo Libro de este Historia)" (Ordóñez y Aguiar in León 1907: 134). A few other morsels, ostensibly based on the Votan-authored manuscript, are given by Ordóñez y Aguiar in the first part of his work, but, again, they add nothing substantial to Cabrera's summary of its contents.

Brasseur de Bourbourg's (1851, 1857–1859, 1861) occasional references to Ordóñez y Aguiar's account of Votan, based on the "Fragmentos" he had access to, add little that is significantly new, with the exception of a claim (1861: lxxxviii, footnote 3) that a group of "grandes ruinas" were named Valum-Votan, situated "a deux lieues environ du village de Teopizca, situe a 7 l. de Ciudad-Real." However, he (1851: 54–56) professes to quote a passage from the "Fragmentos" that is worth quoting in full since it conveniently encapsulates the Ordóñez y Aguiar version:

> Votan dice, escribió un cuaderno del origen del los Indios y su transmigración a estas partes. El principal argumento de su obra se reduce a probar que desciendo de Nino: que es el del linage de los Culebras, que tras su origen de Chivin, que es el primer hombre que Dios embió en esta región a repartir y poblar las tierras que hoy llamamos América. Dice la derrota que trajo, y añade que después de establecido en ella, hizo varios viajes a Valum-Chavin. Dice que los viajes que hizo fueron cuatro. En el primero dice que habiendo salido de Valum-Votan, tomó el camino por el parage nombrado Casas de las trece Culebras; de allí fué a Valum-Chivin, de donde pasó a la ciudad grande, y vió fabricar la gran casa de Dios. De allí pasó a la ciudad antigua y dice que vió con sus propios ojos las ruinas de un gran edificio que los hombres por mandado de su abuelo, construyeron para subir al cielo, y que los hombres con quienes conversó le aseguraron que aquel edificio fué el lugar donde Dios dió a cada familia un distinto idioma. A su regreso de la ciudad grande del templo de Dios, dice que estuvo a primera y segunda vez a registrar todo lo ahugerado y señalado por él. Añade que pasó por un camino subterráneo que atraviesa toda la tierra hasta la raíz del cielo. En esta ocasión, dice Votan, que este camino no fué otra cosa que un ahugero de culebra, porque él es hijo de Culebra.

SUMMARY

It would probably be unwise to attempt to artificially combine these two quite dissimilar accounts of Votan. The first, that of Núñez de la Vega, can be summed up thus (straining out the most obvious biblicisms):

(1) Votan, the third day sign in the list, was the great hero-ancestor of the Tzeltal/Tzotzil, the first to "divide and apportion" the land and who apparently wandered about from place to place; (2) he was lord of the two-tongued wooden drum, *teponaztli*; (3) he assigned every group its own language; (4) in Huehuetan (an important center of ancient Xoconochco) he placed tapirs ("dantas"; or is this really, as Thompson [1950: 73] suggested, a misreading for "mantas" = mantles?) and a great treasure, consisting of sealed clay jars, a room (*pieza*) where the "figures of the old heathen Indians which are in the calendar" (i.e., the day signs?) were carved in stone, objects of jade (*chalchihuitl*), and other "superstitious figures," in a dark house (*casa lobrega*),

which he formed by blowing; (5) he appointed as custodian a female chief, with guardians (*tapianes* = Nahuatl *tlapiani* or *tepiani*); (6) this was identified with a cave (undoubtedly a sanctuary) near Huehuetan, where in 1691 the chieftainess (priestess?) and her guardians delivered up everything contained in it to the bishop, who ordered it to be publicly burned in the plaza of the town; (7) Votan was greatly revered by all the Indians, and in a certain province was held to be "the heart of the towns"; (8) in the bishop's time, there still existed a lineage in the town of Teopisca (located between San Cristóbal de las Casas and Comitan), which had always borne the name of the hero.

Combining Cabrera and Ordóñez y Aguiar, we get the following rather murky account: (1) Votan, which meant "heart," the third (or the ninth) of that line, starting from Valum Chivim, conducted seven families from Valum Votan (the land of Votan) to the Chiapas area (his founding of Palenque is likely an Ordóñez y Aguiar invention), where he assigned lands to his followers; (2) he was a member of a group known as Serpents (Chan) of the line of "Chivim" and was descended from "Imox" (or Nino); (3) seeking "the root of heaven," he undertook four trips to Valum Chivim; (4) returning, he discovered seven families of another group, called Tzequiles ("men with petticoats"), who founded a town called Tzequil, from their ethnic name; (5) in return for having taught them "the refinement of manners," he was taught certain religious matters and became the leader of all "these united families"; (7) he left behind a "Probanza" containing his history.

COMMENT

The Tzeltal manuscript supposedly used by Ordóñez y Aguiar and Cabrera has apparently disappeared. Without being able to consult it, it is impossible to appraise accurately his and Cabrera's version of its contents. Our knowledge of this pair's general approach and methods of analyses, however, hardly inspires us with much confidence in their accounts of it. In spite of Ordóñez y Aguiar's conviction that his manuscript was the same as that cited by Núñez de la Vega, there can be no certainty of this. Although vaguely coinciding, there are a number of important incidents in the Núñez de la Vega version that neither Ordóñez y Aguiar nor Cabrera mentions. Also, it is significant that Boturini made a fruitless attempt to locate Núñez de la Vega's manuscript—even going so far as to address an inquiry to the then bishop of Chiapas, to no avail (Boturini 1746: 115). The translation of Votan as "heart" seems well established (Brinton 1882b: 217). Also accepted by most students is Seler's (1900–1901: 49; 1904b: 294–295) association of Votan with the Central and Southern Mexican jaguar/earth deity, Tepeyollotl, whose name literally translates "hill-heart." The use of Votan for the third *tonalpohualli* day (variants of which—Waton, Woton—are also found in the modern Chuh and Jacalteca day lists) strongly supports this view, for Tepeyollotl, often fused with Tezcatlipoca, was in fact the patron of both the third day in the Central Mexican system, Calli (House), and the third *tonalpohualli trecena*, beginning 1 Mazatl (Deer). His putative association with tapirs in the Núñez de la Vega account may be significantly related to a similar association in the case of the modern Kekchi earth gods (Thompson 1950: 74).

However, the relevant question for our purposes is whether Votan can also be associated with Quetzalcoatl—as has been frequently assumed from the beginning of ancient Mexican studies. Apart from the generalized culture-hero aspect of both, Votan's wanderings, and his burial, or hiding, of treasure, there are virtually no specific similarities between the Topiltzin Quetzalcoatl of Tollan Tale and the surviving accounts of the Chiapas hero god. It is conceivable, of course, that some of the traditional tales surrounding Topiltzin Quetzalcoatl—which may have moved into, or through, Chiapas—could have colored what appears otherwise to have been a localized, indigenous legend. If so, however, this influence seems to have been, at best, a very generalized one.

A certain additional case could perhaps be made for a vague association with Ehecatl Quetzalcoatl. This deity, however, seems to have been clearly present in Chiapas under a distinct name, Cuculchan, which, like the Yucatecan Kukulcan, is an exact Tzeltal/Tzotzil translation of Quetzalcoatl. A marginal annotation to Núñez de la Vega's (1702: 132) ninth pastoral letter reads: "En los Repertorios más generales tienen pintado el 7. signo en figura de hombre y de culebra, que llaman Cuchulcha[n], y han explicados los maestros, que es culebra de plumas, que anda en el agua: este signo corresponde a Mexzichuaut, que quiere decir Culebra nebliñosa, o de nueue. Torquemada. 299."

In another marginal note (to number 78, LXXIV, p. 19), this statement is found:

> Tienen pintada cierta laguna rodeada de los Naguales, en figura de diuersos animales, y algunas de los Maestros Nagualistas tienen por Señor, y dueño de ellos al Cuculcham, y assi para darlos le hacen cierta deprecación, con que le piden licencia, la qual esta en lengua Popoluca (que llamaua Baha, en su primitivo gentilísimo), y el Obispo la hizo traducir en Mexicana.

The "seventh sign," as Seler (1900–1901: 42) suggested, probably is the seventh *trecena* of the *tonalpohualli*, beginning 1 Quiahuitl (Rain). In the Borgia Group of ritual/divinatory pictorials, Tlaloc is the usual patron of this period, although both the Central Mexican codices *Borbonicus* and *Telleriano-Remensis/Vaticanus* A depict, in addition, a god who combines the attributes of Tlaloc and Ehecatl Quetzalcoatl, and who, in the latter, bears the calendric name Nahui Ehecatl (4 Wind). This putative Chiapas variant of Ehecatl Quetzalcoatl is probably very closely related to the Guatemalan

Gucumatz, discussed below. Although Gucumatz seems to be referred to in the *Popol Vuh* as U Qux Cho, "the Heart of the Lake," and U Qux Palo, "the Heart of the Sea," these terms, like U Qux Cah, "the Heart of Heaven," or the Sky, applied particularly to Huracan, seem to be generic appellations of deity. They probably, in themselves, should not be construed as convincing evidence for identification with Votan—or Tepeyollotl.

In sum, a local version of Ehecatl Quetzalcoatl does seem to have been present in Chiapas under the name Cuculchan. Reminiscences of Topiltzin Quetzalcoatl, on the other hand, if they are present at all in the legend of Votan, a culture hero seemingly related to a Central/Southern Mexican jaguar-earth deity, Tepeyollotl, are so tenuous as to be practically nondiscernible.

V. Highland Guatemala

In contrast to the situation in Chiapas, where only the vaguest reminiscences of Topiltzin Quetzalcoatl may have survived, if at all, in Highland Guatemala a number of references in the native histories appear to refer either to this personage or to successors who bore similar names and/or titles. This is hardly surprising in view of the fact that most of the Highland Guatemalan traditions concur in naming Tollan as the homeland of the ancestors of various ruling dynasties in this predominantly Mayance-speaking region—the two most powerful at Gumarcaah/Utatlan (Quiche) and Iximche/Tecpan Cuauhtemallan (Cakchiquel). Even without these explicit statements, the patently Nahua names (e.g., Chimalacat, Iztayul, Tepepul, Acxopil, Ixcaquat, Ucelut, Chicumcuat, Atunal, etc.) of certain of these dynasts would in themselves point to an ultimate Central Mexican origin for their lineages.

There are still a number of challenging problems surrounding these Tollan to Highland Guatemala migrations, e.g.: whether they were the direct result of the collapse of the Toltec empire, or earlier (or both); the precise date(s) of the major movement(s); and where the Nahua-speaking Pipil fit into this picture. Concerning this last question, it has been suggested that they were the descendants of Toltec invaders who, unlike their brethren who set themselves up as a ruling elite over such groups as the Quiche, Cakchiquel, and Zutuhil, successfully resisted linguistic

Mayanization. However, others have favored the view that the ancestors of the Pipil initially entered Guatemala in pre-Toltec times. For our purposes, it is sufficient to emphasize the likelihood of these Toltec connections as explaining the existence in the Highland Guatemalan indigenous histories of what appear to be clear references to the great priest/ruler of Tollan. The most important of these will be discussed in turn, beginning with those that chronicle the history of the Quiche-speaking dynasty of Gumarcaah/Utatlan.

1. The *Popol Vuh*

THE SOURCE

This renowned work is an account, in Quiche, of the creation of the world, followed by a lengthy narration of some of the most colorful and imaginative cosmogonical and hero myths recorded for any indigenous New World group, concluding with a continuous (but undated) chronicle of the various branches of the Gumarcaah/Utatlan dynasty, from earliest beginnings in Tollan until the mid-sixteenth century. On internal evidence, it has been speculated (Recinos and Goetz 1953: 30) that it was composed between 1554 and 1558. However, apart from a consensus view that it can probably be assigned to the mid-sixteenth century, no precise date for its composition has yet been established. The original manuscript, now lost, was discovered in Chichicastenango in 1701–1703 by the Dominican Fray Francisco Ximénez, who copied the Quiche text and translated it into Spanish, in both a literal and a free rendering. The latter version was extensively quoted and paraphrased by Ordóñez y Aguiar in his *Historia de la creación del cielo y de la tierra,* but this work, discussed above, was not published (in part) until 1907. Ximénez's paraphrastic translation was finally published in its entirety in 1929–1931 (Ximénez 1929–1931, book I).

The first modern publication of the literal Spanish rendering was by Karl von Scherzer in 1857, from a copy of the Ximénez bilingual manuscript he found in the library of the Universidad de San Carlos in 1853–1854. In 1861, Brasseur de Bourbourg published—with many changes, inaccuracies, and omissions—the Quiche text, from the same or a virtually identical copy of the Ximénez manuscript that had come into his possession, with a French translation. He baptized it with the name by which it has been known ever since. This soon became the "standard" version of the *Popol Vuh*, and many later editions in various languages were derived from it. With the doubtful exception of the German translation of Pohorilles (1913), only the French translation of Raynaud (1925) and the Spanish translation of Villacorta Calderón and Rodas N. (1927) pretended to be genuine new translations from the original Quiche (i.e., the 1861 Brasseur de Bourbourg version, the only one available during this period). In 1944, an accurate version of the Quiche text, based on photographs of the copy of the Ximénez manuscript that Brasseur de Bourbourg had taken to Paris and which had been acquired in 1911 by the Newberry Library, Chicago (Ayer Ms. 1515), with a new German translation, was published in Germany by Leonhard S. Schultze Jena. Three years later, a new Spanish translation by Adrián Recinos, also based on the Newberry manuscript, was published in Mexico, without the Quiche text (second edition, 1953). The first complete English version of the *Popol Vuh* was a translation of this last (Goetz, Morley, and Recinos 1950). In addition to the many editions of the document itself, an extensive interpretative and explanatory literature on the *Popol Vuh* has emerged through the years (see, especially, Recinos 1953: bibliography).

Apparently the *Popol Vuh* was composed by a Spanish-educated member of the Quiche aristocracy, probably in Santa Cruz del Quiche in the mid-years of the sixteenth century, based on oral tradition(s) and, possibly, a pictorial history(ies) as well. His identity, in spite of numerous speculations, remains unknown. Although strong biblical influence is evident in the opening paragraphs, the bulk of the narration is authentically aboriginal in flavor. Perhaps the most striking feature of the *Popol Vuh* is its obvious blending of native Highland Guatemalan (Mayance) and foreign, putatively Toltec (= Nahua) elements.

PROBABLE REFERENCES TO TOPILTZIN QUETZALCOATL

The pertinent passages of the *Popol Vuh* can be roughly grouped into two categories: (1) those that appear to refer to Topiltzin Quetzalcoatl of Tollan, although under a different name, and (2) those that refer to (a) a feathered-serpent creator god and (b) a prominent ruler, who, like Topiltzin Quetzalcoatl, bore the name and/or title of this deity. The most important references in the first category are found in a long passage describing a pilgrimage undertaken by certain leaders of the ancestors of the Gumarcaah dynasty while they were residing on the sacred mountain, Hacavitz, still en route from Tollan to their eventual destination in historic Quiche territory. This mountain (called Hacavitz Chipal in the *Título de los señores de Totonicapan*) was identified by Brasseur de Bourbourg (1861: 235) with one of those that rises, to the north of Rabinal, near the Río Chixoy. "Dawn" had come for the émigrés, and the four original leaders—Balam Quitze, Balam Acab, Mahucutah, and Iqui Balam—had recently disappeared, the first-named leaving behind the sacred bundle, the Pizom Gagal, which corresponds to the Central Mexican *tlaquimilolli* (Mendieta 1945, I: 105, following Olmos). Qocaib, Qoacutec, and Qoahau, the sons, respectively, of Balam Quitze, Balam Acab, and Mahucutah, resolved to return to the "East," on the other side of the sea, whence their fathers had led the group from Tollan, to receive the formal investiture of royal authority (*ta xbe quicama ri ahauarem*). There, Ahau Nacxit, "Lord of the East" (*rahaual ah relebal quih*), the Great Lord, the only Supreme Judge (*hu catoltzih*) of all the kingdom, receives them, and presents them with the royal insignia (*retal ahauarem*) and all of their visible symbols (*romohel v vachinel*). These include the insignia of Ahpop and Ahpop Camha, the titles of the holders of the two supreme offices of the Gumarcaah dynasty, and of the grandeur and sovereignty of the latter—as well as the dais (*muh*), the throne (*galibal*), the bone flutes (*zubac*), the drum (*cham-cham*), the yellow beads (*titil canabah* = *chalchihuitl?*), puma and jaguar claws (*tzicvuil coh, tzicvuil balam*), the heads and hoofs of the deer (*holom, pich queh*), the canopies (*macutax*), snail shells (*tot*), *tatam* (meaning?), tobacco (*gus*), little gourds (*buz*), *caxcon* (meaning?), parrot feathers (*chiyom*), and standards of royal heron feathers (*aztapulul*) (for identifications, see Recinos 1953: 220–222; Seler 1902–1923, III: 95–96; cf. Schultze Jena 1944: 145). In addition, they obtain "the paintings of Tollan" (*u tzibal Tulan*), i.e., pictorial historical annals. The three return in triumph to reassume their rule, now "legitimatized" by their possession of the requisite insignia of authority presented to them by Ahau Nacxit. Soon after, they lead their people from Hacavitz, and the long migration continues (Recinos 1953: 223–229; Schultze Jena 1944: 143–147). The analysis of this passage involving Nacxit, Lord of the East, will be undertaken below.

A later passage, in the second category, possibly also relates to Topiltzin Quetzalcoatl but, if so, in a general associational sense rather than involving a direct reference. Aside from the notable conqueror, Quicab, the eighth-generation ruler, Gucumatz was the most prominent of the Gumarcaah dynasty rulers. It was during his reign that the capital was moved from Chi Izmachi to Gumarcaah, where it remained until the coming of Pedro de Alvarado in 1524. It was Gucumatz who consolidated the power of his dynasty. Recinos (1953: 241–242; cf. Schultze Jena 1944: 163–164) translated the relevant passage thus:

> No fué poco lo que hicieron, ni fueron pocos los pueblos que conquistaron. Muchas ramas de los pueblos vinieron a pagar tributo al Quiché; llenos de dolor llegaron a entragarlo. Sin embargo, su poder no creció rápidamente. Gucumatz fué quien dió principio al engrandecimiento del reino. Así fué el principio de su engrandecimiento y del engrandecimiento del Quiché.

Gucumatz bears the name or title of an important creator god who plays a prominent role in the opening cosmogonical section of the *Popol Vuh*. This name, as has been recognized from the beginning (e.g., Brasseur de Bourbourg 1861: 3), is composed of two elements: *guc*, green feathers (more specifically, those of the quetzal bird), and *cumatz*, serpent, and is the literal Quiche rendering of Quetzalcoatl. Gucumatz is also a title borne by one of the highest members of the "great house" (Nim Ha) of Cavec, which supplied the two chief officeholders of the Gumarcaah dynasty as a whole (Ahpop and Ahpop Camha). His deeds are described thus (Recinos 1953: 232–233; cf. Schultze Jena 1944: 155):

> Verdaderamente, Gucumatz era un rey prodigioso. Siete días subía al cielo y siete días caminaba para descender a Xibalba; siete días se convertía en culebra y verdaderamente se volvía serpiente; siete días se convertía en águila, siete días se convertía en tigre: verdaderamente su apariencia era de águila y de tigre. Otros siete días se convertía en sangre coagulada y solamente era sangre en reposo.
>
> En verdad era maravillosa la naturaleza de este rey, y todos los demás Señores se llenaban de espanto ante él. Esparcióse la noticia de la naturaleza prodigiosa del rey y la oyeron todos los Señores de los pueblos. Y éste fué el principio de la grandeza del Quiché, cuando el rey Gucumatz dió estas muestras de su poder. No se perdió su imagen en la memoria de sus hijos y sus nietos. Y no hizo esto para que hubiera un rey prodigioso; lo hizo solamente para que hubiera un medio de dominar a todos los pueblos, como una demostración de que sólo uno era llamado a ser el jefe de los pueblos.

In addition to these notices concerning Nacxit and, later, the "prodigious" ruler Gucumatz, there are a few other scattered references in the earlier portion of the *Popol Vuh* that may be relevant to our theme. As indicated above, Gucumatz, also Tepeu Gucumatz ("majestic, mighty Gucumatz"), plays a key role in the opening cosmogonical passages (Recinos 1953: 81–98; Schultze Jena 1944: 3–17). Apparently conceived, as with so many Mesoamerican deities, both singly and plurally, Gucumatz and certain fellow deities (one of whom, Huracan [*hu*(*n*) *racan* = "one (his) foot"], may, according to some students, have been related to the Central Mexican Tezcatlipoca) undertake the task of creating the earth and all upon it, including mankind. Here, Gucumatz obviously corresponds to the Central Mexican Ehecatl Quetzalcoatl in his role as creator god, the great fructifier.

The episode (Recinos 1953: 98–112; Schultze Jena 1944: 17–35), narrated after the destruction of the race of wooden men by a great flood and their transformation into monkeys (equivalent to the Atonatiuh or 4 Atl [Water] Sun of the Central Mexican cosmogonical myths), featuring Vucub Caquix (7 Macaw), his sons Zipacna and Cabracan, and their destruction at the hands of the hero twins Xbalanque and Hunahpu, may also be vaguely connected with the Topiltzin Quetzalcoatl of Tollan Tale. This possibility is suggested by the name of the wife of Vucub Caquix, Chimalmat, probably equivalent to Chimalman, who, as noted above, in various of the earlier Central Mexican versions of the tale is the name of the mother of Topiltzin Quetzalcoatl. In addition, Caso (through Jiménez Moreno 1941b: 32) suggested that Cabracan, which can possibly be translated "four (his) foot" (*cab-r-can*), was the Quiche analogue of Nacxitl (but cf. Recinos 1953: 100, who preferred the translation "gigante doble" or "terremoto," and Schultze Jena 1944: 217, who opted for "Der mit zwei Beinen"), which would increase the resemblance to the tale. Vucub Caquix would then correspond to Mixcoatl/Totepeuh.

In most respects, however, the Vucub Caquix episode differs considerably from the Topiltzin Quetzalcoatl tale. Neither Vucub Caquix himself nor his son Cabracan much resembles his putative Mexican counterparts. If Vucub Caquix is a calendric name, it is probably equivalent to 7 Tziquin or Ahmak of the Quiche system and thus to 7 Cuauhtli (Eagle) or Cozcacuauhtli (Vulture) of the Central Mexican system. I find no record, however, that either of the latter dates was assigned as a calendric name to any form of Mixcoatl. The personalities of Mixcoatl-Totepeuh and Vucub Caquix can be made to correspond to a certain extent. The former is a great conqueror and the latter's aspirations reach so high as to become the sun and the moon; otherwise, there is little in common between them. Cabracan appears to have been an earthquake god, the leveler of mountains. He might, with great strain, be remotely linked to Topiltzin Quetzalcoatl through a dubious intermediary, Votan (= Tepeyollotl, an earth god who probably was connected with earthquakes?), but this is stretching vague analogies to extremes. Zipacna (= Central Mexican Cipactonal [Cipactli (Earth Monster) day sign]?) does not really fit at all.

In sum, although the tale of Vucub Caquix and his sons might be interpreted as reflecting some slight influence from the Topiltzin Quetzalcoatl of Tollan Tale, it can hardly be considered a genuine Quiche version of even a portion of it. At best, it might be considered to have been a native Highland Guatemalan tale to which a Toltec coloring, particularly in assignment of personal names, had been overlaid.

Lastly, the problem of the god Tohil should be mentioned. This deity—who seems to have functioned as the special "national god" of the Quiche ruling dynasty, more particularly as the patron deity of the dominant lineage of Cavec—was given, while still in Tollan, to the most prominent of the four original leaders of the ancestors of the Gumarcaah dynasty, Balam Quitze, the founder of that house (Recinos 1953: 184; Schultze Jena 1944: 109). He also was taken as patron deity by the other two principal divisions of the Quiche aristocracy as a whole, Tamub and Ilocab. After providing his followers with fire, created by twirling in his sandal (i.e., probably functioning as a fire drill), he thereafter plays an important role as the guide and protector of his worshippers, even after his transformation into stone at the moment of "dawn" on Mount Hacavitz, when the sun rose for the first time. Immediately following the description of this event occurs this pertinent passage (Recinos 1953: 199–200; cf. Schultze Jena 1944: 123):

> Pero fué aquí donde se multiplicaron, en la montaña, y esta fué su ciudad; aquí estaban, además, cuando aparecieron el sol, la luna y las estrellas, cuando amanció y se alumbro la faz de la tierra y el mundo entero. Aquí también comenzaron su canto, que se llama Camucu; lo cantaron, pero solo el dolor de sus corazones y sus entrañas expresaron en su canto. ¡Ay, de nosotros! En Tullan nos perdimos, nos separamos, y allá quedaron nuestros hermanos mayores y menores. ¡Ay, nosotros hemos visto el sol!, pero ¿dónde están ellos ahora que ya ha amanecido?, les decían a los sacerdotes y sacrificadores de los yaquis.
>
> Porque en verdad, Tohil es el nombre del dios de los yaquis, el llamado Yolcuat-Quitzalcuat.
>
> Nos separamos allá en Tullan, en Zuyva, de allá salimos juntos y allí fué creada nuestra raza cuando vinimos, decían entre si.
>
> Entonces se acordaron de sus hermanos mayores y de sus hermanos menores, los yaquis, a quienes les amaneció allá en el país que hoy se llama México.

The importance of this passage, which is largely self-explanatory, lies in its flat identification of Tohil with Quetzalcoatl, god of the "Yaqui." As has been recognized since Brasseur de Bourbourg's day, this term, which in Nahuatl means "ido o partido para alguna parte," i.e., émigrés (Molina 1944, part II: 31, verso), was applied by the Quiche and their Mayance-speaking neighbors to the Toltecs and the Nahua-speakers in general.

Tohil (Totohil in the *Annals of the Cakchiquels*) has usually, beginning with Ximénez, been translated "rain" or "rainstorm" (cf. Brinton 1881: 633–634: "the Just one, the Comforter, the Avenger, based on a Yucatecan root, *toh*, "pagar deudas"). Toh, with definitely this meaning, is the day in the Quiche calendar that corresponds to the Central Mexican Atl (Water). The deity of the people of Rabinal, who is explicitly identified with Tohil (Recinos 1953: 200), was called Hun Toh, 1 Toh. Based on this etymology, it has usually been assumed that Tohil was a rain and fertility god, although other roles have also been suggested. The former view would square well with his identification with Ehecatl Quetzalcoatl, who, among his other aspects, functioned importantly as a fertility god connected with the rain and the wind.

It has also been suggested that Tohil might be a corrupted version of Topil(tzin). However tempting, in view of the reasonable etymology of the name discussed above, it does not seem likely. The phonetic shift, from *p* to *h*, appears to have no precedent. Tohil's command to draw blood from the ears in sacrifice (Recinos 1953: 191) might provide a tenuous link between the Quiche deity and Topiltzin Quetzalcoatl of Tollan, who, as was brought out above, was particularly associated with this penitential ritual—but this view hardly deserves to be pushed too far.

SUMMARY

(1) Soon after their "dawn" at Mount Hacavitz and the disappearance of their four original leaders, the ancestors of the Gumarcaah dynasty, en route from Tollan to their eventual home in Highland Guatemala, send the sons of three of the departed chiefs to the "East," across the sea, to request the insignia of royal authority from Lord Nacxit; (2) the latter, the great lord and supreme judge, grants this favor, and the envoys return with all of the necessary titles and symbols of majesty, which are itemized in detail, plus pictorial historical annals; (3) Gucumatz, the Quiche equivalent of Quetzalcoatl, is an important creator god who plays, together with Huracan ("One [his] Foot"), a key role in the cosmogony of the *Popol Vuh*; (4) this same name was borne by one of the most prominent rulers of Gumarcaah, the founder of that center, and a renowned conqueror and sorcerer-transformer (*nahual*); (5) Ah Gucumatz was also a title borne by the fifth most important member of the Great House of Cavec, the leading lineage that supplied the two top positions in the Quiche political hierarchy; (6) the special patron god of of Cavec, Tohil (probably "rain" or "storm"), who also seems to have functioned as the "national god" of the Gumarcaah aristocracy as a whole, is specifically identified with "Yolcuat Quitzalcuat," god of the "Yaqui," the migrating, Nahua-speaking Toltecs and/or their congeners.

COMMENT

Comment on this *Popol Vuh* material will be deferred until all of the relevant Highland Guatemala data can be considered together, below.

2. *Titulo de los señores de Totonicapan*

THE SOURCE

The history of this important supplement to the history of the Gumarcaah dynasty provided by the *Popol Vuh* was summarized by Recinos (1950: 211–213). It was a document in Quiche, dated September 28, 1554, which, in

1834, the natives of Totonicapan/Chinekenha had translated for them into Spanish by the priest of Sacapulas, Dionisio José Chonay, following which it was deposited in the local court's register of public documents. The original manuscript subsequently disappeared, but the Chonay translation was discovered in Totonicapan in 1860 by Brasseur de Bourbourg, who made a literal copy that, after his death, came eventually—via Pinart—into the possession of the Comte de Charencey. He translated it into French and in 1884 published both the Spanish and French versions in the *Bulletin des Actes de la Société de Philologie* and separately. The Brasseur de Bourbourg copy was presented to the Bibliothèque Nationale, Paris, by Charencey's widow, where it is presently located (Fonds Américains, 77). In 1950, it was republished by Recinos, with an introduction and notes (Recinos 1950: 211–242)—which version, three years later, was translated into English (Recinos and Goetz 1953: 163–196).

Recinos (1950: 211–212) opined that the Chonay translation "está escrita con claridad y elegancia y parece ser un traslado fiel de las historias del pueblo quiché." The *Título* covers much of the same ground as the legendary-historical portion of the *Popol Vuh* (the opening pages dealing with the creation were intentionally omitted by the translator), in a more abbreviated fashion. The narrative abruptly terminates during the reign of the great conqueror, Quicab, who established the boundaries of the empire of the Gumarcaah dynasty at its height (which included Totonicapan). It was ostensibly signed by the surviving colonial Quiche co-rulers, Don Juan de Rojas and Don Juan Cortés, and other high nobles of the dynasty. It was apparently composed at their order, by a party(ies) unknown except for chapter 4, putatively written by Diego Reynoso, a noble Quiche. As Recinos has suggested, it may have been written in Santa Cruz del Quiché, where most of the top surviving members of the Gumarcaah dynasty resided during the sixteenth century. For the most part, the *Título* corroborates the *Popol Vuh* but occasionally departs significantly from it, as well as frequently supplying interesting new details.

PROBABLE REFERENCES TO TOPILTZIN QUETZALCOATL

The first relevant passage is found near the opening of the account, when the three principal divisions of the ancestors of the Gumarcaah dynasty—the Cavec, the Tamub, and the Ilocab—are on the point of departing from Tollan ("Pa Tulan, Pa Civan," located, as in the *Popol Vuh*, in "la otra parte del océano," "donde sale el sol"). Balam Quitze, the chief of the four leaders of the Cavec, is unanimously chosen supreme leader; then "el gran padre Nacxit les dió un regalo llamado Giron-Gagal." This gift is carried by the emigrants on their long, arduous journey to Highland Guatemala, where, after residing some years in Hacavitz Chipal, "por primera vez desenvolvieron el regalo que el anciano Nacxit les dió cuando salieron de allá del Oriente, y este regalo era lo que los hacía temer y respetar." After repulsing, by trickery and sorcery, an attack by "los pueblos de Vukamag," they decide (Recinos 1950: 222): "Ya es tiempo de enviar embajadores a nuestro padre y señor Nacxit: que sepa el estado de nuestros negocios, que nos proporcione medios para que en lo sucesivo jamás nos venzan nuestros enemigos, para que nunca depriman la nobleza de nuestro nacimiento, que designe honores para nosotros y para todos nuestros descendientes y que, en fin, mande empleos para los que lo merezcan."

Qocaib and Qocavib, the sons of Balam Quitze, are elected for this important mission by majority vote. The former sets off for the east, the latter for the west. Qocaib, overcoming dangers, accomplishes his mission, while his brother, "encontrando algunos obstáculos en las orillas de la laguna de México, regresó sin hacer cosa alguna." He is more successful at seducing the wife of his brother. The latter eventually returns in triumph, bringing from Naxcit the titles of Ahpop, Ahtzalam, and Tzamchinimital, among others, and displaying the insignia that must accompany these dignities: jaguar and eagle claws, hides of other animals, and stones and sticks. Qocaib's subsequent encounter with his errant wife and newborn "son" does not concern us here (Recinos 1950: 216–222).

Chapter IV of the *Título* seems to be an insert. It begins: "Oíd lo que os voy a decir, lo que voy a declarar, yo Diego Reynoso, Popol Vinak, hijo de Lahuh-Noh," who goes on to relate how the great and wise leaders determined on a second journey to the "East." This time, Qocaib, Qocavib, Qoacul, Acutec, "y poco después," Nim Chocoh Cavek (who afterwards took the title of Chocohil Tem) all undertake the journey. They reach the presence of Nacxit, "allá en donde sale el sol," and explain their mission. Nacxit receives them, considerately listens to their request, and grants what they desire, the insignia and badges, and explains their use.

After a listing of the new dignities and the presentation of a brief genealogy, "los nahuales" (i.e., Tohil, Avilix, and Hacavitz), the patron gods of the three divisions of the Quiche, unexpectedly order the chiefs to hide their images on three different hills before the sun rises again. This done, at dawn, making obeisance to the Morning Star, the chiefs offer incense to their gods, crying (Recinos 1950: 225):

> Dos y tres veces damos gracia a vos, criadores de todo lo que nos rodea, os damos gracias porque hemos vuelto a ver el sol y estrellas, y vos, antigua patria nuestra, recibid nuestros votos. Dijeron quemando el incienso cuyo humo subió primero recto en prueba de que fué agradable al Dios grande, y luego se inclinó hacia el sol en prueba de que aquellas ofrendas y aquellos votos, nacidos del oculto del corazón, habían llegado a la presencia de nuestro padre Nacxit.

Assembling their subjects, the chiefs, with Balam Quitze as spokesman, bid farewell to their people, exhorting them to conserve (Recinos 1950: 226):

> . . . el don precioso que nos dió nuestro padre Nacxit, aun ha de servir, porque (no) hemos hallado todavía el lugar en que nos hemos de establecer. Engendrad hijos dignos de las dignidades de Ahpop, Ahpop Camhá, Galel, Atzivinak, etc.; haced hijos llenos del fuego y majestad de que nos dotó nuestro padre Nacxit.

By the next dawn, the leaders are gone, but their sons remain, who take their names. After some time, the group continues its migration, "cargando siempre consigo el don de Nacxit." Eventually reaching a place called Chiqui Tuha, they encounter an old man named Cotuha hunting quail, whom they accept as fourth leader to fill the gap caused by the fact that Iqi Balam had left no son. They also discover there "una piedra semejante a la que les dió Nacxit" (the place is called Cotuha or Tzutuha at this point; concerning the latter, cf. *Popol Vuh* in Recinos 1953: 238). Moving on, they reach Chi Qabauilanic; "lo llamaron así porque les sirvió la piedra de Nacxit de que usaban para sus encantos." After further wanderings, they reach Chi Izmachi. Here, the titles and dignities created by Nacxit are formally proclaimed, with Cotuha recognized as prince and lord, bearing the titles Ahpop and Ahpop Camha; the latter title was also given to Iztayul, son of Conache. Then the offices "que debía haber en la república, según las instrucciones de Nacxit," are itemized.

After a fitting celebration, Cotuha sends two of his retainers to request the hand of the daughter of the Zutuhil ruler of Malah in marriage "según las instrucciones de Nacxit." During this episode, he is once referred to as "Cotuha Gucumatzel." After narrating certain further incidents during the reigns of Cotuha and Iztayul, the account skips abruptly, at the beginning of chapter 7, to the death of Cotuha and the accession of Qika-Cavizimah (*sic* for Quicab). During the remainder of the account, which largely concerns the conquests and boundary fixing of Quicab, there is no further mention of Nacxit. Finally, it is worth noting that the title Gucumatz is listed as one belonging to one of the noble signatories at the end of the document.

SUMMARY

(1) In Tollan, Nacxit, called "the great father" and "the aged," presents the ancestors of the Gumarcaah dynasty, about to depart for Highland Guatemala, with a sacred bundle (*giron gagal*), which contains a stone used in magical incantations; (2) finally reaching Hacavitz Chipal, they unwrap the greatly feared and respected gift; (3) after repulsing the attacks of their enemies, they send two envoys, Qocaib and Qocavib, the sons of their principal leader, one to the "East," one to the "West," to request from Nacxit the

insignia of royal authority; (4) the latter encounters obstacles around the "lake of Mexico" and returns empty-handed, but the former accomplishes his mission; (5) according to an apparent insert chapter, a second delegation, composed of the two previous envoys and three others, Qoacul, Acutec, and Nim Chocoh Cavek, is sent to Nacxit in the east, which also succeeds in obtaining from him the desired titles and insignia; (6) the further references to Nacxit are either to the magic stone or to the titles and instructions he earlier provided the envoys; (7) Cotuha, who is the first to be proclaimed chief ruler after the founding of Chi Izmachi, in one passage is called "Cotuha Gucumatzel"; (8) Gucumatz is also listed as the title of one of the signers of the document.

3. Titulos de los antiguos nuestros antepasados, los que ganaron estas tierras de Otzoyá antes de que viniera la fe de Jesucristo entre ellos, en el año de mil y trescientos

THE SOURCE

This is the Spanish translation of an original document, in Quiche, that will be referred to hereafter more briefly as the *Título de Izquin Nehaib*, which was submitted as a brief in a real property litigation by "una de las más antiguas e ilustres familias de Totonicapan," around the middle of the eighteenth century. The court ordered an exact translation, which was deposited in the archive of the Department of Totonicapan. A copy of this translation was made in the second half of the nineteenth century and was placed in the museum of the Sociedad Económica in Guatemala City. The official publication of that organization, *La Sociedad Económica* (volume 4, numbers 34–36), published it in 1876, with a brief introduction giving the background information summarized above. It was republished in 1941 in the *Anales de la Sociedad de Geografía e Historia de Guatemala* (volume 17, number 3: 244–252).

Although of anonymous authorship, as are most of the Highland Guatemalan *títulos*, it was probably composed by a member of the Izquin Nehaib division, judging from the prominence given to that lineage, second only to Cavec in importance. It narrates, somewhat confusedly as to sequence, an extensive series of conquests by various members of the Gumarcaah dynasty in the region of southwestern Guatemala and adjacent portions of the Chiapas coast (Soconusco). As published, it does not bear a date, but since it was ostensibly signed by Pedro de Alvarado, it would have to predate 1541 (Recinos, in one place [1953: 23], assigns the impossible date of 1524 to the document, but elsewhere [p. 30] states that it "parece haber sido escrito varios años después de la conquista de Utatlán").

PROBABLE REFERENCES TO TOPILTZIN QUETZALCOATL

This source is particularly difficult to handle, due primarily to its seemingly very confused (relative) chronology. The accuracy of the translation from the Quiche is also impossible to gauge without the availability of the original for comparison; certainly the orthography is occasionally corrupt. As published, it is divided into three parts. The first describes a series of conquests by an alliance of over one hundred Quiche towns, represented by the heads of the various "calpules" and led by Quebec and Izquin Nehaib, of a number of places in western Guatemala, many of which are identified as being of Mam affiliation. The only date in the document is found here: "el año de mil y trescientos." The second section describes a similar sweep of conquests, apparently somewhat later, this time led by "Don Quicab" against "los indios de la costa que eran Achíes." "Trece principales y trece cabezas de calpules," who "llevaban consigo trece pueblos de gente," are named as reinforcing Quicab, including "Ahcucumatz" and "Tepeucucumatz." The third part, by far the longest, describes another campaign, this time led by "Don Mahocotah," against certain towns in far western Guatemala and eastern Soconusco: "Naguadecat" (Nahuatlan), "Ayudacat" (Ayotlan), Mazatlan, and "Tapaldecat" (Tapachula), with the important assistance of "Don Francisco Izquin Nehaib." After the attack on the last named town, the name of "un cacique" is suddenly introduced for the first time, none other than "Cucumatz Cotuha." Encountering two great ceiba trees, at his command "el cacique y principales allí pusieron . . . sus armas de águila . . . por señal de su mojon y a donde habían llegado a su conquista" (cf. *Título de los señores de Totonicapan* 1950: 240, there in connection with Quicab). The account (*Título de Izquín Nehaib* 1941: 247) goes on:

> Luego de allí se fué hacia el mar a conquistar y a ganar más tierras y a holgarse en el mar, y el dicho cacique por estar contento y tener gratos a sus soldados, se volvió águila y se metió dentro del mar haciendo de muestra de su conquista batiendo el mar, y después de haber salido del mar se holgaron mucho sus soldados de ver su hazaña, dándole la bienvenida.

The account then abruptly returns to the campaign of Mahocotah and Don Francisco Izquin Nehaib. Cucumatz Cotuha is not mentioned again. On his triumphal return to Chi Izmachi Gumarcaah, Mahocotah is welcomed by three great lords, "Don Balam Acul, Don Ikibalam, and Don Mahocotah el viejo," after which, as was customary, he renders an accounting of his campaign to "su rey Quiche Culaha" (later given as Bulaha, a title also listed in the *Título de los señores de Totonicapan*, as well as Tulaha). The loot is guarded by a "tesorero" and a "contador," the latter called Gucumatz. The remainder of the narrative concerns events that immediately preceded the Conquest, as well as an account of that event, featuring particularly the deeds of Tecum, the native commander at the Battle of Quetzaltenanco, which broke the Quiche power.

SUMMARY

A summary of this limited material is hardly necessary. Apart from providing more evidence of the common use of "G(C)ucumatz" as a title, it contains a passage that seems on the face of it puzzlingly out of place yet provides an interesting vignette concerning the career of the sorcerer-ruler Gucumatz. It may also be significant that here again the name is linked with that of Cotuha, apparently as that of a single individual. But why was this brief anecdote involving Gucumatz/Cotuha inserted at this place, while recounting a campaign of conquest ostensibly led by another leader? Why is he—or they—seemingly placed in time *after* Quicab? Why are Ikibalam, "Mohotocah al viejo," and Balam Acul (= Balam Acab?), who in the *Popol Vuh* and the *Título de los señores de Totonicapan* are three of the original four leaders who guided the ancestors of the Gumarcaah dynasty from Tollan, named as contemporaries of a leader who, on the face of it, seems to fit generations later? Various explanations present themselves, but since these problems, however interesting in themselves and important for the pre-Hispanic history of Highland Guatemala, are not directly relevant to our inquiry, they must be left unexamined. For our purposes, it is merely sufficient to add to the record these puzzling notices of the activities of one of the most important members of the Gumarcaah dynasty, who bore as a name or title the exact equivalent of Quetzalcoatl.

4. Papel del origen de los señores

THE SOURCE

This is a brief history of the Gumarcaah dynasty, accompanied by a crude genealogical chart, contained in the *Descripción de Zapotitlan y Suchitepec enviada al rey por el corregidor Juan de Estrada,* November 22, 1579, now in the Benson Latin American Collection of the University of Texas, Austin. The *Papel del origen de los señores* and a facsimile of the chart were published by Recinos in his edition of the *Anales de los Cakchiqueles* (1950: 245–247; English translation: Recinos and Goetz 1953: 237–239).

Up to the reigns of "Cocayb" and "Cocaybim," the *Papel* closely agrees with the *Título de los señores de Totonicapan*; but from this point on it is radically divergent from both this source and the *Popol Vuh.* This seems to be explained partly by the fact that the *Papel* is obviously, with two or three possible exceptions, giving the *titles* of the rulers (cf. list of the Great Houses of Cavec in the *Popol Vuh*), rather than their proper or calendric names. The title of the third ruler after Qocayb is given as Ahau Cumatz, which seems to correspond to the *Popol Vuh*'s fifth of the Great Houses of Cavec, Ahau Ah Gucumatz. Since this fits appropriately in the position assigned to Gucumatz and Cotuha in that document, it probably represents the same person. No details are given concerning his reign, which is not even mentioned in the text proper (only in the caption on the genealogy).

5. The *Fuentes y Guzmán Genealogy*

The *Recordación florida* of Francisco Antonio de Fuentes y Guzmán, a late seventeenth-century Guatemalan historian (and great-great-grandson of Bernal Díaz del Castillo), contains (Fuentes y Guzmán 1932–1933, I: 5–11; II: 386–391) a sequential listing of the members of the Gumarcaah dynasty that, in spite of its being ostensibly based on certain lost native-authored histories, is obviously quite synthetic and badly garbled. Although it contains no directly relevant material, it is worth mentioning because Lehmann (1922: 294–296) suggested that "Jiutemal" (= Ihuitimalli), who is named as the founder of the Cakchiquel dynasty and son of the first great Quiche ruler, Acxopil (Nahua: "toe"), is to be identified with the individual of the same name who is associated with Topiltzin Quetzalcoatl in Alvarado Tezozomoc's *Crónica Mexicana* (here called "Timal") and in the "Toltec Elegy," the *Teponazcuicatl*, as well as the Toltec ruler who succeeded Totepeuh, according to the *Anales de Cuauhtitlan*. This possibility will be briefly reconsidered below.

This completes the survey of the available sources (certain others, listed in Recinos and Goetz 1953, bibliography, are still unpublished) providing significant information concerning the history of the Gumarcaah dynasty that contain information relating to the subject of our inquiry. Next to be considered are sources that contain comparable historical data concerning the rival dynasty of Iximche, which ruled over the Cakchiquel-speakers southeast of the Quiche region.

6. The *Annals of the Cakchiquels*

THE SOURCE

This ninety-six-page document in Cakchiquel, second only to the *Popol Vuh* in fame and importance, presents a fairly detailed history of the Iximche dynasty from the point of view of its second most important lineage (*chinamit*), the Xahil, whose surviving leaders resided at Solola in the sixteenth century. The narrative begins before the departure from Tollan (with a glance at the creation of man, etc., much briefer than the corresponding section in the *Popol Vuh*). The latest date named is 1619–1620 (at least one leaf, however, perhaps more, is missing at the end). As to its authorship, Brinton (1885: 57–58), followed substantially by Mengin (1952: 11), broke it down thus—

pre-1560: father of Francisco Hernández Arana (grandson of Hunyg, head [Ahpoxahil] of the Xahil, who died in 1521); 1560–1583: Francisco Hernández Arana himself; post-1583: Francisco Díaz. Recinos (1950: 17–18), correcting Brinton, believed that all of the account, up to about 1581, was the work of Francisco Hernández Arana and that Francisco Díaz, a relative, carried it down to at least 1604. He further pointed out that "en la última época, varias personas tuvieron acceso al libro cakchiquel convirtiéndolo en una especie de diario de la comunidad indígena . . . (Sololá)." The manuscript is in one uniform hand, probably that of a professional scribe, and undoubtedly represents a rescript (1620–1650?) of an earlier document that was actually a compilation, its later entries at least, in different hands. Both Recinos and Mengin, in opposition to Brinton and Raynaud, held that it was not a *título* or legal document filed as evidence in a court proceeding, but a straight historical chronicle.

First used by the early eighteenth-century ecclesiastical historian Francisco Vázquez (1714–1716), it was discovered in 1844 in the archive of the Franciscan monastery in Guatemala City by the Guatemalan scholar Juan Gavarrete, who lent it to Brasseur de Bourbourg in 1855. The latter translated those portions dealing with pre-Conquest events and the Conquest into French, presented Gavarrete with a copy of this translation, and carried the original to France. The French scholar, although utilizing it in his historical writings, never published his translation. However, a Spanish translation of it, by Gavarrete, was published in Guatemala in 1873. In 1884, Brinton acquired both the original manuscript and the Brasseur de Bourbourg translation from Alfonse Pinart. A year later he published the same portion of the Cakchiquel text that had been translated by Brasseur de Bourbourg, accompanied by an English translation. Later translations of the same portion are those of Raynaud (1925, French translation; 1927, 1937, Spanish translations of his French translation); Villacorta Calderón (1934, first publication of complete Cakchiquel text); Teletor (1946, only those portions not translated by previous students); and Recinos (1950, Spanish translation of bulk of complete document [for listing of sections untranslated by him, see Carrasco 1951]); and Recinos and Goetz (1953, English translation of most of the Recinos edition). In 1952, a photographic facsimile of the original manuscript, now in the library of the University Museum, Philadelphia, was published in Denmark, with an introduction by Ernst Mengin.

The *Annals of the Cakchiquels* provides a more detailed dynastic history than that of the *Popol Vuh* and has the additional advantage of listing exact dates for its important events, unfortunately starting very late, from May 18, 1493. Like the *Popol Vuh*, it was probably based both on oral tradition and pictorial records of an essentially genealogical nature. For our purposes, however, it contains significantly less material that possibly relates to Topiltzin Quetzalcoatl than the Quiche sources already considered.

PROBABLE REFERENCES TO TOPILTZIN QUETZALCOATL

The *Annals* provides a considerably more detailed Tollan-to-Highland Guatemala migration itinerary than do the Quiche sources, reminiscent in this respect of many Central Mexican historical annals. In the midst of one of these detailed listings, the following incident is related. The ancestors of the Iximche dynasts, after arriving at Zakiteuh, Zakiqua, Niqah Zubinal, Niqah Chacachil, Tzulahuah, Ixbacah, Niqah Nimxor, Niqah Moinal, and Niqah Carchah, in Recinos's (1950: 67–68, § 25) translation:

> llegaron ante los hijos de Valil, los hijos de Tzunún; llegaron ante Mevac y Nacxit que era en verdad un gran rey. Entonces los agasajaron y fueron electos Ahauh Ahpop y Ahpop Qamahay. Luego los vistieron, les horadaron la nariz y les dieron sus cargos y las flores llamadas Cinpual. Verdaderamente se hizo querer de todos los guerreros. Y dirigiéndose a todos, dijo el Señor Nacxit: "Subid a estas columnas de piedra (*vapal ahab*), entrad a mi casa. Os daré a vosotros el señorío, os daré las flores Cinpuval Taxoch. No los he concedido la piedra a otros," agregó. Y en seguida subieron a las columnas de piedra. De esta manera se acabó de darles el señorío en presencia de Nacxit y se pusieron a dar gritos de alegría.

They then encounter the Pokomam, at Nimpokom ("Great Pokom"), Raxchich, and Pazaktzuy.

After many more wanderings and adventures, including their "dawn," the ancestors of the Iximche dynasts (more specifically, the ancestors of the leaders of the Xahil lineage) reach the forest of Chiqohom. At this time, the leader of the *chinamit* of Baqahol seems to have been in the political ascendancy. The second of the two original founders of the Xahil lineage, Gagavitz, "el que vino de Tulan," had died, leaving two sons, Caynoh and Caybatz. The latter are sent by the Galel Xahil and the Ahuchan Xahil, the leaders of the Xahil, to Tepeuh, lord of Cauke, whose residence is called Cuztum ("Fortress") Chixnal. This ruler had made himself feared because of his witchcraft (*nahual*). He was "el primero que se engrandeció" and to whom all the tribes (*amag*) paid tribute. Caynoh and Caybatz are appointed his tribute collectors, which task they perform so successfully that they "se convirtieron en hijos de Tepeuh," "fueron en verdad amados por él." Next follows an account of certain adventures the two undergo while engaged in collecting tribute from the Zutuhil south of Lake Atitlan (the Ahtziquinahay), after which Caynoh and Caybatz return in triumph to Chiqohom and assume command of the Xahil as Ahpoxahil and Ahpop Camahay, respectively. Tepeuh does not reappear in the account.

SUMMARY

(1) While engaged in their migration from Tollan to their historic capitals in Highland Guatemala, the leaders of the ancestors of the Iximche dynasty (the Xahil lineage and probably the other chief lineages as well) are received by "the great king," Nacxit, and invested with certain insignia of royalty: pierced septums, flowers, etc. (the problem of the geographical locus of this incident will be discussed below); (2) later, after reaching "the forest of Chiqohom," the Xahil leaders come under the domination of the leading political power of the time, Tepeuh of Cauke, a great sorcerer; (3) Caynoh and Caybatz, the two sons of Gagavitz, one of the two founders of the Xahil, become the tribute collectors of Tepeuh, and, after a series of adventures with the Zutuhil, assume the leadership of their lineage.

COMMENT

Although not specifically called the Quiche ruler, Tepeuh is probably Gucumatz (cf. Brasseur de Bourbourg 1857–1859, II: 485, who identifies him with Iztayul). Tepeuh Gucumatz could be identified with the great creator god who plays such an important role in the opening sections of the *Popol Vuh*. The title "Tepeucucumatz," mentioned in the *Título de Izquin Nehaib*, will be recalled. It may have been the full name, or title, of the first of the later Gumarcaah rulers to be prominently featured in the Quiche histories. Although his capitals in these accounts are Chi Izmachi and, later, Gumarcaah, Cauke (modern Santa María Cauque) was undoubtedly within his jurisdiction. At any rate, the chronology fits, as well as his prowess as a sorcerer and his extensive political power.

7. The *Historia de los Xpantzay*

THE SOURCE

Heinrich Berlin assigned this title to six documents that formed part of a legal *expediente* instituted in 1658 by the natives of Tecpan Guatemala against a Spanish *hacendado*. They were discovered by him in the archive of the Escribanía del Gobierno y Sección de Tierras de Guatemala and he assigned the letters from A to F to them. The originals are in Cakchiquel, accompanied by Spanish translations made in 1659. The three documents that provide the most valuable historical information (A, D, and F) were newly translated into Spanish by Recinos. His translations of these and the old translations of the remaining documents (B, C, and E) were published by Berlin in 1950, without the Cakchiquel text. The first three provide historical data of exceptional importance concerning the Xpantzay lineage of the Cakchiquel, which, like nearly all of the politically important lineages in Highland Guatemala, traced its descent directly back to Tollan (its founder bore the Nahua name Chimal Acat, "Shield Reed"). Incidental information on the Iximche dynasty as a whole is also included, providing a valuable supplement to—and essential corroboration of—the *Annals of the Cakchiquels*. In spite of this importance, however, no careful study of these documents, aside from the brief introduction by Berlin, has been made. Certain obscurities in the text make interpretation difficult at times, but the general meaning of most of the text seems clear.

The documents were probably in the possession of "Pedro López Expanxay, alcalde" of Tecpan Guatemala, who is named as one of the principal litigants on the indigenous side and who may have been the head of the lineage at the time. Document A, according to Berlin, in spite of its heading, *Título original 1524 años*, appears to be a copy of a document originally composed in the second half of the sixteenth century; it contains no material directly relevant to our theme. Document D, from internal evidence, was originally drawn up in 1554 by Alonso Pérez, who considered himself the legitimate head of the Xpantzay at that time, although the present manuscript appears to be a copy made subsequent to 1602. It, as well as the unsigned Document F, likewise dated 1554 and also seemingly copied after 1602, contains valuable material concerning Gucumatz of the Gumarcaah dynasty.

POSSIBLE REFERENCES TO TOPILTZIN QUETZALCOATL

As indicated, Document A, although it contains important historical information generally, provides none specifically relevant to our theme. Document D, on the other hand, which narrates the succession of the leaders of the Xpantzay lineage from Chimal Acat, who "vino de Tulan Zuyva," to Alonso Pérez, the 1554 claimant, contains brief but significant information concerning Gucumatz.

The migration from Tollan is described, with the principal stopping places listed in order. Finally reaching Chiqohom (cf. *Annals of the Cakchiquels*), they move on to "Mukubal Zib Bitol Amag," while Xpantzay Noh, son of the recently deceased Chimal Acat, heads the lineage (Berlin 1950: 48):

> Allí recibieron las flechas y los escudos frente a los quichés de la tribu de Cavec, en Chi-Izmachí-Gumarcaah. Gobernaba entonces al Señor Gugucumatz [*sic*]. Allí los quichés de Cavec, casaron a sus hijas con los zotziles y tukuches [two of the four major divisions of the Cakchiquel dynasts], y en celebración se dieron las manos, tomaron sus bebidas y les hicieron casas de palos para dormir.

They then move on, now under the leadership of Xpantzay Ahmak, who has succeeded Xpantzay Noh, to "Chiavar Xupitakah, Avar Civan, Avar Tinamit." There Huntoh and Vukubatz, the Ahpozotzil and Ahpoxahil, the supreme co-rulers of the dynasty, embark on a series of conquests as allies of the "quichés de Cavec." The death of Xpantzay Ahmak is then recorded, followed (Berlin 1950: 48) by: "Y allí murió al rey Gugucumatz, el padre de Qikab. Fue recogido a la orilla de un río, no tuvo padre ni madre, fué un rey prodigioso."

Soon after, bitter dissensions cause a breaking of the alliance (or their tributary status) with the Quiche of Cavec, and "Iximché sobre el Ratzamut" is founded by the two co-rulers who succeeded Huntoh and Vucubatz, Lahuh Ah and Oxlahuh Tziy.

Document F presents an exceptionally interesting, if at times obscure, account of the Cakchiquel-Quiche alliance in the times of Gucumatz and Quicab, the latter described here, as in Document D, as the son of the former. It begins with the Zotzils and Tukuches at Mukubal Zib Bitol Amag (Berlin 1950: 50): "No tenían armas ni escudos, solo el Señor Gugucumatz se había fortalecido allá en Izmachí-Gumarcaah. Los zotziles y tukuchés tenían escondidas sus armas y sus joyas entre las matas y la corteza de los árboles." Later it is explained that they were ". . . brujos y hechiceros que practicaban sus artes hasta el amanecer. No hacían la guerra sino unicamente sus brujerías."

Gucumatz undertakes to persuade them to join him in a campaign against the town of Cohaa, where great wealth would await them as recompense for their aid. Apparently at this time Huntoh and Vucubatz were important military commanders ("Ahpop Achtí") under Rahamun and Xiquetzal. The Zotzil and Tukuche, however, decline the honor, protesting their lack of ability in the military sphere, as well as pointing out that they possess no weapons. Gucumatz is insistent, offering to supply them from his own arsenal. Reluctantly, they acquiesce. At this point (Berlin 1950: 51), the rulers of the "quichés de Cavec" are named: Qonache, Gagavitz, Balam Aka, and Balam Quitze (*sic*). Arriving on the battlefield, the Zotzil and Tukuche, after an initial reluctance to lead the attack, are freshly persuaded to advance (to Mukchee), whereupon the Quiche leave them to carry on the fight alone. Through their powers of sorcery, they triumph and capture prisoners. Returning to the temples of the Quiche gods, Avilix and Tohohil, they upbraid their erstwhile allies for their lack of support. Gucumatz, however, newly insists on their support in an attack on Tecum Ziqom Puvak, the ruler of Cohaa, who has killed his daughter and son-in-law. Then the death of Gucumatz and birth of Quicab are described (Berlin 1950: 52):

> El Señor [Gucumatz] le dijo a un corcobado: "Anda corcobado, a aparecerle a la Señora y le dirás: 'el Señor ha muerto,' así lo dirás cuando llegues allá. Si la Señora no está allí cinco o seis días después de tu llegada que se ponga a tejer la Señora y verá al muerto." Así le dijo al corcobado. "Está bien, Señor," contestó el corcobado. Y en seguida salió fuego del Señor. El corcobado llegó ante la Señora; luego se intodujo a su cámara. Y cuando él llegó ante ella, le dijo lo que mandaba decir el rey. Los quichés de Cavec se quedaron esperando. Luego nació Qikab.

> Cuando nació estaban ardiendo todos los pueblos . . . Entonces nació el Señor Qikab, hijo de Gugucumatz. Llevó la noticia el jorobado. Obra de encantamiento fué su nacimiento. Entonces vieron el prodigio junto los zotziles y tukuches.

The account then abruptly skips to a later time when Quicab, now a boy, gathers his warriors for another attack on Cohaa. Addressing them, he says (Berlin 1950: 52):

> "Vosotros, Señores, nuestros guerreros, escuchad ahora mis palabras, yo soy el rey, id a conquistar la ciudad de Cohaa. Los huesos de mi padre están allí en Cohaa. Que entre la gente al amanecer y recoja su calavera." Así dijo. "Y que no se revuelva la calavera con los huesos. Juntaos y traed los huesos de mi padre." Esto les dijo el rey a los quichés.

However, Quicab's warriors refuse, fearing to die like his father, pointing out that "El Señor murió porque le tenían envidia." Quicab insists even more strongly, but they still decline, suggesting that he send the Zotzil and the Tukuche. More hassling, now involving the latter also, takes place, at one point "los Señores" reminding the ruler: "Y si muriera al rey como en otro tiempo murió Gugucumatz, que era rey prodigioso?" Finally all consent, and the attack is launched. "Los zotziles y tukuches destruyeron la ciudad con sus encantamientos." The town is captured and burned, and a great quantity of wealth secured. The Quiche hide so much of their loot that they are insulted by the Zotzil and the Tukuche. Quicab is successful in his aim and recovers the bones of his father. The account then goes on to describe a further series of conquests in which the Zotzil and Tukuche—and the Xpantzay—play a prominent role, coming down to the time when they break with their allies, or overlords, the Quiche of Cavec.

SUMMARY

Documents D and F of the *Historia de los Xpantzay* supply the following information concerning Gucumatz of the Gumarcaah dynasty: (1) having no parents, discovered on the bank of a river, this "rey prodigioso" is ruling when the Cakchiquel dynasts are residing first at Mukabal Zib Bitol Amag, later at Chiavar Zupitakah, during the successive reigns of the pairs of co-rulers, Rahamun-Xiquetzal and Huntoh-Vucubatz; (2) in the latter document, the Zotzil and the Tukuche, two of the four great divisions of the Cakchiquel ruling house, having abandoned their weapons and now living by the practice of sorcery, are persuaded by Gucumatz, over their considerable reluctance, to join him in a military campaign, during which they distinguish themselves after they are abandoned by the Quiche of Cavec; (3) Gucumatz, vengeance bound after the killing of his daughter and son-in-law by Tecum Ziqom Puvac, ruler of Cohaa, again endeavors to enlist the services of his

Cakchiquel allies; (4) however, Gucumatz dies, apparently fighting before Cohaa, and his body is captured and left in the latter town; (5) his son Quicab, born miraculously after his death, when of age rallies his warriors and allies and, after overcoming considerable reluctance on their part, captures and destroys Cohaa, recovering the bones of his father.

COMMENT

Although these narrations, focusing on various military campaigns conducted by the two most prominent pre-Hispanic Quiche rulers, Gucumatz and Quicab, aided by their Cakchiquel allies, are flavored with events that recall some aspects of the Topiltzin Quetzalcoatl of Tollan Tale, no connection with the latter of any consequence could reasonably be claimed for them. On the other hand, they probably do reflect the Toltec dynastic tradition as it had survived in Highland Guatemala and which seems have included at least faint echoes of the tale—some of whose elements could have been incorporated into the local traditions concerning the careers of their most important past rulers. In any case, we proceed now to a general consideration of the relevant Highland Guatemalan data that have been summarized above.

Discussion of the Highland Guatemala Sources

The most interesting passages in this group of sources are those that concern Nacxit. Although his name is not explicitly combined with either Quetzalcoatl or Topiltzin, the likelihood seems very strong that he is to be identified either with the Toltec ruler whose career we are attempting to reconstruct or an important successor who bore his name(s) as a title. As we have seen, no less than four apparently independent primary Central Mexican sources give Nacxitl as an additional name for Topiltzin Quetzalcoatl. Furthermore, just as important as this identity in names is the identity of role, i.e., the powerful, revered ruler, dispenser of all legitimate political authority, which role, as noted above, was precisely that ascribed to Topiltzin Quetzalcoatl of Tollan (cf. Seler 1902–1923, III: 96–97).

Although a close connection between the Highland Guatemala Nacxit and the preeminent priest/ruler of Tollan seems eminently plausible, a number of challenging problems remain. One, which has puzzled many investigators, is the placement of Nacxit's seat of authority in the "East," from where, according to all of the accounts but one (*Annals of the Cakchiquels*), the ancestors of the Highland Guatemala dynasts had departed. Various hypotheses to account for this seeming directional anomaly have been advanced. Seler (1902–1923, III: 574–575) suggests that this notion of an eastern origin was connected with Zuiva, often linked with Tollan, apparently located in Tabasco, which for the inhabitants of Central Mexico represented the eastern region par excellence. He also suggests that "Toltec traders" (perhaps better, Toltec ancestors of the Guatemala dynasts) may have actually reached Highland Guatemala from the east, i.e., through Tabasco, across the Petén, and up the Río Motagua Valley. The migration itinerary of the *Annals of the Cakchiquels*, however, as Recinos (1950: 41) pointed out, would seem to support an entrance into the central Guatemalan highlands from Chiapas, i.e., the *west*, which direction in fact is specified as the point of origin in this source. Lehmann (1922: 301–302) believed this concept of an eastern origin to have been an idea markedly Mexican, arising in late times after the regions of the east were considered to be the authentic land of the Toltecs, i.e., where their culture had survived in its purest form. He also suggested, much more dubiously, that the complex of ideas revolving around the "East" arrived in Highland Guatemala together with a supposed "Acatl reform" of the Toltec calendar, since this calendric sign was assigned to the direction east.

Certain mythological conceptions may have entered into this characteristically Highland Guatemalan concept of the importance of the "East," thereby distorting the actual geographic situation. A certain case might also be made for a second Tollan in Tabasco (as noted above, the *Annals of the Cakchiquels* names no less than *four* Tollans), conceivably founded as a commercial and military base by émigrés from the home center. This hypothetical Tollan would have been located in the "East" from the point of view of the original Tollan and could have served as the immediate point of departure of the Toltec-connected groups who moved into Highland Guatemala (and Yucatan?). However, this putative Tollan of the "East," assuming its existence, was directly connected with the original Central Mexican homeland, since the song, "Camucu," recalling "nuestros hermanos mayores y menores," the Yaqui, the Toltecs, who stayed behind, ostensibly in the "East," refer to the "país que hoy se llama México" (Recinos 1953: 200).

Recinos made an interesting attempt to pinpoint some of the areas associated with Nacxit. He (1953: 222–223) believed that the journey of Qocaib and Qocavib, described in the Reynosa insert in the *Título de los señores de Totonicapan*, could be reconstructed thus: the former went by the east coast of Yucatan to Chichen Itza, where the court of Nacxit was located, while the latter probably followed the courses of the Ríos Chixoy and Usumacinta to Tabasco. The "Lake of Mexico," where Cocavib encountered obstacles that frustrated his design, Recinos identified with the Laguna de Terminos (where he [in Recinos 1953: 200] also located Zuiva). Assuming this account can be taken fairly literally, a certain case might be made for *two* Nacxits, one with his seat at Tollan in the west (west of the "Lake of Mexico," i.e., Lake Texcoco), and the other in the east, in the Gulf Coast region, at the "other" Tollan. Chichen Itza, or even Mayapan, as alternative identifications for the latter also probably cannot be ruled out entirely. As will be seen, the former city was for a long period the greatest "Toltec" center in northern Yucatan, while at the latter center, which succeeded it in power, its most famous ruler, Hunac Ceel, may be referred to in the *Chilam Balam of Tizimin* as "Ah Nacxit Kukulcan."

In the *Título de los señores de Totonicapan* it is clear that Nacxit was already ruling in Tollan before the departure of the ancestors of the Gumarcaah dynasty, for he presented them with the *giron gagal*, the sacred bundle of power, at that time. If Nacxit can be assumed to have been a single historical person, his seat of authority most likely would have been here, the Central Mexican Tollan. If, on the other hand, the "great father Nacxit" was merely the embodiment of Toltec authority in the person of the leader of the moment who bore this title, he could be located almost anywhere that Toltec power had been established.

In this connection, it may be significant that the *Annals of the Cakchiquels* account of Nacxit does not seem, on the face of it, to involve a journey comparable in length to those described in the two Quiche accounts. Locating Nacxit's residence in the Cakchiquel chronicle is particularly difficult. The last place listed in the migration itinerary, just before the Nacxit incident, is Carchah, which seems to be identifiable with the modern town of that name just northwest of Coban in the Alta Vera Paz (Recinos 1950: 67). Whether the next two proper names are really towns is not certain, but a case can be made. The first, Valil, may be identifiable (Moran n.d.; Raynaud 1937: 21) with (San Agustín) Acasaguastlan, in the upper Río Motagua valley, just to the east of the Vera Paz, where, at least in colonial times, Nahua is reported to have been spoken (Brinton 1887b). Tzunun ("Sparrow"), which follows, cannot be located, but a Chi Tzunun Choy ("In the Lake of the Sparrows") is listed earlier as a town on Lake Atitlan, and, later, Tzununhuyu ("Sparrow Mountain") is named, immediately after the encounter with the Pokomam (in or near their territory south of Acasaguastlan?). The name linked with that of Nacxit, Mevac ("maíz quebrado [o quebrantado] por una primera molienda [o mano]," according to Raynaud 1937: 21), has not been explained; it might refer either to a person or a place, probably the former.

Recinos (1950: 68), in line with his previous views on the location of the Nacxit of the Quiche sources, also places the Nacxit of the Cakchiquel *Annals* in Chichen Itza, stressing the seeming mention of stone columns that are so plentiful at this site. On the other hand, if the identification of Valil with Acasaguastlan is valid, a possible secondary center of Toltec power in the upper Río Motagua region could be indicated, where Nahua speech may have survived. Thus, it could have been here, rather than in the distant "East" (unless this upper Motagua region *is* the "East" of the Quiche records), that the ancestors of the Iximche dynasts received their investiture from a local representative of Toltec authority who bore the title Nacxit.

Another possibility, of course, is that this passage in the *Annals* is so condensed that the pilgrimage aspect, perhaps once present, has disappeared from the account.

As is clear from the prayer addressed to Nacxit, the Spanish translation of which was quoted above, he was also considered to be in some sense divine. The parallel here with Topiltzin Quetzalcoatl of Tollan is, again, very close. Furthermore, it is known (Moran n.d.) that, as a god, Nacxit was also worshipped by the neighboring Pokomam and perhaps other Highland Guatemala groups whose dynasties claimed a Toltec origin or had come under heavy Toltec influence.

The insignia and titles that Nacxit dispensed are particularly interesting. The latter correspond, although rarely in meaning, to the lengthy lists of similar titles so characteristic of the Nahua-speaking groups of Postclassic Central Mexico and their neighbors. Like the Highland Guatemala groups, they probably had inherited them from their Toltec predecessors. Only some of those mentioned in the Guatemalan records, however, such as jaguar and eagle claws, are known to have been important at the time of the Conquest in Central Mexico. It is possible that various of the Toltec symbols and rituals surrounding persons of authority survived in purer form on the Guatemalan periphery than in their area of origin—although some fusion with preexisting Mayance patterns must have taken place, since chieftainship, judging from the elaborate tombs, was quite important in Highland Guatemala during the Classic period.

Another difficult problem is that of Gucumatz. Does this important member of the Gumarcaah dynasty bear any specific relationship to the renowned priest/ruler of Tollan apart from their nomenclatural identity? Two similarities are noteworthy: (1) his prominence as ruler, the first of the later Gumarcaah dynasts to be singled out for extended treatment, together with his role as founder of the last Quiche capital (cf. Topiltzin Quetzalcoatl's founding—in some of the accounts—of Tollan); and (2) his miraculous origin and prowess as a sorcerer. There is no question of a direct identification here, but perhaps it is possible that some elements in the career of Topiltzin Quetzalcoatl—which might have been remembered by the putative Toltec groups who moved into Highland Guatemala—could have rubbed off on this important Quiche ruler who bore a name, or title, of identical meaning.

Various obscurities surround Gucumatz, especially as his career is described in the *Popol Vuh*. For example, in one passage it is stated that he was both Ahpop and Ahpop Camha in the fourth generation. Later, he is linked with a co-ruler, the Ahpop Camha, Cotuha, in the fifth generation. On the other hand, if this fuller *Popol Vuh* account were lacking, on the basis of other Quiche sources a cogent case could be made for merging Cotuha and Gucumatz into a single person, the latter name serving as a title. Gucumatz,

Ah Gucumatz, and/or Tepeu Gucumatz were unquestionably used titularly and might well have been borne by any ruler in addition to other names and titles. Every highborn native Highland Guatemalan appears to have borne at least three distinct appellations: his calendric name, his "proper" name, and his title (or titles) of rank. In the dynastic lists, all three types are encountered. The confusion this nomenclatural variance might have caused, even in pre-Hispanic times, is obvious. Conceivably, three rulers listed consecutively as, say, Hun Toh, Tepepul, and Ah Tohil could actually be the same individual under three different designations. In the immediate case, it will be recalled that the *Título de los señores de Totonicapan* calls Cotuha "Cotuha Gucumatzal." The *Título de Izquin Nehaib* also refers to "Gucumatz Cotuha" as a single person. Recinos (1950: 231) interpreted this double name as signifying "brujo, capaz de convertirse en serpiente emplumada," but a titular interpretation is perhaps more likely.

In the Quiche accounts, the antecedents of Gucumatz are remarkably obscure. His precise relation to the preceding and succeeding rulers is nowhere clearly stated. Only in a Cakchiquel source, the *Historia de los Xpantzay*, Document D, is it specified that he was of miraculous origin and that Quicab was his son (this last, also in Document F). Clearly, as in the case of our hero, the career of this ruler was later surrounded with a considerable amount of fable and legend. In any case, although they share this quality, the best evidence indicates that Gucumatz can only be related to Topiltzin Quetzalcoatl in a general associational fashion.

In pre-Hispanic Highland Guatemala, as everywhere in Mesoamerica, the further one works back in time the more the smoke of legend obscures the fire of genuine history. This is particularly well illustrated by the chronological placement of the four great early heroes and founders of the Gumarcaah dynasty—Balam Quitze, Balam Acab, Iqui Balam, and Mahucutoh—who are shuffled about from source to source in a somewhat disconcerting fashion. The deeds of Gucumatz and Quicab are certainly more worthy of credence, particularly those of the latter, but the marvelous still plays an important role. Unfortunately, the loss of the historico-genealogical pictorial records kept by the Highland Guatemala ruling lineages makes it difficult to decide how much of this chronological confusion and legendary embellishment existed before the Conquest and how much of it might have been the result of colonial breakdown.

Finally, to return to the Tohil problem. The statement in the *Popol Vuh* will be recalled: "Porque en verdad, el llamado Tohil es el mismo dios de los yaquis, cuyo nombre es Yolcuat Quitzalcuat." The prefix "Yolcuat" has been variously interpreted. Brasseur de Bourbourg (1861: 246) etymologized it as "yol-cohuatl, serpent a sonnettes, du mot yolli, coeur ou sonnette, et de cohuatl, serpent." Yohualli Ehecatl, "Night (and) Wind," a generic appellation of deity, applied especially to Tezcatlipoca (Sahagún 1946: passim), was Seler's (1904a: 234) choice. This might find support in the additional name, "Yagualiecatl," applied to Quetzalcoatl, as creator god, in the opening cosmogonical section of the *Historia de los Mexicanos por sus pinturas* (García Icazbalceta 1891: 228). Lehmann (1922: 298), on the other hand, opted for "youalcoatl," "serpent of the night." All of these interpretations may have some cogency, although it is clearly quite dubious to derive *ehecatl* from *cuat*, which unquestionably means serpent in the word "Quitzalcuat."

VI. The Pipil

Remarkably little is known concerning the important Nahua-speaking groups of Highland Guatemala and western El Salvador, to whom the term Pipil is usually applied. Although a common view is that they entered Guatemala as part of the general Toltec movement southward, there is some evidence—traditional, linguistic, and archaeological—that not all of these Nahua-speakers arrived at the same time or as part of the same movement (on the "Pipil question" see, especially: Lehmann 1920, II: 978–1075; Thompson 1948: 11–15; Schultze Jena 1935; Sapper 1936). The Nahua advance guard may have reached the area somewhat before the rise of the Central Mexican Tollan to political and cultural importance. The final, Nahua(tl)-speaking arrivals (Tlaxcalteca, Acolhuaque, Mexica, et al.) came, in a sense, with Pedro de Alvarado. There is no specific evidence that any of the ruling dynasties of these Nahua groups traced their origin back to Tollan. Since we lack any of their original histories, however, which certainly once existed (Fuentes y Guzmán 1932–1933, II: 90–92, utilized one, now lost), it is difficult to decide on this question. A certain case can be made that some of the ancestors of the Guatemalan and Salvadoran Pipil did migrate from Central Mexico during or soon following the Toltec era, along with the ancestors of the Gumarcaah, Iximche, and related dynasties who became linguistically Mayanized. If this supposition is valid, then some reminiscences of Topiltzin Quetzalcoatl of Tollan among the Pipil might have survived, perhaps under the name Nacxit, his designation, as we have seen, in the traditional histories of their Mayance-speaking neighbors. However, no concrete evidence supporting this possibility is extant.

One fact is certain. Quetzalcoatl was worshipped as a *god* by at least one Pipil group in the region of Asunción Mita (ancient Mictan), Guatemala, which seems to have been an important Nahua-speaking center in late pre-Hispanic times. This we know from the 1576 letter to Philip II by the *oidor* of the Audiencia de Guatemala, García de Palacio (1860: 66, 70, 72), which contains the fullest account of the customs (but, unfortunately, not the history) of the Pipil of that region. Together with the notices of Fuentes y Guzmán and Torquemada, the information in this epistle is practically all we have (there is a useful summary in Thompson 1948: 11–15). Quetzalcoatl is named as one of two "ídolos" (the other a goddess, "Itzqueye," "Obsidian Skirt") to whom sacrifices were made at appropriate times in the calendar and after battles. As far as I am aware, this notice places the cult of the god Quetzalcoatl, under that name, the furthest south in Mesoamerica that it has been reported. He may have been connected with Topiltzin Quetzalcoatl of Tollan, but, in the absence of any confirming evidence, this question must remain open. If eventually an original Pipil history is ever brought to light, it seems possible that it might contain at least some reference to Nacxit. Various references (e.g., Fuentes y Guzmán 1932–1933, part 2, book 2, chapter 5; Thompson 1948: 14) make it very likely that at the time of the Conquest Pipil pictorial histories, fully comparable to those of their Toltec-descended Mayance-speaking neighbors, were in existence and have since been lost. Hopefully, more ethnohistorical documentation concerning the Guatemalan/Salvadoran Pipil is waiting to be discovered.

VII. Nicaragua

The most powerful native group in western Nicaragua at the time of the Conquest were the Nahua-speakers, usually called the Nicarao, who occupied most of the narrow strip of fertile land between Lake Nicaragua and the Pacific, the Isthmus of Rivas. Our knowledge of them, as of their linguistic brethren, the Pipil of El Salvador and Guatemala, is very fragmentary. The most important information was recorded by Oviedo y Valdés (1851–1855, book 42, chapters 2 and 3), who summarized the transciption of an interrogatory concerning their religion, history, and customs compiled by a Mercedarian ecclesiastic, Fray Francisco de Bobadilla, who was sent by Pedriarias Dávila, the governor of Nicaragua, to the village of Teoca in 1528. The replies of the chiefs and the elders to a standard list of questions were duly recorded by the public notary of the *consejo* of Granada. It provides a fascinating insight into the indigenous point of view toward their gods and traditions.

The Nicarao apparently possessed no tradition of a Tollan origin, or, if so, it was not elicited by the interrogators or recorded. Instead, some of their leaders stated that they had migrated from afar, from "Ticomega" and "Maguatega," in the west, to escape the oppression of unnamed masters. No estimate of the time of this movement is given. Torquemada (1943–1944, I: 331–333), however, reporting another tradition relating to this group, states that their ancestors migrated from Soconusco, oppressed by their old enemies the Olmec, who had conquered them a span of time before which could be measured by the lives of seven or eight very old men. Lehmann and Long, followed by Thompson (1948: 11), suggested that these "lives" were really the 104-year periods called *huehueliztli* in Central Mexico, which would take the Olmec conquest (the migration probably took place not long after) back to about the eighth or ninth century. Even if these "lives" are accepted literally, this conquest would probably only date to a generation or two later. As we shall see below when discussing the chronology of Topiltzin Quetzalcoatl, a ninth- or tenth-century date is not too early for a Tollan connection for the Nicarao, although the "fall" of this center probably occurred much later.

In spite of this possibility, the names Topiltzin, Quetzalcoatl, and Nacxit do not appear in Oviedo's version of Bobadilla's interrogatory—unless "Theobilche" (Oviedo y Valdés 1851–1855, IV: 101), probably equivalent to the Nahuatl Teopiltzin, "son of god" or "esteemed son," could be construed rather as Topiltzin. The two chief gods, the creators, are called "Tamagastad" (or "Tamagostat") and "Cipattonal." The latter equates with the Central Mexican Cipactonal, who apparently is equivalent to Xpiyacoc of the Xpiyacoc/Xmucane pair in the *Popol Vuh*. The identification of the former is more difficult. Since elsewhere the sacrificing priest is called "tamagast," undoubtedly the equivalent of *tlamacazqui*, it is probable that the god's name was similarly derived. As noted above, this term for a type of priest was applied in Central Mexico to Quetzalcoatl and, occasionally, to Tlaloc (the Nicarao rain god, however, is called "Quiateot," literally "Rain God"). It is barely possible, then, that the Tamagastad of the Nicarao equals Ehecatl Quetzalcoatl in his role as creator.

The ruler "Miseboy" informed Bobadilla that, in addition to "Tamagostat" and "Cipattonal," "Oxomogo," "Chalchitguegue," and "Chicoziagat" were important creator gods (*teotes*; *dioses mayores*). The first-named clearly equates with Oxomoco of the Central Mexican Cipactonal/Oxomoco pair. The second must equal Chalchiuhtlicue, the water goddess. The last name is particularly intriguing, but somewhat uncertain as to its correct interpretation—perhaps Chicuace Acatl, 6 Reed, or, less likely, Chicome Acatl, 7 Reed. On the former date, according to the *Historia de los Mexicanos por sus pinturas* (García Icazbalceta 1891: 235), Centeotl, the maize deity, was created. As we saw, the latter date was associated with Quetzalcoatl, including Topiltzin Quetzalcoatl, in Central Mexico. The latter half of the name alone, *ciagat*, on the other hand, could be interpreted as Ce Acatl, Quetzalcoatl's most common calendric name.

In any case, the name of the "dios del ayre" is given as "Chiquinuat y Hecat," i.e., Chiconahui Ehecatl, 9 Ehecatl (Wind), another of Quetzalcoatl's important Central Mexican calendric names. Thus—as among the Pipil of the Asunción Mita, Guatemala, area—a version of Quetzalcoatl, in spite of the lack of mention of that specific name, clearly functioned as a significant member of the Nicarao pantheon, as wind god. He might also have been connected with Topiltzin Quetzalcoatl of Tollan, but, in the absence of any concrete evidence of Nicarao-Tollan ties, this seems quite unlikely.

VIII. Tabasco-Campeche

The swampy lowland area of Tabasco marked the western boundary of Mayance-speaking territory (Chontal, or Putun). A great commercial crossroads in pre-Conquest times due to its key Gulf Coast location, this zone contained at least eight Nahua-speaking towns (Scholes and Roys 1948: 15–47). As suggested above, it is not entirely inconceivable that during Toltec times another Tollan—which, as is well known, in addition to its literal meaning, "Place of Reeds," also connoted "Metropolis"—had been established in this region.

However, knowledge of the histories of the Nahua-speaking communities of Tabasco at the time of the Conquest is nil. Only for the Chontal/Putun of the adjoining province of Acallan (southern Campeche) do we have available a substantial historical tradition. In the source that presents this tradition, the *Paxbolon-Maldonado Papers* that consist of *probanzas* of the merits and services of Don Pablo Paxbolon, ruler of colonial Tixchel, and his son-in-law Francisco Maldonado (1612–1614), the "devil" of the ruler of Izamkanac, capital of Acallan, is called "Cukulchan" (Scholes and Roys 1948: 56–57, 395), obviously the Chontal/Putun version of Kukulcan. Unfortunately, aside from this mere mention, no information concerning this god is extant, although he may have played essentially the same role here as in Yucatan—and thus might have borne some relationship to Topiltzin Quetzalcoatl of Tollan. The possible Toltec background of the Acallan ruling dynasty (Scholes and Roys 1948: 77–79) would make this connection more likely. It must be recognized, however, that positive evidence is lacking.

IX. Yucatan

In the late pre-Hispanic period, most of this peninsula was, for Mesoamerica, an unusually homogeneous linguistic zone—in spite of a striking degree of political fragmentation at Contact. Contrary to an older view that once enjoyed wide currency, it is now clear that there was probably about as much time depth to the cultural record in pre-Hispanic Yucatan as in any other portion of the Lowland Maya region. And it was here, together with Tabasco and adjoining territory, that Maya high culture, although in some state of decline from earlier achievements, was still generally flourishing at the time of the Conquest. Since it is generally agreed that there had been important Toltec and/or Toltec-connected movements, ultimately from Central Mexico into Postclassic northern Yucatan, the presence of some recollections of Topiltzin Quetzalcoatl in the historical traditions that were current in this area in the early sixteenth century might be expected. Although the relevant ethnohistorical material is rather sparse, it is of considerable importance. The key sources will, as usual, be taken up in turn by date.

1. The "Catechism" of Francisco Hernández in Fray Bartolomé de Las Casas's *Apologética historia de las Indias*

THE SOURCE

The *clérigo* Francisco Hernández came to Yucatan in 1541 as Francisco de Montejo II's chaplain. In 1545, while in Campeche, he was appointed by the newly elected bishop of Chiapas, Fray Bartolomé de Las Casas, to undertake a proselytizing mission in the interior, since he appears to have had some command of the indigenous language (Landa 1941: 67). Within a year, Hernández sent to Las Casas a *relación* concerning the beliefs of the natives among whom he was laboring, which the latter abstracted in chapter 123 of his *Apologética historia de las Indias* (Las Casas 1909). As Seler (1902–1923, I: 670) noted, the bulk of it constitutes a portion of the Catholic catechism with certain names of Maya gods inserted.

THE POSSIBLE TOPILTZIN QUETZALCOATL MATERIAL

The relevant portion reads (Las Casas 1909, I: 329):

> . . . y que afirmaban más, que antiguamente vinieron a aquella tierra veinte hombres (de los quince señala los nombres, que porque es mala letra y porque no hace al caso aquí no los pongo; de los otros cinco dice

> el clérigo que no halló rastro); el principal dellos se llamaba Cocolcan; a este llamaron dios de las fiebres o calenturas; dos de los otros del pescado; otros dos de los cortijos o heredades; otro que truena, etc.; traían las ropas largas, sandalias por calzado, las barbas grandes, y no traían bonetes sobre sus cabezas; los cuales mandaban que se confesasen las gentes y ayunasen, y que algunos ayunaban el viernes porque había muerto aquel día Bacab; y tiene por nombre aquel día himis, al cual honran y tienen devoción por la muerte de Bacab. Los señores todas estas particularidades saben, pero la gente popular solamente cree en las tres personas Icona, y Bacab, y Echuac, y Chibinas, la Madre de Bacab, y en la madre de Chibinas, llamada Hischen, que nosotros decimos haber sido Santa Ana. Todo lo de suso así dicho me escribió aquel padre clérigo, llamado Francisco Hernández, y entre mis papeles tengo su carta.

COMMENT

This is probably the earliest mention of Kukulcan in Yucatan. It is also one of the strangest. As Seler suggested, the god of "fever" label may indicate Kukulcan's role as rain/wind god. The same student felt that his position as first in a series of twenty divinities indicated that he was the patron of the first of the twenty day signs or of the twenty *trecenas*, implying that his "companions" were the patrons of the other nineteen. Their apostolic mission, their costumes and beards (it is significant that they are not described as white men), and their institution of the custom of fasting are all reminiscent of some of the later Central Mexican sources concerning Topiltzin Quetzalcoatl (Seler specifically cited Alva Ixtlilxochitl's account). The extremely garbled nature of the passage, however, cautions us to utilize it only with great caution.

2. Fray Diego de Landa's *Historia de las cosas de Yucatán*

THE SOURCE

An extended discussion of the most important source on late pre-Hispanic and early colonial northern Yucatecan culture would be superfluous after Alfred Tozzer's (1941: vii–x) scholarly introduction to his copiously annotated edition. Landa's complete work has never been found. In 1863, Brasseur de Bourbourg discovered a copy, or abstract (made in 1616?; see Genet 1928–1929, I: 10–11), of a portion of it in the library of the Real Academia de la Historia, Madrid, which he published (incompletely) in 1864, with a French translation. Since then, a number of editions have appeared, some of them complete, including two English translations. Tozzer's 1941 edition (Landa 1941) is now the one most used by English-speaking students, perhaps more for its valuable notes and appendices than for its translation of the texts—although the latter seems to be on the whole quite accurate. My quotes are from the Pérez Martínez edition of 1938.

Genet (1928–1929, I: 12–18) and Tozzer (Landa 1941: vii) have discussed the problem of Landa's sources. On his own statement, Juan (Nachi) Cocom, a Christianized member of the important Cocom dynasty of Sotuta, supplied him with some information. There is also strong evidence that Gaspar Antonio Chi (concerning whom more below), connected with the rival Tutul Xiu dynasty of Mani, aided the bishop, particularly with the historical traditions. It seems that, in addition, Landa made occasional use of certain Spanish writers such as Oviedo y Valdés, López de Gómara, Las Casas, and, possibly, Cervantes de Salazar. The date of 1566 is believed to be close to the date of completion of the work, while its author was in Spain.

Of Landa himself, a considerable amount is known (Landa 1941). Born in Toledo, in 1524 he entered the Franciscan order at age sixteen. He arrived in Yucatan in 1549, where he resided until 1563, when he returned to Spain to justify his inquisitorial policies during a determined campaign to wipe out native idolatry. Exonerated, he returned as bishop of Yucatan in 1573, remaining there until his death in 1579. During his first residence in the country, he had excellent opportunities for collecting data concerning native traditions, while engaged in his vigorous activities to obliterate all trace of the pre-Hispanic religious/ritual system. Although Landa was no Sahagún, what remains of his work could be considered even more important for our knowledge of late pre-Hispanic northern Yucatecan culture—due to the lack of other comparable accounts—than the monumental treatise of his brother Franciscan is for the culture of the natives of the Basin of Mexico.

THE POSSIBLE TOPILTZIN QUETZALCOATL MATERIAL

The first relevant passage is found early in his work (Landa 1938: 71–73; 1941: 20–26), just after a summary description of the ruins of Chichen Itza and a brief outline of the well-known tale of the three lords who ruled there. Its importance warrants a full quotation.

> Que es opinión entre los indios que con los Yzaes que poblaron Chichenizá, reinó un gran señor llamado Cuculcán. Y que muestra ser esto verdad el edificio principal que se llama Cuculcán; y dicen que entró por la parte de poniente y que difieren en sí entró antes o después de los Yzaes o con ellos, y dicen que fué bien dispuesto y que no tenía mujer ni hijos; y que después de su vuelta fué tenido en México por uno de sus dioses y llamado Cezalcuati y que en Yucatan también lo tuvieron por dios por ser gran republicano, y que esto se vió en el asiento que puso en Yucatan después de la muerte de los señores para mitigar la disensión que sus muertos causaron en la tierra.
>
> Que este Cuculcán tornó a poblar otra ciudad tratando con los

> señores naturales de la tierra que él y ellos viniesen (a la ciudad) y que allí viniesen todas las cosas y negocios; y que para esto eligieron un asiento muy bueno a ocho leguas más adentro en la tierra que donde ahora está Mérida, y quince o dieciséis del mar; y que allí cercaron de una muy ancha pared de piedra seca como medio cuarto de legua dejando sólo dos puertas angostas y la pared no muy alta, y en el medio de esta cerca hicieron sus templos; y que el mayor, que es como el de Chichenizá, llamaron Cuculcán; y que hicieron otro redondo y con cuatro puertas, diferente a cuantos hay en aquella tierra, y otros a la redonda, juntos unos de otros; y que dentro de este cercado hicieron casas para los señores, entre los cuales solamente repartieron la tierra dando pueblos a cada uno conforme a la antigüedad de su linaje y ser de su persona. Y que Cuculcán puso nombre a la ciudad, no el suyo como hicieron los Ahizaes en Chichenizá, mas llamóla Mayapán que quiero decir el pendón de la Maya, porque a la lengua de la tierra llaman maya; y los indios llaman Ychpa, quiere decir dentro de las cercas.
>
> Que este Cuculcán vivió con los señores algunos años en aquella ciudad y que dejándolos en muchas paz y amistad se tornó por el mismo camino a México, y que de pasada se detuvo en Champotón, que para memoria suya y de su partida, hizo dentro del mar un buen edificio al modo del de Chichenizá, a gran tiro de piedra de la ribera, y que así dejó Cuculcán perpetua memoria en Yucatan.
>
> Que partido Cuculcán, acordaron los señores, para que la república durase, que el mando principal lo tuviese la casa de los Cocomes por ser la más antigua y más rica y por ser el que la regía entonces hombre de más valor.

Aside from this long passage, which was probably derived from either Juan Cocom or Gaspar Antonio Chi, Landa provides almost no additional material relating to this "gran señor." However, in his treatment of the eighteen annual feasts, he does describe the ceremonies during Xul (1938: 196–198; 1941: 157–158) that were dedicated to Kukulcan, who, according to some, "había ido el cielo con los dioses, y por eso lo tuvieron por dios y le señalaron templo [or tiempo] en que como a tal le celebrasen su fiesta." This ceremony was celebrated everywhere until the destruction of Mayapan, and subsequently only in the province of Mani, ruled by the Tutul Xiu lineage. However, the other provinces, "en reconocimiento de lo que debían a Cuculcán," regularly presented to those of Mani four or five sumptuous feather banners for use in the ceremony. This last, called Chic Kaban, consisted of a great procession, led by the priests and lords, to the temple of Kukulcan, where for five days fasts were conducted, offerings presented, and many rituals, including comic ones, were performed. The climax came on the final day, when Kukulcan was believed to descend in person from heaven to receive the services, vigils, and offerings tendered to him.

SUMMARY

Landa's sparse but important information can be summarized as follows: (1) with the Itza who established themselves ("poblaron") at Chichen Itza, a great lord named Kukulcan reigned, who had entered the country from the west, although it was uncertain whether he had come with the Itza, before, or after; (2) he was deified for his statesmanship and his exemplary chaste character, and the principal temple of the city was named after him; (3) he ended the political disturbances that followed the death of the three lords of Chichen Itza and founded a new city, called Mayapan, "the standard of the Maya" and Ichpa, "within the enclosures," which he arranged with the local lords was to be the administrative capital of the entire country and within whose walls were constructed both residences for the ruling families, who divided the land between them, and temples, one large like that of Chichen Itza and similarly named Kukulcan, and another round in form, unlike any other in Yucatan; (4) Kukulcan resided there with the lords some years but, leaving them in peace and friendship, eventually returned to Mexico by way of Champoton, where, in his memory, a temple was built just offshore; (5) in Mexico, he was held to be a god and called Quetzalcoatl; (6) he left a perpetual remembrance in Yucatan, and, after his departure, the Cocom lineage was chosen to exercise supreme authority; (7) a cult was established in his honor, which was celebrated annually at Mayapan until its fall and, after that, only at Mani, the capital of the Tutul Xiu–ruled province of that name; (8) the lords of the other provinces, however, sent feather banners to Mani for use in the ceremony, which consisted of the usual processions, offerings, and sacrifices—at the end of which Kukulcan was believed to descend from heaven personally to receive the offerings and adoration.

COMMENT

As suggested above, it seems probable that this tradition concerning Kukulcan stemmed from Juan Cocom or Gaspar Antonio Chi. If from the latter, it would represent a Tutul Xiu version, just as that to be examined next. Landa's own ambiguity concerning the exact nature of Kukulcan's relationship to the Itza of Chichen Itza has given rise to many problems; this will receive further consideration below. In any case, Landa, or his informant, clearly associated this great Yucatecan statesman with (Topiltzin) Quetzalcoatl, although failing to point out that his Yucatecan Maya name is an exact translation of the Nahuatl version. His return to Mexico is interesting (cf. Olmos) and, as we shall see, within the Yucatecan corpus is found only in this source. It is significant that Landa does not mention any Yucatecan belief that he was expected to return. A noteworthy feature of this synopsis is that Kukulcan is actually more involved with Mayapan than with Chichen Itza. The restricted nature of his cult in historic times is also made clear.

3. The *Historical Recollections* of Gaspar Antonio Chi

THE SOURCE

The sketchy biography of this important early colonial Yucatecan native was worked out by Blom (1928), Morley and Roys (1942), and Tozzer (Landa 1941: 44–46). Born about 1531 at the Tutul Xiu capital of Mani, Gaspar Antonio Chi was connected with the ruling dynasty of that place on his maternal side. Unusually well educated for a full-blooded indigene, with a mastery of Spanish and Nahuatl in addition to his native Yucatecan Maya, he became an important church and administrative functionary and finally the royal interpreter at Mérida. His aid to Landa has already been mentioned. A number of the *encomenderos* of Mérida, obligated by the *relaciones geográficas* questionnaire of 1577 to provide relevant data on their holdings, in answering questions 14 and 15 relating to native history and customs, were provided nearly identical material by Gaspar Antonio Chi. Jakeman (1952; cf. Roys 1962: 50–56) carefully reconstructed this information from twelve separate replies (first published in their respective *relaciones geográficas* in *Relaciones de Yucatán*, 1898–1900, I), which, in effect, almost amounts to a single *relación* of great value for both the late pre-Hispanic history and Conquest-period ethnography of the northern peninsula.

THE POSSIBLE TOPILTZIN QUETZALCOATL MATERIAL

The text of what Jakeman called the "Third Narration," which was apparently read to the *encomenderos* of (1) Kisil and Sitilpech, (2) Kitelcan and Cabiche, (3) Tocanto and Tepacan, and (4) Isamal and Santa María, about February 13, 1581, reads, in the wording of the first (the others are practically identical; Jakeman 1952: 15–16):

> En vn tienpo estubo toda esta tierra debajo del domynyo de vn señor estando en su ser la ciudad antigua de chichinysa a quien fueron trebutarios todos los señores desta provincia y avn de fuera de la provincia, de inxico guauhtemal [y] mananapa [*sic*, for Mexico, Guatemala, and Chiapas] y otras provincias les enbiauan presentes en señal de pax y amystad y andando al tienpo poblada mayapan quando se hizo señor della tutuexiv [Tutul Xiu] y con la mudanca de los tienpos se fueron mundando las costunbres hasta que cada provincia y pueblos vino a tener señores y casiques particulares y ansi quando los conquistadores vinieron a esta[s] provincias divisas . . . les dizese que los primeros pobladores de chichinisa no fueron ydolatras hasta que Rul Rau [*sic*, for Kukulcan] capitán mexicano entró en estas partes al qual enseño la ydolatria o la nesesidad como ellos dizen los enseño a ydolatrar.

The second, sixth, and seventh narrations, probably all dictated in 1581 (Jakeman 1952: 29), add a few details of interest, namely that Chichen Itza was considered to be the first city established in Yucatan after the flood, that its hegemony lasted over two hundred years, and that the nonidolatrous pattern lasted up to eight hundred years before—or, in another version, less than a thousand years. The most important alternate version is found in the "Sixth Narration" (*Relación de Kinacama o Moxopip*), where it is stated (Jakeman 1952: 23) that idolatry did not prevail in the land until:

> . . . los mexicanos entraron en ella y la poseyeron un capitán que se dezia quetzalquat en la lengua mexicana que quiere dezir en la nuestra plunaxe de culebra y entre ellos a la sierpe le ponen este nombre porque dizen que tiene plumaje y este capitán suso dicho yntroduxo en esta tierra la ydolatria y uso de ydolos por dioses los quales hazia de palo y de barro y de piedra y los hazia adorar y les ofrescian muchas cosas de caca y de mercadurias y sobre todo la sangre de sus narizes y orejas y corazones de algunos que sacrificaban en su serbicio.

Finally, in the "Fifth Narration" (*Relación de San, Panabchan y Muna*, ca. February 20, 1581), the "cerro hecho a mano que era el templo de Cuculcan ydolo principal" in Mayapan is described, with four steep stairways (over one hundred steps each) and a sanctuary with four doors, the principal one facing north.

SUMMARY

(1) Yucatan had originally been under the domination of the lords of Chichen Itza, whose power lasted over two hundred years and whose political influence extended as far as Mexico, Chiapas, and Guatemala; (2) after living without "idolatry" for eight hundred or a thousand years, the "Mexicans" entered and possessed the land, under a leader called Quetzalcoatl, or Kukulcan; (3) the latter instructed them in the making of wood, stone, and clay idols, as well as offerings and sanguinary sacrifices, both individual bloodletting and the heart-extraction sacrifice; (4) later, in Mayapan, a great four-sided pyramid (named after him) was raised to his cult.

COMMENT

These brief notices are of considerable importance, coming as they do from an individual who must have been fully conversant with the traditions of the leading dynasty with which he was connected. With the exception of the expected exaggeration of the importance of the Tutul Xiu, the historical outline that this tradition records generally agrees with other reliable information, both archaeological and ethnohistorical.

As in Landa, Kukulcan/Quetzalcoatl is once again a Mexican "captain." Here, however, his political role is subordinated to his role as disseminator of a new type of religious cult. As in Landa, Kukulcan's precise relationship to those who ruled in Chichen Itza is somewhat ambiguous. From the order of events presented and the statement in one version ("Second Narration," *Relación de Chunchuchu y Tabi*; Jakeman 1952: 12–14) that the lords of this city and their vassals were not idolaters, it is implied that Kukulcan did not enter the picture until after the two-hundred-year period of Chichen Itza's hegemony. The material presented here concerning Kukulcan is actually just a brief reference, included to explain the presence of idolatry in historic times in northern Yucatan. It provides only a tantalizing hint of a rich historical tradition highly relevant to our inquiry, no reasonably complete version of which, unfortunately, has survived.

Additional References

This about exhausts the significant references to Kukulcan/Quetzalcoatl in Yucatecan sources written in Spanish. The *Relación de Motul* (*Relaciones de Yucatán* 1898–1900, I: 75–88; Jakeman 1954), dated February 20, 1581, contains a brief reference to Kukulcan as introducer of idolatry into Yucatan, very similar to those in Chi's *Historical Recollections*—which is probably derived from the same source. Torquemada (1943–1944, II: 57) ends his account of the Central Mexican Quetzalcoatl by stating that this god was also venerated, under the name Kukulcan, in Yucatan, where he had entered from the west. Then follows the significant statement, found only in Torquemada: "Decían de este, que descendían de él los Reies de Yucatan, que llamaron Cocomes, que significa Oidores." These remarks may have been taken from another manuscript of Landa, perhaps that of his complete *Relación de las cosas de Yucatán*.

Fray Diego López de Cogolludo, a Franciscan missionary who composed a historical survey of Yucatan in 1688, utilizing a number of important primary sources, some of them lost, merely refers to Kukulcan as "un ídolo de uno, que había gran capitán entre ellos," probably borrowing from Chi or Landa here. He further states that "tuvieron por Dios a Quetzalcohuat el de Cholula, llamándolo Kukulcan," expressly citing Torquemada (López de Cogolludo 1954–1955, I: 352).

Gaspar Antonio Chi's own *relación*, written in 1582 (English translation, in Tozzer/Landa 1941: Appendix C), which presents much the same material as his *Historical Recollections* in a more condensed form, does not mention Kukulcan/Quetzalcoatl. Herrera y Tordesillas (1601–1615) copied the passage quoted above, from the manuscript of Landa to which he had access in Spain, but presents no significant new material. Such other important early Yucatecan sources as Sánchez de Aguilar (1639), Ciudad Real (1872 [ca. 1588]), Lizana (1893 [1633]), and the *Valladolid Lawsuit of 1618* (in Brinton 1882a: 113–118) make no mention of him.

4. Historical References in the *Books of Chilam Balam*

THE SOURCES

The remainder of this section will deal with a particular body of materials in the Yucatecan Maya language, some of which contain brief allusions to the subject of our inquiry. The nature of these sources, collectively called the *Books of Chilam Balam*, has been repeatedly discussed (e.g., Brinton 1882a; Tozzer 1917, 1921; Weitzel 1931; Roys 1933; Barrera Vásquez and Rendón 1948; Barrera Vásquez and Morley 1949) and will not be entered into here. Suffice it to say that what historical and religious lore has survived in Yucatecan Maya is almost entirely contained in these remarkably eclectic compilations. Unfortunately, all are late copies (the earliest probably dates only from sometime in the eighteenth century). Although certain of the passages are obviously based on materials that go back to the sixteenth century (possibly ultimately derived from pre-Hispanic hieroglyphic screenfolds), during the repeated recopying process substantial changes seem to have been frequently made, passages garbled and incorrectly copied, and numerous interpolations inserted. A critical dissection of these annalistic hodgepodges is requisite to any realistic treatment of them. Although most modern students fully recognize this, it is still occasionally neglected (e.g., Makemson 1951), with unfortunate results.

THE POSSIBLE TOPILTZIN QUETZALCOATL MATERIAL

The most important sources in this group that contain some material relevant to our theme, however slight, are: (1) the *Chilam Balam of Chumayel*, apparently compiled by a Don Juan Josef Hoil of that town about 1782—although Roys (1933: 6; 1954: 8) believed that its language indicated that it was probably "a careful copy of a much older manuscript"—which has been published in facsimile (Gordon 1913) and translated in its entirety twice (Spanish: Mediz Bolio 1930; English: Roys 1933); (2) the anonymous *Chilam Balam of Tizimin*, which Roys (1954: 8) inclined to date "shortly after the middle of the eighteenth century" and which has been completely translated once, quite inaccurately, into English (Makemson 1951), although the sequential Katun count has been translated various times (e.g., Brinton 1882a; Martínez Hernández 1927; Barrera Vásquez and Morley 1949) and the prophetic material utilized by Roys (1949b; 1954); (3) the *Codex Pérez*, a compilation (see Barrera Vásquez 1939; Roys 1949a) made by the Yucatecan scholar Juan Pío Pérez during the second third of the nineteenth century that includes the so-called *Chilam Balam of Mani*, portions of that of *Ixil*, and many other miscellaneous materials copied from sources similar to the *Chilam Balam* books, primarily from Mani, that date from the late sixteenth to the early nineteenth century, published in its entirety, with Spanish translation, by Solís Alcalá (1949), and partially by many others; (4) the *Chilam Balam of Kaua*, also of unknown authorship, the first prophetic series of which is believed by Roys (1954: 8) to date from the last decade of the eighteenth century and which is still for the most part unpublished ("Katun Prophecies," Series I: Roys 1954; 20 day-sign auguries: Barrera Vásquez 1943).

There are three types of material in these sources that are pertinent to our inquiry: (1) the *Maya Chronicles*, consisting of five sequential Katun counts; (2) certain brief passages that describe isolated historical events or series of events; and (3) the prophecies, most of which contain important—but often very obscure—historical allusions.

It is interesting and significant that in the five *Maya Chronicles*—which in reality seem to be only three primary accounts (Brinton 1882a; Martínez Hernández 1927; Barrera Vásquez and Rendón 1948; Barrera Vásquez and Morley 1949)—not once does the name Kukulcan or Quetzalcoatl appear. It is barely possible, however, that the name of the earliest leader of the Tutul Xiu in the first section of Chronicle I (*Mani*), Holon Chan Tepeu, might be a circumlocutory way of describing a leader who bore the title Kukulcan/Quetzalcoatl. As Barrera Vásquez and Morley (1949: 27) pointed out, Holon here probably signifies "leader," and Chan may well stand for "serpent." Tepeu is undoubtedly Nahua, as in Highland Guatemala, and probably has the same meaning it had there, "majestic, admirable, powerful," etc.—thus: "Majestic Lord Serpent," or some such, certainly an apt description for a leader who might have borne the title Quetzalcoatl or its Yucatecan Maya equivalent, Kukulcan. Since the Tutul Xiu dynasty was most likely of Toltec—or at least Nahua—descent, it would not be surprising to find their first leader bearing this title. This is only a possibility, however, and I would not particularly urge it.

Three isolated historical passages do contain brief references to the Yucatecan version of our hero. The first, which Roys (1949a: 101) called "Historical Narrative of the Fall of Chichen Itza," is found in the *Chilam Balam of Tizimin* (22–23) and the *Codex Pérez* (120–121). It has been translated into English by Roys (1962: 80; cf. Makemson 1951: 45–47) and into Spanish by Barrera Vásquez (Barrera Vásquez and Rendón 1948: 223–225) and Solís Alcalá (1949: 237–239). It is an extremely obscure passage but apparently provides important additional information concerning the so-called Hunac Ceel Episode that led to the conquest of Chichen Itza in a Katun 8 Ahau. It perhaps stemmed from Ah Canul sources. According to Landa, members of this group were the descendants of the Nahua-speaking mercenaries who were introduced into Mayapan by the ruler of that place to aid him in maintaining his control over the northern peninsula. Roys's translation follows:

> (Katun) 8 Ahau was the time when Ix Chan Chab swept the market place. Then descended the word of Oxlahun-ti-ku ("13 gods"). 8 Ahau at Chichen; Oxlahun-ti-ku (was) its aspect. Thrice greeted be your seat! This was the rule, when it came at the command of Oxlahun-ti-ku; 8 Ahau was when it occurred at Chichen, when the ruler of the people of Uxmal was painted (on the record of the katuns?). Then occurred the trampling on the back of Chac-xib-chac by Ah Nacxit Kukulcan; then came the general questioning (*katlam*) of the Ah Itza. Then came purse-snatching strife, overturning-things strife, blowgun strife. Then was when sin was introduced; it came through Lord 8 Ahau also. Then occurred the . . . of the ceiba tree. So it occurred a second time because of the Ah Chac-xib-chac at Chichen, whatever thing would be its charge (or destiny) in the future. At one time, one shot (suddenly) it would be. It was Katun 8 Ahau also, when it occurred (to) Ah Ulil Itzmal. This, then was the time he (Ah Chac-xib-chac) sniffed (at the plumeria), when he was deceived, because a sin was committed against Ah Ulil Ahau, against the woman, wife of his fellow ruler. This was the establishing of the katun. It occurred in the 17th (Mani version, 16th) . . . , the command (or prophecy) of the rule of mighty (or holy) Itzam-caan ("sky-lizard"). There came forth the rattlesnake with Hapai-can. Then Ah Itzmal Ul Ahau was deceived. Then occurred the giving in tribute the son of mighty (or holy) Itzmal in order to feed Hapai Can, during the misery of Ah Itzmal-thul. Then arrived Yax-bolai ("green beast of prey"). Then arrived the buzzard in the heart of the sky with Chac-bolai and Chac-xib-chac. Miserable is his soul, when he undergoes his misery here at Izamal, deceived by the sin of the ruler of the Canul. This was because he gave as tribute his son to Hapai Can. Then when it was learned about by Kukulcan, then he was beheaded and he was killed by Ah Kukil Can. They saw it, they heard it, all the children of Itzmal-thul, who gave in tribute what was swallowed by Hapai Can. These were the subjects who bore the sin of their ruler. Then began the testing of Ah Itzam-caan. Then came the introduction of the sin of the ruler of Canul. Then came forth the rattlesnake (or chief teacher, a homonym) at the mouths of the wells here at Maxcanu, at Tuchican. When the ruler came forth, 13 was his charge, then he was begotten by his father.

Another pertinent reference is found in the *Chilam Balam of Chumayel*, in a section that Roys entitled "Memoranda Concerning the History of Yucatan." As usual, difficult to understand, this passage apparently compares the coming of two sets of "foreigners," with consequences that were at least in part the same: the Itza earlier, and the Spaniards later. The relevant passage, in Roys's (1933: 83; cf. Mediz Bolio 1930: 26) translation: "At that time the course of humanity was orderly. The foreigners made it otherwise when they arrived here. They brought shameful things when they came.

They lost their innocence in carnal sin; they lost their innocence in the carnal sin of Nacxit Xuchit, in the carnal sin of his companions."

The passage then goes on to describe other misfortunes that apparently were the result of the arrival of these foreigners, who are seemingly identified as the Itza ("these, they say, were the Itza").

The third allusion is found in part II of the *Codex Pérez* (*Chilam Balam of Mani*), in a passage (pages 126–127) interpolated into a chronological discussion correlating Christian years (1392–1800) with a series of twenty-four-year Katunob and their thirty-nine bearers (Katun 8 Ahau, year 7 Cauac–13 Ahau, 12 Cauac), preceded by an introduction apparently written on May 10, 1756 (year 7 Cauac, day 19 Muan). It reads, in Roys's (1962: 80–81; cf. Solís Alcalá 1949: 248–251) translation:

> Now Katun 11 Ahau, according to its reign, was when the foreigners entered our land here, in order to bring us into Christianity. It then began, as they say, but it was (Katun) 8 Ahau, before the coming of the foreigners. This was when occurred the introduction of treachery to them, the holy men (a term applied to the Itza in the Chronicles).... This was when began the introduction of treachery to them (*keban than*). They understood the arrival of the time of the opening of the 13-cluster plumeria flower through the agency of Hunac Ceel, the halach uinic of Mayapan within the walls (of Mayapan). It was he who caused the odor of the plumeria to come forth to his (Chac-xib-chac's) nose, so that he would desire the woman. Now this was because the time drew near, the arrival of the time, the katun, given to them by their great rulers. These were Cetzalcuat (Quetzalcoatl), and Ah Buluc Am ("11 spider"), as he was called by their priests and their wise men. This was Montezuma.

Of special interest among the surviving examples of Yucatecan Maya literature are the prophecies. There is nothing quite comparable to them from elsewhere in Mesoamerica. Roys (1933: 132–187; 1949a: 90–91; 1949b: 157–159; 1954: 5–8) subjected them to the most careful analysis. He distinguished four distinct classes: those that related to (1) the days; the Kinob; (2) the Tunob (360-day periods; one series, within a Katun 5 Ahau, preserved in the *Chilam Balam of Tizimin* and the *Codex Pérez*); (3) the Katunob (two series of thirteen each, preserved in the *Chilam Balams of Chumayel, Tizimin*, and *Kaua*, and the *Codex Pérez*); and (4) a special class that related to the coming of foreign conquerors and a new religion. The same student edited a critical text and English translation of the Tun prophecies (1949b) and an English translation—accompanied by an extensive analysis—of Series I of the Katun prophecies (1954). As Roys demonstrated, there is important historical material contained in these obscure renderings, in spite of their being couched in the future tense as "prophecies." The material relevant to our inquiry is very slight—but certainly worthy of mention.

In the Tun prophecies, there is only one mention of Kukulcan. This is in the Tun 6 Cauac, which is called a "time of struggling" and pestilence, when they "break each other's limbs." It is also stated (Roys 1949b: 176, 183; cf. Makemson 1951: 23; Solís Alcalá 1949: 223), in Roys's translation: "This is the time when it came to pass that Kukulcan tightened that which was loose, in the katun when he who shakes the rattle sits on his buttocks."

In spite of the greater richness of Series I of the Katun prophecies in incidents of pre-Hispanic history than Series II, there does not seem to be a single explicit reference to Kukulcan/Quetzalcoatl or Nacxit. In Series II, however, in the prophecy for Katun 4 Ahau, this passage occurs (Roys 1933: 161; 1954: 26): "Katun 4 Ahau is the seventh *Katun* according to the count. The *Katun* is established at Chichen Itza. The settlement of the Itza shall take place. The quetzal shall come, the green bird shall come. Ah Kantenal shall come. Blood-vomit shall come. Kukulcan shall come with them for the second time. The word of God. The Itza shall come."

Accompanying this passage in the *Chilam Balam of Chumayel* is a drawing of "The Lord of the Katun." It is unusual in that feathers seem to be indicated, as well as stars. Roys interpreted the former as a portrayal of the feathered serpent and the latter as possibly indicating the four (*sic*) Venus periods of the *Codex Dresden*, since Quetzalcoatl was the Venus god.

The corresponding version in the *Chilam Balam of Tizimin* (Barrera Vásquez and Rendón 1948: 140–141; cf. Makemson 1951: 66) is nearly identical, but it is stated that both the blood-vomit and Kukulcan shall come for the *fourth* time. As Roys (1954: 26) pointed out, however, "the addition of a single letter turns 'second' (*ca*) into 'fourth' (*can*)." In addition, it is possible that the first Tun prophecy, for 13 Kan, that states (Roys 1949b: 165, 179), "Mayapan was the aspect of the change of the katun, at the time of the descent of the children of the quetzal, the children of the green bird," contains an allusion to Kukulcan/Quetzalcoatl, recalling Torquemada's (1943–1944, II: 52) statement that the Cocom dynasty of Mayapan claimed descent from this personage.

Roys, Tozzer, and others expressed their belief that the fourth class of prophecy actually had reference to an expected return to Yucatan of Kukulcan/Quetzalcoatl, although the Spanish priests suppressed his name. However, the positive evidence for this is slight. Neither the name Kukulcan nor Quetzalcoatl appears in these prophecies. But in one (Roys 1933: 62, 169), seemingly the famous one of Chilam Balam of Mani himself predicting the coming of the Spaniards (see Tozzer 1921: 120–130), which has been preserved in a number of versions, in a continuation found only in the *Chumayel*, in Roys's translation:

> He is ruler over us; he is the true God over our souls. But those to whom the word is brought, lord: thrice weighed down is their strength, the

> younger brothers native to the land. Their hearts are submerged in sin. Their hearts are dead in their carnal sins. They are frequent backsliders, the principal ones who spread (sin). Nacxit Xuchit in the carnal sin of his companions, the two-day rulers. (They sit) crookedly on their thrones; crookedly in carnal sin. Two-day men they call them. For two days (endure) their seats, their cups, their hats. They are the unrestrained lewd ones of the day, the unrestrained lewd ones of the night, the rogues of the world. They twist their necks, they wink their eyes, they slaver at the mouth, at the rulers, lord. Behold, when they come, there is no truth in the words of the foreigners to the land. They tell very solemn and mysterious things, the sons of the men of Seven-deserted-buildings, the offspring of the women of Seven-deserted-buildings, lord.

SUMMARY AND COMMENT

These scattered notices in the various *Books of Chilam Balam* fail to present us with a very coherent picture of Kukulcan/Quetzalcoatl in northern Yucatan, but they add a few details of interest. Perhaps the most significant is the use of the designation Nacxit—already familiar to us—for this figure, in addition to his standard "feathered serpent" epithet. When it first appears, in the "Historical Narrative of the Fall of Chichen Itza," it seems to concern Ah Nacxit Kukulcan as the conqueror of Chac xib chac, apparently the ruler of Chichen Itza—which event in chronicles I, II, and III, based on a single source, is rather accomplished by Hunac Ceel and "The Seven Men of Mayapan" (*uuctulob ah mayapanob*), all with pure Nahua names (Barrera Vásquez and Morley 1949: 34–36). Seler (1902–1923, I: 676), therefore, took the Nacxit Kukulcan of the *Chilam Balam of Tizimin* to stand for these Nahua conquerors. Spinden (in Tozzer 1941: 34; cf. Roys 1962: 72), on the other hand, took it to stand as a title for Hunac Ceel, believing him to be of the Cocom dynasty that again, following Torquemada, claimed descent from Quetzalcoatl/Kukulcan.

In the two other occurrences of the term Nacxit, in the "Memoranda Concerning the History of Yucatan" and in the continuation of the prophecy, both in the *Chilam Balam of Chumayel*, it is combined with Xuchit (Nahua *xochit*, "flower") and is associated in both accounts (probably derived from the same source, since the passages, although in different contexts, are basically similar) with "carnal sin" (*nicte*, also the name of the exotic plumeria flower). This putative "sin" is possibly connected with the "plumeria love charm," so intimately bound up with the Hunac Ceel episode, but perhaps more likely indicates some association of Kukulcan/Quetzalcoatl/Nacxit with the introduction of new rites into Yucatan. Perhaps these were of a phallic nature, for which archaeological evidence exists at Chichen Itza (Temple of the Phalli; scene in reliefs on vault of North Temple, Great Ball Court).

The *Codex Pérez* mention of "Cetzalcuat," in the passage quoted above, which also refers to the Hunac Ceel episode and the plumeria love charm, is quite obscure. Roys (1962: 80) believed that he could be identified with the Ah Nacxit Kukulcan of the *Chilam Balam of Tizimin* passage, but this is by no means certain. The association with Ah Buluc Am, Eleven Spider, and "Montezuma" is particularly puzzling. Roys (1962: 81) suggested some connection with Motecuhzoma I, ruler of Mexico Tenochtitlan, 1440–1469—during which time Mayapan may have been abandoned and possibly the Hunac Ceel incident occurred. The same association of the latter two names, without mention of Kukulcan/Quetzalcoatl, is found in the Tun prophecies, for Katun 5 Ahau (Roys 1949b: 171, 181). As far as is known, the former name or title is never associated, in Central Mexican sources, with either of the rulers of Mexico Tenochtitlan who bore the name Motecuhzoma. Its appearance in this Yucatecan source might represent a colonial interpolation—after the fame of the unfortunate ninth Tenochca ruler had spread widely throughout Middle America.

The Series II Katun prophecy for Katun 4 Ahau that directly associates Kukulcan with the Itza constitutes an apparent confirmation of Landa's statement concerning the coming of Kukulcan to Chichen Itza. The coming for the second time could be interpreted in different ways. It has often been connected with the statement in chronicles I–III (Barrera Vásquez and Morley 1949: 32) that this coming of the Itza to Chichen Itza in Katun 4 Ahau was a *return* to this center, after a previous abandonment. This first occupation of Chichen by the Itza, however, has been questioned, even on the basis of the statements in the *Chronicles* themselves. An alternate interpretation would merely see in it a prediction of Kukulcan's expected return.

The other brief references to Kukulcan are also difficult to interpret, particularly the one in the Tun prophecies that speaks of "tightening that which is loose." This is not too surprising, however, for many of the cryptic allusions in the prophetic materials of the *Books of Chilam Balam* are, to put it mildly, quite baffling. Much more could be said about the Yucatecan references to a personage(s) that might be a version of Topiltzin Quetzalcoatl. However, further discussion will be reserved for the next chapter, expressly devoted to questions of interpretation—when the relevant archaeological evidence will also be taken into account.

Itzamna

Before leaving Yucatan, a word is in order concerning the Yucatecan sky god and culture hero Itzamna. From the few scattered notices relating to him, it seems possible that elements of Ehecatl Quetzalcoatl—and perhaps Topiltzin Quetzalcoatl as well—are present in his supernatural personality. The most important original information concerning Itzamna can be found in Landa

(1938: 149–154, 168, 187, 189; 1941: 142–147, 153, 155–162), López de Cogolludo (1954–1955, I: 326–327, 352), Fray Gabriel de San Buenaventura (quoted in Beltrán de Santa Rosa 1746: 16), Román y Zamora (1897: 51–52), Hernández (in Las Casas 1909, I: 329), the *Vienna Dictionary* (quoted in Roys 1944: 100), the *Relación de Capocolche y Chocola* (in *Relaciones de Yucatán*, 1898–1900, I: 183), Lizana (1893: 4–5), the *Relación de Valladolid* (in *Relaciones de Yucatán*, 1898–1900, I: 161), *The Ritual of the Bacabs* (in Gates 1931: 15), and various brief mentions in the *Chilam Balam* books. From these data, quite limited in scope, we derive a picture of a celestial, solar, and fertility deity, son of the creator (occasionally identified with him), consort of Ixchel or her daughter, Ixchebelyax (probably the young moon goddess), originally a man, the first great priest, inventor of the calendar and hieroglyphic writing, with power over healing ("god of medicine"), who led a migration of people into Yucatan from the east (or west? cf. confusion in López de Cogolludo 1954–1955, I: 326), assigning all the place-names and dividing the land. Thompson (1939: 152–160; 1950: 11) assembled the evidence in favor of interpreting Itzamna as the great celestial reptilian monster (one at each cardinal point) so ubiquitous in Classic Maya art, comparable to the *xiuhcoatl* of Central Mexico, while recognizing his anthropomorphic aspect as well (God D or K?).

Itzamna's role as the arch-priest, inventor of the calendar and writing, and his place-name assignments are reminiscent of Topiltzin Quetzalcoatl. In any case, it appears likely that the Contact-period Yucatecan conception of Itzamna had been influenced to some extent by the impact of Toltec religious patterns and traditional history—and overtones of the great priest/ruler of the Toltecs may well be included in his supernatural personality. Itzamna is, however, as far as I am aware, never expressly identified or even closely associated with Kukulcan, and it is possible that all of these aspects of Itzamna were indigenously Yucatecan Maya.

X. Archaeological Evidence Possibly Relevant to the Topiltzin Quetzalcoatl of Tollan Tale

I (Nicholson 1955a) have previously discussed the problem of correlating the information derived from archaeological excavation with that gleaned from native Mesoamerican historical traditions. The obvious truth was stressed that these two categories of sources provide histories of quite different aspects of the culture, the former revealing much about material culture development, the latter presenting a sequence of largely political and dynastic events. Synchronically meshing these two sets of data is, at best, difficult. However, in certain favorable circumstances the "gap" between them can be successfully bridged and at least tentative correlations hypothesized.

One of these cases might be the present one. As we shall see, it is possible that leaders who succeeded to the title of Quetzalcoatl are portrayed in two major Toltec-period centers. It is perhaps even conceivable that Topiltzin Quetzalcoatl himself, assuming for the moment the possibility of his historicity, is represented at one of them.

Before proceeding to examine this tantalizing possibility, one matter should be cleared up at the outset. Since we are only interested here in archaeological evidence directly relevant to the Topiltzin Quetzalcoatl of Tollan Tale, the mere occurrence of the feathered-serpent icon in and of itself by no means demonstrates any necessary connection with the priest/ruler of Tollan. This point was ably discussed by Armillas (1947) and will not be entered into here. The feathered serpent, a celestial monster connected with rain and fertility that had appeared in different parts of Mesoamerica at least by the Early Classic (especially at Teotihuacan), is far more ancient than the period during which Topiltzin Quetzalcoatl may have flourished. It is distributed much more widely—on the basis of present evidence, apparently from Costa Rica in the southeast and even well beyond the northern frontier of Mesoamerica into the U.S. Southwest and Southeast—than the available archaeological data would indicate that any knowledge of Topiltzin Quetzalcoatl of Tollan ever penetrated.

On the other hand, since there is reason to believe that the Toltec priest/ruler might well have promoted the cult of this old creator-wind-fertility god whose name he bore, the occurrence of his most striking symbol *could* in certain cases have relevance to our inquiry. The ubiquitous plumed serpents of Tula and Chichen ltza, therefore, may have reflected at least the influence, if not the actual presence, of the figure with whom we are concerned. However, the systematic plotting of the distribution in time and space of the feathered-serpent motif, while a valuable archaeological inquiry in itself, is not directly germane to the problem that concerns us.

Again, the two relevant sites are Tula, Hidalgo (= Tollan) (Figure 1, Color Plate 11), and Early Postclassic Chichen Itza, Yucatan (Figure 2). Most archaeologists have agreed that many Toltec culture patterns were imported into Chichen Itza from Central Mexico—from Tula/Tollan itself or its neighborhood. The first five seasons of the Instituto Nacional de Antropología e Historia's intensive excavations at Tula, Hidalgo, were reported in a preliminary way (Acosta 1940, 1941, 1942, 1943, 1944, 1945), and three useful syntheses of the work have also appeared (Ruz Lhuillier 1945; Marquina 1951: 145–164; Dutton 1955). From this literature and from my own visits to the site, the ubiquity of the feathered serpent as a motif is abundantly clear. This mythological creature is present in the form of columns (Mound B; Color Plate 11), as a recurrent motif on cornices projecting above sloping banquettes (sometimes alternating with the *mixcoatl*, "cloud serpent," icon); as a balustrade device (Pyramid C); as the "patron" of warrior figures, undulating behind them (East Altar, Colonnade of Mound B: ceramic vessel in Vienna's Naturhistorisches Museum [Fuhrmann 1923: 85]); as decorations on the heel caps of the sandals of the giant caryatid warrior columns of Pyramid B; and, apparently, in an intertwined motif on Charnay's (1887: 95) ball game ring. In addition, the "man-bird-serpent" motif is one of the basic design elements on the facing of Pyramid B. The feathered serpent undulating behind a figure (Topiltzin Quetzalcoatl?) carved on the rocky cliff of the Cerro de la Malinche, opposite Tula, contrary to most published statements, on the other hand, is clearly Late Postclassc/Aztec in date, not Toltec (see Figure 3).

The most tantalizing depiction at Tula, however, is found on the south face of the lower section of Pillar 11, discovered, along with many others,

Figure 1. Aerial view of the great central plaza and surrounding structures, Tula, Hidalgo. From López Luján, Cobean, and Mastache 1995: 161 (46). Courtesy of Michael Calderwood (photographer) and Jaca Book (Milan).

Figure 2. Tatiana Proskouriakoff's reconstruction drawing of Chichen Itza (seen from the north), Yucatan. From Proskouriakoff 1946: no. 21.

Figure 3. Drawing of Late Postclassic relief carving putatively depicting Topiltzin Quetzalcoatl. He wears the "priestly jacket" (xicolli)*, and is performing autosacrifice. He is backed by an undulating feathered serpent and is identified by the date 1 Acatl (Reed). Cerro de la Malinche, near the site of Tula, Hidalgo. From Meyer 1939: 126 (fig. 2).*

during the 1941 season in the plaza north of Pyramid B (Acosta 1941: figure 3; Dutton 1955: plate 9h) (Figure 4). This is the upper portion of a warrior figure, attired in standard Toltec fashion but wearing a unique helmet (probably an eagle head with stone knife edging, common in the Mixteca-Puebla–style pictorials) and also sporting a full beard. His name sign is apparently a feathered serpent. In addition, he wears a long nose rod and an ear disk with an exceptionally long rodlike pendant issuing from the center (cf. Figure 5).

A stela found at Tula in 1935 by Mujica y Diez de Bonilla, now in the Museo Nacional de Antropología (Ruz Lhuillier 1945: figure 12), depicts an elaborately attired personage, also wearing a full beard. Bearded figures are also depicted: (1) on the pottery vessel in Vienna, previously cited, with the feathered serpent as "patron" and also wearing a large ear disk with a long rod depending from its center); and (2) on another vessel, definitely known to be from Tula, which was first published over a century ago by Brantz Mayer

Figure 4. South side of surviving lower section of Pillar 11 (III), Pyramid B, Tula, Hidalgo, depicting a standing figure, in typical Toltec warrior attire, wearing a putative eagle head helmet and a prominent beard. He is identified (name or rank?) by what appears to be an abbreviated image of a feathered serpent. Photograph by Robert H. Cobean. Cf. discussions of this intriguing figure in de la Fuente, Trejo, and Gutiérrez Solana 1988, Kristan-Graham 1988, and Jiménez García 1998.

and is now also in the Vienna museum (Fuhrmann 1923: 84). Discussion of these Tula bearded figures will be deferred until similar figures from Chichen Itza can be cited for comparison. This is about all of the archaeologically derived data so far uncovered at Tula that would appear to have possible direct relevance to the Topiltzin Quetzalcoatl of Tollan Tale. Hopefully, more will be revealed as excavation at the site continues.

Figure 5. Incised shell pendant, reportedly found in Tula, Hidalgo. The warrior figure, backed by a version of the feathered serpent, displays interesting resemblances to the Tula pillar relief illustrated in Figure 4, including the avian helmet, the ear plug, and the beard. The piece is in the collection of the Museo Nacional de Antropología, Mexico City. From Indian Art of Mexico and Central America *by Miguel Covarrubias, © 1957 by Alfred A. Knopf, a division of Random House, Inc. Used by permission of Alfred A. Knopf, a division of Random House, Inc.*

Over eight hundred airline miles away, in a far different clime, a great contemporary center may provide additional relevant archaeological material. Certainly, Chichen Itza, far more than Tula itself (as so far excavated), fairly crawls with feathered serpents, a motif that haunts the iconography of the site. Every type at Tula, with the possible exception of the sandal cap motifs, has apparently also been found here, plus some that are apparently absent from the Central Mexican site—e.g., façade friezes (but see Marquina 1951, lámina 46), heads at the tops and bases of stairway balustrades, and "sky dragons" on metal plaques (much of the extensive bibliography of Chichen Itza archaeology, which cannot be cited here *in extenso,* is included in Ruppert 1952: 167–169).

In addition, there are a number of depictions of figures with full beards, some of which display the feathered serpent as their "patron." The best examples are: (1) on the east face of the pilaster (h-2) of the west jamb of the principal entrance to the Castillo vestibule (e.g., Charnay 1887: 345; Willard 1941: 160, 164; Figures 6 and 7); (2) on the sculpted frieze on the rear wall of the North Temple (Maudslay's C) of the Great Ball Court, which takes one of its names from the presence of this figure (reconstructed by Miguel Ángel Fernández and frequently reproduced; e.g., Marquina 1951: photo 439 [Figure 8]; cf. Breton 1917: 190, who doubted the presence of the beard); and (3) on a number of gold plaques from the Sacred Cenote (Lothrop 1952: Disks A [Figure 9], B, C, D, E [Figure 10], and I, figures 29, 30, 31, 32, 33, and 36; two warriors on Disks F and H, figures 34 and 36, display well-defined mustaches but no beards).

The bearded figures on the plaques are all wearing typically Toltec attire, usually that of the fully equipped warrior, with *atlatl* and spears. Without exception, they wear the turquoise mosaic bird device on the front of their headdresses (on Disks A and C they also wear the long nose rod, considered by Tozzer to be typically "Maya" rather than Toltec). With the possible exception of Disk I, these bearded warriors are the principal figures of the scene and on Disks B, C, D, and E are backed up by attendants or spear bearers in less sumptuous attire. On Disks D and B, unfeathered rattlesnakes undulate behind these figures. Two similar serpents are portrayed on Disk I; these have bunches of feathers streaming out the ends of the tails. In all of the scenes, the bearded warrior is either attacking or interrogating (?) figures in Yucatecan Maya costume (on these distinctions, see Tozzer 1930).

The two carved bearded figures both lack weapons. The one in the North Temple of the Great Ball Court is seated, covered by a mantle, wearing a simple headband with three feathers attached, before a curious standing figure that may represent a sacred image. Behind him, seated on low cushions (?), are five personages wearing great "feather bonnets." Facing him, on the other side of the putative sacred image, are seven seated figures, all wearing large turbans with swirling feathers attached. Undulating behind him is a classic Toltec-style feathered serpent.

Figure 6. Relief carving on the east face of pilaster (h-2) of the west jamb flanking the northern doorway of the sanctuary atop the highest pyramid temple, El Castillo, at Chichen Itza, Yucatan. The figure, in fairly typical Toltec garb, wears a prominent, long, pointed beard. From Charnay 1887: 345.

Figure 7. Close-up photo of upper portion of Pilaster h-2, El Castillo, Chichen Itza, Yucatan. Although retouched, as with many of Willard's photos, it constitutes an essentially accurate depiction of the carving—which Willard maintained was a portrait of Kukulcan. From Willard 1941: 165.

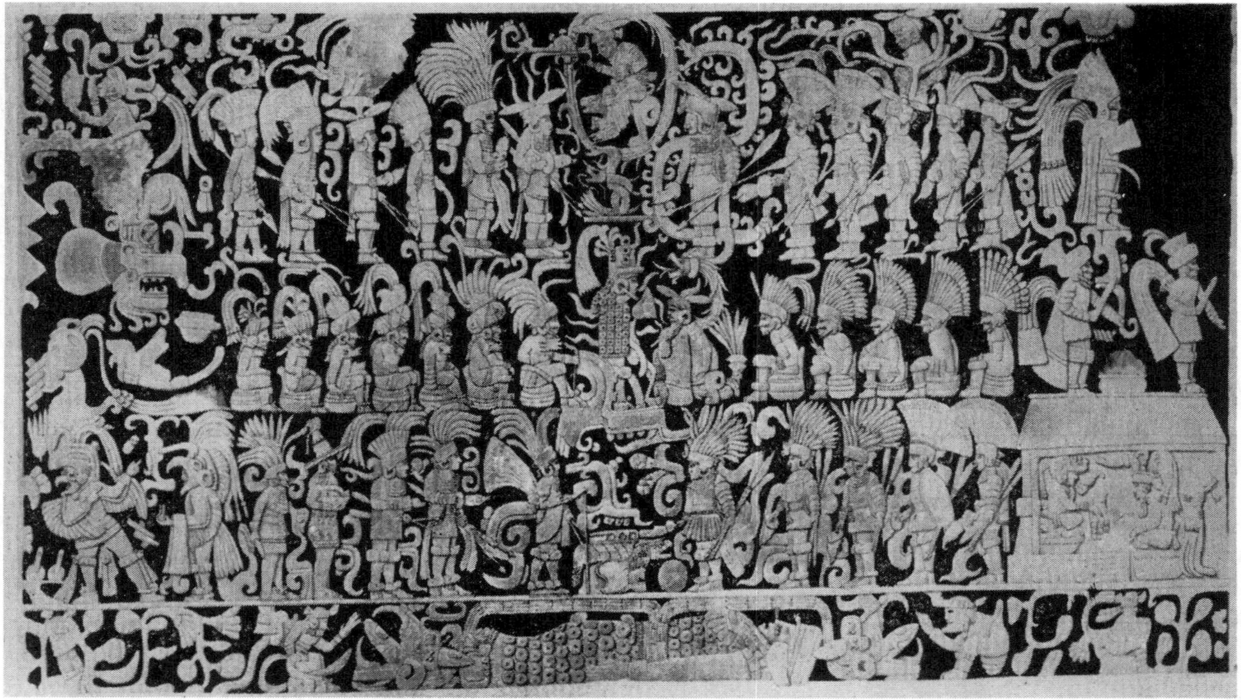

Figure 8. Complex ritual scene carved in relief on the rear wall of the North Temple of the Great Ball Court, Chichen Itza, Yucatan. Reconstruction drawing by Miguel Ángel Fernández. A berobed bearded personage, wearing a simple feather headdress and backed by a feathered serpent, is seated at the center of the scene. Behind him and fronting him are numerous seated figures wearing elaborate feather headdresses, while numerous standing figures, in a variety of costumes, occupy the upper and lower registers. From Marquina 1964: 866 (fot. 439). Courtesy of the Instituto Nacional de Antropología e Historia (Mexico).

Figure 9. Drawing (by Kisa Noguchi) of depiction of a putative "Toltec" personage, wearing a long pointed beard, confronting a smaller "Maya" figure, on the upper fragment of Disk A, dredged up from the Sacred Cenote, Chichen Itza, Yucatan. From Lothrop 1952: 43 (fig. 29a). Courtesy of the Peabody Museum of Archaeology and Ethnology, Harvard University. Cf. Figure 6.

The Castillo figure wears the typical headdress, feather-crested, fronted with the mosaic bird device and with the "butterfly" or stylized bird pectoral on the chest. In both hands, instead of weapons, he is holding what appear to be bundles of cords or perhaps, as Seler suggested, grass. Both patron feathered serpent and name sign are lacking.

These bearded warrior figures from Tula and Chichen Itza have elicited considerable speculation. Beards, of course, were—and are—sometimes sported by Mesomerican indigenes, and figures of men and/or gods with beards are sporadically represented in various pre-Hispanic Mesoamerican artistic traditions. But the beards on these Tula and Chichen Itza personages are particularly distinguished by their luxuriance and length. Also striking is the close similarity between the bearded figure on Acosta's Pillar 11 at Tula and that on Chichen Itza's Cenote Disk A, for both are wearing very similar earplugs and long nose rods—although their headdresses differ sharply. It is also likely that these figures are human figures, portrayed with considerable fidelity to costume and general appearance, rather than deities. How then to interpret them? A somewhat romantic approach (e.g., Willard 1941) might interpret them as actual depictions of our hero, complete to his beard, which, as we have seen, is ascribed to him in some of the Central Mexican accounts. This interpretation would imply that Topiltzin Quetzalcoatl of Tollan and the Yucatecan Kukulcan/Quetzalcoatl mentioned by Landa and Chi were one and the same, a point that will be examined below.

Figure 10. Drawing (by Kisa Noguchi) of depiction on gold Disk E, from the Sacred Cenote, Chichen Itza, Yucatan, of two "Toltec" warriors, the principal one, associated with a version of the feathered serpent, wearing a long pointed beard. From Lothrop 1952: 48 (fig. 33). Courtesy of the Peabody Museum of Archaeology and Ethnology, Harvard University.

In my view, an alternative explanation deserves more serious consideration. Each priest in late pre-Conquest Central Mexico—and probably wherever Toltec influence was strong—was apparently considered to have been an embodiment of Topiltzin Quetzalcoatl, the patron of the priestly school, the *calmecac*, and the preeminent sacerdotal archetype. This concept evidently applied particularly to the high priests—and at Tollan, Mexico Tenochtitlan, Tetzcoco, and possibly other leading Central Mexican centers, it is known that they bore his name as the title of their offices. Although statements are lacking that they wore the attire and insignia ascribed to their archetype, they may well have done so on appropriate occasions. I suggest as a hypothesis, therefore, that these bearded figures at Tula and Chichen Itza could represent actual historical individuals who bore the titles Quetzalcoatl, Topiltzin, Nacxit[l]), and/or Kukulcan and who might have worn artificial beards in memory of the great priest/ruler whose role and tradition they were emulating and perpetuating.

In the next chapter, I shall return briefly to a consideration of the archaeological evidence when discussing the wider problem of the possible historicity of at least some aspects of the Topiltzin Quetzalcoatl of Tollan Tale. Before leaving the present topic, however, mention should be made of Seler's (1902–1923, I: 683–691) theory that the complicated series of reliefs on the rear wall of the Lower Jaguars Temple (Maudslay's E) of the Great Ball Court was a depiction of the immolation of Topiltzin Quetzalcoatl, depicting the various groups of personages who participated in his last rites. Although some likely connection with Quetzalcoatl is indicated by the fact that the strange figure in the center of the second row from the bottom—which Seler suggested represented a "cenotaph figure of Quetzalcoatl Kukulcan" in the process of being immolated—has as its patron a large, striking feathered serpent, I do not believe Seler's intriguing suggestion can really be taken very seriously.

Lastly, it should be emphasized that the patron role of the feathered serpent was particularly ubiquitous at Chichen Itza. This is evidenced most strikingly in the frescoes of the Upper Jaguars Temple, where these undulating creatures are depicted behind figures that appear to represent the military commanders of the attacking "Toltec" armies. The famous scene of human sacrifice from the Temple of the Warriors (Morris, Charlot, and Morris 1931, II: plate 145) is also patronized by the feathered serpent—which both indicates the importance of the latter's cult as well as provides indisputable evidence of its sanguinary character at Chichen Itza.

This about sums up the archaeological evidence that appears to be directly relevant to our theme. As always, the problem is one of interpretation. It is tempting to take a bold, speculative approach and embrace the notion that at least some of the bearded personages associated with the feathered serpent depicted at Tula and Chichen Itza might be actual portraits of our hero. However, so many dangerous assumptions are involved here that I feel that it is definitely exceeding the bounds of responsible scholarship to so interpret these images. In any case, as corroboration of the great importance of the feathered serpent in Toltec and Toltec/Maya iconography—and undoubtedly in the religious/ritual systems of these two great centers as well—as well as the probable existence of leaders who bore the title Quetzalcoatl and/or its variants, this archaeological evidence is of considerable significance.

XI. Some Interpretations of the Basic Data Presented

In the preceding sections there has been passed in review a mass of Mesoamerican documentary and archaeological data surely or possibly relating to the figure I have been calling, in the interests of standardization, Topiltzin Quetzalcoatl of Tollan. The documents, taken together, constitute a rich, fascinating, confused, and contradictory corpus, a remarkable mélange of intricately blended historical, legendary, and mythological elements. It could be—and has been—approached from many angles. In this study, in addition to presenting the basic raw data in considerable detail, I am particularly interested in sifting out what genuinely historical features this complex tale may or may not contain.

The present chapter has three principal aims: (1) to reconstruct, depending most heavily on the six basic "core sources," what I have designated the Basic Topiltzin Quetzalcoatl of Tollan Tale as it was apparently current in much of the Nahuatl-speaking area of Central Mexico at the time of the Conquest; (2) to examine the key problem of the degree of possible historicity in the tale as it is presently available to us; and (3) to briefly discuss various chronological, geographical, nomenclatural, and etymological aspects of the tale, including its relevance to the Toltec problem.

A. The Basic Topiltzin Quetzalcoatl of Tollan Tale

In spite of numerous contradictions and inconsistencies, various of the Central Mexican sources, particularly the six "core" accounts, probably provide a reasonably adequate notion of what was actually taught in the *calmecac(s)* of the leading communities of the Basin of Mexico—and, undoubtedly with certain variants, the Basin of Puebla and neighboring regions as well—concerning Topiltzin Quetzalcoatl of Tollan. It seems unlikely that anything like a rigidly standardized version existed, even within one major center, such as Mexico Tenochtitlan, much less throughout a larger territory. Based, as indicated earlier, on narrative chants and/or epic poems, straight oral historical tradition, and pictorial histories, the epic saga of the great priest/ruler of the Toltecs, in the process of transmission over time, had doubtless been repeatedly revised, reorganized, embellished, cut, and even deliberately distorted for propagandistic purposes by the custodians of the historical and religious lore of the many polities whose ruling houses claimed some connection with legend-thronged, imperial Tollan, widely recognized as the source of all "legitimate" political power in Late Postclassic Central Mexico. However, a fundamental version of the tale, displaying a certain degree of uniformity in the major events, can be tentatively reconstructed, utilizing what appear to be the earliest and most reliable accounts. It naturally divides itself into seven principal episodes:

1. *Birth*: Father: Mixcoatl, or variant (Iztac Mixcoatl, Camaxtli, Totepeuh), a semidivine conqueror, possibly the earliest important quasi-historical figure in Central Mexican tradition, founder of the Toltec power (not in Tollan but in some center to the northwest?).

Mother: Chimalma(n), or variant (Coatlicue, Coacueye, Cihuacoatl; all names of earth-fertility goddesses), identified in two sources as a native (chieftainess?) of (Teo)huitznahuac, apparently conquered by Mixcoatl/Camaxtli. A miraculous conception seems to have been a genuine variant—and her death in childbirth may also have been an integral episode of the basic tale.

Place: Varies considerably: (Teo)colhuacan, (Teo)huitznahuac, Michatlauhco, and Tollan itself are mentioned.

Time: Year 1 Acatl most common; day with same designation much rarer, although this can be implied from calendric name. Days 7 Acatl and 9 Ehecatl are significant variants.

2. *Youth*: Only one source specifically names his grandparents as those who raised him. Another specifies a person with the name of the earth goddess, Cihuacoatl/Quilaztli, as playing that role. His father's death at the hands of his uncles (only variant, his brothers) may also belong to the basic tale. His search for his father's bones, his burial of them, and his erection of a temple (Mixcoatepetl) to his progenitor's memory—and, after a struggle, his disposal of his malevolent uncles, led by the usurper Atecpanecatl (Apanecatl)—also seem to have been well-established episodes in the basic tale.

3. *Enthronement*: The exact manner of his accession to the supreme political and priestly office among the Toltecs varies considerably. According to one leading version, after acceding to this position he leads his people first to Tollantzinco and later to Tollan, acting as its founder. According to another, he becomes ruler in a Tollan already established. Deciding which version is more "basic" here is difficult; but the latter better fits the archaeological evidence.

4. *Apogee*: The details of his beneficent, quasi-theocratic rule in Tollan vary, but the general pattern is the same. His role as chaste, penitent arch-priest and religious innovator (particularly autosacrificial rites) is clearly fundamental. His generally pacifistic bent and aversion to human sacrifice are certainly more common than his contrasting role as a military conqueror. However, the two may not have been absolutely irreconcilable within the framework of pre-Hispanic Mesoamerican ideology. His culture-hero role does not seem to be as important as is often assumed—although his teaching of certain skills and crafts is emphasized in some accounts. His "invention" (reform, modification?) of the calendar was probably basic. His celibacy fits his role as sacerdotal archetype—but is frequently omitted. His skill as a

sorcerer (*nahualli*) is occasionally made explicit but more frequently implied. His construction of four precious "houses of oration," with colors associated with the cardinal directions, definitely seems to have been basic, although, as usual, details vary. His association with round temples is not mentioned in the core accounts and would seem to belong more aptly with Ehecatl Quetzalcoatl.

5. *Downfall*: This episode, like the preceding, varies considerably in details, but the different versions compare well in overall pattern. Tezcatlipoca, sometimes with associates, as Topiltzin Quetzalcoatl's chief antagonist is unquestionably basic. The precise motivation for their confrontation is not always made very clear, but, aside from the pure malevolence of the "Smoking Mirror," a conflict of cults with differing attitudes toward human sacrifice is mentioned in two of the core sources and might be implied in others. Precedent to his flight, Topiltzin Quetzalcoatl's destruction and/or burial of his treasures appears to have been fundamental and may have possessed about the same degree of romantic fascination for the ancient Mexicans as for their treasure-obsessed modern descendants. The "breaking of his vows" episode—with possible sexual overtones—that constitutes the climax of his conflict with Tezcatlipoca and dramatically underscores the latter's final triumph is only clearly present in one core account but is described with such a wealth of detail that it might qualify as basic (but too novelistic?). The other incidents connected with Tezcatlipoca's persecution of his rival vary greatly. This might have been expected, for just here was presented an exceptionally favorable opportunity for the exercise of the creative imagination of the storyteller without seriously affecting the basic structure of the tale. Above all, Tezcatlipoca, congruent with his fundamental supernatural personality, very much exercises the role of the arch-sorcerer—with emphasis on his transformational powers.

6. *Flight*: After abandoning Tollan and his high office, Topiltzin Quetzalcoatl's long trek to the Gulf Coast is highlighted in all six of the core accounts—as well as in most of the others—and constitutes one of the most fundamental elements of the tale, although the details vary enormously. No two of the primary sources closely agree, for instance, on the itinerary of the flight. The terminus is nearly always (Tlillan) Tlapallan, Tlatlayan, or a recognizable variant. Chalollan is a common waystop—but in some of the later accounts is the scene of events that have little or nothing to do with Tollan and may belong to a largely independent cycle (ultimately of Olmeca Xicalanca origin?).

7. *Death or Disappearance*: The fate of Topiltzin Quetzalcoatl after reaching Tlapallan displays two principal variants, both apparently basic: (1) disappearance, often across the sea, and (2) death and subsequent cremation. The transformation of Topiltzin Quetzalcoatl's soul into the planet Venus is also

common enough to be considered fundamental. Only one of the six core sources emphasizes his expected return and consequent confusion with Cortés and the Spanish invaders. However, it is frequent enough in the supplementary accounts, some of them among our earliest and seemingly most reliable, to be tentatively included as an integral aspect of the basic tale. The date of Topiltzin Quetzalcoatl's death/disappearance varies, but the year or day 1 Acatl is most common. Four Tochtli is a significant variant in one core source.

A kind of tragic "drama in seven acts," then, can be tentatively reconstructed as the most fundamental version of the tale as known from the core group of Central Mexican sources. The fundamentally neutral term "tale" was chosen for it advisedly, without the technical connotation of "folktale," although folkloric elements are certainly prominently embedded in it. "Legend," although possibly apt, would, to many, connote too small a degree of historicity. "Myth" would clearly be a misnomer, unless one is willing to take an outright Brintonian stand on its interpretation.

A pertinent problem is the extent of the spatial distribution of the basic tale at the time of the Conquest. It appears likely that most of the important polities of the Basin of Mexico preserved some version of it. The basic tale, as reconstructed above, probably represented, above all, the tradition of Mexico Tenochtitlan, which, as indicated, seems to have perpetuated—undoubtedly modified to enhance the political interests of the Mexica—the tradition of Colhuacan. The Sahaguntine version, which lines up reasonably well with the others, was apparently collected in Tlatelolco. Unfortunately, the specific communities of origin of the others cannot be clearly pinpointed. In any case, most of the earlier and more authentic versions of the tale, whatever their provenience, probably reflected some degree of Colhuaque/Tenochca influence. It would be quite interesting—and surely revealing—if we had at our disposal and could compare the "official" versions of the tale, say, of Mexico Tenochtitlan, Tlatelolco, Tetzcoco, Tlacopan, Cuauhtitlan, Xaltocan, Xochimilco, Cuitlahuac, Mizquic, Chalco, etc., with one another. Such a hope certainly can never be realized. Consequently, while recognizing the possibility that the putatively Colhuaque/Tenochca version of the tale may not have been all that predominant outside of the Mexica capital, with the limited number of sources available to us we probably have little recourse but to accept, as a working hypothesis, the likelihood that it was.

As for the versions ostensibly from the Basin of Puebla—where some Toltec culture patterns may have survived in even purer form than in the Basin of Mexico, above all at Cholollan—aside from the brief allusions to Topiltzin Quetzalcoatl or some analogous figure in the *Historia Tolteca-Chichimeca*, the *Relación de Cholula*, and the *Relación de Andrés de Tapia*, we cannot be certain that any of the extant versions actually derive from this region. It does seem possible, however—as noted—that the accounts of Motolinía and Olmos were collected here. It is particularly unfortunate that, in view of the importance of Quetzalcoatl at this great mercantile/pilgrimage center, the prevailing Chololteca version of the tale has, as far as we know, not been preserved. The few snatches of the tale from Pueblan sources that have survived appear to line up reasonably well with those surely or ostensibly from the Basin of Mexico—although his "missionary" role may have been given somewhat more emphasis here (e.g., in Tapia, Olmos, and Motolinía, assuming their Pueblan origin).

Outside of these two Central Mexican areas, it is much more difficult to reconstruct the late pre-Hispanic distribution of versions of the tale. Certainly, as we saw, for most of Oaxaca, Chiapas, and Veracruz/Tabasco there is scant evidence for its presence—although the feathered-serpent concept and creator/fertility gods similar to Ehecatl Quetzalcoatl appear to have played some role in the religious/ritual systems of these areas. Principally based on the evidence of the pictorial histories, a case can be made for the preservation of at least some elements of the basic tale in the Mixteca. It is also possible that various of the Nahua-speaking enclaves south and east of the main Central Mexican concentration (i.e., those in eastern Veracruz, Tabasco, Oaxaca coast, and Chiapas), at least those connected with migrations from the region of Tollan, preserved some reminiscences of Topiltzin Quetzalcoatl. Our information concerning these groups is so fragmentary, however, that at this stage of our knowledge—or better, ignorance—this would be pure speculation.

Moving on to Highland Guatemala, El Salvador, and Nicaragua, versions of both Ehecatl Quetzalcoatl and Topiltzin Quetzalcoatl, as we have seen, were almost certainly present among various of the Mayance- and Nahua-speaking groups that dominated these regions. However, genuinely significant elements of the basic tale appear to have been virtually lacking. The best case is the possible influence it might have exerted on the Gucumatz/Quicab tradition of the Gumarcaah and Iximche dynasties of Highland Guatemala. Again, it is to be much regretted that more historical data have not been preserved from the traditions of the Nahua-speakers of these regions—for the Toltec impress on the political aspect of some of the indigenous polities of Highland Guatemala was clearly very strong. Their overall sociopolitical structures, characterized by their pervasive aristocratic orientation with emphasis on the careful tracing of dynastic descent, elaborate investiture ceremonies, and multitudinous titles, among other features, clearly reflected this. And all of these "Toltecasized" sociopolitical patterns were intimately connected with the great authority figure, the "legitimatizer" par excellence, Nacxit (= Topiltzin Quetzalcoatl). Thus, even if the Central Mexican version of the basic tale itself might have been hardly known in

Highland Guatemala, at least its protagonist had made a powerful impact there as the paramount symbol of political authority and legitimacy.

The Yucatecan situation is somewhat similar, but here there was more emphasis on certain putatively historical happenings that seem to relate to our hero or cognate personages. Kukulcan/Quetzalcoatl was clearly identified as a great Nahua leader, whose impact on the culture of the northern peninsula is described as profound, particularly in the religious sphere. Nor was his political role slighted, for here too it would seem "legitimate" political authority for the most part traced back to his career and deeds of "statesmanship." On the other hand, just as in Highland Guatemala, there is slight evidence for the preservation of other significant elements of the basic tale.

In sum, it would seem that the rich full tale of the life of Tollan's great priest/ruler was probably largely confined to Central Mexico, particularly the Basin of Mexico and, secondarily, the Basin of Puebla—with a possible significant extension into the Mixteca. Outside of these regions, where Toltec-descended rulers had evidently labored most successfully to perpetuate and record the proud dynastic traditions of their forebears, wherever Tollan-connected émigrés had penetrated in strength, some reminiscences of their archetypical lord and priest might well have survived—together with characteristic Central Mexican sociopolitical patterns that were believed to have derived from his authority and legitimatization. This was clearly true, at any rate, for Highland Guatemala and northern Yucatan, where the Toltec eastern *völkswanderung* seems to have achieved its greatest political success.

B. The Possible Historicity of the Topiltzin Quetzalcoatl of Tollan Tale

This section will focus on one of the central problems with which this study is concerned. All of the available important documentary versions of the tale and the most significant allusions to its protagonist have been paraphrased and summarized. A "basic" version, which was probably close to that current at Contact in the priestly schools of the leading Central Mexican polities, has been tentatively reconstructed. The relevant archaeological evidence has been discussed. It is already evident, from preliminary remarks made in the commentary sections, that I believe that a certain amount of genuine historicity probably does adhere to Topiltzin Quetzalcoatl. The problem to be further explored here, stated most simply, is: How much?

Clearly, mythological, legendary, and folkloristic elements played a significant role in the genesis and development of the tale. However, it has long been recognized that the mere presence of "impossible" supernaturalistic incidents or improbable apocryphal material in an account of the career of an historical figure in itself by no means negates his/her historicity. The cycle of marvelous legends that grew up in Asia surrounding the personality and career of Alexander of Macedon, for example, hardly robs him of his real existence. Closer to home, the cycle of similar kinds of tales that emerged early in colonial New Spain concerning the unfortunate Motecuhzoma II of Mexico Tenochtitlan hardly shakes our faith in his historicity. Few of the great have escaped this myth- and legend-making process, which represents a fundamental propensity throughout human history.

In spite of a considerable literature produced by historians and students of legend and folklore concerning this question, it is obvious that no set of hard-and-fast rules have been formulated for determining what past events actually did or did not occur. Obviously, incidents that fly in the face of accepted agreement concerning what is possible or impossible in nature, commensurate with the latest findings of science, must, by definition, be rejected. In the present case, all of those aspects of the tale that smack of the miraculous or frankly supernatural can at the outset be eliminated. These would include the miraculous birth, the anthropomorphizing of animals, the sorcery of both Topiltzin Quetzalcoatl and his rival Tezcatlipoca (particularly the numerous tricks and transformations of the latter), Topiltzin Quetzalcoatl's stellar apotheosis, and all of the other "magical" elements of the tale. Cutting away this outer layer of the marvelous, we arrive at a core of events in his career that *could* have occurred—but, of course, this potentiality in itself does not necessarily demonstrate that they *did* occur.

An important methodological note is in order here. As I have emphasized in another place (Nicholson 1955a), in analyzing a native tradition preserved almost exclusively in the writings of Spaniards or Spanish-educated indigenes and mestizos, there are two distinct steps involved. The first must be directed to the transmitting source. The key question here is: does it more or less accurately record the version(s) of the tale that might have been included in the "official" histories of the leading centers of late pre-Hispanic Central Mexico and taught in their *calmecac(s)*? The date of composition, the author's identity and profession, his motivation for writing, the place where his version was collected, the identity and status of his informants—all these facts, where ascertainable, must be taken into consideration in appraising the authenticity and reliability of a version of the tale only available through a transmitting source.

This indispensable critical spadework completed—and assuming that it has been determined that we are dealing with a reasonably reliable transmittal of a "*calmecac* version" of the tale—the second and much more difficult step remains. This is the determination of the degree of historical reliability, if any, of the indigenous tradition itself. There are fewer signposts to guide us here. On the chronological side, the potential accuracy of the Central Mexican native year count is patent, but the problem of the recurring 52-year cycles is ubiquitous. And it has become further exacerbated with the demonstration (e.g., Kirchhoff 1950, 1955b; Jiménez Moreno 1940, 1953, 1955) that different year counts—and, much more dubiously, possibly different *tonalpohualli* day counts as well—were current in Central and Southern Mexico in the last few centuries before the Conquest. That propagandistic distortion was frequent is known from comparing accounts of the same events from different, often rival, polities. For various important events of the last pre-Hispanic century and shortly before, a number of accounts from different localities are available—and a careful comparative analysis often aids significantly in determining their historical reliability. For earlier events, however, particularly those that extend back to the Toltec period, the paucity of material provides few opportunities to undertake comparisons of this kind.

Clearly, the more independent accounts that record the same event, or set of events, that are available, the greater the likelihood of their actual historicity. However, the determination of genuine independence, i.e., in our case the provenience of versions of the tale from different centers, is often difficult. In view of the crucial importance to our inquiry of these determinations, in earlier sections I devoted particular attention to bibliographical and textual analysis. If the record keepers of, say, Mexico Tenochtitlan, Tetzcoco, Tlacopan, Cuauhtitlan, Cholollan, and Tlaxcallan all more or less agreed in their versions of the career of our hero, its chances for some degree of historicity would obviously be considerably increased. If, in addition, similar versions could be identified from Oaxaca, Veracruz/Tabasco, Chiapas, Highland Guatemala, and northern Yucatan, the case would, of course, become even stronger. Unfortunately, too few primary sources narrating the career of Topiltzin Quetzalcoatl of Tollan have survived, even in Central Mexico, to permit anything like this type of broad-spectrum comparative historical analysis. From my summaries of the few that are available, variants and contradictions even in the six core sources were all too obvious. Nevertheless, in spite of these problems, I still feel that a certain case can be made for some measure of historicity for the tale of Topiltzin Quetzalcoatl of Tollan.

That a genuine interest in history existed in pre-Hispanic Mesoamerica has long been recognized and is apparent from many lines of evidence. I (Nicholson 1955a) have called this a "chronicle consciousness" and stressed that the tools were available that made reasonably accurate historical record keeping possible—and which is attested by the number of verbal and pictorial histories that have survived in one form or another. A cultural climate existed—particularly the political interests of the paramount ruling dynasties—that was conducive to the maintenance of narrative histories. In any case, one thing is clear. For the Conquest-period Central Mexican groups within whose corpus of traditional lore the Topiltzin Quetzalcoatl of Tollan Tale occupied a stellar position, it was considered historical in a very different way from the cosmogonical events that usually preceded it. Topiltzin Quetzalcoatl, in spite of his concomitant quasi-divinity, was essentially a man who lived at a stated time and who moved through a world specifically located in space. More striking than his partial godhead was his very human, earthbound role as the great priest/ruler of the Toltecs, the fountainhead of all later legitimate political power. Motecuhzoma II was clearly claiming descent from an ancestral, terrestrial ruler—albeit a semidivine one—not a purely celestial deity.

The tale had become fully integrated into the world historical scheme of the late pre-Hispanic Central Mexican peoples whose culture was derived most strongly from that of Tollan. And it is precisely at this point in time that the outlines of actual past events begin to emerge from out of the mythic mist of the preceding era. Now the flesh-and-blood kind of history that names persons, places, and dates can be cautiously added to the record of imperishable artifact style change and diffusion as reconstructed by the archaeologist. And herein lies the special significance of the tale: its location at this key juncture of "documented" history and "dirt" archaeology.

The analogy that can be drawn, for example, with the Homeric epics, the Sanskrit Vedas, the Genesis Patriarchal tales, the Chinese Huang Ti cycle, and the Arthurian romances, among others, is intriguing. In all of these well-known cases, scholars most familiar with the evidence have increasingly recognized the frequent existence of the valid historical pearl concealed within the rough outer shell of the marvelous. Archaeology has frequently provided dramatic corroboration of the essential historicity of at least the general cultural milieu surrounding these narrations—and even sometimes the likely historicity of the legendary heroes that are characteristically featured in them. The Topiltzin Quetzalcoatl of Tollan Tale appears to provide one of the best New World parallels to these classic Old World examples.

Apart from the usual analytic tools of the documentary historian, the evidence from archaeological excavation usually provides the most convincing corroboration of historicity. However, its value must not be overrated. An ancient artifact, monument, or edifice is a concrete "fact," but its accurate interpretation is often extremely difficult. Archaeologists working in Central Mexico are not as fortunate as the Assyriologists and Egyptologists, for example, who, with the discovery of contemporary written inscriptions, can often unequivocally establish the existence of rulers whose names figure in king lists often drawn up, in final form, hundreds of years after their deaths. A partial exception is provided by certain monuments with representations of the latest rulers of Mexico Tenochtitlan, some with accompanying dates in the native calendric system (Nicholson 1955b)—but here the time span covered is frustratingly brief.

Assuming for the moment the possibility of his historicity, buildings or monuments constructed at Topiltzin Quetzalcoatl's order at Tollan—or possibly even at Chichen Itza—*may* have already been discovered, but no convincing demonstration of this can be offered at the present time. And the problem of the possible "portraits" of Topiltzin Quetzalcoatl at these two centers has already been discussed—with no definitive resolution. However, although it hardly demonstrates the actual existence of Topiltzin Quetzalcoatl of Tollan, the archaeological evidence of the importance of the feathered-serpent icon in these two major Toltec-period centers and its direct association with leadership patterns does at least provide a background that enhances the *possibility* of his historicity.

In spite of the difficulties involved, historians and anthropologists with historical interests must advance hypotheses to be tested by future archaeological discoveries and/or the application of more rigorous analyses of existing data. As with experimental science, in this way historical understanding advances and expands. The following hypothesis concerning Topiltzin Quetzalcoatl is offered, therefore, with this end in mind. It proposes nothing that is startlingly new, but it may at least possess the virtue of being based on a broader evidential corpus than most of those advanced by previous researchers.

First, and most importantly, I believe that it is quite possible that there was an "original" Topiltzin Quetzalcoatl, an actual person who lived on this earth but who later apparently became inextricably fused (and confused) with more than one deity—and probably with later rulers as well. I believe, if this proposition has any validity, that it is unlikely that he was an outsider, a "foreign missionary," but almost certainly an indigene who was born somewhere in northwestern or central Mexico (the problem of the locus of his birth will be discussed below). As to his parentage, there is considerable evidence that the personage who is most frequently named as his father, Mixcoatl/Camaxtli (I agree with Jiménez Moreno that Totepeuh was probably a variant name), although merged with the deity of this same name(s), may also have been a quasi-historical figure. If so, he seems to have undertaken a series of conquests in Central Mexico. Rather speculative attempts have been made to plot the extension of these putative conquests and his consequent "empire" (see Müller 1949: maps 1 and 2, pp. 20–30, for the most part following the ideas of Jiménez Moreno). Some students have regarded him as the real founder of Toltec power, or, as Jiménez Moreno (1945: 12) put it, "una especie de Gengis-Khan indígena, elevado después a la categoría de un díos." The Mexican scholar also believed that he might, at the head of a conquering horde of Nahua, have been the destroyer of Teotihuacan. Space limitations preclude further discussion of this interesting figure who bears such a significant relationship to Topiltzin Quetzalcoatl—but, again, that some degree of historicity attaches to him is, in my view, a distinct possibility.

On the maternal side, Chimalma(n)/Cihuacoatl/Coatlicue, most commonly named as his progenitress, is a much more shadowy figure. Some of the earliest versions of the tale recount her death in childbirth, TQ's upbringing by his grandparents, and the killing of his father by his brother(s), the uncle(s) of our hero. Accurately judging the historicity of these elements, undeniably of the type that so often appears in legends and folktales, is obviously very difficult. And the same goes for Topiltzin's avenging of his father's death, culminating in the elimination of his murderer(s). Just how he came to the throne of Tollan is also obscure, for here even the core accounts are quite divergent. Perhaps only further archaeological evidence can clarify, if ever, whether he "founded" Tollan, becoming its first ruler, or whether he acceded in some fashion to an established throne in an already flourishing center. In any case, the sources are in general agreement that, once installed, he ruled there for some time in prosperity.

As Tollan's ruler, he must have played the familiar Mesoamerican double leadership role, i.e., sacerdotal *and* secular. He was credited with the introduction of new autosacrificial rites, and he probably was a significant religious innovator who attempted to advance the cult of an old creator/fertility god symbolized by the feathered serpent, whose name he seems to have adopted as a title. In addition, he apparently operated as a patron of arts and crafts and certain intellectual activities, particularly calendric calculations. Although the core sources do not stress it and no list of conquests after his accession is extant (as noted, those of the *Leyenda de los soles* probably represent way stops on his "flight," rather than genuine conquests), he most likely made efforts to build up the military power of his polity, for his role as political legitimatizer is so strongly stressed in so many accounts. In short, he seems, like Harun-al-Rashid, to have ruled at a time of great prosperity and cultural and political growth, a "golden age," and to have been given a great deal of credit for it.

The causes for his downfall may always remain obscure, but the theory accepted by many students, that it involved a religious conflict, is, I believe, as good a hypothesis as any. His aversion to human sacrifice may have been a genuine feature of the tale, since so many of the basic accounts stress it—but it is somewhat difficult to square with the archaeological evidence and the nature of his cult, fused with that of Ehecatl Quetzalcoatl, in late pre-Hispanic Central Mexico. Tezcatlipoca may, as has also frequently been suggested, personify the rival religious system. At any rate, those who preserved the tradition after Topiltzin Quetzalcoatl's departure obviously believed that he had been the victim of a kind of systematic persecution, whatever its motivation.

Some of the details of his flight may actually be historical, while others are obviously apocryphal. Certainly, many fantastic elements have been added (e.g., his impressing parts of his body into solid stone, a motif that has a remarkably wide distribution throughout the world). Deciding on the historicity of his residence in Chollollan, which apparently at this time was an Olmeca Xicalanca center and possibly a political rival of Tollan, is particularly difficult. The ethnohistorical evidence definitely would support a scenario in which, after the fall of Tollan, a sizable contingent of émigrés from that center moved into Chollollan, replacing a possible preceding Olmeca Xicalanca dynasty. The descendants of these putative Toltec conquerors seem to have maintained their cultic and historical traditions with particular success—and the syncretic supernatural personality called Quetzalcoatl at the time of the Conquest was the great patron deity of this leading commercial and religious center. Was Topiltzin Quetzalcoatl's "residence" there, included in some versions of the basic tale, projected back into the past by the Toltec-descended Chololteca who regarded him with special veneration? Does their claim, recorded by both Tapia and Gabriel de Rojas, that he *founded* Chollollan actually represent the same historical retrojection process? Against this view is the implication in the *Historia Tolteca-Chichimeca* that he was important there *before* the Toltec conquest (i.e., the existence of the "oracle" of "Topiltzin Quetzalcoatl Nacxitl Tepeuhqui"). Alva Ixtlilxochitl's statement that Quetzalcoatl "preached" to the Olmeca Xicalanca is also significant. Conceivably, the old feathered-serpent creator/fertility god, Quetzalcoatl (apparently going back at least as early as Classic-period Teotihuacan), was important in the Olmeca Xicalanca cult—Xochicalco, with possible Olmeca Xicalanca ties, may also be pertinent here—and their version of this deity became merged with that introduced by their Toltec conquerors.

The problem of the "fate" of Topiltzin Quetzalcoatl is also a challenging one. Tlapallan, whatever it had meant to the Toltecs, was to the late pre-Hispanic Central Mexican peoples obviously a semilegendary place whose location, although in the direction of Yucatan, was not precisely fixed (see below). This brings us to one of the most tantalizing possibilities in pre-Hispanic Mesoamerican history. It has been seriously suggested by various Mesoamericanists that the "historical" Topiltzin Quetzalcoatl of Tollan, after his abandonment of that center, might have led his followers down from the plateau, through Veracruz, Tabasco, and Campeche, and on to Chichen Itza, where he was remembered as the "great Mexican captain" Kukulcan. In certain reconstructions of Central Mexican and northern Yucatecan history, such as Thompson's (1941a), the dates putatively fit rather well. And Thompson was not alone in suggesting that the archaeology can be interpreted to support the view that Toltec groups moved almost directly from Tollan to Chichen Itza. But could it have been the "original" Topiltzin Quetzalcoatl who led them? Rather than "disappearing" across the sea or being cremated and converted into the morning star did he actually lead a military force on to the conquest of northern Yucatan?

This problem will be briefly reconsidered when we discuss the chronology of the tale. I would just like to state here that I feel that this intriguing possibility cannot be flatly discarded but that it is perhaps more likely that the Kukulcan—or Kukulcans—who moved into northern Yucatan were Toltec or Toltec-connected military (and religious?) leaders who bore the title apparently established by the figure with whom we are concerned. And the further possibility might be entertained that for a time *any* leader of a migrating Toltec or Toltecoid group bore this title. This might also explain the presence of similar titles in Highland Guatemala—although it must be recognized that, according to the local chronicles, this type of title was not borne by any of the leaders of the migrating ancestors of the leading dynasties of this region (the important ruler, Gucumatz, appears only after the Gumarcaah dynasty was well established). More importantly, as noted, some of the Highland Guatemalan native histories recorded that the Toltec-connected émigrés who established themselves here clearly recalled that it had been the "great father Nacxit" who had dispensed and confirmed the titles and insignia of rank that they prized so highly (cf. Rojas's [1927] description of similar confirmation rituals in Chololląn). Could this conceivably have been "the" Topiltzin Quetzalcoatl of Tollan? There are serious chronological difficulties here (discussed below), and, again, as in the case with Kukulcan in northern Yucatan, it is perhaps more likely that the Nacxit of these Highland Guatemalan traditions represents the Toltec power of the moment, possibly at Tollan or Tollan Chollolan or even in some secondary Toltec center closer to Guatemala.

So much for the bare outline of what I believe might conceivably have actually occurred with regard to Topiltzin Quetzalcoatl of Tollan. My speculations are not too different in many respects from those that have had a strong influence in Mesoamerican ethnohistory, particularly in Mexico: the reconstructions put forward by Wigberto Jiménez Moreno (never fully expounded or documented but summarized in a number of places; e.g., 1941a, 1941b, 1945, 1946, 1954–1955, and n.d.). I differ with him in that I doubt very much that Toltec power was first established in the Colhuacan of the Basin of Mexico by Mixcoatl/Totepeuh before it was transferred to Tollan. I am also less certain than he of the dates of our hero, nor can I place as much stock in the modern folklore of Tepoztlan as filling in certain details of his career. In addition, I have certain other minor reservations not important enough to specify here. Jiménez Moreno represented perhaps the strongest antithesis to the old Daniel Brinton (1876: 195) thesis, which the pioneer Americanist scholar summed up thus:

> The central figure of Toltec mythology is Quetzalcoatl. Not an author on ancient Mexico but has something to say about his glorious days when he ruled over the land. No one denies him to have been a god, the

> god of the air, highest deity of the Toltecs, in whose honor was erected the pyramid of Cholula, grandest monument of their race. But many insist that he was at first a man, some deified king. There were in truth many Quetzalcoatls, for the high priest always bore his name, but he himself is a pure creation of the fancy, and all his alleged history is nothing but a myth.

Two leading earlier exponents of this anti-Brintonian "historical school" of interpretation of the Topiltzin Quetzalcoatl of Tollan Tale were Adolf Bandelier (1884), whose discussion of the problem was one of the best published up to that time, and Herbert Spinden, whose enthusiasm for a historical Quetzalcoatl is well summed up in the following passage (Spinden 1928: 173–175):

> Quetzalcoatl, perhaps the most remarkable figure in ancient American history, was emperor, artist, scientist, and humanist philosopher. He established orders of knighthood as well as the coronation ceremony used by the later Mexican kings. He developed the various industrial arts and built up a wide trade in cotton, cacao, and other products. As a patron of the peripatetic merchant he appears under the name Nacxitl, which means Four-way Foot. Apotheosis being an idea strongly fixed among the Toltecs, Quetzalcoatl was deified as Ehecatl, God of Winds, on account of his support of the Mayan god of rainstorms, and for his astronomical work he was further deified as God of the Planet Venus.

Seler, who always recognized some historical elements in the tale, after 1906 preferred a largely mythological interpretation, seeing in it a typical lunar myth (Seler 1902–1923, III: 305–351). The *Leyenda de los soles* version, on the other hand, he interpreted as a morning star myth. Two of his students, Walter Krickeberg and Walter Lehmann, maintained a more historical tack than their mentor, particularly the latter, without ever completely discarding the Selerian moon god hypothesis. An important Mexican student, Alfonso Caso, although he never expressed his ideas on the subject in detail, obviously leaned strongly to the historical side. Paul Kirchhoff, a leader in Mesoamerican ethnohistorical studies, fitted squarely within the historical tradition, although he differed sharply from Jiménez Moreno in regard to Topiltzin Quetzalcoatl's chronology, of which more below.

Granted at least the possibility that a real person initially sparked this influential tale, can we deduce anything very positive about him? Why was his impact on the historical consciousness of the Late Postclassic Toltec-connected Mesoamerican polities so great? Although certainty here can obviously never be attained, perhaps some more or less cogent hypotheses can be advanced. I believe that the strongest case can perhaps be made for Topiltzin Quetzalcoatl as a significant religious innovator. Of all his many roles, this seems to have made the greatest impression. At the same time, his role as a preeminent political authority figure appears to have impacted almost as powerfully on his dynastic successors.

Mesoamerica was clearly an area where a combined religious-secular leadership pattern had evolved to an unusually high degree. It provided an exceptionally favorable cultural climate for a gifted individual of high station to make his historical mark on society. Topiltzin Quetzalcoatl may well have been such a person. I am not suggesting that we might be confronted here with a Mesoamerican Buddha, Zoroaster, Jesus Christ, or Mohammed, for no comparable systematized body of religious doctrine seems to have stemmed from his life or teachings, but his impact on cult activities in Mesoamerica may have been considerable. That he introduced autosacrifice can be seriously questioned, for there is abundant evidence that it was well established in Mesoamerica long before the Toltec period, particularly in the Lowland Maya area. However, he might have promoted considerably greater emphasis on it, enhancing the crucial role that it is known to have played in the religious/ritual system of Late Postclassic Central Mexico.

Apart from this probable important religious role, his parallel political role, although obviously quite significant, can only be discerned in a shadowy fashion. It is, in fact, somewhat contradictory. In some accounts, his fundamentally pacifistic orientation is stressed, while others emphasize his role as dynastic founder and legitimizer—which implies a strong authoritarian, imperialistic persona. On the intellectual side, the ascription to him of the role of calendar inventor probably cannot be taken too seriously. The Central Mexican version of the Mesoamerican calendric system certainly existed in a well-developed form long before his time. On the other hand, it is possible that he reorganized or "reformed" it, perhaps about the time the Toltecs first adopted it. Here future archaeological work may clarify this aspect of the tale. Our knowledge of the specific mechanics of the Toltec calendric system is not very satisfactory. As pointed out above, Topiltzin Quetzalcoatl's culture-hero aspect, in the usual sense of the term, is not as emphasized in the basic core sources as one might have anticipated. However, his role as teacher, particularly in matters of religion and ritual, is often stressed.

Aside from any question of Topiltzin Quetzalcoatl's actual historicity, the impact of the tale on the later peoples of Central Mexico who most strongly carried on the Toltec cultural and dynastic tradition was unquestionably quite powerful. So strong, in fact, among the Tenochca—whose rulers claimed direct descent from him—that it appears to have played a significant role in influencing Motecuhzoma II's conduct vis-à-vis the European invaders. Above all, it is probable that, as the great sacerdotal archetype, the example of his life and career, whether genuinely historical or not, provided an influential model for the Late Postclassic Central Mexican priesthood, whose leaders, as noted, often bore his name(s) as a title of their office.

It might be legitimately queried at this point whether this hypothesis concerning the possible historicity of Topiltzin Quetzalcoatl aids our understanding of cultural-historical processes during Early Postclassic Central Mexico. Jiménez Moreno's influential hypothesis viewed him as an active civilizing agent, due to his upbringing with his mother's people of superior culture, the Huitznahuaca, whom he identified with the southern Nahuas connected with the major ceremonial center of Xochicalco, Morelos. Although, in my view, the evidence for the passing of Topiltzin Quetzalcoatl's youth in the Morelos region, as Jiménez Moreno and some others have speculated, is quite tenuous, that he might have played a significant role in the Toltec acquisition of certain more advanced elements of Mesoamerican high culture might be entertained as a working hypothesis. Archaeologically, the period in Central Mexico between the collapse of Teotihuacan and the rise of Tollan is still poorly understood. Although Toltec culture was obviously quite eclectic, incorporating diverse elements from earlier traditions, the precise manner in which this process occurred still poses major problems for the archaeologist and ethnohistorian.

Again, assuming that Topiltzin Quetzalcoatl fits chronologically near the beginning of the Toltec period, he might have been a key player in the emergence of this new cultural synthesis that, in essence, was to persist until the time of the Conquest. Although few anthropologists would embrace the "Great Man" school of cultural-historical interpretation, the catalytic role of certain key individuals in history cannot be denied. This is especially true when a less civilized group is in the process of attempting to acquire the skills of a more advanced group, which may to some extent have been the Toltec situation during Topiltzin Quetzalcoatl's period. A strong personality at the political and religious helm during such a time has been known to enhance and expedite this acculturative process. Familiar examples might include Alexander, Charlemagne, Kublai Khan, Peter the Great, Ataturk, et al. At any rate, I offer this as a subsidiary hypothesis to be tested by further research, both archaeological and ethnohistorical. It could help explain the extent of Topiltzin Quetzalcoatl's impact on the Mesoamerican historical consciousness. Such a "civilizing" role, in addition to that of a religious innovator, would likely have left a significant mark on the vigorous young Toltec polity(ies), ostensibly eager to mount the cultural and political Mesoamerican ladder. In view of their considerable success in both spheres, it would hardly be surprising that the memory of the leader who may have provided an influential cultural stimulus at a crucial time in their early history would be preserved (cf. Imhotep in Old Kingdom Egypt).

Lastly, a word concerning the fusion process that undoubtedly occurred after the disappearance of our hero from the scene. The major deity Quetzalcoatl at the time of the Conquest was a very complex one, obviously the end product of a long process of conceptual syncretism. To adequately analyze this multifaceted supernatural personage would necessitate a thorough study of its own. I undoubtedly oversimplified a very complicated situation when I hinted earlier that the Conquest-period Quetzalcoatl was a blend of the putatively historical Toltec priest/ruler and the old feathered-serpent fertility/creator/wind god I have denominated, to distinguish him from the former, Ehecatl Quetzalcoatl. Pedro Armillas (1947: 164–165, 176) suggested that at least six distinct aspects could be factored out of the "final" Quetzalcoatl: (1) the Creator; (2) the Venus God (in a double aspect as morning and evening star: Tlahuizcalpantecuhtli/Xolotl); (3) the Wind God (Ehecatl proper); (4) the Culture Hero; (5) the historical figure, or figures; and (6) a rain/fertility deity. Nor does this list, in my view, exhaust the possibilities. Although Armillas felt that the first three lacked a "relación natural," I believe that the first, third, and sixth did constitute related concepts within the framework of pre-Hispanic Mesoamerican ideology and might well have been somewhat merged from an early period. On the other hand, it is possible that some or all were originally distinct supernatural concepts and/or personalities.

David Kelley (1955) suggested that certain aspects of this complex deity were only brought in by the southern representatives of the widespread Uto-Aztecan linguistic family, the Nahua-speakers. I feel, however, that his evidence requires a more intensive critique and analysis before all of his propositions can be accepted. The Venus god aspect was perhaps the most peripheral; when it was added to the "Quetzalcoatl complex" would be difficult to ascertain. The occasional association of symbols that probably connote the planet Venus or a bright star with the feathered serpent in Toltec art may indicate that this association goes back at least to the Early Postclassic, if not earlier. In the tale, of course, Topiltzin Quetzalcoatl is brought into intimate relation with the planet by his conversion into it at the end of his life. It probably cannot be assumed, however, that no association between Venus and Topiltzin Quetzalcoatl existed until this time. Again, here is a problem concerning which archaeology may eventually be able to throw considerable light. As interesting as this and related problems are, they are not directly relevant to the theme of this study and must be left with this brief glance.

Granted the possibility that Topiltzin Quetzalcoatl might once have lived and breathed on this earth, he must have operated in a very definite area of space and moved through a specific period of time. Some attention, therefore, should be devoted to the spatial and temporal aspects of the tale.

This will be done in two special sections below. Before this, however, a section will be devoted to brief consideration of a significant problem: Topiltzin Quetzalcoatl's relation to the broader question of the position of the Toltecs within the framework of pre-Hispanic Mesoamerican culture history. Finally, a last section is devoted to consideration of certain nomenclatural and etymological aspects of the tale, which can enrich to some extent our understanding of it.

C. Supplementary Aspects of the Tale

1. Topiltzin Quetzalcoatl vis-à-vis the "Toltec Problem"

Some brief consideration of the relevance to this problem of the Topiltzin Quetzalcoatl of Tollan Tale is in order, although space limitations permit only the most cursory of treatments. A thorough analysis would necessitate a study at least as long as the present one. This problem, which from the beginning has concerned nearly all serious students of Mesoamerican culture history, entered an entirely new phase with the Tula excavations commencing in 1940, after—to considerably oversimplify—having passed through Caso's (1941a: 85) well-known "ingenuous," "skeptical," and "critical" stages (Tozzer [1957: 27] aptly suggested a fourth stage, "baffling"). Now that the heated debate has simmered down (in spite of Séjourné's (1954a, 1954b) attempts to revive it), most students agree that the Toltecs of the late pre-Hispanic Central Mexican historical traditions had their capital at what are now the ruins of Tula, Hidalgo. As a corollary, they have been divorced from the earlier center of Teotihuacan—although a post-Teotihuacan Toltec (Mazapan) occupation has been located in the outskirts of the site.

There are probably few Brintonians left who would dismiss the Toltecs as creatures solely of mythical imagination—although probably few ethnohistorians would agree with Kirchhoff (1955a: 164) when he expressed his optimistic conviction that there was sufficient documentation on the Toltecs "para aclarar todos los problemas fundamentales de la historia de ese pueblo." That they, or at least their aristocracy, spoke "Nahuat" or some other closely related archaic version of Nahuatl seems well established by a number of lines of evidence, aside from the express statements of Sahagún and Alva Ixtlilxochitl. That they exercised political control over a large area of Central Mexico also seems likely, although the exact boundaries of their dominion are difficult to determine. The *Historia Tolteca-Chichimeca* provides valuable data on this point, but they have been subject to differing interpretations. The *Anales de Cuauhtitlan* includes a list of the dominant polities of the Toltec empire, which differs markedly from the more dubious one of Chimalpahin. That the Toltec culture pattern was basically similar to and clearly provided the foundation for that which prevailed in Central Mexico in 1519 also appears to be virtually certain. Toltec chronology, in spite of much hypothesizing, still remains quite murky. Not even the time of Tollan's "fall" can really be fixed with much precision, much less the date of the establishment of this center. This question will be briefly discussed in the section devoted to the chronology of the tale.

The primary source material on the Toltecs is not really very extensive. Apart from a number of sources that mention them incidentally, only a select few provide sufficient information enabling us to form any kind of substantial picture of their overall culture pattern and history. The most important of these are, in roughly chronological order: the *Historia de los mexicanos por sus pinturas*, the *Juan Cano Relaciones*, the *Historia Tolteca-Chichimeca*, the *Histoyre du Mechique*, the *Leyenda de los soles*, the *Codex Vaticanus* A, Sahagún, the *Anales de Cuauhtitlan*, the *Memorial breve* and the *relaciones* of Chimalpahin, and the *relaciones* and *Historia Chichimeca* of Alva Ixtlilxochitl. In addition, such sources as the *Teponazcuicatl*, no. 18 of the *Cantares Mexicanos*, previously analyzed, Durán, and Muñoz Camargo provide a few scraps of some significance. About the only Toltec material in some of these sources is precisely that which occurs in the narration of the Topiltzin Quetzalcoatl of Tollan Tale. Clearly, the tale was so intimately bound up with the overall history of the Toltecs that the two are at times practically coterminous—with the usual addition of that of Huemac and the final downfall.

On Toltec origins we are very poorly informed. Apparently the illumination of authentic historicity is flickering so low at this point as to be almost undiscernible. Some of our otherwise best Toltec sources, such as the *Anales de Cuauhtitlan*, are virtually silent on this point. Alva Ixtlilxochitl is the most detailed, but, as usual, inconsistent and contradictory. He is the only chronicler to present a detailed early Toltec migration itinerary, but a careful analysis of the place-names reveals two entirely different origin points, one in the northwest and another in the southeast (for an attempt to reconcile them, see Jiménez Moreno 1954–1955: 225–226, and n.d.; cf. Melgarejo Vivanco 1949: 48–52). The *Juan Cano Relaciones* provide a somewhat more consistent account, bringing the Toltecs clearly from the northwest, from the legendary Teocolhuacan. A preliminary stopover at Tollantzinco is mentioned in various of these sources, but at times it seems to be confused with the stopover of Topiltzin Quetzalcoatl at that place (e.g., *Anales de Cuauhtitlan*).

Toltec history, once Tollan had risen to prominence, is skimpy and contradictory. Only five important lists of rulers have survived: *Juan Cano Relaciones*, *Leyenda de los soles*, *Anales de Cuauhtitlan*, Chimalpahin Cuauhtlehuanitzin, and Alva Ixtlilxochitl. They do not generally agree in their names, much less in chronology. The problem of confusion between "proper" name, calendric name, and title apparently also plagues us here. It is uncertain how many rulers succeeded each other in Tollan or whether the names of possible co-rulers have been arranged sequentially in a misleading fashion, as Kirchhoff (1955a: 190–193) suggested for Colhuacan. Three stand out with special prominence: Mixcoatl/Totepeuh, Topiltzin Quetzalcoatl, and Huemac. With one exception, they are listed in that order, although in three of the later sources, as noted, the last two are treated as contemporaries. Although the first two usually stand in the relation of father and son, Huemac's antecedents are much vaguer and often unmentioned.

The "fall" of Tollan and the consequent diaspora of its people are, as would be expected, more fully covered in the sources than the antecedents of the Toltecs and their history during the flowering of their capital. This was clearly the most momentous, well-remembered incident in pre-Hispanic Central Mexican political history until the turbulent events of the late fourteenth and fifteenth centuries in the Basin of Mexico and, not surprisingly, left a profound mark on the historical consciousness of Tollan's successor polities. The central figure of the Toltec denouement is Huemac—although when Topiltzin Quetzalcoatl is described as his contemporary, he and Huemac usually share in the debacle. The specific reasons given for the dissolution of the Toltec empire vary, but "heavenly wrath" (often symbolized by Tezcatlipoca's sorcery), famine, and warfare are prominently mentioned. Also stressed in some of the sources was the at least partial survival of Toltec culture and Toltec dynastic connections at certain key centers, particularly at Colhuacan, Xico, Cholollan, and, most significantly, Mexico Tenochtitlan.

Of considerable importance in any consideration of the Toltec problem are the Highland Guatemalan and northern Yucatecan traditions that connect the origins of prominent ruling dynasties in those areas to Tollan. If we had no other evidence than the names of some of these dynasts, we could be practically certain that the dominant speech of Tollan—and probably cognate and successor centers—was Nahuan. In addition, the Highland Guatemalan records supply valuable fragments of information on Toltec investiture ceremonies, sociopolitical organization, titles of rank, religion, mythology, and calendrics. The Nicaraguan data recorded by Bobadilla via Oviedo also cast some light on Toltec—or Toltecoid—cultures. These far southern émigrés, separated by centuries from direct contact from their linguistic relatives in Central Mexico, appear to hve preserved certain cultural features that in the latter area had either disappeared or had become significantly modified by the time of the Conquest. As indicated earlier, however, not all of these southeastern Nahuan movements seem to have been connected with Toltec dispersions. Some may have been substantially earlier. Even those that moved out of the specifically Toltec orbit may not necessarily have occurred at the same time but more likely in different waves connected with different events. Interestingly, it appears that the northern Yucatecan and Highland Guatemalan émigrés—who had become linguistically Mayanized—had retained the clearest recollection of their Tollan origin. This could be misleading, however, since it is just for these Mayanized dynasties that we have the fullest historical records, while for the Pipil of Guatemala and El Salvador, for example, who successfully maintained their original tongue, virtually none of their history has survived.

This, then, in broad outline, sans specific chronological and geographical factors, is the overall picture that can be derived from the principal sources concerning the Toltec rise and fall. What is most significant for our purposes is that the central figure in this drama is almost invariably Topiltzin Quetzalcoatl, wherever he may be placed in relative time. From one point of view, the "Toltec problem" and the "Quetzalcoatl problem" are so intimately related as to be nearly synonymous. Thus, some attention to the former is obviously demanded in any study of the latter. No thorough analysis of all of the available information concerning theToltecs has yet been undertaken. The early research of such students as Seler, Lehmann, Krickeberg, and, more recently, Linné, Vaillant, Jiménez Moreno, Kirchhoff, Acosta, and others, needs to be followed up with greater attention to critical methodology. More exhaustive investigations in the relevant ethnohistorical sources might result in some significant increases in our knowledge, but it seems likely that even more information on Toltec culture patterns and culture history will result from further archaeological excavations, particularly at Tula itself. Although the ethnohistorical traditions usefully inform us concerning how much the late pre-Conquest Central Mexican peoples recollected of Toltec glories, working in the Toltec ruins themselves should bring us even closer to the vanished reality we seek to reconstruct.

2. Chronological Aspects

The absolute chronology of Postclassic Mesoamerica, which is based largely on ethnohistorical evidence, is still, in spite of the considerable advance in our knowledge in recent years, in a rather nebulous state. The best-known areas are Central and Southern Mexico, but even here considerable confusion and doubt prevail. As noted earlier, as if the situation had not been difficult enough before, the demonstration (see, especially, Jiménez Moreno 1940, 1953, 1955; Kirchhoff 1950, 1955b) of the existence of different calendric systems in these regions has further compounded the chronological problems. No longer can we automatically transcribe any Central/Southern Mexican native date into the Mexica system. Even in a single chronicle, such as the *Anales de Cuauhtitlan*, various systems can sometimes be discerned, due to the number of independent sources that were utilized in its compilation. And even within a single tradition, such as that recounted in the *Juan Cano Relaciones*, it is possible that two, or even three, distinct year counts have been employed in different sections (Jiménez Moreno 1955: appendix; this particular example, however, has yet to be convincingly demonstrated). Neither of the two leading investigators in this area, Jiménez Moreno and Kirchhoff, has published more than a fraction of the evidence for the different systems he has proposed—which do not exactly agree. But the door into greater chronological understanding of the Central/Southern Mexican ethnohistorical sources was opened by their pioneer efforts (in which Alfonso Caso and Robert Barlow also played a significant part). Already certain ostensible contradictions in the dating of some of the events in these sources have been tentatively resolved by these new discoveries.

Even before the revelation of the existence of various independent year counts, the chronological picture in Central Mexico before the fourteenth century was never very clearly in focus. The repetitive 52-year cycles have always created serious chronological difficulties. Even without this problem, however, there was always the possibility that, due to the turbulent years following the fall of Tollan, the continuity of the year count had been interrupted in both the Basins of Mexico and Puebla. An additional complicating factor must have been the tendency on the part of certain leading polities to exaggerate their political importance by elongating the duration of their histories. Also, the seeming lack of full understanding of the mechanism of the native calendar on the part of some of the later chroniclers, such as Alva Ixtlilxochitl, has further complicated attempts to establish an acceptable chronology for Postclassic Central Mexico.

The chronology of Topiltzin Quetzalcoatl is essentially the chronology of the Toltecs, whose relative position is now in little doubt: in archaeological terms, between the collapse of Teotihuacan and the rise of such ceramic styles as Aztec II (Tenayuca) and the disappearance of Effigy Plumbate and Fine Orange. Unfortunately, it is difficult to date the former event with any precision. A round date of circa A.D. 750/800 might be accepted by many archaeologists, although others would probably prefer to slide it down by as much as one or two centuries.

The dates of the alpha and omega of Tollan, its rise to political preeminence and its fall, are the chronological hinges of Early Postclassic Central Mexico. If they could be pinned down securely within even a century, half the battle would be won. Jiménez Moreno's (1954–1955: 222–224) dates for these events, based on the *Anales de Cuauhtitlan*'s 1 Tecpatl for the beginning of the Tollan dynasty under Mixcoamazatzin and a similar year, five cycles (260 years) later for the fall, were 908 and 1168 (Mexica year count; Mixteca/Popoloca year count, which Jiménez Moreno believed may have been the Toltec system: 896 and 1156). He arrived at these dates by adding three 52-year cycles to 752, the date arrived at by counting back along the continuous year count from 1 Acatl, A.D. 1519. Unfortunately, the *Anales de Cuauhtitlan's* long continuous year count is clearly contrived and artificial, which Jiménez Moreno himself recognized by his sliding forward the three 52-year cycles.

Another important early source that provides an ostensibly continuous year count, although not in the native system, is the *Juan Cano Relaciones*. According to the explicit statement of its compilers, the continuous year count of this Colhuaque tradition went back 765 years before 1532 (= A.D. 767), or, according to another statement in the *Origen*, 783 years (= A.D. 749). However, figuring by dead reckoning from 1532, systematically adding the durations of the reigns and other events, we arrive in the *Relación* at A.D. 772 and in the *Origen* at 778. A number of other mathematical inconsistencies in these two accounts further create confusion—as does the fact that the one exact native date that can be deduced does not fit properly into the count. To make matters worse, if Jiménez Moreno was correct, three distinct year counts were employed in this tradition. All of these inconsistencies create challenging difficulties in attempting to utilize the *Juan Cano Relaciones* to set up a reliable absolute chronology for Postclassic Central Mexico. However, if its overall chronological scheme can be generally accepted, this important early source indicates that the Toltecs became established sometime in the late eighth or early ninth century and that Topiltzin Quetzalcoatl ruled, first over Teocolhuacan for sixteen years and later, after a migration lasting ten years, for four years at Tollantzinco and ten or twelve at Tollan, during the late ninth century.

The year count of the *Historia de los Mexicanos por sus pinturas*, another quite early source, has the advantage, in its opening sections, of convertibility into the native system. Later, however, during the narration of the Mexica migration, the continuity seems to be broken by omissions. The break is not substantial, however, and it probably can be reasonably calculated that the year count of this source goes back to sometime in the late tenth century (986). This would place Topiltzin Quetzalcoatl in the eleventh century (birth:

1 Acatl, 1051; departs from Tollan, 2 Acatl, 1091), considerably later than in the *Juan Cano Relaciones*. The *Leyenda de los soles*, so similar in many respects to the *Historia*, does not provide us with anything like a continuous year count, although it does give some spot native dates and some durations for Topiltzin Quetzalcoatl and the Toltec period (e.g., birth: 1 Acatl; death: 4 Tochtli, fifty-six years later). Because of the 52-year cycle repetition problem, however, it is very difficult to fit them into an overall continuous annual sequence.

The *Historia Tolteca-Chichimeca* provides an ostensible continuous year sequence back to the time of the fall of Tollan, which has been calculated (Berlin 1947), assuming all dates were in the Mexica system, to 1116, the native year 1 Tecpatl, when the Tolteca Chichimeca arrive at Tollan from Colhuacatepec. Tollan's collapse occurs only one year later(!), 2 Calli, 1117, when the Nonoalca Chichimeca desert the city—with the Tolteca Chichimeca finally making their departure in 2 Tochtli, 1130. However, Jiménez Moreno was convinced that three separate year counts could be identified in this source: Mexica, Mixtec/Popoloca, and "Tetzcocano." In his correlation chart (Jiménez Moreno 1953; 1955: appendix), he shifted the conquest of Cholollan by the Tolteca Chichimeca from the ostensible 1168 to 1292, adding two 52-year cycles and regarding the native date for it, 1 Tecpatl, to be in the Tetzcocan count rather than the Mexica (2 x 52 + 20 = 1292). Making the same adjustment for the 1 Tecpatl year at the beginning of the count would shift it forward to 1240. Jiménez Moreno, however, did not include the earlier dates in his chart, and he apparently still favored a twelfth-century date for the fall of Tollan. Apart from the problem of possible independent year counts, it seems likely that the continuity of this chronicle, like that of the *Anales de Cuauhtitlan*, is at least partly artificial and its earlier dates, in particular, should not be taken too literally.

Among the later sources, spot dates in the native system are provided by both Chimalpahin and Alva Ixtlilxochitl, who make their own equations with Christian dates, following the Mexica system. According to the former, Topiltzin Quetzalcoatl flourished between the years 4 Tochtli, 1002, and 1 Acatl, 1051. I have already expressed my doubts as to the reliability of Chimalpahin's version of the tale; I would also apply this same skepticism to his chronology. Alva Ixtlilxochitl's dates (birth of Meconetzin/Topiltzin: 1 Acatl, 900; abandonment of Tollan: 1 Tecpatl, 1011 [*sic*, for 1012]) may be based on an authentic tradition available to him, but his whole account is so aberrant that they must be seriously questioned.

The other dates in the primary sources associated with Topiltzin Quetzalcoatl are largely brief statements, such as that he was born, departed from Tollan, and died or disappeared on a certain day or in a certain year. The most frequently encountered date, of course, is 1 Acatl, either explicitly or implicitly. Deciding whether there is any historicity here is obviously quite difficult. Although it is often given as his birth *year*, individuals in ancient Mesoamerica normally took their calendric name from the *day* of their birth. Even if Topiltzin Quetzalcoatl actually was born on this day, which repeated every 260 days, this obviously is of no value in pinning him down chronologically. And supposing that 1 Acatl was the authentic *year* of his birth or demise, it aids us little in placing him more precisely in time. In my view, the chronological aspect of the Topiltzin Quetzalcoatl of Tollan Tale is one of the least satisfactory aspects of our understanding of it. Attempts, such as those of Spinden (1930: 34) and Thompson (1941a: 105–106), to fix his dates with such precision that they can be correlated with astronomical phenomena can only be regarded as highly tenuous at best.

Before leaving Central Mexico, to illustrate the chronological extremes that are encountered it is revealing to compare the dates of Sahagún for the fall of Tollan with those provided by the Xaltocan genealogy of Pablo Nazareo. The former, in the Spanish version of the *Historia* (Sahagún 1946, I: 12; II: 48), provides two dates for this event: (1) about one thousand years before 1569, or 569, after it had flourished as the Toltec capital for about an equal period of time; and (2) 1,890 years before 1571, or 319. For the Nahuatl version of the latter passage in the *Florentine Codex,* which contains the same date, Anderson and Dibble (in Sahagún 1950–1982, part IX: 15) give this translation: "This (the fall of Tollan) was in the year one thousand, one hundred and ten; from there the count reacheth and endeth at this year, 1565." Alternatively, if the figure 1,110 is to be taken as the duration of time that had elapsed since the fall until 1565, we arrive at the date 455, which is certainly closer to the others.

In striking contrast to these Sahaguntine dates are those that can be estimated based on the genealogy of the rulers of Xaltocan named in the well-known Latin letter of Pablo Nazareo (Paso y Troncoso 1939–1942, 10: 89–129), the sixteenth-century *cacique* of that community (reconstructed in Jiménez Moreno 1950). In this scheme, Huemac ("Vemactevctli") is specified as the great-great-great-great-grandfather of Motecuhzoma Ilhuicamina, who died in 1469. If this can be taken literally, it would place Tollan's fall most likely sometime in the thirteenth century. These two dramatically contrasting dates, both found in primary sources of considerable value, are typical of the challenging chronological problems that have plagued all students of pre-Hispanic Mesoamerica since the commencement of serious research into its history.

There is some evidence from outside Central Mexico relevant to the chronology of the Toltecs and Topiltzin Quetzalcoatl. Unfortunately, it is also unsatisfactory from the standpoint of absolute time. The long chronological sequence worked out by Caso for the Mixteca pictorial histories, back to 692, might bear some relevance to the problems we have been discussing, for the place sign of Tollan may be depicted—but comment must be deferred. The Highland Guatemala situation provides little aid due to lack of pre-1493 absolute dates in the important chronicles of this area. Robert Wauchope (1949), employing the generation-counting method, calculated the entry to Highland Guatemala of the ancestors of the Gumarcaah and Iximche dynasties as occurring in the early fourteenth century (1303 for the accession of Balam Quitze). He fixed at 1383 the visit to Nacxit to obtain the requisite titles and the insignia of dynastic rank. Clearly, accepting Wauchope's estimates, a twelfth-century date for the fall of Tollan would appear to be too early. And, assuming that the putative Toltec move into Guatemala was connected with the collapse of Tollan, a late thirteenth-century date would more satisfactorily fit his calculations. Likewise, if 1383 is approximately accurate for the time of Nacxit, this seems much too late for Topiltzin Quetzalcoatl and would further strengthen the titular interpretation previously suggested.

However, I am not convinced that the dynastic lists of the Highland Guatemala chronicles are complete. The last few rulers appear to be authentic, but it seems possible that as we move back in time a certain amount of nomenclatural consolidation and/or simple omission of names occurred—a well-known phenonemon that has characterized genealogical record keeping in many other parts of the world. Certainly, if other evidence supports an earlier date for the fall of Tollan, I do not believe these Highland Guatemalan chronicles by themselves negate it. Alonso de Zorita's statement (1891: 225–226) that he had seen, in the province of Utatlan, "pinturas" that went back over eight hundred years, could, if taken literally, support a somewhat earlier date for the Toltec move into Guatemala—assuming that these pictorial histories might have been of Toltec inspiration.

The northern Yucatecan situation is hardly clearer. Although exact dates in the indigenous calendric system are available for certain events that might be interpreted as coeval with the Toltec period, interpretations have varied widely. The Katun count operative in Yucatan in late pre-Hispanic times poses the same kind of repetition problem as with the 52-year cycles in Central Mexico—although the time span involved is much greater (around 256 versus 52 years).

Two important reconstructions of northern Yucatecan history place the Itza entry into Chichen Itza, the Xiu entry into Uxmal, and the Hunac Ceel Incident, which may have resulted in the virtual abandonment of the first-named center, considerably later than was previously held by many students. In the Tozzer (1957) scheme, Toltec Chichen Itza (Chichen II-III, B') lasts from 948 to 1224. Between 1224 and 1244, in a Katun 4 Ahau, the Itza arrive from Chakanputun. With them is a "Kukulcan II." Tozzer believed

"Kukulcan I," a much more shadowy figure, might have been associated with the original, much earlier Toltec entry. He placed the founding of Mayapan, with Kukulcan II prominently involved, in Katun 13 Ahau, 1263–1283. The Tutul Xiu were at Uxmal in Katun 10 Ahau, 1421–1441. He would place the Hunac Ceel Episode and the "end of Chichen" in Tun 10 (1451) of the Katun 8 Ahau, which fell between 1441 and 1461. He would also place the fall of Mayapan during this period. In this proposed reconstruction, nearly all of the events narrated in the northern Yucatecan sources, particularly the *Books of Chilam Balam*, can be dated only to the final phases of the Toltec period (hegemony of Chichen Itza) and the period of the dominance of Mayapan (Chichen IV) and later (Chichen V).

The Tozzer scheme owed much to the views of Ralph Roys (for the latter's own scheme, utilizing the *Chilam Balam* prophetic material, see Roys 1954: 8–30). The reconstructions of Barrera Vásquez and Morley (1949), based primarily on the *Maya Chronicles*, were very different and pushed the chronology much further back in time. Thompson (1954) represented a kind of chronologically intermediate view—and his reconstruction was clearly preferred by most Mesoamericanists. Although he identified the Toltec stylistic wave at Chichen Itza as being connected with the Itza invasion (for him, the Katun 4 Ahau from 987 to 1007), which Tozzer and Roys rejected, they all agreed that the Toltecs or strongly Toltec-influenced groups first moved into northern Yucatan during the tenth century.

This virtual unanimity would be more significant if it were not for the fact that most of these students in advancing their schemes for northern Yucatan seem to have been influenced to some degree by the chronological reconstructions of the Central Mexican specialists, especially those of Jiménez Moreno, rather than working them out independently. In support of this relatively early date for the Toltec advent in northern Yucatan is the tradition recorded by Chi that Chichen Itza had dominated the northern peninsula for over two thousand years, ending, it would seem, eight hundred or a thousand years before the recording of the tradition (i.e., 600–800), when Quetzalcoatl/Kukulcan entered and introduced "idolatry." Actually, if the apogee of Chichen Itza could be placed after this entry, it would appear to fit the archaeological and Central Mexican ethnohistorical evidence much better. Sánchez de Aguilar's (1639: 101–102) statement that the Mexicans had conquered Yucatan six hundred years before the Conquest is also significant here.

It is clear from the ethnohistorical evidence that there was probably more than one important movement of Nahua-speakers, ultimately from Central Mexico, into northern Yucatan. Probably not all were directly connected with the Toltecs proper, although the one that first introduced the "Mexican" style at Chichen Itza might have stemmed more or less directly from Tollan. Interestingly, the Tutul Xiu, probably originally a Nahua-speaking group, provide one intriguing item of evidence in favor of their relatively early appearance in the peninsula. Their name, Tutul Xiu, is Nahua for "Turquoise Bird" (= Classical Nahuatl: Tototl Xihuitl). This may well have had reference to the devices featuring this depiction that are so common on Toltec-style headdresses in the art of Chichen Itza of this period—and which are also common at Tula. Probably a badge of rank, the Nahua name of this headgear might well have been applied as a kind of titulary nickname to the Toltec-connected ancestors of the dynasty ruling at Mani in the sixteenth century. If so, a cogent case could be made for a much earlier Yucatecan presence for the Tutul Xiu, back to Toltec Chichen Itza, than either Roys or Tozzer (cf., however, a similar earlier suggestion of the latter [in Landa 1941: 30]). The brief Xiu Family Tree (Morley and Brainerd 1956: plate 22), which Roys (1954: 19) cited in support of his shorter Tutul Xiu chronology, I would not regard as controlling, since various generations may have been skipped due to genealogical condensation and/or loss of records—as has been suggested for Highland Guatemala.

If Topiltzin Quetzalcoatl of Tollan is dated to the beginning of Toltec history—perhaps most likely to sometime in the tenth century—and if the Roys-Tozzer reconstruction is correct, he can hardly be equated with the Kukulcan who accompanied the Itza to Chichen Itza between 1224 and 1244. On the other hand, Kirchhoff (1955a) argued strongly for positioning Topiltzin Quetzalcoatl at the end of the Toltec period, rather than near its commencement, where he would correlate well with Tozzer's "Kukulcan II." For his late dating of our hero, Kirchhoff relied principally on the later native and mestizo historians Chimalpahin, Alva Ixtlilxochitl, and Muñoz Camargo. In contrast, as we have seen, the earlier accounts generally tend to support the view that Topiltzin Quetzalcoatl's career unfolded at or near the beginning of the Toltec epoch—or, in any case, not at its end, a position that clearly belonged to Huemac. Kirchhoff argued skillfully and ingeniously for his reconstruction, but such clear-cut statements (not explicitly cited by Kirchhoff) as that in the *Historia de los Mexicanos por sus pinturas* that Topiltzin was the *first* ruler of Tollan are difficult to argue away. And since, as noted, most of the other members of the core group support a reconstruction of the Tollan dynasty in which Topiltzin Quetzalcoatl ruled well before Huemac, this version, in my view, is to be preferred. Topiltzin Quetzalcoatl's contemporaneity with Huemac, even though it appears to be supported by no less an authority than Sahagún, may be due largely to post-Conquest condensation and confusion.

The Tozzer suggestion of *two* Kukulcan/Quetzalcoatls entering Yucatan, one with the initial Toltec wave in the tenth century and the second with the Itza in the thirteenth, was an ingenious way of resolving certain chronological difficulties. I have already discussed the considerable evidence for the titular use of these names, which Tozzer justifiably cited in support of his scheme. However, my own feeling—and it is little more—is that it is likely that there was only one *outstanding* figure in northern Yucatan who bore these names, although the deeds of lesser leaders who bore them as titles might have been merged with him by the time these historical traditions were recorded after the Conquest.

Another significant item of evidence relevant to Toltec chronology comes from the traditions of the Nahua-speakers of distant Nicaragua. As pointed out earlier, this might have been sometime in the eighth or ninth century. Although the Bobadilla interrogatory makes no mention of a Tollan origin, citing two little-known places instead, it seems possible, judging from what is recorded concerning their religion, mythology, and calendar, that the ancestors of the Nicarao emigrated—perhaps near the beginning of that period—from somewhere within the Toltec cultural orbit. If so, Torquemada's tradition, noted above, might provide additional evidence for a fairly early date for Toltec beginnings. The evidence of glottochronology (Swadesh 1954–1955) also would support a substantially early date (about the sixth century) for the initial dispersion of the Nahua-speakers, although these earliest movements were probably pre-Toltec (cf. Jiménez Moreno 1954–1955: 120–122).

From this necessarily brief review, it is clear that the chronology of the Toltec period and Topiltzin Quetzalcoatl still presents quite challenging problems. No two leading students seem to closely agree, a clear reflection of the highly contradictory nature of the evidence. The whole question needs a very intensive critical reexamination, utilizing all relevant evidence throughout Mesoamerica. Until this is done, it is probably safe to say that most students would still tend to favor a ninth- or tenth-century date for the rise of the Toltec empire and a twelfth- or thirteenth-century date for its dissolution. Again, I believe, contrary to Kirchhoff's reconstruction, that the preponderance of evidence still supports the view, particularly identified with Jiménez Moreno, that Topiltzin Quetzalcoatl can best be dated at or soon after the establishment of Tollan as a major political center and that his departure probably marked a serious disruptive episode in the history of Tollan rather than its final collapse. As for the dates associated with Topiltzin Quetzalcoatl's life and career, their contradictory nature and the fact that they are extremely difficult to place within a continuous count due to the repetitive 52-year-cycle problem largely negate their value in locating our hero more precisely in time. This must come from consideration of all of the relevant evidence, ethnohistorical, archaeological, and linguistic. Much research remains to be done, which, if prosecuted thoroughly, might well lead to a considerably improved understanding of the chronology of imperial Tollan and its most famous ruler.

3. Geographical Aspects

While it is not my intention to discuss each and every place associated with Topiltzin Quetzalcoatl, some comment on the spatial aspect of the tale is called for, to complement the discussion of the temporal dimension just concluded. Most of the relevant places can be at least generally located on the map (see the map of Postclassic Mesoamerica, pp. lxii–lxiii), although some may always defy precise pinpointing. Only those that are particularly important or involve problems of special interest will be considered here.

The first of these is the place of Topiltzin Quetzalcoatl's birth. The three leading candidates—aside from Tollan itself—are (Teo)colhuacan, (Teo)huitznahuac, and Michatlauhco. Although Jiménez Moreno and others have identified the first with the Colhuacan of the Basin of Mexico, I believe the evidence is compelling that, at Contact, it was a semilegendary place of origin—with the most obvious meaning of "sacred curved, or bent place." It also figured prominently in various of the migration narratives of the Late Postclassic Central Mexican peoples, including those of the ancestors of the Azteca/Mexica, and was believed to be located somewhere off to the west or northwest. Most of the colonial native annals, for instance, when describing the 1529 West Mexican *entrada* of Nuño de Guzmán, specify Colhuacan, Teocolhuacan, or Hueycolhuacan as his destination. A large town, in what is now the state of Sinaloa, on Mexico's north Pacific coast, was given this name by Nuño de Guzmán's native auxiliaries and still bears a corrupted form of it, Culiacan. Kirchhoff (1955a: 178), following a suggestion of Martínez del Río, advanced the notion that the Colhuacan/Teocolhuacan of the Azteca/Mexica migration accounts could be identified with another Culiacan, in Guanajuato. However, as with the perennial game of attempting to establish the actual locations of Aztlan and Chicomoztoc, I would regard as basically futile any attempt to pin down with geographical precision a place whose location, according to the *Juan Cano Relaciones*, even the natives themselves were uncertain of at the time of the Conquest. In any case, it is of considerable interest that one important early tradition placed the birth of Topiltzin Quetzalcoatl and the scene of his early life in a fundamentally mystical place of origin at some distance from Central Mexico.

Huitznahuac, "spiney or thorny place," clearly meant "south" in a generic sense (variants: *huitzlampa*, *huitztlan*) and has so been interpreted in this context. It has also been identified (e.g., Müller 1949: map 1) with a community in the southern Basin of Mexico, near Chalco. Jiménez Moreno (1945: 13) suggested that it referred to the general region of Morelos and adjoining areas, the territory of the southern Nahua who, in his reconstruction, had preceded the Toltecs into Central Mexico.

Michatlauhco, "barranca of the fish," is only named in the *Histoyre du Mechique* as Topiltzin Quetzalcoatl's birthplace. Jiménez Moreno (1945: 13), in line with his conviction that Morelos was the scene of his early life, suggested that this place (otherwise unknown, as far as I am aware) was located in this region, near Tepoztlan. He did not cite any concrete evidence in support, however, and the location of Michatlauhco appears to be unknown.

A number of places in the general region of Tollan are named in connection with Topiltzin Quetzalcoatl, especially in Sahagún and the *Anales de Cuauhtitlan*. Jiménez Moreno (1945: 10–11), with the aid of an unpublished eighteenth-century map, was able to identify certain of these places, which were (and, in some cases, are) still known under their ancient names at that time. An important place obviously near Tollan was Nonoalco, which was also the general term for the southern Gulf Coast region. It has yet to be exactly located, although Jiménez Moreno suggested that the modern "Cerro de Magoni," to the west of Tula, might be equated with the Nonoalcatepetl.

Perhaps the most interesting geographical aspect of the tale is the itinerary of Topiltzin Quetzalcoatl's "flight." Its general route, in a southeastward direction, from Tollan through the Basin of Mexico, between the twin volcanoes into the Basin of Puebla, then down into the Gulf Coast lowland, where Topiltzin Quetzalcoatl dies or disappears somewhere in southern Veracruz, Tabasco, or further east, can readily be traced. The majority of place-names along the route can be identified. Some, such as the Tepehuitonco and Ayanco of the "Toltec Dirge," Teponazcuicatl, assuming they really belong to the itinerary, cannot. Two especially interesting ones are Zacanco and Cuixcoc. They have been located in northeastern Guerrero (Jiménez Moreno 1954–1955: 226), where a community bearing the former name still exists. There is also some evidence from Chimalpahin Cuauhtlehuanitzin that similarly named places were located in the Chalco area of the Basin of Mexico, which would appropriately fit their position in the overall itinerary. Two others from the *Leyenda de los soles*, Tzonmolco (the temple of the Fire God and a merchant ward in Mexico Tenochtitlan) and Mazatzonco, although probably lying between the Basin of Mexico and Oaxaca, are more difficult to locate.

At the terminus of his journey, three names stand out: Coatzacoalco, Acallan, and (Tlillan) Tlapallan (with two others intimately associated with this last: Tlatlayan and Poctlan). The location of the first two is well known: the first ("sanctuary of the serpent"), at the mouth of the modern river of that name, and the second ("place of canoes"), in the Río Candelaria drainage, in southern Campeche. Tlillan Tlapallan ("the place of the black and red colors" or "the place of writing"), on the other hand, seems to have been a more mythical place. Seler, followed by Jiménez Moreno, suggested that its name might have had reference to the Maya country, the area of "writing" par excellence; certainly, it was located in that direction. Melgarejo Vivanco

(1949: 47) believed that it could be located precisely, to the extent of identifying it, together with Poctlan ("place of smoke") with two towns in Veracruz (near Totutla and Axocuapan, respectively). Another Tlapallan, the "old," he believed was that mentioned in the *Relación de Espíritu Santo* (Coatzacoalco) of 1580 and in an unpublished document of 1591—which he identified with a *ranchería* of Chinameca, near Jaltipan (1949: 47, 491). Tlatlayan ("place of burning") has been identified (Covarrubias 1947: 137) with a modern village of that name in the district of Los Tuxtlas, Veracruz. All of these putatively precise identifications may be tantalizing, but I believe that to the Conquest-period inhabitants of the plateau Tlapallan and associated places were located in the same vague way as Teocolhuacan, Chicomoztoc, and other localities that were connected with semilegendary origins and migrations.

This is well brought out by the references to (Hue)Tlapallan in the letters of Cortés and Pedro de Alvarado. The reference in the 1526 fifth *Carta y relación* of Cortés (1946: 601–602) is particularly revealing:

> . . . tengo noticia de muy grandes y ricas provincias y de grandes señores en ellas, de mucha manera y servicio, en especial de una que llaman Hueitapalan, y en otra lengua Xucutaco, que ha seis años que tengo noticia della y por todo esto camino he venido en su rastro, y tuvo por nueva muy cierta que está ocho o diez jornadas de aquella villa de Trujillo, que puede ser cincuenta o sesenta leguas, y desta hay tan grandes nuevas que es cosa de admiración lo que della se dice, que aunque falten los dos tercios hace mucha ventaja a esta de Méjico en riqueza e iguálale en grandeza de pueblos y multitud de gente y policía della.

The parallel to Teocolhuacan is particularly close. These places were essentially legendary and, in colonial times, smacked more than a little of El Dorado. The location of Cortés's "Hueitapalan," so far east in Honduras, is interesting. His account is paralleled by Pedro de Alvarado's (1924: 87) statement in his 1524 second letter to Cortés, during his conquest of Guatemala, that he planned to search for the province of "Tepalan," located fifteen days' journey into the northern interior (from Santiago, Guatemala), where there was a city as great as Mexico Tenochtitlan, with large flat-roofed stone buildings. The mystical, "fabulous kingdom" aspect of Tlapallan is also well brought out by Torquemada's (1943–1944, II: 50) citing of the questioning of Sahagún concerning its location by the natives (Xochimilca) themselves.

What is perhaps most significant about the geographical aspect of the tale is that the world of Topiltzin Quetzalcoatl, with certain exceptions—particularly his place of origin and that of his death or disappearance—was essentially quite specifically located in space. The majority of the places mentioned probably would have been familiar to most hearers of the tale at the time of the Conquest—and it could be argued that this geographic specificity does perhaps add some additional support for its at least partial historicity.

4. Nomenclatural and Etymological Aspects

Although it is beyond the limits of this study to enter into detailed etymologies of all of the indigenous language names in the relevant sources, some remarks on certain of the most important, particularly the names applied to Topiltzin Quetzalcoatl himself, are in order.

Beginning with his parents, the name of his father, Mixcoatl ("cloud serpent"), presents no problems, but Totepeuh has been interpreted in two different ways. Lehmann (1938: 69) preferred "unser Berg" (*to-tepe-uh*), in which he has been followed by others. A more likely etymology, however, is probably "conqueror," or "our glory" (*tepeuani*, "conquistador, o vencedor de batalla"; Molina 1944, part II: 101, verso). A direct relation to the Tepeuh of the Highland Guatemala chronicles seems very likely.

Chimalma(n), his mother's name, was translated "Ruhender Schild" by Lehmann (1938: 72). The simpler etymology, "shield-hand" (*chimal[li]-ma[itl]*), seems more likely, however, perhaps alluding to the manner of her encounter with Mixcoatl (cf. Acolman, *Acol[li]-ma[itl]-n*). Her probable identification with the earth goddess has already been noted.

As for our hero himself, Topiltzin (*to-pil[li]-tzin*), "our prince" or "our son," has been generally accepted from the beginning. Quetzalcoatl (*quetzal[li]-coatl*) literally translates "quetzal feather snake." "Feathered serpent," although not literal, seems acceptable. "Precious snake" is a reasonable supplementary interpretation, due to the precious nature of the long green tail feathers of this highly prized bird, *Pharomachrus mocinno*. "Precious twin" is not impossible, since *coatl* did have this double meaning (Molina 1944, part II: 23, recto; Mendieta 1945, I: 119), but the romantic fancies derived from this etymology are hardly justified. Tlamacazqui, "priest," largely speaks for itself.

Perhaps the most interesting of the proper names is Nacxit(l). The usual etymology is "four foot" (*na[hui]-[i]cxitl*), which seems acceptable. It has often been interpreted (e.g., Lehmann 1922: 293) as referring to the four cardinal points (from which the wind blows). Jiménez Moreno (n.d.: 52), however, made a tantalizing suggestion that is worthy of serious consideration. He pointed out that a calendric sign exists in the system of Xochicalco that represents a *foot*. This was almost surely a day sign. Four Foot, then, could well have been another calendric name for our hero, derived from the earlier *tonalpohualli* day-sign system of Xochicalco and perhaps other Epiclassic cultures. There is archaeological evidence that this great Morelos center exerted a significant cultural influence on the young, growing Tollan. Interestingly, Sahagún (1946, I: 56; 1950–1982, part II: 19) also gives this name as one of the "brothers" of Yacatecuhtli, the merchant deity, who bears considerable resemblance to Quetzalcoatl. It has even been suggested, somewhat dubiously, that Y(i)-acatecuhtli is actually a corrupted form of Ce Acatl Tecuhtli, thus Quetzalcoatl (Jiménez Moreno, cited in Acosta Saignes 1945: 39).

As noted, Nacxit possessed special importance in Highland Guatemala (cf. Cab-ra-kan = One Foot). Assuming its validity, this calendric interpretation opens up some tantalizing possibilities that involve the problem of the nature of the relationship between Xochicalco and Tollan. Unfortunately, the equivalence of the Xochicalco foot glyph to the corresponding day sign in the system current in Central Mexico at the time of the Conquest is uncertain. Ehecatl is a possibility (cf. Caso 1955: 22–23, who equates Ehecatl with "ojo de reptil"). If so, it is undoubtedly significant that Nahui (4) Ehecatl is given by the interpreters of the *Codices Telleriano-Remensis* and *Vaticanus* A as the name for a god (especially revered by the rich merchants, who celebrated an important ceremony on that day [Sahagún 1946, I: 359]). Iconographically, he is a hybrid of Tlaloc and Ehecatl Quetzalcoatl and functioned as the patron of the seventh *tonalpohualli trecena* beginning 1 Quiahuitl (Rain). The Stuttgart jade image of a macabre aspect of Quetzalcoatl (Seler 1902–1923, III: 241–261) also bears this date.

An interesting name, mentioned only in the *Historia Tolteca-Chichimeca*, is "Tepeuhqui." It is highly probable that, like Totepeuh, this name bears an intimate relation to the Highland Guatemalan Tepeuh, and in this context probably signifies "the mighty one," "the glorious one," etc. (*qui* is merely an adjectival suffix). Alva Ixtlilxochitl's "Meconetzin" does seem to signify, as he states, "son, or child, of maguey" (*me*[*tl*]*-cone*[*tl*]*-tzin*), but this name is found in no other source and cannot be considered one of the standard appellations of our hero. Tlahuizcalpantecuhtli, "lord of the house of dawn," although strictly speaking the name of the Venus god who essentially constituted a distinct supernatural personality, can perhaps be considered, in a broad sense, another name of Topiltzin Quetzalcoatl, due to his conversion into that star—as can Xolotl, "monster," or "double," who possibly, in one aspect, was considered the god of the Evening Star. Sahagún (1946, I: 325–326; 1950–1982, part IV: 59–60) also gives Tlilpotonqui, "he who is feathered in black," as another name for Quetzalcoatl in his capacity as patron of the priestly school, the *calmecac*. This may refer to one of his distinctive insignia, the neck fan, *cuezalhuitoncatl*, of alternating red and black feathers (see Seler 1902–1923: 436–437).

The commonest of the calendric names, of course, is Ce (1) Acatl (Reed), which hardly calls for extended explanation. Chiconahuil (9) Ehecatl (Wind) may belong also to Topiltzin Quetzalcoatl—but perhaps more fitly to Ehecatl Quetzalcoatl. As previously noted, one of the interpreters of the *Codex Telleriano-Remensis* gives it as an alternative birth date for Topiltzin Quetzalcoatl. In Chalco (*Histoyre du Mechique* 1905: 31) and the southern Basin of

Puebla (Motolinía 1903–1907: 347), the Creator went under this name, just as in distant Nicaragua. The importance in the Mixteca pictorial histories of a god and/or legendary ancestor bearing this name has already been cited—and the twin hero gods of the Cuilapan cosmogony bore it as a calendric name. The Stuttgart jade image of the skeletal Quetzalcoatl also bears this date, as does a stone mask in the Berlin Museum für Völkerkunde, described by Seler (1902–1923, III: 174–176), where it functions as the calendric name of an image of Ehecatl Quetzalcoatl carved on its back. Other days in the native calendar associated with Quetzalcoatl are 7 Acatl (birth date according to the *Codices Vaticanus* A and *Telleriano-Remensis*) and 1 Ehecatl (Sahagún 1946, I: 385–386).

This multiplicity of names for both historical individuals and gods is typically Mesoamerican. In the case of the latter, it probably functioned as a device to express more than one aspect of the divinity. Both Ehecatl Quetzalcoatl and Topiltzin Quetzalcoatl were characteristic in this regard.

XII. Conclusions

In addition to summarizing and analyzing all of the available primary documentary accounts concerning him—plus some consideration of the possibly relevant archaeological evidence—the central problem of this study was to clarify, if possible, the cultural-historical role of the most prominent figure in pre-Hispanic Central Mexican tradition: Topiltzin Quetzalcoatl of Tollan. With historical problems, no definitive "solutions" can, of course, be offered. As Kroeber (e.g., 1952: 79) repeatedly stressed, the student of history, in anthropology or elsewhere, rather than "solving" or "proving,"

> . . . infers greater or lesser probabilities—probabilities of fact, of relation, of significance. His whole business, beyond the assemblage of materials, is a judicial weighing of possibilities and a selection and combination of these into the most coherent whole or pattern. The process is one of progressive reconstruction, until the total fabric, with all its ramifications and complications, attains the most harmonious fit possible of all its parts.

The most significant question to be raised at this point, after this long verbal safari through one particularly dense patch of the tangled jungle of Mesoamerican ethnohistory, is: Does a coherent whole or pattern emerge in regard to Topiltzin Quetzalcoatl? I suggest that the answer depends largely on what level is being sought. The time is hardly ripe for a depth probe into the psyche of our hero. On the other hand, I also feel that solar mythologists and kindred souls will find little enlightenment in the tale. Although we see him only through a glass darkly, perhaps the lineaments of a flesh-and-blood individual are sufficiently discernible that we can begin to seriously consider the contribution he may have made to the cultural-historical process in Postclassic Mesoamerica. It was earlier suggested that Topiltzin Quetzalcoatl may have occupied one of those key transitional bridges between two distinct cultural levels, which often provide fortuitously positioned leaders with exceptional opportunities for initiating positive cultural innovation and achievement. Certainly, accepting some degree of historicity for the tale, it seems unlikely that it would have been just an ordinary life and public career that impacted so strongly on the historical consciousness of the Mesoamerican groups that had most clearly inherited and/or been influenced by the Toltec tradition.

At the beginning of the data presentation section it was pointed out that by the very fact of organizing the material in a certain way, some interpretation of the data was unavoidably anticipated. It has long been recognized that "raw facts" never simply "speak for themselves." In itself, the process of organizing the data to present them in a meaningful fashion entails selectivity, judgment of relevance and significance, and some degree of interpretation. My system of data presentation revealed that I regarded one particular set of sources, the "core" group, as possessing the greatest reliability and value for our knowledge of what I designated the Basic Topiltzin Quetzalcoatl of Tollan Tale. These six accounts, which in general outline compare reasonably well with each other, provided the principal raw data for my reconstruction of the tale.

I fully recognize that, by focusing instead on the later accounts, a very different version of the basic tale would emerge (e.g., Kirchhoff 1955a). In support of my choices, I would like to reiterate my conviction that all of them convey the authentic ideology of the pre-Hispanic *calmecac* much more effectively than more "rational" and "logical"—i.e., significantly Europeanized—accounts of the late sixteenth- and early seventeenth-century Spanish-educated native and mestizo chroniclers. It is also obvious from my organizational scheme that I believe that the white-skinned "foreign missionary" version of the tale is largely late and unreliable—although it must be recognized that it first appears as early as the account of Fray Andrés de Olmos. In its more fully developed form, however, it appeared somewhat later and has, in my view, unduly influenced the thinking of many scholars concerning the career of Topiltzin Quetzalcoatl and his impact on Mesoamerican civilization.

To sum up my views—at the risk of a certain amount of repetition—I would like to suggest the following conclusions, or, more accurately, hypotheses, concerning the subject of this study:

(1) Topiltzin Quetzalcoatl was conceivably a genuine historical figure prominently involved with an early stage of Toltec history; (2) if so, he later seems to have become blended and, occasionally, to some extent confused with certain supernatural personalities, particularly an ancient fertility/rain/wind/creator deity, Ehecatl Quetzalcoatl; (3) possibly the son of an important early conqueror, Mixcoatl/Totepeuh, he assumed the secular and sacerdotal leadership of a vigorous group of Nahua-speakers established at Tollan; (4) while in power, he appears to have introduced or presided over the introduction of significant cultural innovations, especially in the religious sphere but also in other aspects of the culture; (5) due to circumstances that are obscure but which may have primarily involved opposition to his religious doctrines, a conflict developed in Tollan to such proportions that Topiltzin Quetzalcoatl was forced to leave, probably with a sizable number of followers; (6) heading generally in a southeastward direction, with a possible stopover in Cholollan, he reached the Gulf Coast and either moved further eastward, disappeared, or died; (7) the suggestion that "the" Topiltzin Quetzalcoatl of Tollan actually led a group into northern Yucatan and established a new political capital there, Chichen Itza, has often been made and is certainly conceivable, although an alternative hypothesis invoking different leaders bearing the names Kukulcan, Quetzalcoatl, Nacxit, etc., as *titles* seems more likely; (8) in addition to his religious role, which is stressed in the sources from both Central Mexico and northern Yucatan, Topiltzin Quetzalcoatl appears also to have functioned importantly as a political leader/consolidator and was best remembered by the Toltec-connected dynasts of Highland Guatemala as the dispenser of all valid political authority; (9) the evidence for a widespread belief in his eventual return to reclaim his power, which might have significantly influenced Motecuhzoma II of Mexico Tenochtitlan—who apparently was considered to be the direct dynastic successor of Topiltzin Quetzalcoatl—during his initial dealings with Cortés, is quite strong.

Finally, in this study I have attempted to provide my fellow scholars with a useful compilation of basic data concerning Mesoamerica's most celebrated priest/ruler, with a preliminary analysis and interpretation of this extensive corpus of primary source material. Future studies, my own hopefully included, will no doubt move forward, building on the mass of information that I have presented in such detail. If Kroeber was right in emphasizing that sound culture history is essentially the interrelating of patterns and configurations into increasingly wider and more meaningful contexts, then no historical study is ever "final" in more than the most relative sense. Like Topiltzin Quetzalcoatl, I do solemnly prophesy a return to this problem on the part of many future students, building steadily upon the work of one another. This study is intended to be one more link in that chain of greater understanding.

References Cited

Abrams, H. Leon Jr.

1973 "Comentario sobre la sección colonial del *Códice Telleriano-Remensis.*" *Anales del Insituto Nacional de Antropología e Historia*, ser. 7, 3: 139–176.

Acosta, Jorge

1940 "Exploraciones en Tula, Hidalgo, 1940." *Revista mexicana de estudios antropológicos* 4, no. 3: 172–194.

1941 "Los últimos descubrimientos arqueológicos en Tula, Hidalgo." *Revista mexicana de estudios antropológicos* 5, nos. 2–3: 239–248.

1942 "La ciudad de Quetzalcoatl, exploraciones arqueológicas en Tula, Hidalgo." *Cuadernos americanos*, año 1, vol. 2, no. 2: 121–131.

1943 "Los colosos de Tula." *Cuadernos americanos*, año 2, vol. 12, no. 6: 138–146.

1944 "La tercera temporada de exploraciones arqueológicas en Tula, Hidalgo, 1942." *Revista mexicana de estudios antropológicos* 6, no. 3: 125–157.

1945 "Las cuarta y quinta temporadas de exploraciones arqueológicas en Tula, Hidalgo, 1943–1944." *Revista mexicana de estudios antropológicos* 7, nos. 1–3: 23–64.

Acosta, José de

1590 *Historia natural y moral de las Indias*. Seville: Juan de León.

1962 *Historia natural y moral de las Indias*. 2nd edition, revised. Edición preparada por Edmundo O'Gorman, con un prólogo, tres apéndices, y un índice de materias. Biblioteca americana. Serie de cronistas de Indias, 38. Mexico City: Fondo de Cultura Económica.

1963 *Historia natural y moral de las Indias: Vida religiosa y civil de los Indios.* Prólogo y selección, Edmundo O'Gorman. Biblioteca del estudiante universitario, 83. Mexico City: Universidad Nacional Autónoma de México.

1977 *Historia natural y moral de las Indias.* Introducción, apéndice, y antología por Barbara G. Beddall. Valencia: Valencia Cultural.

1987 *Historia natural y moral de las Indias.* Edición de José Alcina Franch. Madrid: Historia 16, Crónicas de América, 34.

Acosta Saignes, Miguel

1945 *Los pochteca: Ubicación de los mercaderes en la estructura social tenochca.* Acta Anthropologica 1, no. 1. Mexico City: Escuela Nacional de Antropología e Historia.

Acuña, René

1973 "Problemas del *Popol Vuh.*" *Mesta, Revista de literatura-creación-teoría-interpretación* 5: 123–176.

1984–1988 Editor, new versions of all of the 1579–1585 series *relaciones geográficas* of Nueva España, published by the Instituto de Investigaciones Antropológicas of the Universidad Nacional Autónoma de México—cited under their authors' names.

Alva Ixtlilxochitl, Fernando de

1829 *Horrible crueldades de los conquistadores de México y de los Indios que los auxiliaron.* Carlos María Bustamante, ed. First publication of the *Relación Décima Tercera* of the *Noticia de los Pobladores.* Mexico City: Imprenta de Alejandro Valdés.

1838 *Cruautes horribles des conquérants du Mexique, et des indien qui les aiderent à soumettre cet empire à la couronne d'Espagne.* French translation of the *Relación décima tercera* of the *Noticia de los pobladores.* In Henry Ternaux-Compans, *Voyages, relations et mémoires originaux por servir à l'histoire de la découverte de l'Amérique*, vol. 8. Paris: Arthus Bertrand.

1848 *Historia chichimeca* and *Relaciones.* In Kingsborough 1830/31–1848, vol. IX: 197–468.

1891–1892 *Obras históricas de Don Fernando de Alva Ixtlilxochitl.* Publicadas y anotadas por Alfredo Chavero. 2 vols. Mexico City: Oficina Tipográfica de la Secretaría de Fomento.

1952 *Obras históricas de Don Fernando de Alva Ixtlilxochitl.* Publicadas y anotadas por Alfredo Chavero. Prólogo de esta edición por el Sr. Lic. J. Ignacio Dávila Garibi. 2 vols. Reprint of 1891–1892 Chavero edition. Mexico City: Editora Nacional, S.A. 2nd edition, 1965.

1975–1977 *Obras históricas.* Incluyen el texto completo de las llamadas *Relaciones* e *Historia de la nación chichimeca* en una nueva versión establecida con el cotejo de los manuscritos mas antiguos que se conocen. Edición, estudio introductorio y un apéndice documental por Edmundo O'Gorman. Mexico City: Universidad Nacional Autónoma de México, Instituto de Investigaciones Históricas, Serie de historiadores y cronistas de Indias, 4, 2 vols.

Alvarado, Pedro de

1924 *An Account of the Conquest of Guatemala in 1524*. Edited by S. J. Mackie. New York: The Cortés Society.

1953 *Two Letters of Pedro de Alvarado*. In Fuentes 1963: 183–196.

1954 *Relación hecha por Pedro de Alvarado a Hernando Cortés*. Mexico City: José Porrúa e Hijos Sucs.

Alvarado Tezozomoc, Hernando

1878 *Crónica mexicana escrita por D. Hernando Alvarado Tezozomoc hacia el año de MDXCVII*. Anotada por el Sr. Lic. D. Manuel Orozco y Berra y precedida del *Códice Ramírez*, manuscrito del siglo XVI intitulado, *Relación del origen de los Indios que habitan esta Nueva España según sus historias*, y de un examen de ambas obras, al cual va anexo un estudio de cronología mexicana por el mismo Sr. Orozco y Berra. Mexico City: Imprenta y Litografía de I. Paz.

1944a *Crónica mexicana*. Escrita hacia el año de 1598. Notas de Manuel Orozco y Berra. Mexico City: Editorial Leyenda, S.A.

1944b *Crónica mexicana*. Selección y introducción por Mario Marsical. Mexico City: Secretaria de Educación Pública, Biblioteca Enciclopédia Popular, 33.

1949 *Crónica mexicayotl*. Traducción directa del Náhuatl por Adrián León. Universidad Nacional Autónoma de México, Instituto de Historia, en colaboración con el Instituto Nacional de Antropología e Historia. Mexico City: Imprenta Universitaria. 2nd edition, 1975.

1975 *Crónica mexicana escrita por D. Hernando Alvarado Tezozomoc hacia el año de MDXCVII*. Anotada por el Sr. Lic. D. Manuel Orozco y Berra. Reprint of 1878 Orozco y Berra edition. Biblioteca Porrúa, 61. Mexico City: Editorial Porrúa, S.A. 2nd edition, 1987.

Alvarez Lomeli, María Cristina

1969 *Descripción estructural del maya del "Chilam Balam de Chumayel."* Mexico City: Universidad Nacional Autónoma de México, Seminario de Estudios de la Escritura Maya, Cuaderno 1.

1974 *Textos coloniales del "Libro de Chilam Balam de Chumayel" y textos glíficos del "Códice de Dresde."* Universidad Nacional Autónoma de México, Coördinación de Humanidades, Centro de Estudios Mayas, Cuaderno 10.

Anónimo Mexicano

1903 In *Anales del Museo Nacional de México* 7: 115–132.

Anonymous Conqueror

1917 *Narrative of Some Things of New Spain and of the Great City Temestitan, Mexico, Written by the Anonymous Conqueror, a Companion of Hernán Cortés*. M. H. Saville, translator and annotator. Documents and Narratives Concerning the Discovery and Conquest of Latin America, no. 1. New York: The Cortés Society.

1941 *El conquistador anónimo: Relación de algunas cosas de la Nueva España, y de la gran ciudad d Temestitán México escrita por un compañero de Hernán Cortés*. Edited by León Díaz Cárdenas. Mexico City: Editorial América.

1963 *The Chronicle of the Anonymous Conqueror*. In Fuentes 1963: 165–181.

1967 *Relación de algunas cosas de la Nueva España y de la gran ciudad Temestitan México, hecha por un gentilhombre del señor Fernando Cortés*. Francisco de la Maza, trans. Biblioteca José Porrúa Estrada de Historia Mexicana, dirigida por Jorge Gurría Lacroix, Primera Serie, La Conquista. Mexico City: José Porrúa e Hijos, Sucs.

1970 *Le Conquistador Anonyme*. Traduction, introduction et notes de Jean Rose. Mexico City: Institut Francais d'Amérique Latine.

Armillas, Pedro

1947 "La serpiente emplumada: Quetzalcoatl y Tlaloc." *Cuadernos americanos*, año 6, vol. 31, no. 1: 161–178.

Aubin, Joseph Marius Alexis

1885 *Mémoires sur la peinture didactique et l'écriture figurative des anciens Mexicains*. Introduction by E. T. Hamy. Mission Scientifique au Mexique et dans l'Amérique Centrale, Recherches Historiques et Archéologiques, Première Partie: Histoire. Paris: Imprimerie Nationale.

Bancroft, Hubert Howe

1882–1883 *The Native Races of the Pacific States*. 5 vols. San Francisco: A. L. Bancroft and Company. 1st edition, New York, 1974–1975.

Bandelier, Adolph F. A.

1884 *Report of an Archaeological Tour in Mexico, in 1881*. Papers, Archaeological Institute of America, American Series, 2. Boston: Published for the Institute by Cupples, Upham, and Company.

Barlow, Robert H.

1945 "La crónica 'X': Versiones coloniales de la historia de los mexica tenochca." *Revista mexicana de estudios antropológicos* 7, nos. 1–3: 65–85.

Barrera Vásquez, Alfredo

1939 "El Códice Pérez." *Revista mexicana de estudios antropológicos* 3, no. 1: 69–83.

1943 "Horoscopos mayas o el pronóstico de los 20 signos del tzolkin." *Registro de cultura yucateca* 1, no. 6. Mérida.

Barrera Vásquez, Alfredo, and Sylvanus G. Morley

1949 "The Maya Chronicles." *Contributions to American Anthropology and History* 10, no. 48: 1–86. Washington, DC: Carnegie Institution of Washington Pub. 585.

Barrera Vásquez, Alfredo, and Silvia P. Rendón, trans. and eds.

1948 *El libro de los "Libros de Chilam Balam."* Mexico City: Biblioteca Americana. Serie de Literatura Indígena. Fondo de Cultura Económica.

Baudot, Georges

1971 "Les premières enquetes ethnographiques américaines. Fray Toribio Motolinía: Quelques documents inédits et quelques remarques." *Cahier du Monde Hispanique et Luso-Brésilien* (Caravelle) 17: 7–35.

1977 *Utopie et histoire au Mexique: Les premiers chroniquers de la civilisation mexicaine (1520–1569)*. Toulouse: Editions Edouard Privat.

1983 *Utopía e historia en México: Las primeros cronistas de la civilización mexicana (1520–1569)*. Traducción del Francés por Vicente González Loscertales. Madrid: Espasa-Calpe, S.A.

1995 *Utopia and History in Mexico: The First Chroniclers of Mexican Civilization (1520–1569)*. Translated by Bernard R. Ortiz de Montellano and Thelma Ortiz de Montellano. Niwot: University Press of Colorado.

Beltrán de Santa Rosa, Pedro

1746 *Arte de el idioma maya reducido a succintas reglas, y semilexicon yucateco . . . año de 1742*. Mexico City: Viuda de Don J. Bernardo de Hogal.

Berlin, Heinrich

1947 "Ensayo sincronológico." In *Historia tolteca-chichimeca* 1947: xi–xvi.

1950 "La historia de los Xpantzay." *Antropología e historia de Guatemala* 2, no. 2: 40–53.

Beyer, Hermann

1920 "Las cruces en el manto de Quetzalcoatl." *Revista de revistas*, año XI, no. 543: 21.

Bierhorst, John

1974 *Four Masterworks of American Indian Literature: Quetzalcoatl/The Ritual of Condolence/Cuceb/The Night Chant*. Edited, and with commentaries and new translations, by John Bierhorst. New York: Farrar, Straus and Giroux.

1985a *Cantares Mexicanos: Songs of the Aztecs*. Stanford: Stanford University Press.

1985b *A Nahuatl-English Dictionary and Concordance to the "Cantares Mexicanos," with an Analytic Transcription and Grammatical Notes*. Stanford: Stanford University Press.

Blom, Frans

1928 "Gaspar Antonio Chi, Interpreter." *American Anthropologist* 30, no. 2: 250–262.

Boban, E. Eugène

1891 *Documents pour servir à l'histoire du Mexique*. 2 vols. and atlas. Paris: E. Leroux.

Boone, Elizabeth Hill

1988 "The Nature and Earlier Versions of Diego Durán's *Historia de las Yndias* in Madrid." In *Smoke and Mist: Mesoamerican Studies in Memory of Thelma D. Sullivan*. Edited by J. Kathryn Josserand and Karen Dakin, sections coordinated by H. B. Nicholson, Doris Heyden, Karen Dakin, and Nicholas A. Hopkins. Oxford: BAR (British Archaeological Reports) International Series 402 (i), Part i: 41–58.

Boturini Benaducci, Lorenzo

1746 *Idea de una nueva historia general de la América Septentrional*. Madrid: Imprenta de Juan de Zúñiga.

Brasseur de Bourbourg, Charles Etienne

1851 *Lettres pour servir d'introduction à l'histoire primitive des nations civilisées de l'Amérique septentrionale adresées à Monsieur le Duc de Valmy. Cartas para servir de introducción à la historia primitiva de las naciones civilizadas de la América Setentrional.* México City.

1857–1859 *Histoire de nations civilisées du Mexique et de l'Amérique-Centrale durant les siècles antérieurs à Christophe Colomb.* 4 vols. Paris: Arthus Bertrand.

1861 *"Popol Vuh." Le Livre sacré et les mythes de l'antiquité américaine, avec les livres héröiques et historiques de Quichés.* Collection de documents dans les langues indigènes, pour servir à l'étude de l'histoire et de la philologie de l'Amérique ancienne, 1. Paris: Arthus Bertrand.

Breton, Adela C.

1917 "Preliminary Study of the North Building (Chamber C), Great Ball Court, Chichén Itzá, Yucatán." In *Proceedings of the 19th International Congress of Americanists* (Washington, DC, 1915): 187–194.

Bricker, Victoria R.

1990a *A Morpheme Concordance of the "Book of Chilam Balam of Chumayel."* New Orleans: Middle American Research Institute, Tulane University, Publication 59.

1990b *A Morpheme Concordance of the "Book of Chilam Balam of Tizimin."* New Orleans: Middle American Research Institute, Tulane University, Publication 58.

Brinton, Daniel G.

1876 *The Myths of the New World: A Treatise on the Symbolism and Mythology of the Red Race of America.* 2nd edition, revised. New York: Holt.

1881 "The Names of the Gods in the Kiché Myths of Central America." *Proceedings of the American Philosophical Society* 19: 613–647.

1882a *The Maya Chronicles.* Philadelphia: Brinton's Library of Aboriginal American Literature, no. 1.

1882b *American Hero-Myths: A Study in the Native Religions of the Western Continent.* Philadelphia: H. C. Watts and Co.

1885 *The Annals of the Cakchiquels.* Philadelphia: Brinton's Library of Aboriginal American Literature, vol. 6.

1887a *Ancient Nahuatl Poetry, Containing the Nahuatl Text of XXVII Ancient Mexican Poems.* With a translation, introduction, notes, and vocabulary by Daniel G. Brinton. Philadelphia: Brinton's Library of Aboriginal American Literature, no. VII. Reprint edition, 1969 New York: AMS Press.

1887b "On the So-Called Alagüilac Language of Guatemala." *Proceedings of the American Philosophical Society* 24: 366–377.

1893 "The Native Calendar of Central America and Mexico: A Study in Linguistics and Symbolism." *Proceedings of the American Philosophical Society* 31: 258–324.

Brotherston, Gordon

1979 *Image of the New World: The American Continent Portrayed in Native Texts*. London: Thames and Hudson.

Brotherston, Gordon, and Ana Gallegos

1990 "El *Lienzo de Tlaxcala* y el *Manuscrito de Glasgow* (Hunter 242)." *Estudios de cultura náhuatl* 20: 117–140.

Bruce, Robert D.

1976–1977 "The *Popol Vuh* and the *Book of Chan K'in*." *Estudios de cultura maya* X: 173–208.

Burgess, Dora M. de, and Patricio Xec

1955 *Popol Wuj*. Quetzaltenango: Tipografía "Él Noticiero Evangélico."

Burgoa, Fray Francisco de

1674 *Geográfica descripción de la parte septentrional del Polo Ártico de la América, y Nueva Iglesia de las Indias Occidentales, y sitio astronómico de esta provincia de predicadores de Anteqvera Valle de Oaxaca*. 2 vols. Mexico City: En la Impr. de Iuan Ruyz.

1934 *Geográfica descripción*. 2 vols. Publicaciones del Archivo General de la Nación, 25–26. Mexico City: Talleres Gráficos de la Nación.

1989 *Geográfica descripción de la parte septentrional del Polo Ártico de la América y Nueva Iglesia de las Indias Occidentales y sitio astronómico de esta provincia de predicadores de Antequera, Valle de Oaxaca*. 2 vols. Breve presentación por Barbro Dahlgren. Biblioteca Porrúa, 97–98. Mexico City: Editorial Porrúa.

1996 *Geográfica descripción de la parte septentrional del Polo Ártico de la América*. 2 vols., facsimilar. Mexico City: Grupo Editorial Miguel Angel Porrúa.

Burland, Cottie A.

1947 "Einige Bemerkungen über den *Codex Vindobonensis Mexicanus I*." *Archiv für Völkerkunde* 2: 101–107.

1953 *Magic Books from Mexico*. Harmondsworth: Penguin.

1955 *The Selden Roll: An Ancient Mexican Picture Manuscript in the Bodleian Library at Oxford*. Monumenta Americana herausgegeben von der Ibero-Amerikanischen Bibliothek zu Berlin, Schriftleitung: Gerdt Kutscher, II. Berlin: Verlag Gebr. Mann.

Bustamante, Carlos María de

1840 *La aparición de Ntra. Señora de Guadalupe de México comprobada con la refutación del argumento negativo que presenta D. Juan Bautista Muñoz, fundándose en el testimonio del P. Fr. Bernardino Sahagún, ó sea, historia original de este escritor que altera la publicada en 1829 en el equivocado concepto de ser la única y original de dicho autor*. Mexico City: Imprenta de Ignacio Cumplido.

Cabrera, Pablo Félix

1822 *Teatro crítico americano, or, a Critical Investigation and Research into the History of the Americas*. In Antonio del Río, *Description of the Ruins of an*

Ancient City Discovered Near Palenque, in the Kingdom of Guatemala, 30–123. London: H. Berthoud, and Suttaby, Evance and Fox.

Cakchiquels, Annals of: Editions of this chronicle are listed by their editors and translators.

Cárdenas, Salvador de

1905–1907 *Relación de Ahuatlan y su partido*. In Paso y Troncoso 1905–1907, V: 91–99.

1985 (1581) *Relación de Ahuatlan y su partido*. In *Relaciones geográficas del siglo XVI*. Edición de René Acuña. Tomo segundo: 65–85. Mexico City: Universidad Nacional Autónoma de México, Instituto de Investigaciones Antropológicas, Etnohistoria, Serie Antropológica, 59.

Carmack, Robert M.

1966 "El Ajpop Quiche, Kúkúmatz: Un problema de la sociología histórica." *Antropología e historia de Guatemala* 18, no. 1: 43–47.

1967 *Toltec Influence on the Postclassic Culture History of Highland Guatemala*. New Orleans: Middle American Research Institute, Tulane University, Publication 26: 49–92.

1973 *Quichean Civilization: The Ethnohistoric, Ethnographic, and Archaeological Sources*. Berkeley, Los Angeles, London: University of California Press.

1979a *Evolución del reino quiché*. Traducción de Danilo A. Palma. Guatemala City: Editorial Piedra Santa.

1979b *Historia social de los Quichés*. Publicación/Seminario de Integración Social Guatemalteca, no. 38. Guatemala City: Editorial "José de Pineda Ibarra," Ministerio de Educación.

1981a "New Quichean Chronicles from Highland Guatemala." *Estudios de cultura maya* XIII: 84–103.

1981b *The Quiché Mayas of Utatlán: The Evolution of a Highland Guatemala Kingdom*. Norman: University of Oklahoma Press.

Carmack, Robert, and Francisco Morales Santos, eds.

1983 *Nuevas perspectivas sobre el "Popol Vuh."* Papers presented to the Primer Congreso sobre el Popol Vuh, Santa Cruz del Quiché, June 4–8, 1979. Guatemala City: Editorial Piedra Santa.

Carmack, Robert M., John W. Fox, and Russell E. Stewart

1975 *La formación del reino Quiché*. Guatemala City: Instituto de Antropología e Historia, Publicación Especial, no. 7.

Carmack, Robert M., and Alfonso Efra Tzaquitzal Zapeta

1993 *Título de los señores Coyoy*. Transcripción k'iche' de Robert M. Carmack; traducción k'iche'-español de Alfonso Efra Tzaquitzal Zapeta. 2nd ed. Guatemala City: Comisión Interuniversitaria Guatemalteca de Conmemoración del Quinto Centenario del Descubrimiento de América.

Carrasco, Pedro

1950 *Los Otomíes*. Mexico City: Universidad Nacional Autónoma de México, Publicaciones del Instituto de Historia, primera serie, no. 15.

1951 "Review of Recinos 1953." *American Antiquity* 20, no. 2: 181–182.

Carrera Stampa, Manuel

1945 "Algunos aspectos de la historia de Tlaxcala de Diego Muñoz Camargo." In *Estudios de historiografía de la Nueva España*, H. Díaz-Thome, ed., 91–142. Mexico City: Publicaciones del Centro de Estudios Históricos, El Colegio de México.

Caso, Alfonso

1941a "El complejo arqueológico de Tula y las grandes culturas indígenas de México." *Revista mexicana de estudios antropológicos* 5, nos. 2–3: 85–95.

1941b *Culturas mixteca y zapoteca*. Biblioteca del Maestro, 23. Culturas Precortesianas, 1. Mexico City: El Nacional.

1949 "El mapa de Teozacoalco." *Cuadernos americanos*, año 8, vol. 47, no. 5: 145–181.

1950 "Explicación del reverso del *Codex Vindobonensis*." *Memoria de el Colegio Nacional*, 5, no. 5: 9–46.

1951 "Base para la sincronología mixteca y cristiana." *Memoria de el Colegio Nacional* 6, no. 6: 49–66.

1954 *Interpretación del Códice Gómez de Orozco*. Mexico City: Talleres de Impresión de Estampillas y Valores.

1955 *El calendario mexicano*. Mimeographed.

1960 "The Historical Value of the Mixtec Codices." *Boletín de estudios oaxaqueños* 16: 1–7.

1961 "Los lienzos mixtecos de Ihuitlan y Antonio de León." In *Homenaje a Pablo Martínez del Río*, 237–274. Mexico City: Instituto Nacional de Antropología e Historia.

1964 "Mixtec Writing and Calendar." In *Handbook of Middle American Indians*, vol. 3, part 2: *Archaeology of Southern Middle America*, Robert Wauchope, general editor; Gordon Willey, volume editor, 948–961. Austin: University of Texas Press.

1965 *Los calendarios prehispánicos*. Mexico City: Universidad Nacional Autónoma de México, Instituto de Investigaciones Hisóricas, Serie de Cultura Náhuatl, Monografías, 6.

1977–1979 *Reyes y reinos de La Mixteca: Diccionario biográfico de los señores mixtecos*. 2 vols. Mexico City: Fondo de Cultura Económica.

Chapman, Anne M.

1960 *Los nicarao y los chorotega según las fuentes históricas*. San José: Publicaciones de la Universidad de Costa Rica, Serie Historia e Geografía, No. 4.

Charnay, Désiré

1887 *The Ancient Cities of the New World, Being Voyages and Explorations in Mexico and Central America from 1857–1882*. Translated by J. Gonino and H. S. Conant. New York: Harper and Brothers.

Chavero, Alfredo

1880 "Apéndice: Explicación del códice geroglífico de Mr. Aubin." Appendix in Durán 1867–1880, II: 1–172.

1887 *Historia antigua y de la conquista*. México a través de los siglos, 1. Mexico City: Balleseca y Comp.

Chávez, Adrián, trans.

1979 *Pop wuj (Libro de Acontecimientos): Traducción directa del manuscrito del Padre Jiménez*. Mexico City: Ediciones de la Casa Chata, Centro de Investigaciones Superiores del INAH.

1987 *Pop wuj = poema mito-histórico ki-che*. Traducido del texto original por Adrián I. Chávez, prólogo de Carlos Guzman Bökler, nota preliminar y revisión, Adolfo Colombres. Buenos Aires: Ediciones del Sol, Biblioteca de Cultura Popular, 7.

Chávez Orozco, Luis

1933 *La civilización nahoa*. Mexico City: Cuadernos de Divulgación Histórica de la Secretaria de Educación Pública, Talleres Gráficas de la Nación.

Chilam Balam, Books of: These works are cited by their editors and translators.

Chimalpahin Cuauhtlehuanitzin, Domingo Francisco de San Antón Muñón

1889 *Annales de Domingo Francisco de San Antón Muñón Chimalpahin Quauhtlehuanitzin, sixième et septième relations (1258–1612)*. Pub. et tr. sur le manuscrit original par Rémi Siméon. Paris: Maisonneuve et C. Leclerc, Bibliothèque Linguistique Américaine, 12. Nendeln: Kraus Reprint edition, 1968.

1949 See Rendón 1949.

1949–1952 *Diferentes historias originales de los reynos de Culhuacan, y de México, y de otras provincias*. El autor de ellas dicho Don Domingo Chimalpahin. Manuscrit Mexicain No. 74. Liber in lingua mexicana manuscriptus ut est conservatus in Biblioteca Nationis Gallicae Parisiensi sub numero LXXIV. Cum praefatione in lingua Britannica, Gallica, Germanica et Hispana atque indice paginarum edidit Ernst Mengin. Corpus Codicum Americanorum Medii Aevi, vol. III. 3 vols. Copenhagen: Einar Munksgaard.

1958 *Das "Memorial breve acerca de la fundación de la ciudad de Culhuacan" und weitere ausgewählte Teile aus den "Diferentes historias originales"* (Ms. Mexicain No. 74, Paris), von Domingo de San Antón Muñón Chimalpahin Quauhtlehuanitzin. Aztekischer Text und deutscher Übersetzung von Walter Lehmann und Gerdt Kutscher. Stuttgart: W. Kohlhammer Verlag, Quellenwerke zur alten Geschichte Amerikas aufgezeichnet in Sprachen der Eingeborenen, Herausgegeben von der Ibero-Amerikanischen Bibliothek zu Berlin, Schriftleitung: Gerdt Kutscher, VI.I.

1963 *Die Relationen Chimalpahin's zur Geschichte México's*. Teil 1: Die Zeit zur Conquista 1521. Text herausgegeben von Günter Zimmermann. Universität Hamburg, Abhandlungen zur dem Gebiet der Auslandskunde,

Band 68—Reihe B (Völkerkunde, Kulturgeschichte und Sprachen), Band 38. Hamburg: Cram, De Gruyter & Co.

1991 *Memorial breve acerca de la fundación de la ciudad de Culhuacan.* Domingo Francisco de San Antón Muñón Chimalpain Cuauhtlehuanitzin. Estudio, paleografía, introducción, notas e índice analítico por Victor M. Castillo F. Mexico City: Universidad Nacional Autónoma de México, Instituto de Investigaciones Históricas, Serie de Cultura Náhuatl, Fuentes, 9.

1997 *Codex Chimalpahin: Society and Politics in Mexico Tenochtitlan, Tlatelolco, Texcoco, Culhuacan, and Other Nahua Altepetl in Central Mexico: The Nahuatl and Spanish Annals and Accounts Collected and Recorded by Don Domingo de San Antón Muñón Chimalpahin Quauhtlehuanitzin.* Edited and translated by Arthur J. O. Anderson and Susan Schroeder; Wayne Ruwet, manuscript editor, Susan Schroeder, general editor. 2 vols. Norman: University of Oklahoma Press, The Civilization of the American Indian Series, Vols. 225, 226.

n.d. "Memorial breve acerca de la fundación de la ciudad de Culhuacan." Spanish translation by Miguel Barrios. Ms.

[Ciudad Real, Antonio de]

1872 *Relación breve y verdadera de algunas cosas de las muchas que sucedieron al padre fray Alonso Ponce . . .* [ca. 1588]. Colección de documentos inéditos para la historia de España, 57–58. Madrid: Imprenta de la Viuda de Calero.

Clavigero, Francisco Javier

1883 *Historia antigua de México y de su conquista, sacada de los mejores historiadores españoles, y de los manuscriptos y pinturas antiguas de los Indios.* Traducida del Italiano por J. Joaquín de Mora. 2 vols. Mexico City: Dublán.

Cline, Howard F.

1964 "The Relaciones Geográficas of the Spanish Indies." *Hispanic American Historical Review* 44, no. 3: 341–374.

1972 "The Chronology of the Conquest: Synchronologies in *Codex Telleriano-Remensis* and Sahagún." *Journal de la Société des Américanistes* 62, no. 1: 9–33.

Cline, Sarah L.

1988 "Revisionist Conquest History: Sahagún's Revised Book XII." In *The Work of Bernardino de Sahagún: Pioneer Ethnographer of Sixteenth-Century Aztec Mexico,* J. Jorge Klor de Alva, H. B. Nicholson, and Eloise Quiñones Keber, eds., vol. 2: 93–106. Albany: Institute for Mesoamerican Studies, The University at Albany, State University of New York, Studies on Culture and Society.

Codex Bodley

1830/1831 In Kingsborough 1830/1831–1848, I: 154–193.

1960a Alfonso Caso, *Interpretación del Códice Bodley 2858*. Mexico City: Sociedad Mexicana de Antropología.

1960b Alfonso Caso, *Interpretation of the Codex Bodley 2858*. Translated by Ruth Morales and revised by John Paddock. Mexico City: Sociedad Mexicana de Antropología.

1964 In Kingsborough 1964–1967, vol. II: 31–99. Estudio e interpretación, José Corona Núñez.

Codex Colombino-Becker I

1961 *Codices Becker I/II; Museum für Völkerkunde, Wien, Inv. Nr. 60306 und 0307*. Kommentar und Beschreibung: Karl Anton Nowotny. Graz: Akademische Druck- u. Verlagsanstalt, Codices selecti phototypice impressi, vol. 4.

1964 *Codices Becker I/II; Museo de Etnología de Viena, No. inventario 60306 y 60307*. Comentario, descripción y corrección de Karl Anton Nowotny. Traducción española de Baron W. v. Humboldt, revisada por Gastón García Cantú. Mexico City: Instituto Nacional de Antropología e Historia, Codices selecti phototypice impressi vol. 4.

1966 Alfonso Caso, *Interpretación del Códice Colombino*. Las glosas del Códice Colombino: Mary Elizabeth Smith. Mexico City: Sociedad Mexicana de Antropología.

1974 Nancy Troike, "The Codex Colombino-Becker." Ph.D. dissertation, University of London.

1997 *Códice Alfonso Caso: La vida de 8-Venado, Garra de Tigre (Colombino-Becker I)*. Introducción: Miguel León-Portilla. Mexico City: Patronato Indígena, AC.

Codex Telleriano-Remensis

1830/1831 In Kingsborough 1830/1831–1848, I: 1–47, V: 127–158, VI: 95–123.

1899 *"Codex Telleriano-Remensis," manuscrit mexicain du cabinet de Ch. M. Le Tellier, archevêque de Reims, à la Bibliothèque nationale (ms. mexicain no. 385) reproduit en photochromographie aux frais du duc de Loubat et précédé d'une introduction contenant la transcription complète des anciens commentaires hispano-mexicains par le Dr. E. T. Hamy*. Anger, France: Imp. Burdin, Section Orientale de l'Imp. Camiseteia, Paris.

1964 In Kingsborough 1964–1967, I: 151–337. Estudio e interpretación, José Corona Núñez.

1995 Eloise Quiñones Keber, *Codex Telleriano-Remensis: Ritual, Divination, and History in a Pictorial Aztec Manuscript*. Foreword by Emmanuel Le Roy Ladurie. Illustrations by Michel Besson. Austin: University of Texas Press.

Codex Vaticanus A

1830/1831 In Kingsborough 1830/1831–1848, II:159–206, V: 159–206, VI: 155–232.

1964 In Kingsborough 1964–1967, III: 7–313. Estudio e interpretación, José Corona Núñez.

1979 *Codex Vaticanus 3738 ("Cod. Vat. A," "Cod. Ríos") der Biblioteca Apostolica Vaticana.* Farbreproduktion des Codex in Verkleinertem Format. Introductory note by Hans Biedermann. Codices Selecti, Phototypice Impressi, Vol. LXV, Codices e Vaticanis Selecti, quam simillime expressi, Jessu Joannis Pauli PP. II, Consilio et Opera Curatorum Bibliotecae Apostolica Vaticanae. Vol. XXXVI. Graz: Akademische Druck- und Verlagsanstalt.

1990 Il *manoscritto messicano vaticano 3738, detto il Codice Rios, riprodotto in fotocromografia a spese di sua eccellenza il duca di Loubat per cura della Biblioteca Vaticana.* Rome: Stabilimento Danesi.

1996 *Religión, costumbres e historia de los antiguos Mexicanos: Libro explicativo del llamado Códice Vaticano A, Codex Vatic. Lat. 3738 de la Biblioteca Apostólica Vaticana.* Introducción y explicación: Ferdinand Anders/ Maarten Jansen. Graz: Akademische Druck- und Verlagsanstalt; Mexico City: Fondo de Cultura Económica.

Codex Vindobonensis

1929 *Codex Vindobonensis Mexic. 1; Faksimileausgabe der mexikanischen Bilderhandschrift der National-Bibliothek in Wien.* Reproduktion der Kunstanstalt Max Jaffe; eingeleitet durch Walter Lehmann und Ottokar Smital. Vienna: Verlag für Nord-und Südamerika Kunstanstalt M. Jaffé.

1963 *Codex Vindobonensis Mexicanus 1.* Österreichische Nationalbibliothek, Wien. History and description of the manuscript MS, Otto Adelhofer. Graz: Akademische Druck- und Verlagsanstalt, codices selecti phototypice impressi, vol. 5.

1967 In Kingsborough 1964–1967, vol. IV: 51–183. Estudio e interpretación, José Corona Núñez.

1974 *Codex Vindobonensis Mexicanus 1 vollständige Faksimile-Ausgabe im Original format.* History and description of the manuscript, Otto Adelhofer. Graz: Akademische Druck- und Verlagsanstalt, Codices selecti phototypice impressi, vol. 5.

1992 *Origen e historia de los reyes Mixtecos: Libro explicativo del llamado Códice Vindobonensis, Codex Vindobonensis Mexicanus 1, Österreichische Nationalbibliothek, Vienna.* Introducción y explicación: Ferdinand Anders, Maarten Jansen, y Gabina Aurora Pérez Jiménez. Madrid: Sociedad Estatal Quinto Centenario; Graz: Akademische Druck- und Verlagsanstalt; Mexico City: Fondo de Cultura Económica.

Codex Xolotl: See Dibble 1951, 1980.

Codex Zouche-Nuttall

1902 *Codex Nuttall: Facsimile of an Ancient Mexican Codex Belonging to Lord Zouche of Harynworth, England.* With an introduction by Zelia Nuttall. Cambridge: Peabody Museum of American Archaeology and Ethnology, Harvard University.

1974 *Códice Nuttall: Reproducción del facsímile editado por el Museo Peabody de la Universidad de Harvard.* Introducción por Zelia Nuttall. Mexico City: La Estampa Mexicana.

1975 *The Codex Nuttall: A Picture Manuscript from Ancient Mexico.* The Peabody Museum facsimile edition edited by Zelia Nuttall. With new introductory text by Arthur G. Miller, The Center for Pre-Columbian Studies, Dumbarton Oaks. New York: Dover Publications, Inc.

1987 *Codex Zouche-Nuttall: British Museum London (Add. Ms. 39671).* Vollständige Faksimile-Ausgabe im Original Format. Vorwort, Ferdinand Anders. Introduction, Nancy P. Troike. Graz: Akademische Druck- und Verlagsanstalt, codices selecti photoypice impressi, vol. 84.

1992 *Crónica mixteca: El rey 8 Venado, Garra de Jaguar, y la dinastía de Teozacualco-Zaachila.* Libro explicativo del llamado *Códice Zouche-Nuttall,* Ms. 39671 British Museum, Londres. Introducción y explicación: Ferdinand Anders, Maarten Jansen, y Gabina Aurora Pérez Jiménez. Madrid: Sociedad Estatal Quinto Centenario; Graz: Akademische Druck- und Verlagsanstalt; Mexico City: Fondo de Cultura Económica.

Códice Ramirez: See Tovar.

Códice de Yanhuitlan

1940 *Códice de Yanhuitlán.* Edición en facsimile y con un estudio preliminar por Wigberto Jiménez Moreno y Salvador Mateos Higuera. Mexico City: Secretaría de Educación Pública, Instituto Nacional de Antropología e Historia, Museo Nacional.

Colston, Steven A.

1973a "Fray Diego Durán's *Historia de las Indias de Nueva España e islas de la tierra firme*: A Historiographical Analysis." Ph.D. dissertation, Department of History, University of California, Los Angeles.

1973b "The 'Historia Mexicana' and Durán's *Historia.*" *Journal de la Société des Américanistes* 62, no. 1: 35–42.

1974 "Tlacaelel's Descendants and the Authorship of the 'Historia Mexicana.'" *Indiana: Beiträge zur Völker- und Sprachenkunde, Archäologie und Antropologie des Indianischen Amerika* 2: 35–42.

1977 "A Comment on Dating the 'Crónica X.'" *Tlalocan: Revista de fuentes para el conocimiento de las culturas indígenas de México* 7: 371–377.

1980 "Establishing the Character of the *Codex Durán*: A Historiographer's Approach to Mesoamerican Ethnohistory." Paper presented at the Annual Meeting of the Southwestern Anthropological Association, San Diego, California, April 10, 1980.

1985 "Fray Diego Durán and the Localistic Orientation of His *Historia.*" *Indiana: Beiträge zur Völker- und Sprachenkunde, Archäologie und Anthropologie des Indianischen Amerika* 10: 121–128.

1988 "Fray Diego Durán and His Native Informants." In *Smoke and Mist: Mesoamerican Studies in Memory of Thelma D. Sullivan.* J. Kathryn Josserand and Karen Dakin, eds.; sections coordinated by H. B. Nicholson, Doris Heyden, Karen Dakin, and Nicholas A. Hopkins. Oxford: BAR (British Archaeological Reports) International Series 402 (i), Part i: 59–65.

Córdova, Fray Juan de

1578 *Vocabulario en lengua zapoteca*. Mexico City: Pedro Charte y Antonio Ricardo.

1942 *Vocabulario castellano-zapoteca* (Edición Facsimilar). Introducción y notas de Wigberto Jiménez Moreno. Mexico City: Instituto Nacional de Antropología e Historia, Biblioteca Lingüística Mexicana, I.

Cornyn, John H., ed. and trans.

1931 *The Song of Quetzalcoatl*. Yellow Springs, OH: The Antioch Press.

Corona Núñez, José

1946 "La religión de los tarascos." *Anales del Michoacán*, segunda época, 4: 13–38.

1948 "Esquema de deidades de los tarascos antiguos." In *Cuarta Reunión de Mesa Redonda: Del occidente de México* (celebrada en el Museo Nacional de Historia del 23 al 28 de septiembre de 1946), 139–145.

Cortés, Fernando

1946 *Hernán Cortés: Cartas y relaciones con otros documentos relativos a la vida y a las empresas del conquistador*. Prólogo y notas de Nicolás Coronado. Buenos Aires: Emecé Editores, S.A.

1958 *Hernán Cortés: Cartas de relación*. Nota preliminar de Manuel Alcalá. Mexico City: Editorial Porrúa, S.A., Colección "Sepan cuantos," 7.

1961 *Hernán Cortés: Cartas y documentos*. Introducción de Mario Hernández Sánchez-Barba. Mexico City: Editorial Porrúa, S.A., Biblioteca Porrúa, 2.

1971 *Hernán Cortés: Letters from Mexico*. Translated and edited by A. R. Pagden, with an introduction by J. H. Elliott. New York: An Orion Press Book, Grossman Publishers.

1984 *Hernán Cortés: Cartas de relación*. Edición de Mario Hernández. Madrid: Historia 16, Crónicas de América, 10.

Couch, Christopher

1983 "Fragments of History: Paste-Over Illustrations in the Durán Manuscript." Paper presented at the Annual Meeting, American Society for Ethnohistory, Albuquerque, New Mexico, November 1983.

Covarrubias, Miguel

1947 *Mexico South, the Isthmus of Tehuantepec*. New York: Alfred A. Knopf.

1957 *Indian Art of Mexico and Central America*. New York: Alfred A. Knopf.

Craine, Eugene R., and Reginald C. Reindorp, eds. and trans.

1979 *The Codex Pérez and the Book of Chileam Balam of Mani*. Norman: University of Oklahoma Press, Civilization of the American Indian Series, 150.

Crónica mexicayotl

1948 See Alvarado Tezozomoc 1949.

Cuauhtitlan, Anales de

1885 *Anales de Cuauhtitlan: Noticias históricas de México y sus contornos*. J. F. Ramírez, ed.; F. Galicia Chimalpopoca, G. Mendoza, and F. Sánchez

Solís, trans. In *Anales del Museo Nacional de México* 3, Apéndice, Documentos para la Lingüística de la República: 65–84. Mexico City: Imprenta de Ignacio Escalante.

1938 *Die Geschichte der Königreiche von Colhuacan und Mexico*. Text mit Übersetzung von Walter Lehmann, Dr. med. et phil., Prof. h. c. des Nationalmuseums in Mexico. Quellenwerke zur alten Geschichte Amerikas aufgezeichnet in den Sprachen der Eingeborenen. Herausgegeben vom Ibero-Amerikanischen Institut, Berlin. Stuttgart and Berlin: Verlag von W. Kohlhammer. Also cited as Lehmann 1938.

1945 *Códice Chimalpopoca: Anales de Cuauhtitlan y Leyenda de los soles*. Traducción directa del náhuatl por el licenciado don Primo Feliciano Velázquez. Universidad Nacional Autónoma de México, Instituto de Historia, Publicaciones del Instituto de Historia, Primera Serie, Número 1. Mexico City: Imprenta Universitaria. Cited as Velázquez 1945.

1974 *Die Geschichte der Königreiche von Colhuacan und Mexico*. Text mit Übersetzung von Walter Lehmann, Dr. med. et phil., Prof. h. c. des Nationalmuseums in Mexico. Zweite, um ein Register vermehrte und berichtigte Auflage, herausgegeben von Gerdt Kutscher. Quellenwerke zur alten Geschichte Amerikas aufgezeichnet in den Sprachen der Eingeborenen. Herausgegeben Ibero-Amerikanischen Institut Preussischer Kulturbesitz, Schriftleitung Gerdt Kutscher. Stuttgart, Berlin, Köln, Mainz: Verlag W. Kohlhammer.

1975 *Códice Chimalpopoca: Anales de Cuauhtitlan y Leyenda de los soles*. Traducción directa del náhuatl por Primo Feliciano Velázquez. Mexico City: Universidad Nacional Autónoma de México, Instituto de Investigaciones Históricas, Primera Serie Prehispánica, 1. Paperback reprint edition of Velázquez 1945.

1992a *History and Mythology of the Aztecs: The Codex Chimalpopoca (Annals of Cuauhtitlan* and *Legend of the Suns)*. Translated from the Nahuatl by John Bierhorst. Tucson and London: University of Arizona Press. Paperback reprint edition, 1998.

1992b *Codex Chimalpopoca*. The text in Nahuatl with a glossary and grammatical notes by John Bierhorst. Tucson and London: University of Arizona Press.

Dahlgren de Jordán, Barbro

1953 "Etnografía prehispánica de la costa del golfo." *Revista Mexicana de Estudios Antropológicos* 13, nos. 2–3: 145–161.

1954 *La Mixteca, su cultura e historia prehispánica*. Colección Cultura Mexicana, 11. Mexico City: Imprenta Universitaria. Later reprint editions: 1966, 1979, 1990.

de la Fuente, Beatriz, Silvia Trejo, and Nelly Gutiérrez Solana

1988 *Escultura en piedra de Tula: Catálogo*. Mexico City: Universidad Nacional Autónoma de México, Instituto de Investigaciones Estéticas, Cuadernos de Historia del Arte, 50.

de la Garza, Mercedes, ed.

1985 *Libro de Chilam Balam de Chumayel.* Traducción del maya al castellano, Antonio Mediz Bolio, prólogo, introducción, y notas, Mercedes de la Garza. Cien de México. Mexico City: Secretaría de Educación Pública.

Dibble, Charles E.

1951 *Códice Xolotl.* Editado en colaboración por las Universidades de Utah y de México. Universidad Nacional Autónoma de México, Publicaciones del Instituto de Historia, Primera Serie, No. 22.

1980 *Códice Xolotl.* Edición, estudio y apéndice de Charles E. Dibble. Universidad Nacional Autónoma de México, Instituto de Investigaciones Históricas, Serie *Amoxtli*: 1.

Dorantes de Carranza, Baltasar

1902 *Sumaria relación de las cosas de la Nueva España.* Mexico City: Imprenta del Museo Nacional.

Durán, Fray Diego

1867–1880 *Historia de las Indias de Nueva España y islas de tierra firme.* La publica con un atlas de estampas, notas e illustraciones, José F. Ramírez. 2 vols. and atlas of plates. Mexico City: Imprenta de J. M. Andrade y F. Escalante.

1951 *Historia de las Indias de Nueva España y islas de tierra firme.* La publica con un atlas de estampas, notas e illustraciones, José F. Ramírez. 2 vols. and atlas of plates. Mexico City: Editora Nacional, S.A.

1964 *The Aztecs: The History of the Indies of New Spain.* Translated, with notes, by Doris Heyden and Fernando Horcasitas. Introduction by Ignacio Bernal. New York: Orion Press.

1967 *Historia de las Indias de Nueva España e islas de tierra firme.* Escrita por Fray Diego Durán, Dominico, en el siglo XVI. Edición paleográfica del manuscrito autografo de Madrid, con introducción, notas y vocabulario de palabras indígenas y arcaicas. La prepara y da a luz Angel Ma. Garibay K. 2 vols. Mexico City: Editorial Porrúa, S.A., Biblioteca Porrúa, 36–37.

1971 *Book of the Gods and Rites and the Ancient Calendar by Fray Diego Durán.* Translated and edited by Fernando Horcasitas and Doris Heyden. Foreword by Miguel León-Portilla. Norman: University of Oklahoma Press.

1980 *Ritos y fiestas de los antiguos mexicanos.* Introducción y vocabulario por César Macazaga Ordoño. Series: El arte y la historia de México en libros. Mexico City: Editorial Cosmos.

1989 *Códice Durán.* Proyecto y textos, Electra y Tonatiuh Gutierrez. Mexico City: Arrendadora Internacional.

1990–1991 *Historia de las Indias de Nueva España e islas de tierra firme.* Prólogo, José Rubén Romero Galván; transcripción, Francisco González Varela; revisión, Javier Portús; fotografías, Rafael Doniz. 2 vols. Santander: Banco Santander; Mexico City: Ediciones Equilibrista; Madrid: Turner Libros.

1994 *The History of the Indies of New Spain.* By Fray Diego Durán. Translated, annotated, and with an introduction by Doris Heyden. The Civilization of the American Series, vol. 210. Norman and London: University of Oklahoma Press.

1995 *Historia de las Indias de Nueva España e islas de tierra firme*. Estudio preliminar, Rosa Carmelo y José Rubén Romero. 2 vols. Consejo Nacional para la Cultura y las Artes. Mexico City: Cien de México.

Dutton, Bertha P.

1955 "Tula of the Toltecs." *El Palacio* 62, nos. 7–8: 195–251.

Dyckerhoff, Ursula

1970 "Die "Crónica Mexicana" des Hernando Alvarado Tezozomoc: Quellenkritische Untersuchungen." Dissertation zur Erlangung der Doktorwürde der Philosophischen Fakultät der Universität Hamburg. Hamburger Reihe zur Kultur- und Sprachwissenschaft, Band 7. Herausgeber Arbeitskreis anthropologischer Wissenschaften an der Universität Hamburg.

Edmonson, Munro S.

1971 *The Book of Counsel: The "Popol Vuh" of the Quiche Maya of Guatemala*. Munro S. Edmonson. New Orleans: Middle American Research Institute, Tulane University, Publication 35.

1974 *Sixteenth-Century Mexico: The Work of Sahagún*. Edited by Munro S. Edmonson. A School of American Research Book. Albuquerque: University of New Mexico Press.

1982 *The Ancient Future of the Itza: The "Book of Chilam Balam of Tizimin."* Translated and annotated by Munro S. Edmonson. Austin: University of Texas Press, The Texas Pan American Series.

1986 *Heaven Born Merida and Its Destiny: The "Book of Chilam Balam of Chumayel."* Translated and annotated by Munro S. Edmonson. Austin: University of Texas Press, The Texas Pan American Series.

Ehrle, Franz

1900 "Introduction." In *Codex Vaticanus* A, 1900.

Estrada, Juan de, and Fernando de Niebla

1955 (1579) "Descripción de la Provincia de Zapotitlan y Suchitepéquez." *Anales de la Sociedad de Geografía e Historia de Guatemala* 28: 68–84.

1982 *Relación de Zapotitlán*. In Relaciones Geográficas del Siglo XVI: Guatemala. Edición de René Acuña. Mexico City: Universidad Nacional Autónoma de México, Instituto de Investigaciones Antropológicas, Etnohistoria, Serie Antropológica, 45.

Estrada Monroy, Agustín

1973a *Popol Vuh*. Versión actualizada, basada en los textos quiché, castellano, y anotaciones al manuscrito de fray Francisco Ximénez. Guatemala City: Editorial "José de Pineda Ibarra."

1973b *Popol Vuh: Empiezan las historias del origen de los Indios de esta provincia de Guatemala*. Traducido de la lenguas quiché a la castellana por el R. P. fray Francisco Ximénez. Edición facsimilar. Paleografía modernizada y notas por Agustín Estrada Monroy. Guatemala City: Editorial "José de Pineda Ibarra."

Fernández del Castillo, Ignacio B.

1922 "Apuntes para la genealogía de los señores de Teotihuacan." In *La poblacion del Valle de Teotihuacan*, Manuel Gamio, ed., vol. I, VII, 2: 536–547. Mexico City: Dirección de Talleres Gráficos, Secretaria de Educación Pública.

Fowler, William R.

1989 *The Cultural Evolution of Ancient Nahua Civilizations: The Pipil-Nicarao of Central America*. Norman and London: University of Oklahoma Press, Civilization of the American Indian Series, 194.

Fuentes, Patricia de

1963 *The Conquistadors: First-Person Accounts of the Conquest of Mexico*. Preface by Howard F. Cline. New York: Orion Press.

Fuentes y Guzmán, Francisco Antonio de

1932–1933 *Recordación florida . . . del reyno de Guatemala*. 3 vols. Biblioteca "Goathemala" de la Sociedad de Geografía e Historia, 6–8. Guatemala City: Tipografíia Nacional.

1989 *Obras históricas de Francisco Antonio de Fuentes y Guzmán*. Edición y estudio preliminar de Carmelo Sáenz de Santa María. Biblioteca de autores españoles, desde la formación del lenguaje hasta nuestros, Biblioteca de autores españoles, tomos 230, 251, 259. Madrid: Ediciones Atlas.

1995 *Recordación florida primera parte: Libros primero y segundo*. Fundación Guatemalteca para las Letras, Series Ayer y Hoy, 15. Guatemala City: Editorial Artemis-Edinter.

Fuhrmann, Ernst

1923 *Mexiko III*. Kulturen der Erde, Material zur Kultur- und Kunstgeschichte aller Völker, 13. Hagen i. W. und Darmstadt: Folkwang-Verlag G.M.B.H.

Furst, Jill Leslie

1978 *Codex Vindobonensis I: A Commentary*. Preface by Mary Elizabeth Smith. Albany: Institute for Mesoamerican Studies, State University of New York at Albany Publications, no. 4.

García, Fray Gregorio

1729 *Origen de los Indios de el Nuevo Mundo, e Indias Occidentales*. 2nd ed., revised and annotated by Andrés González de Barcia. Madrid: Imprenta de F. Martínez Abad.

1981 *Origen de los Indios de el Nuevo Mundo, e Indias Occidentales*. Facsimile of 1729 edition. Mexico City: Fondo de Cultura Económica.

García de Palacio, Diego

1860 *Carta dirijida al Rey de España por el Licenciado Dr. Don Diego García de Palacio, oidor de la Real Audiencia de Guatemala, año 1576. Being a*

Description of the Ancient Provinces of Guazacapan, Izalco, Cuscatlan, and Chiquimula, in the Audiencia of Guatemala. With an Account of Their Aboriginal Inhabitants, and a Description of the Ruins of Copan. Documents and Relations Concerning the Discovery and Conquest of America. Published in the original with translations, illustrative notes, maps, and biographical sketches by E. G. Squier, 1. New York: Charles B. Norton.

1983 *Carta-relación de Diego García de Palacio a Felipe II sobre la Provincia de Guatemala, 8 de marzo de 1576.* Versión paleográfica, María del Carmen León Cázares. Ed. facsimilar y modernizada, con un estudio preliminar, cuadro lingüístico, glosarios, índice analítico y mapa preparada por Ma. del Carmen León, Martha Ilia Nájera C. y Tolita Figueroa. Mexico City: Universidad Nacional Autónoma de México, Centro de Estudios, Instituto de Investigaciones Filológicas, Fuentes para el Estudio de la Cultura Maya, 2.

1985 *Letter to the King of Spain: Being a Description of the Ancient Provinces of Guazacapan, Izalco, Cuscatlan, and Chiquimula, in the Audiencia of Guatemala, with an Account of the Languages, Customs, and Religion of Their Aboriginal Inhabitants, and a Description of the Ruins of Copan.* Translated and with notes by Ephraim G. Squier, with additional notes by Alexander von Frantzius and Frank E. Comparato, editor. Culver City, CA: Labyrinthos.

García Icazbalceta, Joaquín, ed.

1858–1866 *Colección de documentos para la historia de México.* 2 vols. Mexico City: J. M. Andrade.

1891 *Nueva colección de documentos para la historia de México*, vol. 3: *Pomar y Zurita. Pomar, Relación de Tezcoco, Zurita, Breve relación de los señores de la Nueva España. Varias relaciones antiguas (Siglo XVI).* Mexico City: F. Díaz de León.

1896–1899 *Obras de d. J. García Icazbalceta.* 10 vols. Mexico City: Imprenta de V. Agueros.

1941 *Nueva colección de documentos para la historia de México.* 3 vols. Mexico City: Salvador Chávez Hayhoe.

Garibay Kintana, Ángel María

1945 *Épica náhuatl: Divulgación literaria.* Biblioteca del Estudiante Universitario, 51. Mexico City: Universidad Nacional Autónoma de México.

1952 *Poesía indígena de la altiplanicie: Divulgación literaria.* Biblioteca del Estudiante Universitario, 11. Mexico City: Universidad Nacional Autónoma de México.

1953–1954 *Historia de la literatura náhuatl.* 2 vols. Mexico City: Biblioteca Porrúa, 1, 5. 3rd edition, 1987. Mexico City: Editorial Porrúa.

1961 *Llave del náhuatl: Colección de trozos clásicos, con grámatica y vocabulario, para utilidad de los principiantes.* Segunda edición reviada y aumentada. Mexico City: Editorial Porrúa. 1st edition, 1940.

1964 *La literatura de los Aztecas.* El Legado de la América Indígena, Serie del Instituto Indigenista Interamericano publicada con la colaboración de la Fundación Wenner Gren para Investigaciones Antropológicas, Coordinadores, Miguel León-Portilla y Demetrio Sodi M. Mexico City: Editorial Joaquín Mortiz.

1964–1968 *Poesía náhuatl. I. Romances de los señores de Nueva España, Manuscrito de Juan Bautista Pomar, Tetzcoco, 1582*. Paleografía, versión, introducción, notas y apéndices de Ángel Ma. Garibay K. (1964). II. *Cantares mexicanos, Manuscrito de la Biblioteca Nacional de México*. Primera parte. Paleografía, versión, introducción y notas explicativas de Ángel Ma. Garibay K. (1965). III. Segunda parte (1968). Mexico City: Universidad Nacional Autónoma de México, Instituto de Investigaciones Históricas, Fuentes Indígenas de la Cultura Náhuatl, 4–6.

1965 *Teogonía e historia de los Mexicanos: Tres opúsculos del siglo XVI*. Preparó esta edición Angel Ma. Garibay K. Mexico City: Editorial Porrúa, S.A., Colección "Sepan cuantos," núm. 37.

Gates, William

1931 "The Thirteen Ahaus in the Kaua Manucript, and Related Katun Wheels in the *Paris Codex*, Landa, Cogolludo, and the Chumayel." *Maya Society Quarterly* 1, no. 1: 2–20.

Genet, Jean

1928–1929 See Landa 1928–1929.

Gibson, Charles

1950 "The Identity of Diego Muñoz Camargo." *Hispanic American Historical Review* 30, no. 2: 195–208.

1952 *Tlaxcala in the Sixteenth Century*. New Haven: Yale University Press.

Gibson, Charles, and John B. Glass

1973 "Prose Sources in the Native Historical Tradition. B. A Census of Middle American Prose Manuscripts in the Native Historical Tradition." In *Handbook of Middle American Indians*, vol. 15: *Guide to Ethnohistorical Sources*. Robert Wauchope, general editor; Howard Cline, volume editor; Charles Gibson and H. B. Nicholson, associate volume editors, 322–400. Austin: University of Texas Press.

Gibson, Charles, and George Kubler

1951 *The Tovar Calendar, an Illustrated Mexican Manuscript ca. 1585*. Reproduced with a commentary and handlist of sources on the Mexican 365-day year. New Haven: Memoirs of the Connecticut Academy of Arts and Sciences, 11.

Glass, John B., in collaboration with Donald Robertson

1975 "A Census of Native Middle American Pictorial Manuscripts." In *Handbook of Middle American Indians*, vol. 14: *Guide to Ethnohistorical Sources*. Robert Wauchope, general editor; Howard Cline, volume editor; Charles Gibson and H. B. Nicholson, associate volume editors, 81–252. Austin: University of Texas Press.

Goetz, Delia, Sylvanus G. Morley, and Adrián Recinos, trans.
1948 *"Popol Vuh": The Sacred Book of the Ancient Quiche Maya.* Norman: University of Oklahoma Press.

Gómez Canedo, Lino
1973 "Toribio Motolinía and His Historical Writings." *The Americas: A Quarterly Review of Inter-American Cultural History* XXIX, no. 3: 277–307.

Gómez de Orozco, Federico
1953 "El Conquistador Anónimo." *Historia mexicana* 2, no. 3: 401–411.

Gordon, G. B., ed.
1913 *The Book of Chilam Balam of Chumayel.* Introduction by G. B. Gordon. Philadelphia: University of Pennsylvania, The Museum, Anthropological Publications, vol. 5. Facsimile of original manuscript.
1993 *The Book of Chilam Balam of Chumayel.* Introduction by G. B. Gordon. Laguna Hills, CA: Aegean Park Press, Mayan Studies, 6. Reprint edition of Gordon 1913.

Gropp, Arthur E.
1933 *Manuscripts in the Department of Middle American Research.* New Orleans: Tulane University, Middle American Research Series, no. 5: 217–297.

Hamy, E. T. [Ernest Théodore]
1899 Introduction and commentary in *Codex Telleriano-Remensis* 1899.

Herrera y Tordesillas, Antonio de
1601–1615 *Historia general de las hechos de los castellanos en las islas i tierra firme del mar oceano.* 4 vols. Madrid: Emprenta Real.
1991 *Historia general de los hechos de los castellanos en las islas y tierra firme del mar océano, o, "Décadas."* Edición y estudio de Mariano Cuesta Domingo. 4 vols. Madrid: Universidad Complutense de Madrid.

Himmelblau, Jack J.
1989 *Quiche Worlds in Creation: The "Popol Vuh" as a Narrative Work of Art.* Culver City, CA: Labyrinthos.

Historia de los Mexicanos por sus pinturas
1882 *Anales del Museo Nacional de México* 2: 83–106.
1891 In García Icazbalceta 1891, 3: 228–262.
1941 In García Icazbalceta 1941, III: 228–262.
1965 In Garibay Kintana 1965: 23–66.
1988 See Obadia-Baudesson 1988.

Historia Quiche de Don Juan Torres (Título Tamub)
1957 In Recinos 1957: 23–67.

Historia Tolteca-Chichimeca
1937 *Die mexikanische Bilderhandechrift "Historia tolteca-chichimeca."* 2 parts. K. T. Preuse and E. Mangin, eds. and trans. Baessler-Archiv, Beiträge zur Völkerkunde, 9 and 21. Berlin: D. Reimer.

1942 E. Mengin, ed. Facsimile of original ms. Corpus Codicum Americanorum Medii Aevi, 1. Copenhagen: Einar Munksgaard.

1945 *Historia tolteca-chichimeca.* H. Berlin and S. P. Rendón, eds. P. Kirchhoff, prologue. Spanish translation of the 1937 German translation of K. T. Preuss and E. Mengin. Fuentes para la historia de México, 1. Mexico City: Antigua Librería Robredo de J. Porrúa e Hijos.

1976 *Historia tolteca-chichimeca.* Paul Kirchhoff, Lina Odena Güemes, Luis Reyes García, editors and translators. Mexico City: Instituto Nacional de Antropología e Historia (CISINAH, SEP).

Histoyre du Mechique

1905 Édouard de Jonghe, ed. *Journal de la Société des Américanistes*, nouvelle serie, 2: 1–41. Spanish translation, by André Thevet, of part of BNP MSS Francais 19031.

1961 Spanish translation, by Joaquín Meade, of de Jonghe 1905, with notes by Wigberto Jiménez Moreno. *Memorias de la Academia Mexicana de la Historia* 20, no. 2: 183–210.

1965 Spanish translation, by Ramón Rosales Munguía, in Garibay Kintana 1965: 91–120.

Hochleitner, Franz Joseph, Ana Paula de Paula, and Helmut Krumbach

1987 *Novas interpretacoes de Codex Vindobonensis.* Juiz de Fora: Universidad Federal de Juiz de Fora.

Humboldt, Alexander von

1810–1813 *Vues des Cordillères, et monumens des peuples indigènes de l'Amérique.* Paris: Chez F. Schoell.

Imbelloni, José

1943 "La 'Essaltatione delle rose' del *Códice Vaticano Mexicano 3738*, el 'Nicte Katun' de las fuentes mayas y el 'pecado nefando' de la tradición peruana más remota." *Anales del Instituto de Etnografía Americana, Universidad Nacional de Cuyo* 4: 161–203.

Jakeman, M. Wells, ed. and trans.

1948 The *Relación de Motul*, a Sixteenth-Century Account of Some of the History, Customs, and Religious Beliefs of the Ancient Maya. Provo, UT: Brigham Young University, *Bulletin of the University Archaeological Society* 5: 22–29.

1952 *The "Historical Recollections" of Gaspar Antonio Chi: An Early Source-Account of Ancient Yucatan.* Provo, UT: Brigham Young University Press, Publications in Archaeology and Early History, no. 3.

Jansen, Maarten

1982 *Huisi Tacu, estudio interpretativo de un libro mixteco antiguo: Codex Vindobonensis Mexicanus I.* 2 vols. Amsterdam: Centrum voor Studie en Documenatie van Latijns Amerika.

1983 "El Códice Ríos y Fray Pedro de los Ríos." *Boletín de estudios latinamericanos y del Caribe* 36: 69–81.

1992 "Mixtec Pictography: Conventions and Contents." In *Supplement to the Handbook of Middle American Indians*. Victoria Reifler Bricker, general editor. Vol. 5, *Epigraphy*, edited by Victoria Reifler Bricker, volume editor, with the assistance of Patricia A. Andrews, 20–33. Austin: University of Texas Press.

1996 "Lord 8 Deer and Nacxitl Topiltzin." *Mexicon: Aktuelle Informationen und Studien zu Mesoamerika* 18, no. 2: 25–29.

1997a "La serpiente emplumada y el amanecer de la historia." In *Códices, caciques y comunidades*. M. Jansen y L. Reyes García, coordinador, *Cuadernos de historia latinoamericana* 5: 11–63. AHILA (Asociación de Historiadores Latinoamericanistas Europeos), the Netherlands.

1997b "Un viaje a la Casa del Sol." *Arqueología mexicana (Codices prehispánicas)* 4, no. 23: 44–49.

1998 "Monte Alban y Zaachila en los códices Mixtecas." In *The Shadow of Monte Alban: Politics and Historiography in Postclassic Oaxaca*. Maarten Jansen, Peter Kröfges, and Michel Oudijk, eds. Leiden: Research School CNWS, Leiden University, CNWS Publications, vol. 64: 67–122.

Jansen, Maarten, Peter Kröfges, and Michel Oudijk, eds.

1998 *The Shadow of Monte Alban: Politics and Historiography in Postclassic Oaxaca*. Leiden: Research School CNWS, Leiden University, CNWS Publications, vol. 64.

Jiménez García, E. Elizabeth

1998 *Iconografia de Tula: El caso de la escultura*. Mexico City: Instituto Nacional de Antropología e Historia, Colección Cientifica, Serie Arqueología.

Jiménez Moreno, Wigberto

1938 *Fray Bernardino de Sahagún y su obra*. Mexico City: Pedro Robredo.

1940 "Signos cronográficos del códice y calendario Mixteco." In Jiménez Moreno and Mateos Higuera 1940: 69–76.

1941a "Tula y los toltecas según las fuentes históricos." *Revista mexicana de estudios antropológicos* 5, nos. 2–3: 79–83.

1941b "Advertencia." In Lehmann 1941: 3–10.

1945 "Introducción." In Ruz Lhuillier 1945: 7–18.

1946 "Cronología de la historia precolombina de México." In *México prehispánico, culturas, deidades, monumentos*. Jorge A. Vivo, ed., 114–123. Mexico City: Editorial E. Hurtado.

1950 "The Importance of Xaltocan in the Ancient History of Mexico." *Mesoamerican Notes* 2: 133–138.

1953 Cronología de la historia de Veracruz. *Revista mexicana de estudios antropológicos* 13, nos. 2–3: 312–313. Includes correlation chart: 3-year counts of *Historia Tolteca-Chichimeca*.

1954–1955 "Síntesis de la historia precolonial del Valle de México." *Revista mexicana de estudios antropológicos* 14, primera parte: 219–236.

1955 "Meses con que principiaban al año diversos pueblos y sus consecuencias para la cronología de la historia prehispánica." Paper presented to the

Mesa Redonda of the Sociedad Mexicana de Antropología on Calendric Problems of Ancient Mexico, Castillo de Chapultepec, December 1955.

n.d. "Historia antigua de México." Mineographed from class lecture notes.

Jiménez Moreno, Wigberto, and Salvador Mateos Higuera

1940 *Códice de Yanhuitlán.* Edición en facsimile y con un estudio preliminar por Wigberto Jiménez Moreno y Salvador Mateos Higuera. Mexico City: Instituto Nacional de Antropología e Historia, Museo Nacional, Secretaria de Educación Pública.

Jonghe, Édouard de

1906 "Thévet, mexicaniste." In *Internationaler Amerikanisten-Kongress; vierzehnte Tagung, Stuttgart, 1904*, vol. 1: 223–240. Stuttgart: W. Kohlhammer.

Juan Cano Relaciones: See *Origen de los Mexicanos*, 1891, 1941; *Relación de la genealogía . . .* , 1891, 1941.

Kelley, David H.

1955 "Quetzalcoatl and His Coyote Origins." *El México antiguo* 8: 397–413.

Kingsborough, Lord [Edward King]

1830/1831–1848 *Antiquities of Mexico.* 9 vols. London: Robert Havell and Conaghi, Son, and Co.

1964–1967 *Antigüedades de México, basadas en la recopilación de Lord Kingsborough.* Palabras preliminares, Antonio Ortiz Mena. Prólogo, Agustín Yañez. Estudios e interpretación, José Corona Nuñez. 4 vols. Mexico City: Secretaria de Hacienda y Crédito Público.

Kirchhoff, Paul

1950 "The Mexican Calendar and the Founding of Tenochtitlan-Tlatelolco." *Transactions of the New York Academy of Sciences*, second series, 12, no. 4: 126–132.

1951 "El autor de la segunda parte de la Crónica Mexicayotl." In *Homenaje al Doctor Alfonso Caso*, 225–227. Mexico City: Imprenta Nuevo Mundo.

1955a "Quetzalcoatl, Huemac y el fin de Tula." *Cuadernos americanos*, año 14, vol. 84, no. 6: 163–196.

1955b "Las fechas indígenas mencionadas para ciertos acontecimientos en las fuentes, y su importancia como índice de varios calendarios." Paper presented to the Mesa Redonda of the Sociedad Mexicana de Antropología on Calendric Problems of Ancient Mexico, Castillo de Chapultepec, December 1955.

Klor de Alva, Jorge, H. B. Nicholson, and Eloise Quiñones Keber, eds.

1988 *The Work of Fray Bernardino de Sahagún: Pioneer Ethnographer of Sixteenth-Century Aztec Mexico.* Albany: Institute for Mesoamerican Studies, State University of New York at Albany, Studies on Culture and Society, vol. 2.

Kowalski, Jeff Karl, ed.

1999 *Mesoamerican Architecture as a Cultural Symbol.* New York and Oxford: Oxford University Press.

Krickeberg, Walter

1933 *Los Totonaca: Contribución a la etnografía histórica de la América Central.* Porfirio Aguirre, trans. Mexico City: Talleres Gráficos del Museo Nacional de Arqueología, Historia y Etnografía.

Kristan-Graham, Cynthia Beth

1988 "Art, Rulership and the Mesoamerican Body Politic at Tula and Chichen Itza." Ph.D. dissertation, Department of Art, University of California, Los Angeles. Ann Arbor: U.M.I.

Kroeber, Alfred L.

1952 *The Nature of Culture.* Chicago: University of Chicago Press.

Kutscher, Gerdt

1948 "Le 'Memorial breve' de Chimalpahin." Un manuscrit mexicain inédit de la Bibliothèque Nationale à Paris. *Congrès International des Américanistes, Actes de la Session de Paris, 24–30 Aout,* 1947: 407–418.

Landa, Fray Diego de

1928–1929 *Relation des choses de Yucatan.* 2 vols. J. Genet, trans. Collection de textes relatifs aux anciennes civilisations du Mexique et de l'Amérique Centrale, 1. Paris: Les Editions Genet.

1937 *Yucatan Before and After the Conquest, by Friar Diego de Landa, with Other Related Documents, Maps and Illustrations.* Translated with notes by William Gates. Baltimore: Maya Society Publication no. 20.

1938 *Relación de las cosas de Yucatán.* H. Pérez Martínez, ed., introduction, and notes. Mexico City: Editorial Pedro Robredo.

1941 *Landa's "Relación de las cosas de Yucatán": A Translation.* Edited with notes by Alfred M. Tozzer. Cambridge: Papers of the Peabody Museum of American Archaeology and Ethnology, Harvard University, vol. XVIII. Later reprint editions, 1966, 1975, 1978.

1959 *Relación de las cosas de Yucatán.* Introducción por Angel Ma. Garibay K., 8th ed., con un apéndice en el cual se publican varios documentos importantes y cartas del autor. Mexico City: Editorial Porrúa, S.A., Biblioteca Porrúa, 13. Reprint editions, 1966, 1978.

1975 *The Maya: Diego de Landa's Account of the Affairs of Yucatan.* Edited and translated by A. R. Pagden. Chicago: J. P. O'Hara.

1978 *"Yucatan Before and After the Conquest," by Diego de Landa.* Translated with notes by William Gates. Maya Society Publication no. 20. New York: Dover Publications. Paperback reprint of Gates's 1937 edition.

1985 *Relación de las cosas de Yucatán.* Edición de Miguel Rivera. Madrid: Historia 16, Crónicas de América, 7.

1994 *Relación de las cosas de Yucatán.* Estudio preliminar, cronología y revisión del texto, María del Carmen León Cázares. Consejo Nacional para la Cultura y las Artes. Mexico City: Cien de México.

Las Casas, Bartolomé de

1909 *Apologética historia de las Indias.* 2 vols. Historiadores de Indias, vols. 1–2. Madrid: Bailly, Bailliere e Hijos.

1957–1958 *Apologética historia.* Obras escogidas de Fray Bartolomé de Las Casas, vols. III–IV. Estudio crítico preliminar y edición por Juan Pérez de Tudela Bueso. Madrid: Biblioteca de autores españoles desde la formación del lenguaje hasta nuestros días, tomos XCV–CVI.

1966 *Los Indios de México y Nueva España: Antología.* Edición, prólogo, apéndices y notas de Edmundo O'Gorman de la Academia de la Historia. Con la colaboración de Jorge Alberto Manrique. Mexico City: Editorial Porrúa, S.A., Colección "Sepan cuantos . . . ," núm. 57.

1967 *Apologética historia sumaria.* Edición preparada por Edmundo O'Gorman, con un estudio preliminar, apéndices y un indice de materias. Mexico City: Universidad Nacional Autónoma de México, Instituto de Investigaciones Históricas, Serie de historiadores y cronistas de Indias: 1.

Lehmann, Walter

1906 "Traditions des anciens mexicains." *Journal de la Société des Américanistes* 3, no. 2: 239–297.

1920 *Zentral-Amerika.* 2 vols. Berlin: D. Reimer.

1922 "Ein Tolteken-Klagegesang." In *Festschrift Eduard Seler.* Walter Lehmann, ed., 281–319. Berlin: Strecker und Schröder.

1938 *Die Geschichte der Königreiche von Colhuacan und Mexico.* Text mit Übersetzung von Walter Lehmann, Dr. med. et phil., Prof. h. c. des National-Museums in Mexico. Quellenwerke zur alten Geschichte Amerikas aufgezeichnet in den Sprachen der Eingeborenen. Herausgegeben vom Ibero-Amerikanischen Institut, Berlin. Stuttgart and Berlin: Verlag von W. Kohlhammer.

1941 *Una elegía tolteca.* Paul R. Hendrichs translation of Lehmann 1922, W. Jiménez Moreno, notes. Mexico City: Publicaciones de la Sociedad "Mexico-Alemana Alejandro de Humboldt," folleto no. 2.

Leibsohn, Dana

1993 "The *Historia Tolteca-Chichimeca*": Recollecting Identity in a Nahua Manuscript." Ph.D. dissertation, Department of Art, University of California, Los Angeles.

Leiva, Antonio de

1878 "Relación de Ameca." In *Noticias varias de Nueva Galicia,* 253–282. Guadalajara: Tipografía de Banda, ex-Convento de Santa María de Gracia.

1988 "Relación del Pueblo de Ameca." In *Relaciones geográficas del siglo* (1579) *XVI: Nueva Galicia,* 27–50. Edición de René Acuña. Mexico City: Universidad Nacional Autónoma de México, Instituto de Investigaciones Antropológicas, Etnohistoria, Serie Antropológica, 65.

León, Nicolás

1907 "Bibliografía mexicana del siglo XVIII. Sección primera, cuarta parte, A–Z." *Boletín del Instituto Bibliográfico*, 8.

León-Portilla, Miguel

1964 *Las literaturas precolombinas de México*. Colección Pormaca, 5. Mexico City: Editorial Pormaca.

1969a *Pre-Columbian Literatures of Mexico*. Translated from the Spanish by Grace Lobanov and the author. Norman: University of Oklahoma Press, Civilization of the American Indian Series.

1969b "Ramírez de Fuenleal y las antigüedades mexicanas." *Estudios de la cultura náhuatl* 8: 9–49.

1971 "Religión de los Nicaraos: Analisis y comparación de tradiciones culturales Nahuas." *Estudios de cultura náhuatl* 10: 11–112.

Leyenda de los soles

1903 *Leyenda de los soles, continuada con otras leyendas y noticias: Relación anónima escrita en lengua mexicana el año 1558*. La tradujo al Castellano en homenaje al Congreso Internacional de Ciencias Históricas, que se reunirá en Roma del 2 al 9 de Abril de 1903, Francisco del Paso y Troncoso, Director del Museo Nacional de México (en misión en Europa). Florence: Tipografia de Salvador Landi.

1906 See Lehmann 1906.

1938 See *Anales de Cuauhtitlan* 1938 (2nd edition, enhanced, 1974).

1945 See *Anales de Cuauhtitlan* 1945 (2nd edition, 1975).

1992 See *Anales de Cuauhtitlan* 1992 a/b (Bierhorst English translation).

Lienzo Antonio de León

1961 See Caso 1961.

Lienzo de Ihuitlan

1961, 1965 See Caso 1961, 1965.

Lizana, Fray Bernardo de

1893 *Historia de Yucatán. Devocionario de Ntra. Sra. de Izamal y conquista espiritual*. Mexico City: Imprenta del Museo Nacional. 1st edition, Valladolid: 1633.

López, Atanasio

1931 "Fr. Toribio Motolinía, misionero e historiador de Méjico en el siglo XVI." *Iluminare: Boletín Oficial de la Union Misional del Clero de España* (enero-febrero).

López de Cogolludo, Fray Diego

1867–1868 *Historia de Yucatán*. 2 vols. Mérida: M. Aldana Rivas, 1st edition, Madrid, 1588.

1954–1955 *Historia de Yucatán*. 3 vols. Campeche: Comisión de Historia.

López de Gomara, Francisco

1552 *Ystoria de las Indias. Y Conquista de México*. Zaragoza: Casa de Agustin Millan.

López Luján, Leonardo, Robert H. Cobean, and Alba Guadalupe Mastache E.

1995 *Xochicalco y Tula*. Presentación de Eduardo Matos Moctezuma. Milan: Editoriale Jaca Book.

Lothrop, Samuel K.

1952 *Metals from the Cenote of Sacrifice, Chichen Itza, Yucatan*. With W. C. Root and Tatiana Proskouriakoff; William Harvey, appendix. Cambridge: Memoirs of the Peabody Museum of Archaeology and Ethnology, Harvard University 10, no. 2.

Makemson, Maud

1951 *The Book of the Jaguar Priest, a Translation of the "Book of Chilam Balam of Tizimin," with Commentary*. New York: Henry Schuman.

Mariscal, Mario

1944 Introductions to selections in Alvarado Tezozomoc 1944b.

Marquina, Ignacio

1964 (1951) *Arquitectura prehispánica*. Mexico City: Instituto Nacional de Antropología e Historia, Secretaria de Educación Pública. 2nd edition, enlarged, 1964.

Martínez, Andrea

1990 "Las pinturas del Manuscrito de Glasgow y El Lienzo de Tlaxcala." *Estudios de la cultura náhuatl* 20: 141–162.

Martínez Hernández, Juan

1910 *Los grandes ciclos de la historia maya según el manuscrito de Chumayel*. Mérida: Imprenta de L. Rosado Vega.

1927 *Crónicas mayas*. Carlos R. Menéndez, ed. Maní ms., pp. 1–10; Tizimín ms., pp. 20–24; Chumayel ms. (1st and 3rd chronicles), pp. 24–39. Mérida: Compañía Tipográfica Yucateca.

Maudslay, Alfred P.

1889–1902 *Archaeology. Biologia Centrali-Americana*. 5 vols. London: R. H. Porter and Dulau and Co.

Mayer, Karl Herbert, ed.

1980 *El Libro de Chilam Balam de Tizimin*. Museo Nacional de Antropología, Mexico City (Cod. 35–66). Schwarzweiss-Reproduktion in natürlicher Grösse = Reproducción monocroma de tamaño original. Introduction: Karl Herbert Mayer (English, German, Maya and Spanish). Graz: Akademische Druck- und Verlagsanstalt, Fontes rerum Mexicanarum, vol. 6.

McPheeters, D. W.

1954 "An Unknown Early Seventeenth-Century Codex of the *Crónica Mexicana* of Hernando Alvarado Tezozomoc." *Hispanic American Historical Review* 34: 506–512.

Meade, Joaquín

1950 "Fray Andrés de Olmos." *Memorias de la Academia Mexicana de la Historia* 9, no. 4: 374–452.

Mediz Bolio, Antonio

1930 *Libro de Chilam Balam de Chumayel.* San José, Costa Rica: Imprenta y Librería Lehmann.

Melgarejo Vivanco, José Luis

1949 *Historia de Veracruz.* Vol. I: *Época prehispánica.* Jalapa, Mexico: Enríquez.

1980 *El Códice Vindobonensis.* Jalapa, Mexico: Instituto de Antropología, Universidad Veracruzana.

Mendieta, Fray Gerónimo de

1945 *Historia eclesiástica indiana: Obra escrita a fines del siglo XVI.* 4 vols. Mexico City: Editorial Salvador Chávez Hayhoe.

1971 *Historia eclesiástica indiana.* Obra escrita a fines del siglo XVI. Segunda edición facsimilar, y primera con la reproducción de los dibujos originales del códice. Mexico City: Editorial Porrúa, S.A., Biblioteca Porrúa, 46. Reprint editions, 1980, 1987.

Mengin, Ernst

1952 *Memorial de Tecpan-Atitlan (Solola). Historia del antiguo reino del Cakchiquel dicho de Guatemala.* Facsimile of original ms. Corpus Codicum Americanorum Medii Aevi, 4. Copenhagen: Einar Munksgaard.

Meyer, Enrique

1939 "Noticia sobre los petroglifos de Tula, Hgo." *Revista mexicana de estudios antropológicos* 3, no. 2: 122–128.

Molina, Fray Alonso de

1944 *Vocabulario en lengua castellana y mexicana.* Facsimile of 1571 Mexico City edition. Colección de Incunables Americanos Siglo XVI, 4. Madrid: Ediciones Cultural Hispánica.

Moran, Fray Pedro

n.d. *Manuscript Dictionary of the Pokomam Language.* William Gates photocopy of ms. in Peabody Museum of American Archaeology and Ethnology Library, Harvard University.

Morley, Sylvanus G., and George W. Brainerd

1956 *The Ancient Maya.* 3rd edition. Stanford: Stanford University Press.

Morley, Sylvanus G., and Ralph L. Roys

1942 *Xiu probanzas and family records (Crónica de Oxkcutzcab).* Appendix A: "Mani Land Treaty (1557)." Appendix B: "Family Studies in Yucatan XIX, XX Century Names of Xiu Descendants." Carnegie Institution of Washington, ms. Peabody Museum of American Archaeology and Ethnology, Harvard University.

Morris, Earl H., Jean Charlot, and Ann A. Morris

1931 *The Temple of the Warriors at Chichen Itza, Yucatan.* 2 vols. Washington, DC: Carnegie Institution of Washington Publication 406.

Motolinía [Fray Toribio de Benavente]

1848 *Ritos antiguos, sacrificios e idolatrías de los Indios de la Nueva España, y de su conversión a la fe, y quiénes fueron los que primero la predicaron.* In Kingsborough 1830/1831–1848, IX: 49pp.

1858 *Ritos antiguos, sacrificios e idolatrías de los Indios de la Nueva España.* In García Icazbalceta 1858–1866, I: 1–249.

1869 *Ritos antiguos, sacrificios e idolatrías de los Indios de la Nueva España.* Marqués de Miraflores y Miguel Salva, eds. *Colección de documentos inéditos para la historia de España,* vol. LIII: 297–574. Madrid: Calero.

1903–1907 *Memoriales de Fray Toribio de Motolinía.* Manuscrito de la colección del Señor Don Joaquín García Icazbalceta. Publícalo por primera vez su hijo Luis García Pimentel. Documentos históricos de Méjico, tomo 1. Mexico City: En casa del editor.

1914 *Historia de los Indios de la Nueva España, escrita a mediados del siglo XVI por el R. P. Fr. Toribio de Benavente o Motolinía, de la Orden de San Francisco.* Sácalos nuevamente a luz el R. P. Fr. Daniel Sánchez García, religioso de la misma Orden, teniendo a la vista las ediciones de Lord Kingsborough y de García Icazbalceta. Reprint of 1858 García Icazbalceta edition. Barcelona: Herederos de Juan Gil, Editores.

1941 *Historia de los Indios de la Nueva España.* Reprint of 1914 Barcelona edition. Mexico City: Salvador Chávez Hayhoe.

1950 *Motolinia's History of the Indians of New Spain.* Translated and edited by Elisabeth Andros Foster. Berkeley: Bancroft Library (University of California), The Cortés Society, Documents and Narratives Concerning the Discovery and Conquest of Latin America, new series, no. 4. Reprint edition, 1973, Westport, CT: Greenwood Press.

1951 *Motolinia's History of the Indians of New Spain.* Translated and annotated, with a bio-bibliographical study of the author, by Francis Borgia Steck, O.F.M. Washington, DC: Academy of American Franciscan History Documentary Series, vol. 1.

1956a *Historia de los Indios de la Nueva España.* Reprint of 1914 Barcelona edition. Mexico City: Editora Nacional.

1956b *Relaciones de la Nueva España.* Introducción y selección, Luis Nicolau d'Olwer. *Biblioteca del Estudiante Universitario,* 72. Mexico City: Universidad Nacional Autónoma de México. 2nd edition, 1964.

1966 *Ritos antiguos, sacrificios e idolatrías de los Indios de la Nueva España.* Facsimile of Madrid 1869 edition. Vaduz, Lichtenstein: Krause.

1967 *Memoriales de Fray Toribio de Motolinia.* Facsimile of 1903/1907 García Pimentel edition. Guadalajara: Edmundo Aviña Levy.

1969a *Historia de los Indios de la Nueva España.* Estudio crítico, apéndices, notas y índice de Edmundo O'Gorman. Mexico City: Editorial Porrúa, S.A., Colección "Sepan cuantos . . . ," núm. 129. Various later editions.

1969b "A Critical Edition of the Escorial Manuscript of 'Historia de los Indios de la Nueva España' of Fray Toribio de Benavente (Motolinia)." Sarah

Jane Banks, ed. 2 vols. Unpublished Ph.D. dissertation, University of Southern California.

1970 *Memoriales e Historia de los Indios de la Nueva España.* Estudio preliminar por Fidel de Lejarza. Reprints of 1903/1907 García Pimentel edition of *Memoriales* and 1914 Barcelona edition of *Historia.* Madrid: Ediciones Atlas.

1971 *Memoriales o Libro de las cosas de la Nueva España y de los naturales de ella.* Nueva transcripción paleográfica del manuscrito original con inserción de las porciones de la *Historia de los Indios de la Nueva España* que completan el texto de los *Memoriales.* Edición preparada por Edmundo O'Gorman. Mexico City: Universidad Nacional Autónoma de México, Instituto de Investigaciones Históricas, Serie de Historiadores y Cronistas de Indias, 2.

1979 *Relación de los ritos antiguos, idalatrías y sacrificios de los Indios de la Nueva España, y de la maravillosa conversión que Dios en ellos ha obrado.* Motolinía, Fray Toribio de Paredes. Manuscrito de la Ciudad de México. Introducción, transcripción paleográfica y notas de colación con los manuscritos la Biblioteca del Monasterio de San Lorenzo, El Real de El Escorial, y de "The Hispanic Society of America" de la Ciudad de Nueva York por Javier O. Aragón. Juan Cortina Portilla, ed. Mexico City: Contabilidad Ruf Mexicana S.A.

1985a *Historia de los Indios de la Nueva España.* Edición, introducción y notas de Georges Baudot. Clásicos Castalia. Madrid: Editorial Castalia.

1985b *Historia de los Indios de la Nueva España.* Edición de Claudio Esteva Fabregat, editor. Madrid: Historia 16, Crónicas de América, 16.

1988 *Historia de los Indios de la Nueva España.* Introducción y notas de Giuseppe Bellini. Sección Clásicos del Descubrimiento, El Libro de Bolsillo, 1348. Madrid: Alianza Editorial.

1989 *El Libro Perdido: Ensayo de reconstrucción de la obra histórica extraviada de Fray Toribio.* Trabajo realizado en el Seminario de Historiografía Mexicana de la Universidad Iberoamericana, dirigido por Edmundo O'Gorman. Mexico City: Consejo Nacional para la Cultura y las Artes.

1996 *Memoriales (Libro de Oro,* MS JGI 31). Motolinía, Fray Toribio de Benavente, m. 1568. Edición crítica, introducción, notas y apéndice, Nancy Joe Dyer. Mexico City: El Colegio de México, Centro de Estudios Lingüísticos y Literarios, Biblioteca Novohispana, 3.

Müller, E. Florencia J.

1949 *Historia antigua del Valle de Morelos.* Acta Anthropologica. Mexico City: Escuela Nacional de Antropología e Historia.

Muñoz Camargo, Diego

1843 *Histoire de la Républque de Tlaxcallan.* Henri Ternaux-Compans, trans. In *Nouvelles annales des voyages de géographie et de l'histoire,* vol. 98: 129–204, and vol. 99: 129–197. Paris: Arthus Bertrand.

1892 *Historia de Tlaxcala.* Publicada y anotada por Alfredo Chavero. Se hace esta edición para presentarla como un homenaje a Cristóbal Colón, en la Exposición de Chicago. Mexico City: Oficina Tipografía de la Secretaría de Fomento.

1947–1948 *Historia de Tlaxcala.* Edición cotejada por el historiador Lauro Rosell con la copia de la original del autor que obra n el Archivo del Museo Nacional; las rutas que siguieron los chichimecas, por el Ing. Albert Escalona Ramos, con ilustraciones del Dr. Andrés Angulo y un apéndice. Sexta edición. Mexico City: Ateneo Nacional de Ciencias y Artes de México.

1977 *Historia de Tlaxcala [Crónica del siglo XVI].* Anotada por Alfredo Chavero. Versión enriquecida con 48 láminas del Lienzo de Tlaxcala. Facsimile of 1892 edition. Mexico City: Editorial Innovación, S.A. 2nd edition, 1982.

1981 *Descripción de la ciudad y provincia de Tlaxcala de las Indias y del mar océano para el buen gobierno y ennobleciento dellas.* Edición facsímil del Manuscrito de Glasgow con un estudio preliminar de René Acuña. Mexico City: Universidad Nacional Autónoma de México, Instituto de Investigaciones Filológicas.

1984 *Descripción de la ciudad y provincia de Tlaxcala.* In Relaciones Geográficas del Siglo XVI: Tlaxcala, tomo primero. Edición de René Acuña. Mexico City: Universidad Nacional Autónoma de México, Instituto de Investigaciones Antropológícas, Etnohistoria, Serie Antropológica, 53.

1986 *Historia de Tlaxcala.* Edición de Germán Vázquez. Madrid: Historia 16, Crónicas de América, 26.

1994 *Suma y epíloga de toda la descripción de Tlaxcala.* Paleografía, presentación y notas de Andrea Martínez Baracs y Carlos Sempat Assadourian. Prólogo de Wayne Ruwet. Tlaxcala: Universidad Autónoma de Tlaxcala, Secretaria de Extensión Universtaria y Difusión Cultural, Centro de Investigaciones y Estudios Superiores en Antropología Social, Colección: Historia, Serie: Historia de Tlaxcala, 3. [Muñoz Camargo authorship not certain.]

1998 *Historia de Tlaxcala (Ms. de la Biblioteca Nacional de París).* Paleografía, introducción, notas, apéndices e índices analíticos de Luis Reyes García, con la colaboración de Javier Lira Toledo. Tlaxcala: Gobierno del Estado de Tlaxcala, Centro de Investigaciones y Estudios Superiores en Antropología Social, Universidad Autónoma de Tlaxcala, Colección: Historia, Serie: Historia de Tlaxcala, 5.

Nicholson, H. B.

1955a "Native Historical Traditions of Nuclear America and the Problem of Their Archaeological Correlation." *American Anthropologist* 57, no. 3: 594–613.

1955b "Aztec-Style Calendric Inscriptions of Possible Historical Significance: A Survey." Paper presented at the Mesa Redonda sponsored by the Sociedad Mexicana de Antropología: Calendric Systems of Pre-Hispanic Central Mexico, Castillo de Chapultepec, December 5–12, 1955. Mimeographed.

1957a “Topiltzin Quetzalcoatl of Tollan: A Problem in Mesoamerican Ethnohistory.” Ph.D. dissertation, Department of Anthropology, Harvard University.

1957b “Review of John Paddock et al: *Excavations at Yagul: I.*” *American Antiquity* 23, no. 2, pt. 1: 195–196.

1960 “The Mixteca-Puebla Concept in Mesoamerican Archaeology: A Reexamination.” In *Men and Cultures: Selected Papers from the Fifth International Congress of Anthropological and Ethnological Sciences, Philadelphia, September 1–9, 1956*: 612–617. Edited under the chairmanship of Anthony F. C. Wallace. Philadelphia: University of Pennsylvania Press. Reprinted in other publications: 1966, 1977, and 1981.

1961 “The Use of the Term ‘Mixtec’ in Mesoamerican Archaeology.” *American Antiquity* 26, no. 3, pt. 1: 431–433.

1971 “Religion in Pre-Hispanic Central Mexico.” In *Handbook of Middle American Indians*, vol. 10, pt. 1. Robert Wauchope, general editor, Gordon Ekholm and Ignacio Bernal, volume editors, 395–446. Austin: University of Texas Press.

1978 “The Deity 9 Wind ‘Ehecatl-Queztalcoatl’ in the Mixteca Pictorals.” *Journal of Latin American Lore*, 4, no. 1: 61–92.

1982 “The Mixteca-Puebla Concept Revisited.” In *The Art and Iconography of Late Postclassic Central Mexico: A Conference at Dumbarton Oaks, October 22nd and 23rd, 1977*. Elizabeth P. Benson, organizer; Elizabeth Hill Boone, editor, 227–254. Washington, DC: Dumbarton Oaks, Trustees for Harvard University.

1993 “Reminiscences: The San Diego Museum of Man and Balboa Park in the 1930s and 1940s.” In *Current Topics in Aztec Studies: Essays in Honor of Dr. H. B. Nicholson*. Alana Cordy-Collins and Douglas Sharon, eds., 111–118. San Diego Museum of Man Papers, 30.

1996a “Mesoamerica: Mixteca-Puebla.” In *The Dictionary of Art*. Edited by Jane Turner, vol. 21: 739–741. London: Macmillan Publishers Ltd.; New York: Grove’s Dictionaries Inc.

1996b “Quetzalcoatl.” In *Encyclopedia of Latin American History and Culture*. Barbara A. Tenenbaum, editor in chief, 508–509. New York: Charles Scribner’s Sons.

2000 “The Iconography of the Feathered Serpent in Late Postclassic Central Mexico.” In *Mesoamerica’s Classic Heritage: From Teotihuacan to the Aztecs*. Davíd Carrasco, Lindsay Jones, and Scott Sessions, eds., 145–164. Boulder: University Press of Colorado.

2001a “Feathered Serpent.” In *The Oxford Encyclopedia of Mesoamerican Cultures*. Davíd Carrasco, editor in chief, vol. 1: 396–400. New York: Oxford University Press.

2001b “Topiltzin Quetzalcoatl.” In *The Oxford Encyclopedia of Mesoamerican Cultures*. Davíd Carrasco, editor in chief, vol. 3: 246–247. New York: Oxford University Press.

n.d.a “Ce Acatl Nacxitl Topiltzin Quetzalcoatl = 4 Jaguar of ‘Cattail Frieze’ and Military Ally of 8 Deer ‘Jaguar Claw’?” In press, Festschrift for Mary

Elizabeth Smith, edited by Elizabeth Hill Boone. New Orleans: Middle American Research Institute, Tulane University.

n.d.b "The 'Return of Quetzalcoatl': Did It Play a Role in the Conquest of Mexico?" Paper presented at the 8th Annual Latin American Symposium, February 1997, of the San Diego Museum of Man. In press, Lancaster, California: Labyrinthos Press.

Nicholson, H. B., and Eloise Quiñones Keber

1994 "Introduction." In Nicholson and Quiñones Keber, eds., 1994: vii–xv.

Nicholson, H. B., and Eloise Quiñones Keber, eds.

1994 *Mixteca-Puebla: Discoveries and Research in Mesoamerican Art and Archaeology*. Lancaster, California: Labyrinthos Press.

Nicolau d'Olwer, Luis

1952 *Fray Bernardino de Sahagún, 1499–1590*. Instituto Panamericano de Geografía e Historia, 142. Comisión de Historia, 40. Historiadores de América, 9.

1987 *Fray Bernardino de Sahagún (1499–1590)*. Translated by Mauricio J. Mixco. Foreword by Miguel León-Portilla. Salt Lake City: University of Utah Press.

Nowotny, Karl Anton

1948a "Erläuterungen zum *Codex Vindobonensis* (vorderseite)." *Archiv für Völkerkunde* 3: 156–200.

1948b "Die Ergänzung der zerstörten Stellen im *Codex Vindobonensis* Mex. 1." *Phaidros: Zeitschrift für die Freunde des Buches und der schönen Künste* 2: 145–154.

Núñez de la Vega, Fray Francisco

1702 *Constituciones diocesanas del obispado de Chiapa*. Rome: Caietano Zenobi.

1988 *Constituciones diocesanas del obispado de Chiapa*. Edición preparada por María Carmen León Cazares y Mario Humberto Ruz. Mexico City: Universidad Nacional Autónoma de México, Centro de Estudios Mayas, Fuentes para el estudio de la cultura Maya, 6.

Obadia-Baudesson, Paule, ed.

1988 *Historia de los Mexicanos por sus pinturas*. Paris: l'Association "Oxomoco y Cipactonal."

Ordóñez y Aguiar, Ramón de

1906 *Historia de la creación del cielo y de la tierra, conforme al sistema de la gentilidad americana*. In León 1907: 1–272.

Origen de los Mexicanos

1891, 1941 In García Icazbalceta 1891: xlii–xliv, 281–308; 1941, 3: xxxvi–xxxvii, 256–280.

1991 In Vázquez 1991: 127–158.

Orozco y Berra, Manuel

1880 *Historia antigua y de la conquista de México*. Mexico City: G. A. Esteva.

Oviedo y Valdés, Gonzalo Fernández de

1851–1855 *Historia general y natural de las Indias, islas y tierra-firme del mar océano.* 4 vols. Madrid: Real Academia de la Historia.

1944–1945 *Historia general y natural de las Indias, islas y tierra firme del mar océano.* Prólogo de J. Natalicio González, notas de José Amador de los Ríos. 14 vols. Asunción, Paraguay: Editorial Guaranía.

1959 *Historia general y natural de las Indias.* Edición y estudio preliminar de Juan Pérez de Tudela Bueso. 5 vols. Biblioteca de autores españoles desde la formación del lengua hasta nuestros días, Biblioteca de autores españoles, tomos 117–121. Madrid: Ediciones Atlas.

Paso y Troncoso, Francisco del

1898 *Descripción, historia y exposición del códice pictórico de los antiguos Náuas que se conserva en la biblioteca de la Cámara de Diputados de París (antiguo Palais Bourbon).* Florence: Tipografía de Salvador Landi.

1903 *Leyenda de los soles continuada con otras leyendas y noticias. Relación anónima escrita en lengua mexicana el año 1558.* Biblioteca Náuatl, vol. 5, no. 1: 1–40. Florence: Tipografía de Salvador Landi.

1905–1907 *Papeles de Nueva España, segunda serie, geografía y estadística: Manuscritos de la Real Academia de la Historia de Madrid y del Archivo de Indias en Sevilla.* 7 vols. Madrid: Tipografía "Sucesores de Rivadeneyra."

1939–1942 *Epistolario de Nueva España, 1505–1818.* 16 vols. Biblioteca Histórica Mexicana de Obras Inéditas, segunda serie, 1–16. Mexico City: Libreria Robredo de José Porrúa.

Peñafiel, Antonio

1899 *Cantares en idioma mexicano: impresos según el manuscrito original que existe en la Biblioteca Nacional.* Colección de Documentos para la Historia Mexicana, 2. Mexico City: Oficina Tipográfica de la Secretaria de Fomento.

1904 *Cantares en idioma mexicano: Reproducción facsimiliaria del manuscrito original existente en la Biblioteca Nacional.* Mexico City: Oficina Tipográfica de la Secretaria de Fomento.

Phillips, Henry, Jr.

1884 "Notes Upon the *Códex Ramírez,* with a Translation of the Same." *Proceedings of the American Philosophical Society* 21: 616–651.

Pineda, Emeterio

1845 *Descripción geográfica del departamento de Chiapas y Soconusco.* Mexico City: Imprenta de Ignacio Cumplido.

Pineda, Vicente

1888 *Historia de las sublevaciones indígenas habidas en el estado de Chiapas. Gramática de la lengua Tzel-tal . . . y diccionario de la misma.* Chiapas: Tipografía del Gobierno.

Pohl, John

1994 *The Politics of Symbolism in the Mixtec Codices.* Nashville: Vanderbilt University Publications in Anthropology, 46.

1999 "The Lintel Paintings of Mitla and the Function of the Mitla Palaces." In Kowalski, ed., 1999: 177–205.

Pohl, John, and Bruce Byland

1994 *In the Realm of 8 Deer: The Archaeology of the Mixtec Codices.* Norman: University of Oklahoma Press.

Pohorilles, Noah Elieser

1913 *Das "Popol Wuh." Die mythische geschichte des kice-volkes von Guatemala, nach dem original-texte übersetzt und bearbeitet.* Gesellschaft für vergleichende Mythen Forschung Mythologische Bibliothek, 6, part 1. Leipzig: J. C. Hinrichs.

Pollock, H. E. D.

1936 *Round Structures of Aboriginal Middle America.* Washington, DC: Carnegie Institution of Washington Publication 471.

Pomar, Juan Bautista

1891 *Relación de Tezcoco.* In García Icazbalceta 1891, III: 1–69.

1964 *Relación de Juan Bautista de Pomar (Tezcoco, 1582).* In Garibay Kintana 1964–1968, I: 149–219.

1986 *Relación de la ciudad y provincia de Tezcoco.* In *Relaciones geográficas del siglo XVI: México.* Tomo tercero: 21–113. Edición de René Acuña. Mexico City: Universidad Nacional Autónoma de México, Instituto de Investigaciones Antropológicas, Etnohistoria, Serie Antropológica 70.

1991 *Relación de Tetzcoco.* In Vázquez 1991: 17–99.

Popol Vuh: Editions listed under the names of their editors and/or translators.

Proskouriakoff, Tatiana

1946 *An Album of Maya Architecture.* Washington, DC: Carnegie Institution of Washington Publication 558.

Quiñones Keber, Eloise

1979 "Topiltzin Quetzalcoatl in Texts and Images." Master's thesis, Department of Art, Columbia University, New York.

1984a "Art as History: The Illustrated Chronicle of the *Codex Telleriano-Remensis* as a Historical Source." In *The Native Sources and the History of the Valley of Mexico,* edited by J. de Durand-Forest, 95–116. Proceedings of the 44th International Congress of Americanists, Manchester, 1982. General editor: Norman Hammond. Oxford: BAR (British Archaeological Reports) International Series 204.

1984b "The Illustrations and Texts of the Tonalamatl of the *Codex Telleriano-Remensis.*" Ph.D. dissertation, Department of Art, Columbia University, New York.

1987a "From Tollan to Tlapallan: The Tale of Quetzalcoatl in the *Codex Vaticanus A.*" *Latin American Indian Literatures Journal* 3, no. 1: 76–94.

1987b "The *Codex Telleriano-Remensis* and the *Codex Vaticanus* A: Thompson's Prototype Reconsidered." *Mexicon* 9, no. 1: 8–16.

1990 "Codex Telleriano-Remensis." In *Mexico: Splendors of Thirty Centuries*. Introduction by Octavio Paz. The Metropolitan Museum of Art, New York. Boston/Toronto/London: Little, Brown and Company, A Bullfinch Press Book.

1993 *Paléographie du texte du Codex Telleriano-Remensis*. Paris: SUP-INFOR.

1995a *"Codex Telleriano-Remensis": Ritual, Divination, and History in a Pictorial Aztec Manuscript*. Foreword by Emmanuel Le Roy Ladurie. Illustrations by Michel Besson. Austin: University of Texas Press.

1995b "Collecting Cultures: A Mexican Manuscript in the Vatican Library." In *Reframing the Renaissance: Critical Studies in the Migration and Deception of Visual Culture in Early Modern Europe and Latin America*. Edited by Claire Farago, 341–356. London and New Haven: Yale University Press.

1995c "Painting the Nahua Universe: Cosmology and Cosmogony in the *Codex Vaticanus* A. Part 1. Introduction and Translation." *Latin American Indian Literatures Journal* 11, no. 2: 183–205.

1996 "Creating the Cosmos: The Myth of the Four Suns in the *Codex Vaticanus* A." *Latin American Indian Literatures Journal* 12, no. 2: 192–211.

Radin, Paul

1920 *The Sources and Authenticity of the History of the Ancient Mexicans*. Berkeley: University of California Publications in American Archaeology and Ethnology 17, no. 1.

Ramírez, José Fernando

1854 "Ixtlilxochitl, Fernando de Alva." In *Diccionario universal de historia y de geografía*. Lucas Alamán et al., eds., vol. 4: 33–34. Mexico City: Tipografía de Rafael.

1858 "Noticias de la vida y escritos de Fray Toribio de Benavente Motolinía." In García Icazbalceta 1858–1866, I: xlvi–cliii.

Ramos de Cárdenas, Francisco

1897 (1582) *Relación de Querétaro*. In *Colección de documentos para la historia de San Luis Potosí*. Primo F. Velázques, ed., vol. I: 1–48. San Luis Potosí, Mexico: Imprenta del Editor.

1987 *Relación de Querétaro*. In *Relaciones Geográficas del Siglo XVI: Michoacán*, 205–248. Edición de René Acuña. Mexico City: Universidad Nacional Autónoma de México, Instituto de Investigacion Antropológicas, Etnohistoria, Serie Antropológica 74.

Raynaud, Georges

1925 *Les dieux, les héros et les hommes de l'ancien Guatemala d'après le Livre du Conseil*. Bibliothèque de l'École des Hautes Études Sciences Religieuses 41. Paris: Ernest Leroux.

1937 *Anales de los Xahil de los Indios Cakchiqueles*. Georges Raynaud, French trans.; M. A. Asturias and J. M. González de Mendoza, Spanish trans. 2nd edition. Los Dioses, los Héroes y los Hombres de Guatemala Antigua, 2. Guatemala: Tipografía Nacional.

Recinos, Adrián

1950 *Memorial de Sololá. Anales de los Cakchiqueles*. Traducción directa del original, introducción y notas de Adrián Recinos. *Título de los señores de Totonicapan*. Traducción del original quiché por el P. Dionisio José Chonay; introducción y notas de Adrián Recinos. Mexico City/Buenos Aires: Fondo de Cultura Económica, Biblioteca Americana, Proyectada por Pedro Henríquez Ureña y publicadas en memoria suya, Serie de Literatura Indígena.

1953 *"Popol Vuh": Las antiguas historias del Quiche*. 2nd edition. Traducidas del texto original, con una introducción y notas por Adrián Recinos. Mexico City/Buenos Aires: Fondo de Cultura Económica, Biblioteca Americana, Proyectada por Pedro Henríquez Ureña y publicada en memoria suya, Serie de Literatura Indígena. 1st edition, 1947.

1957 *Crónica indígenas de Guatemala*. Edición, traducción y notas de Adrián Recinos. Guatemala City: Editorial Universitaria.

Recinos, Adrián, and Delia Goetz

1953 *The Annals of the Cakchiquels*. Translated from the Cakchiquel by Adrián Recinos and Delia Goetz. *Title of the Lords of Totonicapán*. Translated from the Quiché text into Spanish by Dionisio José Chonay. English version by Delia Goetz. Norman: University of Oklahoma Press, Civilization of the American Indian Series.

Reina, Bernardo

1925 "Algunas observaciones acerca del *Códice Vaticano 3738* o *Códice Ríos*." *El México Antiguo* 2: 212–219.

Relación de la genealogía y linaje de los señores que han señoreado esta tierra de la Nueva España, después que le acuerdan haber gentes en estas partes

1891, 1941 In Garciá Icazbalceta 1891: xli–xlii, 263–281; 1941, 3: xxxvi, 240–256.

1991 In Vázquez 1991: 101–125.

Relaciones de Yucatán

1898–1900 *Relaciones histórico-geográficas de las provincias de Yucatán*. 2 vols. J. M. Asensio y Toledo, ed. *Colección de documentos inéditos relativos al descubrimiento, conquista y organización de las antiguas posesiones españoles de ultramar*, segunda seria, 11 and 13. Madrid: Est. tip. "Sucesores de Rivadeneyra."

1983 *Relaciones histórico-geográficas de la gobernación de Yucatán (Mérida, Valladolid y Tabasco)*. Edición preparada por Mercedes de la Garza, Ana Luisa Izquierdo, Ma. del Carmen León y Tolita Figueroa, bajo la coordinación de Mercedes de la Garza. 2 vols. Mexico City: Universidad Nacional Autónoma de México, Instituto de Investigaciones Filológicas, Centro de Estudios Mayas, Fuentes para el Estudio de la Cultura Maya, 1.

Rendón, Silvia P.

1949 "La cuarta relación de don Domingo de San Antón Muñón Chimalpahin

Quautlehuanitzin." *Anales del Instituto Nacional de Antropología e Historia* 3: 199–218.

Reyes, Fray Antonio de los

1593 *Arte en lengua mixteca.* Mexico City: En Casa de Pedro Balli.

1889 *Arte en lengua mixteca.* Publiée par le Comte H. de Charencey. Alençon: Typ. E. Renaut de Broise.

Ricard, Robert

1933 "Remarques bibliographiques sur les ouvrages de Fray Toribio Motolinía." *Journal de la Société des Américanistes* 25: 139–151.

Rivera, Miguel, ed.

1968 *Chilam Balam de Chumayel.* Edición de Miguel Rivera. Madrid: Historia 16, Crónicas de América 20.

Robertson, Donald

1959 *Mexican Manuscript Painting of the Early Colonial Period: The Metropolitan Schools.* Yale Historical Publications, History of Art 12. New Haven: Yale University Press.

1968 "The Paste-over Illustrations in the Durán *Codex of Madrid.*" *Tlalocan: Revista de Fuentes para el Conocimiento de las Culturas Indígenas de México* 5, no. 3: 340–348.

1994 *Mexican Manuscript Painting of the Early Colonial Period: The Metropolitan Schools.* Foreword by Elizabeth Hill Boone. 2nd edition. Norman and London: University of Oklahoma Press.

Rojas, Gabriel de

1927 "Relación de Cholula." *Revista mexicana de estudios históricos* 1, no. 6: 158–170.

1985 *Relación de Cholula.* In *Relaciones geográficas del siglo XVI: Tlaxcala.* Tomo segundo: 121–145. Edición de René Acuña. Mexico City: Universidad Nacional Autónoma de México, Instituto de Investigaciones Antropológicas, Etnohistoria, Serie Antropológica 59.

Rolando de León Valdés, Carlos, and Francisco López Pérez, trans.

1985 *"Popol Vuh" = Libro universal de la renovación del tiempo.* Guatemala City: CENALTEX, Ministerio de Educación.

Román y Zamora, Fray Gerónimo

1897 *Repúblicas de Indias, idolatría y gobierno en México y Perú antes de la conquista.* 2 vols. Colección de Libros Raros o Curiosos que Tratan de América, 14–15. Madrid: V. Suárez.

Rosny, Léon de

1869 *Archives paléographiques de l'Orient et de l'Amérique, publiées avec des notices historiques et philologiques,* tomo premier. Paris: Maisonneuve et Cie.

Roys, Ralph L.

1933 *The Book of Chilam Balam of Chumayel.* Translated by Ralph L. Roys. Washington, DC: Carnegie Institution of Washington Publication 438.

1944 "The Vienna Dictionary." *Notes on Middle American Archaeology and Ethnology* 2, no. 41: 93–105. Carnegie Institution of Washington, Division of Historical Research.

1949a "Guide to the Codex Pérez." *Contributions to American Anthropology and History* 10, no. 49: 87–106. Carnegie Institution of Washington Publication 585.

1949b "The Prophecies for the Maya Tuns or Years in the Books of the *Chilam Balam of Tizimin* and *Mani*." *Contributions to American Anthropology and History* 10, no. 51: 153–186. Carnegie Institution of Washington Publication 585.

1954 "The Maya Katun Prophecies of the *Books of Chilam Balam*." Series I. *Contributions to American Anthropology and History* 12, no. 57: 1–60. Carnegie Institution of Washington Publication 606.

1962 "Literary Sources for the History of Mayapan." In H.E.D. Pollock, R. L. Roys, T. Proskouriakoff, and A. L. Smith, *Mayapan Yucatan Mexico*. 25–86. Washington, DC: Carnegie Institution of Washington Publication 619.

1967 *The Book of Chilam Balam of Chumayel*. Translated by Ralph L. Roys. Introduction by J. Eric S. Thompson. Reprint edition of Roys 1933. Norman: University of Oklahoma Press, Civilization of the American Indian Series, vol. 87.

Ruppert, Karl

1952 *Chichén Itzá, Architectural Notes and Plans*. Washington, DC: Carnegie Institution of Washington Publication 595.

Ruwet, Wayne

1994 *Los manuscritos de la Bible Society: Su historia, redescubrimiento y contenido*. In Muñoz Camargo 1994: 27–61.

Ruz Lhuillier, Alberto

1945 *Guía arqueológica de Tula*. Mexico City: Ateneo Nacional de Ciencias y Artes de México.

Sáenz de Santa María, Carmelo, ed.

1989 *Popol Vuh*. Edición de Carmelo Sáenz de Santa María. Madrid: Crónica 16, Crónicas de América, 47.

Sahagún, Fray Bernardino de

1905 *Historia general de las cosas de Nueva España: Edición parcial en facsimile de los "Códices Matritenses" en lengua mexicana que se custodian en las Bibliotecas del Palacio Real y de la Real Academia de la Historia*. Edited by Francisco del Paso y Troncoso. Vol. VI: *Primero Memoriales*: 1–176. Madrid: Fototipia de Hauser y Menet.

1906 "Fray Bernardino de Sahagún O.F.M. Un breve compendio de los ritos idolátricos que los yndios desta Nueva España usaban en el tiempo de su infidelidad. Nach dem vaticanischen Geheimarchiv aufbewahrten von Wilhelm Schmidt." *Anthropos, Ephemeris Internationalis ethnologia et linguistica* I: 320–338.

1938 *Historia general de las cosas de Nueva España por el M. R. P. Fr. Bernardino de Sahagún de la Orden de los Frayles Menores de la Observancia.* Edited by Joaquín Ramírez Cabañas. Wigberto Jiménez Moreno, "Fray Bernardino de Sahagún y su obra." 5 vols. Mexico City: Editorial Pedro Robredo.

1946 *Historia general de las cosas de Nueva España.* Edited by Miguel Acosta Saignes. 3 vols. Mexico City: Editorial Nueva España.

1950–1982 *"Florentine Codex": General History of the Things of New Spain, Fray Bernardino de Sahagún.* Translated from the Aztec into English, with notes and illustrations, by Arthur J. O. Anderson and Charles E. Dibble. In 13 parts. Monographs of the School of American Research, no. 14, parts I–XIII. Santa Fe: The School of American Research and the University of Utah Press. Parts II–IV, XIII, revised, published between 1975 and 1981; parts V–XII reprinted between 1974 and 1979.

1956 *"Historia general de las cosas de Nuva España," escrita por Fray Bernardino de Sahagún, Franciscano, y fundada en la documentación en lengua mexicana recogida por los mismos naturales.* La dispuso por la prensa en esta nueva edición, con numeración, anotaciones y apéndices, Angel María Garibay K. 4 vols. Mexico City: Editorial Porrúa, S.A., Biblioteca Porrúa, 8–11.

1979 *Códice Florentino.* El Manuscrito 218–220 de la colección Palatina de la Biblioteca Medicea Laurenziana. 3 vols. Florence: Giunti Barbera; Mexico City: Archivo General de la Nación. Color photo-reproduction.

1982 *Historia general de las cosas de Nueva España.* Primera versión íntegra del texto castellano del manuscrito conocido como *Códice Florentino.* Introducción paleografía, glosario y notas de Alfredo López Austin y Josefina García Quintana. 2 vols. Mexico City: Fomento Cultural Banamex. Reprint editions: Madrid: Alianza Editorial, S.A., 1988; Mexico City: Editorial Cien, 1989.

1990 *Historia general de las cosas de Nueva España.* Edición de Juan Carlos Temprano. 2 vols. Madrid: Historia 16, Crónicas de América, 55.

1993 *Primeros memoriales.* By Fray Bernardino de Sahagún. Facsimile edition. Photographed by Ferdinand Anders. Norman: University of Oklahoma Press, in cooperation with the Patrimonio Nacional and the Real Academia de la Historia, Madrid, Civilization of the American Indian Series, vol. 200, part 1.

1997 *Primeros memoriales.* By Fray Bernardino de Sahagún. Paleography of Nahuatl text and English translation by Thelma D. Sullivan. Completed and revised, with additions, by H. B. Nicholson, Arthur J. O. Anderson, Charles E. Dibble, Eloise Quiñones Keber, and Wayne Ruwet. Norman: University of Oklahoma Press, in cooperation with the Patrimonial Nacional and the Real Academia de la Historia, Madrid, Civilization of the American Indian Series, vol. 200, part 2.

Sánchez de Aguilar, Pedro

1639 *Informe contra idolorum cultores del obispado de Yucatán.* Madrid: Imprenta por Viuda de Juan Gonçález.

1937 *Informe contra idolorum cultores del obispado de Yucatán*. Mérida: E. G. Triay e hijos, imps. Reprint of 1639 Madrid edition.

Sánchez García, Daniel

1914 "Bio-bibliografía de Fray Toribio de Benavente o Motolinía." In Motolinía 1914: v–xxxv.

Sandoval, Fernando B.

1945 "La relación de la conquista de México en la historia de Fray Diego Durán." In *Estudios de historiografía de la Nueva España*. H. Díaz-Thome, ed., 49–90. Mexico City: El Colegio de México, Publicaciones del Centro de Estudios Históricos.

Sapper, Karl

1936 "Pipiles und Mayavölker." *Ibero-Amerikanisches Archiv* 10: 78–86.

Saravía Enríquez, Albertina

1965 *"Popol Vuh": Antiguas historias de los Indios Quiches de Guatemala*. Ilustradas con dibujos de los codices Mayas. Advertencia, versión y vocabulario de Albertina Saravía E. Mexico City: Editorial Porrúa, S.A., Colección "Sepan cuantos . . . ," 36.

Saravía Enríquez, Albertina, and Juan Rodrigo Guarchaj

1996 *Poopol wuuj = Popol Vuh: K'ichee'-español*. Introducción, versión en español y vocabulario Albertina Saravía E. Traducción al idioma K'ichee' contemporáneo Juan Rodrigo Guarchaj. Guatemala City: Piedra Santa.

Scholes, France V., and Ralph L. Roys

1948 *The Maya Chontal Indians of Acalan-Tixchel, a Contribution to the History and Ethnography of the Yucatan Peninsula*. Washington, DC: Carnegie Institution of Washington Publication 560. 2nd edition, 1968, Norman: University of Oklahoma Press.

Schultze Jena, Leonhard S.

1935 *Indiana II: Mythen in der Muttersprache der Pipil von Izalco in El Salvador*. Jena: Gustav Fischer.

1944 *"Popol Vuh." Das heilige Buch der Quiché-Indianer von Guatemala nach einer wiedergefundenen alten Handschrift neu übersetzt und erläutert von Leonhard Schultze*. Quellenwerke zur alten Geschichte Amerikas aufgezeichnet in den Sprachen der Eingeborenen. Herausgegeben vom Ibero-Amerikanischen Institut, 2. Stuttgart: W. Kohlhammer.

1957 *Alt-Aztekische Gesänge*. Nach einer in der Biblioteca Nacional von Mexiko aufbewahrten Handschrift übersetzt und erläutert von Dr. Leonhard Schultze Jena, Weiland Professor an der Universität Marburg. Nach seinen Tode herausgegeben von Gerdt Kutscher. Quellenwerke zur alten Geschichte Amerikas aufgezeichnet in den Sprachen der Eingeborenen. Herausgegeben von der Ibero-Amerikanischen Bibliothek, Berlin. Schriftleitung: Gerdt Kutscher, VI. Stuttgart: Kohlhammer Verlag.

1977 *Mitos y leyendas de los pipiles de Izalco*. San Salvador: Ediciones Cuscatlan.

Schwartz. Benjamin I.

1975 "The Age of Transcendence." *Daedalus*, Spring: 108.

Séjourné, Laurette

1954a "Tula, la supuesta capital de los toltecas." *Cuadernos americanos*, año 13, vol. 73, no. 1: 153–169.

1954b "Teotihuacan, la ciudad sagrada de Quetzalcoatl." *Cuadernos americanos*, año 13, vol. 75, no. 3: 177–205.

Selden Roll

1954 See Burland 1955.

1964 In Kingsborough 1964–1967, vol. II: 101–113. Estudio e interpretación, José Corona Núñez.

Seler, Eduard

1900–1901 *The Tonalamatl of the Aubin Collection*. A. H. Keane, trans. London: Hazell, Watson, and Viney, Ltd.

1902–1903 *Codex Vaticanus No. 3773 (Codex Vaticanus B)*. A. H. Keane, trans. Berlin and London: A. Asher.

1902–1923 *Gesammelte abhandlungen zur amerikanischen Sprach- und Alterthums-kunde*. 5 vols. Berlin: A. Asher and Behrend.

1904a "The Bat God of the Maya Race." In Eduard Seler et al., *Mexican and Central American Antiquities, Calendar Systems, and History*. English translations supervised by C. P. Bowditch, 233–241. Smithsonian Institution, Bureau of American Ethnology, Bulletin 28. Washington, DC: Government Printing Office.

1904b "The Wall Paintings of Mitla." In Eduard Seler et al., *Mexican and Central American Antiquities, Calendar Systems, and History*. English translations supervised by C. P. Bowditch, 243–324. Smithsonian Institution, Bureau of American Ethnology, Bulletin 28. Washington, DC: Government Printing Office.

1927 *Einige Kapitel aus dem Geschichtswerke des fray Bernardino de Sahagún, aus dem Aztekischen übersetzt*. Edited by Caecelia Seler-Sachs, Walter Lehmann, and Walter Krickeberg. Stuttgart: Strecker und Schröder.

1973 "Einige der 'Cantares Mexicanos': Nahuatl-Text mit deutscher Übersetzung. Aus dem Nachlass herausgegeben von Gerdt Kutscher." *Indiana: Beiträge zur Völker- und Sprachenkunde, Archäologie und Anthropologie des Indianischen Amerika* I: 73–91.

Seler, Eduard, and Gerdt Kutscher

1975 *"Popol Vuh": Das Heilige Buch der Quiché Guatemalas*. In der Übersetzung von Eduard Seler, nach der Abschrift Walter Lehmanns hrsg. von Gerdt Kutscher. Berlin: Gebr. Mann, Stimmen Indianischer Völker, Bd. 2.

Smisor, George T.

1943 "A Ms. of Ramón de Ordóñez y Aguiar." *Tlalocan: Revista de fuentes para el conocimiento de las culturas indígenas de México* I: 71–73.

Smith, Mary Elizabeth

1973 *Picture Writing from Ancient Southern Mexico: Mixtec Place Signs and Maps*. Norman: University of Oklahoma Press, Civilization of the American Indian Series, 124.

Solís Alcalá, Ermilo, trans.

1949 *Códice Pérez*. Ediciones de la Liga de Acción Social. Mérida: Imprenta Oriente.

Spinden, Herbert J.

1925 "A Great American Emperor Revealed." *New York Times Magazine*, May 10: 14–15.

1928 *Ancient Civilizations of Mexico and Central America*. 3rd and revised edition. New York: American Museum of Natural History Handbook Series, no. 3.

1930 *Maya Dates and What They Reveal: A Re-examination of the Evidence in Correlation Between Central America and European Time Counts*. New York: Museum of the Brooklyn Institute of Arts and Sciences, Science Bulletin 4, no. 1.

Swadesh, Morris

1954–1955 "Algunas fechas glotocronológicas importantes para la prehistoria nahua." *Revista mexicana de estudios antropológicos* 14, primera parte: 173–192.

Tapia, Andrés de

1866 *Relación hecha por el señor Andrés de Tapia sobre la conquista de México*. In García Icazbalceta 1858–1866, II: 554–594.

1950 *Relación de Andrés de Tapia*. In Yáñez 1950: 27–82.

1963 *The Chronicle of Andrés de Tapia*. In Fuentes 1963: 17–48.

1988 *Relación de algunas cosas de las que acaecieron al muy ilustre Señor Don Hernando Cortés, Marqués del Valle, desde que se determinó ir a descubrir tierra en la tierra firme del mar océano*. In Vázquez 1988: 59–123.

Tedlock, Dennis, trans.

1985 *"Popol Vuh": The Definitive Edition of the Mayan Book of the Dawn of Life and the Glories of Gods and Kings*. Translated by Dennis Tedlock, with commentary based on the ancient knowledge of the modern Quiché Maya. New York: Simon and Schuster.

1996 *"Popol Vuh": The Mayan Book of the Dawn of Life*. Revised edition. New York: Simon and Schuster.

Teletor, Celso Narcisco

1946 *Memorial de Tecpán Atitlán (última parte)*. C. N. Teletor, trans. Guatemala: Tipografía Nacional.

Tello, Fray Antonio

1891–1945 *Crónica miscelánea . . . de la santa provincia de Xalisco*. 2 vols. Guadalajara, Mexico: Imprenta de "La República Literaria."

Thevet, André

1575 *La cosmographie universelle d'André Thevet, cosmographe du Roy, illustrée de diverses figures des choses plus remarquables veües par l'áuteur, & incogneües de noz anciens & modernes.* 2 vols. Paris: P. L'Huillier.

Thompson, J. Eric S.

1939 "The Moon Goddess in Middle America with Notes on Related Deities." *Contributions to American Anthropology and History* 5, no. 29: 121–173. Carnegie Institution of Washington Publication 509.

1941a "A Coordination of the History of Chichen Itza with Ceramic Sequences in Central Mexico." *Revista mexicana de estudios antropológicos* 5, nos. 2–3: 97–111.

1941b "The Prototype of the Mexican Codices *Telleriano-Remensis* and *Vaticanus A.*" *Notes on Middle American Archaeology and Ethnology* 1, no. 6: 24–26. Carnegie Institution of Washington, Division of Historical Research.

1945 "A Survey of the Northern Maya Area." *American Antiquity* 11, no. 1: 2–24.

1948 "An Archaeological Reconnaissance in the Cotzumalhuapa Region, Escuintla, Guatemala." *Contributions to American Anthropology and History* 9, no. 44: 1–94. Carnegie Institution of Washington Publication 574.

1950 *Maya Hieroglyphic Writing: Introduction.* Washington, DC: Carnegie Institution of Washington Publication 589.

1954 "El area maya norte." *Yan* 4: 2–35.

1971 *Maya Hieroglyphic Writing: An Introduction.* 3rd edition, with new preface and references. Norman: University of Oklahoma Press.

Título C'oyoi

1973 In Carmack 1973, 265–345.

1993 See Carmack and Tzaquitzal Zapeta 1993.

Título de Izquín Nehaib

1876 In *La Sociedad Económica* (Guatemala) 4, nos. 34–36.

1941 In *Anales de la Sociedad de Geografía e Historia* (Guatemala) 17, no. 3: 244–252.

1957 In Recinos 1957: 95–117.

Título de los señores de Totonicapan

1884 Le Comte Hyacinth de Charencey, ed. and trans. In *Bulletin des actes de la Société Philologique* (Alençon) 15: 101–169.

1950 See Recinos 1950.

1953 See Recinos and Goetz 1953.

1983 *El título de los señores de Totonicapán.* Text, traducción y comentario. Edición facsimilar, transcripción y traducción por Robert M. Carmack y James L. Mondloch. Mexico City: Universidad Nacional Autónoma de México, Instituto de Investigaciones Filológicas, Centro de Estudios Mayas, Fuentes para el Estudio de la Cultura Maya, 3.

Torquemada, Fray Juan de

1943–1944 *Monarquia indiana*. 3 vols. Facsimile of 2nd edition, Madrid, 1723. 1st edition, Seville, 1615. Mexico City: Editorial Salvador Chávez Hayhoe.

1975–1983 *Monarquía indiana: De los veinte y un libros rituales y monarquía indiana, con el origen y guerra de los Indios Occidentales, de sus poblazones, descubrimiento, conquista, conversión y otras cosas maravillosas de la mesma tierra*. Edición preparada por el Seminario para el estudio de fuentes de tradición indígena, bajo la coordinación de Miguel León-Portilla. 7 vols. Mexico City: Universidad Nacional Autónoma de México, Instituto de Investigaciones Históricas, Serie de historiadores y cronistas de Indias, 5.

Tovar, Juan de

1860 *Historia de los Yndios mexicanos, por Juan de Tovar*. Cura, et impensis dni. Thomae Phillips, bart. Typis Medio-Montanis, Jacobus Rogers impressit. Cheltenham, England: T. Phillipps and Middle Hill Press.

1878 *Relación del origen de los Indios que habitan esta Nueva España según sus historias*. In Alvarado Tezozomoc 1878.

1944 *"Códice Ramírez," manuscrito del siglo XVI intitulado "Relación del origen de los Indios que habitan esta Nueva España," según sus historias*. Examen de la obra, con un anexo de cronología mexicana por el Lic. Manuel Orozco y Berra. Reprint of 1878 Orozco y Berra edition, with added material. Mexico City: Editorial Leyenda, S.A.

1972 *Manuscrit Tovar: Origines et croyances des Indiens du Mexique, Relación del origen de los Yndios, que havitan en esta Nueva España segun sus historias, tratado de los ritos y ceremonias y dioses que en su gentilidad usavan los Indios de esta Nueva España*. Edition établie d'après le ms. de la John Carter Brown Library par Jacques Lafaye. La traduction en langue française du texte espagnol, due à Constantino Aznar Acevedo, a été relue par Jacques Lafaye. Graz: Akademische Druck- und Verlagsanstalt, Collection UNESCO d'oeuvres représentatives, Série Ibero-Américaine.

1975a *Códice Ramírez*. In Alvarado Tezozomoc 1975 and later reprint editions.

1975b *Códice Ramírez: "Relación del origen de los Indios que habitan en la Nueva España según historias."* Mexico City: Secretaría de Educación Pública, Dirección General de Educación Primaria en el D.F. Núm. 2, Documento núm. 2, Colección de Documentos Conmemorativos del DCL Aniversario de la Fundación de Tenochtitlan.

1987 *Origen de los Mexicanos: Relación del origen de los Indios que habitan esta Nueva España, según sus historias*. Edición de Germán Vázquez Chamorro. Madrid: Historia 16, Crónicas de América, 32.

Tozzer, Alfred M.

1917 "The *Chilam Balam* Books and the Possibility of Their Translation." In *Proceedings of the 19th International Congress of Americanists, 27–31 December, Washington, DC, 1915*, 178–186.

1921 *A Maya Grammar, with Bibliography and Appraisement of the Works Noted.* Papers of the Peabody Museum of American Archaeology and Ethnology, Harvard University, 9.

1930 "Maya and Toltec Figures at Chichen Itza." In *Proceedings of the Twenty-Third International Congress of Americanists, Held at New York, September 17–22, 1928*, 155–164. New York and Lancaster, Pennsylvania: The Science Press Printing Company.

1957 *Chichen Itza and Its Cenote of Sacrifice: A Comparative Study of Contemporaneous Maya and Toltec.* Cambridge, MA: Memoirs of the Peabody Museum of Archaeology and Ethnology, Harvard University, vols. XI (text) and XII (reference material and illustrations).

Troike, Nancy

1974 See *Codex Colombino-Becker I* 1974.

1978 "Fundamental Changes in the Interpretation of the Mixtec Codices." *American Antiquity* 43, no. 4: 553–568.

Tschohl, Peter

1989 "Das Ende der *Leyenda de los Soles* und die Übermittlungsprobleme des *Códice Chimalpopoca.*" *Baessler-Archiv, Neue Folge* XXXVII: 201–279.

Valladolid Lawsuit of 1618: In Brinton 1882a: 113–118.

Vázquez, Germán, ed.

1988 *La conquista de Tenochtitlan.* Edición de Gérman Vázquez. Madrid: Historia 16, Crónicas de América, 40.

1991 *Relaciones de la Nueva España.* Edición de Germán Vázquez. Madrid: Historia 16, Crónicas de América, 65.

Velázquez, Primo Feliciano, trans.

1945 *Códice Chimalpopoca: Anales de Cuauhtitlan y Leyenda de los Soles.* Traducción directa del náhuatl por el licenciado don Primo Feliciano Velázquez Universidad Nacional Autónoma de México, Instituto de Historia, Publicaciones del Instituto de Historia, Primera Serie, Número 1. Mexico City: Imprenta Universitaria.

Veytia, Mariano

1944 *Historia antigua de México.* 2 vols. Mexico City: Editorial Leyenda. 1st edition, Mexico City, 1836.

Villacastín, Francisco de, and Cristóbal de Salazar

1905–1907 *Relación de Coatepec Chalco.* In Paso y Troncoco 1905–1907, VI: 41–65.

1985 (1579) *Relación de Coatepec Chalco.* In *Relaciones geográficas del siglo XVI* (Mexico), tomo primero: 123–176. Edición de René Acuña. Mexico City: Universidad Nacional Autónoma de México, Instituto de Investigaciones Antropológicas, Etnohistoria, Serie Antropológica, 63.

Villacorta Calderón, José Antonio, ed. and trans.

1934 *Memorial de Tepán-Atitlán (Anales de los Cakchiqueles), por Francisco Hernández Arana Xajiliá y Francisco Díaz Gebutá Quej.* Texto y traducción revisados con notas y estudios sobre lingüística guatemalteca, por J. Antonio Villacorta C. Guatemala City: Tipografía Nacional.

1962 *Popol-vuh de Diego Reinoso, Popol-vinac, hijo de Lahuh-Noh.* Guatemala City: Centro Editorial "José de Pineda Ibarra," Ministerio de Educación Pública.

Villacorta Calderón, José Antonio, and Flavio Rodas N., trans.

1927 *Manuscrito de Chichicastenango (Popol Buj): Estudios sobre las antiguas tradiciones del pueblo Quiché.* Guatemala City: Sánchez & de Guise.

Wagner, Henry R.

1944 *The Rise of Fernando Cortés.* Berkeley: Bancroft Library, University of California Press, The Cortés Society.

Wagner, Hermann

1971 "Das 'Reiche Tollan' in der 'Relación de la genealogía' und in den 'Obras históricas' des Fernando de Alva Ixtlilxochitl." *Baessler-Archiv, Neue Folge* XIX: 141–149.

Wallace, Dwight T., and Robert M. Carmack, eds.

1977 *Archaeology and Ethnohistory of the Central Quiche.* Albany: State University of New York, Institute for Mesoamerican Studies, Publication no. 1.

Wauchope, Robert

1949 "Las edades de Utatlan e Iximché." *Publicaciones del Instituto de Antropología e Historia de Guatemala,* 1, no. 1: 10–22.

Weitzel, R. Boland

1931 "The *Books of Chilam Balam* as Tradition." *American Journal of Archaeology* 35: 319–323.

Willard, Theodore A.

1941 *Kukulcan, the Bearded Conqueror.* Los Angeles: Murray and Gee.

Willey, Gordon R.

1976 "Mesoamerican Civilization and the Idea of Transcendence." *British Antiquity,* 50: 205–215.

Ximénez, Fray Francisco

1929–1931 *Historia de la provincia de San Vicente de Chiapa y Guatemala de la orden de predicadores.* J. A. Villacorta C., ed. 3 vols. Biblioteca "Goathemala" de la Sociedad de Geografía e Historia, 3. Guatemala City: Tipografía Nacional.

1965 *Historia de la provincia de San Vicente de Chiapa y Guatemala.* 4 vols. Guatemala City: Ministro de Educación, "José de Pineda Ibarra," Biblioteca Guatemalteca de Cultura Popular, "15 de septiembre," vols. 81–84.

1967 *Escolios a las historias del origen de los Indios.* Escoliadas por el R.P.F. Francisco Ximénez. Guatemala City: Sociedad de Geografía e Historia de Guatemala, Publicación Especial No. 13.

1971–1977 *Historia de la provincia de San Vicente de Chiapa y Guatemala de la orden de predicadores.* Compuesta por Francisco Ximénez. 4 vols. Carmelo Sáenz de Santa María and F. Gall, eds. Paleografía y anotaciones de Carmelo Sáenz de Santa María. David Vela: paleografía (modernizada parcialmente), notas e índice analítico y temático. 1. Ed. de manuscrito original. Guatemala City: Biblioteca "Goathemala" de la Sociedad de Geografía e Historia de Guatemala, vols. 28–29: 24–25.

Xpantzay, La historia de los

1950 See Berlin 1950.

1957 In Recinos 1957: 118–169 (includes paleography of Cakchiquel text).

Yáñez, Agustín, ed.

1950 *Crónicas de la conquista.* Introducción, selección y notas de Agustín Yáñez. Segunda edición. Mexico City: Ediciones de la Universidad Nacional Autónoma de México, Biblioteca de Estudiante Universitario, 2.

Young, John, and J. Henderson Aitken

1908 *A Catalogue of the Manuscripts in the Library of the Hunterian Museum in the University of Glasgow.* James Maclehose & Sons, Publishers to the University.

Zorita, Alonso de

1891 *Breve y sumaria relación de los señores de la Nueva España.* In García Icazbalceta 1891, III: 71–277.

1909 *Historia de la Nueva España.* Colección de Libros y Documentos Referentes a la Historia de América, vol. 9. Madrid: Librería General de V. Suárez.

1963 *Life and Labor in Ancient Mexico: The Brief and Summary Relation of the Lords of New Spain by Alonso de Zorita.* Translated and with an introduction by Benjamin Keen. New Brunswick, RI: Rutgers University Press.

1999 *Relación de la Nueva España: Relación de algunas de las muchas cosas natables que hay en la Nueva España y de su conquista y pacificación y de la conversión de los naturales de ella.* Edición, versión paleográfica, estudios preliminares y apéndices, Ethelia Ruiz Medrano, Wiebke Ahrndt, José Mariano Leyva. 2 vols. Mexico City: Cien de México, Consejo Nacional para la Cultura y las Artes, Dirección General de Publicaciones.

Index

Page numbers in italics indicate illustrations.